WILLIE PEP
"The Will o' the Wisp"

BRIAN HUGHES

© Brian Hughes, Collyhurst and Moston Lads Clubs, 1997.

Published by
Collyhurst and Moston Lads Club.

Typeset, printed and bound by
MFP Design & Print,
Longford Trading Estate,
Thomas Street,
Stretford,
Manchester M32 0JT
Telephone: 0161 864 4540

Other books by the same author:-
THE TOMMY TAYLOR STORY.
JACKIE BROWN - THE MAN, THE MYTH, THE LEGEND.

Table of Contents

Acknowledgements	5
A Genius Named Pep!	7
Reg Gutteridge	11
Hank Kaplan	12
Introduction	14
Don Riley	20
Willie Pep – What a champion	23
Making His Professional Debut	43
Poison Ivy	58
Bitter Taste Of Initial Defeat	79
The Golden Era	86

Manuel Ortiz	98
The Return With Chalky	107
Revenge Over McAllister	123
The Phantom Of Minneapolis	135
Airplane Disaster	144
Miami Bound	160
The Shock	172
Preparing For Saddler	182
What The Papers Said	198
Steady Eddie Falls In Seven	213
Crudeness vs Wizardry – The French Connection	229
My Kidney Punches Made Him Quit	241
World War Four	249
Return To The Big Apple	265
The Lulu Perez Fiasco and The Fix	274
The Best Sports Writer In America	293
Willie's Farewell To Boxing	306
The Comeback	318
Robinson Couldn't Tie Willie Pep's Laces	332
Willie Pep's Record	346

Acknowledgement

Collyhurst and Moston Lads Club acknowledge with gratitude those people who sent us material and photographs for use in this book. Every effort has been made to trace any copyright holders and we apologise to anyone who has not been found or properly acknowledged. Subsequent editions will include any corrections or omissions notified to the club. We would first of all like to thank Hank Kaplin, the foremost boxing historian for his invaluable assistance in putting this book together. Hank was a source of unstinting help and encouragement. Hank, on behalf of everyone at the Lads Club, a million thanks and God bless you! The staff at The Hartford Daily Courant. Claude Abrams of Boxing News, for his support and help with some of the research. Glyn Leach of Boxing Monthly. George Zeleny, for taking time to read the MS and offer help and sugestions. The late, Ray Arcel and his wife for their help with information and material. Nigel Collins, Steve Farhood and The Ring magazine. Bert Randolph Sugar of Boxing Illustrated Mark George from the International Boxing Hall of Fame in Canastota, was also extremely helpful and we thank him for the material he readily sent to us. Pete Heller author of In This Corner and Tyson was also helpful and tremendously encouraging. Pat Macune gave me a wonderful insight in what it was like to be one of Willie Pep's opponents. Pat is a thorough gentleman.

A special thanks must also go to Richard Jones and his son Damian, for their patience when reading and correcting my many mistakes. Simon Crawford of the Rochdale Observer. Peter Collins of the Moston Express. Richard Hernandez for the articles and material on the subject, which he sent from San Antonio. Philip Paul in New York for his valuable help. John Evans and Burt Daly for the many photographs which they willingly put at my disposal. Harold Brown, Joe Mull and Dennie Mancini. Angelo Dundee for reminincing with me about Willie Pep, Angelo is a true first class gentleman. Jimmy Rogers was another who put helpful material at my disposal. Tom Jones our legal adviser who was always ready to help out with sugestions. Thanks also to the many people who willingly helped and to anyone who I may have overlooked, please forgive me I can assure you it is not intentional. Lastly could we say a special thank you to Phil Fitzpatrick of Phoenix Photo Art Restoration. Unit 7. 56-60 Shude Hill, Manchester M4 4AA. And to my friends Doreen and Brian Meadows of Sport Art for their help with the cover and other material. Collyhurst and Moston Lads Club would highly recomend these three wonderful people. I would like to take this opportunity of thanking my wife Rosemarie, for her love, devotion, encouragement and patience. Not forgetting my four children, Anthony, Damian, Christopher and Rachael. All my family must have been absolutely fed up with my endless requests for them to spell and explain certain words, but without complaint they happily obliged. Collyhurst and Moston Lads Club would like to thank Mr. Frank Warren, for his generosity in helping to get this book published. Last but not least, I want to thank Willie Pep himself. I hope he is pleased with our efforts in this tribute to him. Willie in my book you are still the greatest. God bless you!

A Genius Named Pep!

It is said boxing's "Golden Age" started from Jack Dempsey in the 1920's up until the end of Muhammad Ali's first reign as world heavyweight champion in the 1960's. Since then boxing's disintegration has been blamed on incomprehensible politics and fragmented titles which has cost most of its credibility and its walk-up crowds. But the biggest culprit is, without a doubt, television, which largely subsidises it. In this modern age where there are more fights televised than ever before, the familiar cry is often heard: "Television is only interested in seeing knockouts!" Many people in boxing; journalists, trainers, promoters, and matchmakers complain about the art of self-defence being almost extinct. All are in agreement; that today most practitioners of the noble art of self-defence are placing less emphasis on defence in pursuit of crash, bang, wallop techniques, because they have been brainwashed into believing this is the only way to success in the ring. But there is no finer sight in boxing than a match between a boxer versus a puncher. It creates excitement.

The story of Willie Pep, the "Will-o'-the-Wisp," is unsurpassed. This man is the greatest boxing champion pound-for-pound the fight game as ever produced. As a child he was bullied because he was so small and frail, he was forever on the run from the much bigger and meaner kids of his neighbourhood. Yet he became the family bread winner from the tender age of 15. Willie always wanted to be a boxer and he was rejected several times by coaches at the local boxing gym, because he looked like a choir boy with his mop of black curly hair he was so little and weak that they thought he was likely to get hurt. But he persevered and one day he turned up at the gym with his own gloves and demanded he be shown how to box. What followed was spectacular even by boxing standards. He transcended boxing to the level of respectability. He became a dazzling, scientific, boxing perfectionist.

Pep turned professional before his 18th birthday, he fought the cream of the crop of top-class fighters. When asked why he turned professional at such an early age Pep replied: "My family needed the money." His rise up the boxing ladder was absolutely phenomenal to say the least. Fame and riches came his way. For a boxer in the 1940s to make it to the top of the American boxing ladder meant he had to have something extra special. Pep had it in abundance. There were hundreds of fighters in every town and city littered across America, and dozens of fighters in every weight division, they were all hungry to make the mighty dollar. I myself have been fortunate to have seen in action the likes of Jackie Brown, Johnny King, Johnny Cusick, Nel Tarleton, Freddie Miller, Benny Lynch and Howard Winstone, to name but a few wonderful stylish boxers of the lighter weight classes. Yet, I say, without hesitation that Willie Pep was the best of them all!

Pep held the featherweight title for nine years. He fought all over the States, drawing thousands of people through the turnstiles to watch him box. A survivor on an aircraft which crashed in a snowstorm killing five people, Pep was hospitalised for five months wearing a cast from his neck downwards because of the injuries he suffered. Told he would never box again, he took the plaster cast off and within five months was back fighting. It was miracle proclaimed the doctors. Pep sued the airline company for $250,000, but his claim was rejected after he fought again. Pep is a character, a personality cult figure. He has charisma with a capital C. He illuminates the surroundings with his presence. He has been married seven times. Willie Pep was the original "Golden Boy," a tag he hated. He became slightly tarnished in some unsavoury incidents inside and outside the ring. A heavy gambler with the dice and horses, it was a habit which cost him dearly. He was involved in controversy because of his four brutally foul-filled, and disgraceful fights with arch rival, Sandy Saddler, which resulted in his being suspended from boxing in New York. But these incidents should in no way diminish his achievements or his boxing artistry.

The word sensational is one of the most abused in the sporting lexicon but it applies perfectly to the majestic Willie Pep. He was possessed of some sixth sense which told him what an opponent was going to do next. It was called "extra sensory perception." When it was common knowledge that fans in that period would only pay money in order to watch knockout punchers and tough, rough brawlers, he changed it single-handed, through his sophisticated, classical skills inside the ring. Pep was the cream of American boxing. The creme-de-la-creme. Although frail of stature, he strode the rings like a colossus. Muhammad Ali, as brilliant as he was, could not hold a candle to the velvet skills of the immaculate Willie Pep. His fights were contests of sheer craftsmanship between the ropes. In the toughest, roughest twenty-four feet of space in the world he was a master crafsman, the like of which boxing followers will never be privileged to witness again. Pep carried boxing to a different level. There will never be another like him. His achievements will be etched in the record books for ever.

My own fondest memory of Willie Pep was the night he totally rendered Ray Famechon, the destroyer of every British bantam and featherweights of the forties and fifties period, absolutely ineffective by the use of his brilliant feinting, footwork and breathtaking skills. I can close my eyes now and still see the image of Pep dancing, slipping and sliding out of danger. Poor Famechon didn't know what day it was he was so bewildered by Pep's wizardry. And the Frenchman could box and punch with the best of them. Except Willie Pep. Yes, Willie really was something special. The finest boxer I have ever saw. Repeat: Ever! He rose from poverty to become perfection in a business which is notorious for its inevitable hype and sleaze. He was a boxer who maintained a high standard and kept his position as the world's leading fighter.

Earning well over a million dollars with his fists, and losing it all. Yet, who, at 75 is still sprite, agile, active and mentally sharp as a tack. "I didn't believe in taking punches," he often said. Something modern day pugilist would be well advised to learn.

Willie Pep has often been described in various boxing literature as a "natural." Well like the great Joe Louis said many years ago. "There's no such thing as a natural." A baby can not naturally walk. It has to learn. A natural singer has to practice his range. A natural footballer has to practice various manouevres. A natural painter has to paint at every opportunity he gets and practice his brush strokes. The examples are in everything we do in our everyday lives. Willie Pep had what is termed as natural ability, but he will be the first to tell you he had to train to attain his greatness, and train extremely hard. Pep had one of the great teachers, Bill Gore. This man was among the greatest of any era. Like another all-time teacher, Ray Arcel, Gore was a psychologist knowing exactly when to coax or bully his fighter into preparing properly. He was also an Anatomist, an expert masseur. And more than that Bill was a very gentle and patient man. He saved Pep on many occasions because of his quick-silver thinking. A great trainer for an equally great boxer.

Just to conclude, I am honoured to have been asked to contribute my observations on the subject of this book ... Willie Pep. In September 1990 in a poll conducted by Boxing Illustrated to find the top ten slickest boxers of all time, Willie Pep was voted number one. He beat Sugar Ray Robinson, Benny Leonard, Gene Tunney, Muhammad Ali, Sugar Ray Leonard, Jimmy Slattery, Maxie Rosenbloom, Billy Conn and Pernell Whitaker. That was some endorsement of how highly this man was rated. What a fascinating encounter it would have been between Howard Winstone and Willie Pep. A conoiseurs delight. Today, Pep is one of the most sought after speakers on the sportsmans functions and after dinner circuit.

Burt Daly. Manchester. Burt Daly was for years the public relations officer for the Manchester Ex-Boxers Association. A boxing historian, Mr. Daly who, is nearly eighty-years-old is one one the most knowledgeable men about the history of the sport and on individual boxers. He has seen nearly every one of Britain's boxers since the late 1920s to the present day, also countless world champions from other countries. He also owns one of the largest collection of boxing photographs in existence.

REG GUTTERIDGE

Composing a Foreword is a risky game, especially if the writer happens to be a wordy rival in the world of pro hacks.

Brian Hughes' work comes from the streets of Manchester language of honesty, miles apart from the academics of the soft South or the whizz-kids of the old Fleet Street. Brian's work is helping the making of good citizens and, hopefully, the making of world champions along the way.

The modest profits of this book after loads of sweat, toil and probably some tears, will support this famous little amateur club. The subject, Willie Pep, is the perfect example of a real noble art – a champion character with a remarkable story who could pick punches with the craft of a pickpocket. I knew Pep the man without watching him in the flesh, except as referee for Irish John Caldwell's battle in Brazil against the exceptional Eder Joffre. Willie reckoned he suffered more in conflicts with women than in the ring. He once won a round on three judges cards without throwing a punch! I know Willie enjoyed a remarkable career of 26 years with 242 recorded fights (and probably some not listed). You can enjoy living some of them, and his lifestyle, without taking a punch. He was voted "Ring" Fighter of the Year, 1960, and inducted into the Hall of Fame, in 1963. The authors lads, seeking their bits of fame, can learn a lot. Hopefully, it can also provide a little earner.

Reg Gutteridge O.B.E.

Hank Kaplan

It was during the decade of the 1790's that boxing practitioner Daniel Mendoza, still labouring under the primitive rules of John Broughton, harboured a notion that boxing need not continue as a sport dependant upon caveman tactics to attain victory in the ring. He reasoned prize-fighting needed an amalgam to cement the rudimentary combine of muscle, instinct and strategy with artful nuances to make one a more complete fighting machine. "Boxing should be a heady sport, he thought, with defensive techniques and a more effective delivery of punches." For starters, he introduced the concept of the left jab as a tactical tool for use as a probing guide and to deter opponents from invading his safety zone. Mendoza transmitted his theories for all who would listen and those who subscribed to his ideas communicated them to others. The genesis of the boxing art was taking a firm foothold and with slight interventions through the years, continued to improve. That boxing was an artistic form was given credence by James J. Corbett, refined by Benny Leonard and reached it's summit with the coming of Willie Pep. Perfecting the art of hitting while not getting hit took about 75 years from the advent of the Marquess of Queensberry rules to the quintessence of Willie Pep. In paleontological terms that was only yesterday. In all the tomorrow's since the days of Willie Pep, a period of time rapidly approaching another 75 years, boxing has not produced his likeness. Pep's boxing style and techniques were hardly the best kept secret in town. He displayed these prodigious assets better than a couple of hundred times during a quarter century of fisticuffing in most sections of his country. He was there for aspiring boxers to view and emulate, yet the level of his skills and achievements were never reciprocated. His boxing prowess and artisanship, as Brian Hughes will illustrate for you, are attributes which Mother Nature granted to him. His will and inclination brought him to the contact sport so ideally suited to his temperament and unique athletic ability. His synopsis in the record book is but one indicator that Willie Pep was immaculate in the role he was ordained to enact. On 10 September, 1942, America and her allies were embroiled in world conflict against the Nazis. Madison Square Garden in New York was exhibiting the wares of newly-crowned welterweight champion Freddie "Red" Cochrane and Fritzie Zivic in a non-title affair, before Cochrane stowed his title for the duration. On the undercard, appearing in his seventeenth trial of that year, 20-year-old Willie Pep electrified the war-immersed crowd with a first round stoppage of Frank Franconeri, a prospective featherweight out of New Jersey. His performance was an amazing collaborative effort of the athletic senses. In the brief scrap only his offense was perceptible, but his form and co-ordination were poetic, his footwork and delivery flawless. His punches were on the mark and he wasted nothing. Willie Pep had the look of a champion. New Yorkers were viewing Pep for only the second time, but some must have prophesied the wispy tyke would one day undermine the record-keepers and topple all prior crown-bearers from their lofty berths. The word sensational is one of the most abused in the sporting lexicon... but it applies perfectly to Willie Pep.

Hank Kaplan,
Miami Beach,
Florida.
February 1996

Introduction

As a schoolboy just after the war I lived in Collyhurst, an inner-city area of Manchester. There were no television sets and hardly any radios in that grey, drab, bleak period. The main form of entertainment for the whole family was a night out at the cinema, (or the "cini" or "flicks" as it was known by us youngsters). We would study the entertainments pages in the Manchester Evening News or the Manchester Evening Chronicle in search of the theatre which was showing the best adventure films. Whenever a big sporting event took place, such as the Cup Final or the Grand National, Pathe News or Movietone would show the event. This of course proved a huge attraction for the male audience. My favourites were the big boxing championship fights which were shown. It was while watching the boxing matches on the big screen that I first became addicted to the sport. The first contest I vividly remember watching was one which featured Willie Pep. Memory fails me as to exactly who he fought on that particular night, but the vision of this masterful boxer on the silver screen left an indelible impression upon me and has lived with me ever since as I watched transfixed, his image flitting across the silver screen. Yes, watching Willie Pep perform had me glued to my seat.

Collyhurst was a hot bed of boxing in those days. On every grimy, cobbled street seemed to live a former boxer. Jackie Brown, Johnny King,

Jock McAvoy and Johnny "Nipper" Cusick had achieved their greatness while winning-World, British, Empire and European championships from a Collyhurst gym. Jack Bates the trainer of all four champions, was also born and bred in the area and still lived there until his death.
 Willie Pep had a sartorial elegance, he was a thoroughbred among boxers. He was a purist's delight. A masterful boxer, dapper, stylish – a boxer with flair. He was sheer poetry in motion, and also a very proud man. The man who shortened his given name "Papaleo" into the pallindronic "Pep" was boxing's version of the three-card monte player. Now you see him, now you don't. His movement in the ring took on the look of tap dancing with gloves on left his opponents to speculate on their meaning and the fans to listen for accompanying music. Yes, watching Willie Pep in action was rather like drinking a glass of vintage champagne when all the world seems against you. It is invigorating, exciting and effervescent. For not only was Pep one of the most successful boxers, he was also one of the most thrilling.
 When I started coaching youngsters at Collyhurst Lads Club in the early 1960s, I used Willie Pep as an example of how boxing should be executed. "Hit, move, and don't get hit." I had an old film projector (before the days of videos) and some old fight films, among which was the Willie Pep versus Ray Famechon bout. This was a classic. I showed this film so often that one night it just disintegrated and I had to purchase a new one! I decided one of my ambitions was to actually meet Pep and talk about his amazing career. I achieved this distinction in 1994. Willie Pep resides in a quite detached house in Wethersfield, Connecticut. The house where he lives with his seventh wife Barbara is sparkling and the cold winter sun glinted on the silver-framed photographs of his family and some of Willie's famous fights. He was 73 and was the best conditioned 73-year-old I have ever seen. Bright and sparkling, with twinkling eyes, he certainly did not look anywhere near his age. As I studied his features it was hard to believe this was the man the experts proclaimed as the perfect fighting machine. Unlike most old timers, Willie bore no contempt for modern fighters. He was the perfect example of what boxing should be about. A stranger meeting Pep for the first time would not know he was talking to one of the greatest professional boxers of all time. Willie was telling me that he was feeling great. Suddenly, looking deadly serious he said: "I've had 241 professional fights. And I'm all right until I hear a bell. So don't ring any bells!"

When the laughter subsided, I told him I did not wish to discuss his infamous brawls with Sandy Saddler. Though, I explained I obviously intended including his battles with Saddler. (Enough has already been written about those disgraceful, foul-filled battles). In 1948 Pep was knocked out for the first time in his long career by a thin, weak-looking fighter who looked as if a stiff breeze would have knocked him over. Sandy Saddler was the fighters name. The rematch was the highlight of Willie's career. For on the night of 11 February 1949, in that creaky, hallowed arena where dreams are made, Madison Square Garden, Pep made his dream come true by recapturing his featherweight title in what as been described by various writers over the past years as the greatest ever boxing contest they had ever had the privilege to witness.

Willie smiled, looked closely at me and said: "You know, Brian, you must be the first person I've met who doesn't want to cover that issue. I had 241 professional fights, yet every story written about me mentions in detail my four fights with Sandy; every interview I've had with reporters from all over the world seems to revolve around those Saddler fights. I have nothing against Sandy, in fact I have the greatest respect for him and what he achieved. But I had 237 fights that weren't with him. You know, I was never known as a dirty fighter. Check through my career. But those four battles are talked about more than any other."

He then said: "Sometimes I feel like I've been living a hundred years. I've tasted too much, that's the trouble. I've tasted poverty as a child; I tasted what I thought was love and went through a few marriages; I came close to death in a plane crash and then tasted the sweet, pure taste of survival; I've tasted the applause of thousands of people and suffered the stinging and cruel criticism; and I tasted two miserable stints in the Army and the Navy during World War Two; but I've always been truthful and tried to smile through the good, the bad and the ugly times." Willie had me captivated as he regaled me with his past experiences. We got onto the subject of teaching the young boxers in my care, Willie rose from his chair and gave a demonstration as he spoke. "The idea of boxing is to hit and not get hit," he remarked. "You should tell your boxers never to forget that for a moment. Boxing is all about balance. It is stupid to stand and trade punch for punch like you see lots of these kids doing today on television. There's no sense in that. I know the sluggers and big punchers are the darlings of the television audiences, but there is no skill or longevity in doing that."

That Willie Pep has joined the pantheon of truly great world boxing champions and burned off most if not all of his contemporaries is no longer an argument. But where do we place him among the other great champions? To modern day boxing fans many boxing writers are guilty of over rating the old-time boxers. For some reason modern fighters do not get their just credit when compared to past fighters, who are usually overblown in their exploits. That might be so, but they do say greatness is in the eye of the beholder. But this was not the case when analysing the career of Willie Pep, because he was the complete scientific boxer and the supreme professional, incomparable really. Everything he did as a boxer was stamped with unequivocal class. He was a master of the noble art of self-defence. Willie Pep fought as if he didn't like to get hit, which he didn't, having a great respect for his teeth at a very early age. He fought as a survivor, practicing a form of reverse polarity with an uncanny ability to anticipate an opponent's blows and then parry them, pick them off, or just plain beat them with his own form of rat-a-tat punches. Throughout his long career, Pep substituted shiftiness and cunning for a lack of power, most of his 65 inside-the-distance victories coming not from a malicious blow but from his opponents falling to the canvas in utter exhaustion, unable to keep up with the man the press labelled "Willie the Wisp," but which like his own name, would be changed to "Will-'o-the-Wisp."

Many of his opponents described fighting Pep to battling a man in the hall of mirrors, unable to cope with an opponent they couldn't find, let alone hit. Others compared the experience to catching moonbeams in a jar, or chasing a mirage or a shadow. Kid Campeche said after going ten rounds with Pep in which he never won a round: "Fighting Willie Pep is like trying to stamp out a grass fire." But Pep's greatest virtuoso performance came the night he gave the fans a treat, literally, winning a round without throwing a single punch. His opponent on this occasion was Jackie Graves, a top-rated fighter and a ferocious southpaw puncher with more than his share of knockouts. Sportswriters despite their incredulity, found what they had witnessed was absolutely incredible. He had many extra qualities, among them speed and toughness. Can it be really possible for one man to win 229 fights out of a total of 241, and have his last fight when he was 45, two years after being elected to the Hall of Fame? It's impossible to think of boxer in the future equalling just one of his two unbeaten runs of 62 contests and the other of 73 professional bouts. At the tender age of 20, Pep won the world featherweight crown from the hard-hitting Chalkey Wright. He would most certainly have been a teenaged world champion but for boxing politics.

Pep was also known as the "Artful Dodger" by many reporters of the 1940s because of his masterful defensive ability, Willie, the Hartford boxing master fought for five years as a professional before he lost his first contest to Sammy Angott. He then reeled off another 73 straight victories except for one draw. Thus he had but one solitary defeat in 135 consecutive fights. He did not lose another fight until Sandy Saddler beat him in a championship match. In 1941 and 1942 he had 46 fights and won them all. This amount of fights would constitute a full career for modern day fighters. This total and his two long strings of consecutive fights without defeat comprise one of boxing's finest all time records.

Willie was defeated only the once prior to an airplane crash, in 1947, but he nevertheless recovered from his near-fatal injuries when it looked as if his career, if not his ability to walk, were seemingly behind him. Miraculously, five months later, rather than sitting at home and watching his bones mend, he came back not only to walk, but to box, and he made 125 additional ring appearances which included eight world title fights. Widely acclaimed as one of the greatest little men in ring annals, Pep is linked with Joe Louis and Sugar Ray Robinson as the three greatest of their time. But he surpassed both in total fights and victories.

He was elected to the Boxing Hall of Fame in 1963, two years after the Connecticut Sportswriters Alliance had voted him a Gold Key for distinguished service to Connecticut sports. After his retirement in 1959, Pep owned or helped as a host in restaurants and nightclubs in New York, Tampa, and the Hartford area. Despite the fortune he earned, Willie was believed broke when he made a comeback in 1965. He also acted as a guest referee in major bouts in America and overseas. For a brief period he was employed in the State department, but found collecting overdue accounts did not appeal to him. In the 1970s, he was appointed to a post in the boxing division of the Connecticut Consumer Protection Department.

On my visit to Willie Pep's home I was introduced to his charming and beautiful wife Barbara, and her three lovely children. Barbara is over thirty years younger than her husband. "She's my sixth or seventh wife," he smilingly told me. "You know, Brian, all my wives were good housekeepers. When we divorced they kept the houses!" During our conversation,

Barbara asked me if I had read Willie's book "Fridays Heroes" which he wrote many years ago. When I told her "yes" she shot back with the question and answer: "It was good, but not enough was written about Willie himself," she said. Actually the book is a fascinating insight into fighters who appeared on television during the 1950s. But I agreed with Mrs. Pep, not enough was written about the main subject Willie Pep. I assured her my intentions were to put that to rights. Sugar Ray Robinson is described by boxing historians as pound for pound the greatest fighter ever. I have no dispute with this assessment of a truly great champion. Though, equally Willie Pep must be regarded as ounce for ounce the greatest scientific boxer ever! There have been many great fighters, and many great boxers, and many great ring strategists, but there has been only one Will-o'-the-Wisp. The name Willie Pep will forever be remembered as a name put to melody and symphony, a balletic will to grace that made him "Will-o'-the-Wisp. I hope I have managed to convey Willie Pep's brilliance and to record his remarkable achievements and his exploits throughout his amazing career during the toughest period in boxing's history. Yes, this Willie Pep story, a tribute to the "greatest," inspired me to write and use, one-fingered, a typewriter and a simple English dictionary as I laboured on. This then is an in-depth look at his boxing career. Everything in here is perfectly true and accurate as far as I am aware. Please forgive me if I have made any mistakes. But I must confess that though writing this book has been a labour of love, it has also been tremendously difficult. You see, I left school at fourteen hardly able to read, write or spell, and with very little education, which I must confess was largely my own fault. I missed a great deal of schooling through ill health, but in reality I hated going to school. Sit back in your armchair and relax, take a journey back in time to the days when a boxer was a boxer and a fighter really was a fighter. And the greatest of them all was a little fellow called Willie Pep! I hope you enjoy the book.

That Was Greatness—
Willie Pep Was The Greatest!

When I asked Willie Pep to write a few words for this book, he handed me a newspaper cutting which was headlined: "The Round Willie Pep Won Without Throwing A Punch" Don Reily's Eye Opener. "Please include this in the book, because this article says it all for me," said Willie. "I couldn't explain my career any better." After reading Mr. Reily's rivetting description of three minutes in Pep's entire career it brings into perspective how brilliant this man, Pep, really was. When one looks at the hype of some present day boxing champions when making their ring entrance, and compare them to the dignified way the truly great champions such has Willie Pep and Sugar Ray Robinson, to mention just two, who would walk nonchalantly to the ring, makes one wonder about this new era. There was no parachuting into the ring under a cloud of smoke and flashing laser lights, with stereo music blasting the eardrums, no glitzy show business build-up. Pep and Robinson relied solely on their conventional classy and stylish boxing, with not a trace of clownish behaviour and, when the contest was finished, they both showed their composure and showed their opponents respect and dignity. Read on and savour a man who epitomised the art of boxing and needed no false gimmicks.

He was a shadow, dancing, weaving, bobbing, like a cork in a typhoon. There was lightning in his hands. And when you tried to corner him, it was like trying to capture moonbeams in a fruit jar. Willie Pep was there and then he wasn't; a demon, a resin spirit who etched the canvas of the battle pits with the same genius Van Gogh put on the canvas of art. He carried boxing beyond the course, vulgar displays of human carnage. His were classic victories, rarely bloody; more the incredible, skilled surgeon, operating on his foe with the cool, dispassionate dispatch of the antiseptic clinic. The greatest athlete in his particular specialty I have ever seen. Lest I'm engulfed in arguments, let me point out my definition of "greatest." It is the performance by an athlete which can not be copied, indulged in or even approached by his peers. In boxing, Will-'o'-the Wisp' Willie Pep did things in the ring no man has tried or experienced. William Gugliemo Papaleo was a craftsman so masterful, so motivated, so brilliant that the original Phantom of the ropes, Mike Gibbons, turned to me while watching him workout and whispered. "I'd pay anything to watch that boy box." Pep had 241 professional fights. This amazing featherweight won 229, lost 11 and had one draw. His career was interrupted by an airplane crash that ripped his tiny body to shreds. He went through $1.8 million in playgirls, wives, slow ponies and fast dice. Never bitter, always cheerful, Willie today has got things completely under control. "I've got a wife, a brother-in-law and a TV set, and they're all working."

Anyway, this is the story of one round out of his 1,987 rounds; three minutes no man can forget; a story I first wrote for Ring Magazine many years ago, which has been copied many times since, just a few months ago in the New York Times. It was a warm afternoon in '46 and Willie was sitting in the old Nicollet Park boxes, we were watching preliminary boys work out. In two days he'd fight southpaw slugger Jackie Graves in an over-the-weight match in the Mill City Auditorium. It was already a record setting gate and Willie was at his cheery best! He turned to me and said, "Let's have some fun, Don. Tell you what, I won't throw a punch in the third round. See how I come out." Not throw a punch against a TNT hitter like Graves! Incredible! Impossible! It was electric at ringside. I was announcing the fight for WMIN. And I could hardly wait for round three. There was Graves, the Austin assassin, square-jawed and dangerous. There was the slender Pep, on his toes, ever punching, jabbing into the bewildered Graves' face for two rounds, a steady tattoo almost like a machine.

Graves had never seen such blinding speed. Oh, he knew Pep was good. He had told me,"To beat Pep you must be lucky. He's so quick and does so many things." He had no idea how many. Now the third round. In moved Graves still stalking like a tiger. Now, Pep feinted jabs but none landed. Now he switched to southpaw, mimicking Graves, but his right jabs fell short of their target. Pep danced, and weaved. Jackie tried to rush him into a corner and Pep spun him around and was free again, almost laughing. Befuddled, frustrated, Graves again moved in Pep wasn't there. He left his calling card-head feints, shoulder feints, shuffles that make Ali Clod look like a stationary hydrant. For minutes Pep moved, taunted, twirled, tied up Graves but never threw a punch! It was an amazing display of defensive skill so adroit, so cunning, so subtle the 8,000 roaring fans did not notice Pep's tactics were completely without offense. He made Gentleman Jim Corbett's agility look like a broken down locomotive. He made even Sugar Ray Robinson's fluidity, look like cement hardening. Never has boxing seen such perfection. Later, Pep ripped Graves strong body with withering combinations, his hands so fast he led many assaults with right hand leads. The end came in the eighth round and left Graves muttering: "He was so fast I couldn't even see the punches coming. They came from everywhere." Later, I checked the judges score cards. All of them had Pep the winner of the third round. It wasn't even close. Yet he hadn't thrown a punch. No man in ring history could have equalled that display. It was A. J. Foyt winning the Indy 500 without a carburettor. It was Jesse Owens winning the Olympics with a broken ankle. It was Joe DiMaggio going 4-for-4 with a broom handle...That was greatness. Willie Pep was the greatest!

Willie Pep is the greatest boxer I have ever seen...
Sugar Ray Robinson.

Willie Pep-What A champion

"The winner, and new featherweight champion of the world...Willie Pep!, shouted ring announcer, Johnny Addie, as he raised Willie Pep's right hand in token of victory. But hardly anybody in Madison Square Garden could hear him, because of the tumultuous cheering coming from the 20,000 fully satisfied fans, who almost lifted the roof off the famous arena. These were the most amazing scenes ever witnessed at a boxing event; it was simply astounding. The place was absolute bedlam. Everyone was on their feet shaking hands; many were red-faced from the drama, tension and excitement from watching what was described at the time as the greatest featherweight championship fight ever fought. Even the hard-nosed, sceptical, New York reporters were caught up in these wild scenes of undiluted emotion. Not one of them could recall the last time such frenzied passion was displayed by fight fans.

This fight was significant because it had been a contest between two boxers at their peak. Sandy Saddler, the most awesome puncher in the featherweight division in the history of the fight game, against Willie Pep, a pure boxing artist. Usually a match between a pure boxer and a devastating puncher over a long distance would normally see the puncher as the winner. But on this occasion the boxer came out on top. But standing in the ring, Pep looked anything but a winner. His face was swollen, his lips twice their normal size, he was covered in bumps and cuts on the cheekbones, above and below both eyes, which later required several stitches. He looked like a limp, rag doll which had been left out in the pouring rain. But he was the happiest man in the world. He had just fought the greatest fight of his life. A glorious and thrilling contest over 15 epic rounds of pulsating action in which every fibre of his being had been put to the ultimate test. His opponent, Sandy Saddler was also badly bruised, with a bump the size of an egg over one of his eyes. He was also suffering with cuts over both eyes which needed stitching. Sandy was also magnificent. Though beaten he was certainly not disgraced in any way. His time would come again, but on this never-to-be-forgotten occasion the stage belonged to the brilliant boxer known throughout the boxing world as "Will-'o-'the-Wisp." It had been one of the most brutal championship encounters ever seen, and a fight which is still regarded as the best ever featherweight title encounter and still discussed by fans almost 50 years later.

Sat in his crowded dressing-room which was packed with celebrities like Frank Sinatra and Bob Hope, Willie excused himself and went into the shower. As the cold water cascaded down onto his swollen features and his tired, aching body, he started thinking about how it all started. Some of the memories, though painful, would never fade; memories which would fill volumes if set down on paper. A lot of things can happen to a young fighter in his formative years, most of them bad. Family problems, girl problems; he could get caught up with the wrong crowd; drinking or drugs; most commonly, though he could lose his taste for the rigours of training, which is continually un-nerving to most boxers as the perpetual diet is for most jockey's. Willie had experienced the good, the bad, and the ugly throughout his 28 years on this planet.

After he finished showering he was drying himself when a reporter, obviously caught up in the excitement of the proceedings, turned to the new champion and casually asked: "Where did it all start Willie?"

Pep! What a name for a champion, especially when he happened to be a world featherweight champion and the holder of quite a few boxing records. It conjures up a vision of a fast-moving, snappy-punching youngster, who's speedy footwork, leading and countering and magnificent boxing skills had opponents completely dazzled. That, in short, sums up Willie Pep. But there is so much more to the story of this man who is still regarded in the 1990s as the greatest boxer to ever grace a boxing ring.

Pep came from Italian stock, his true name was Gugliemo (William) Papaleo. Both his parents emigrated to America as teenagers. His father Salvatore was 19 when he met Mary, who was 15, and they married shortly afterwards. Neither parent could speak a word of English when they first arrived in America. Both of them originally came from the farming province of Syracussa in Sicily.

Willie was born in Middletown, Connecticut, on 19 September, 1922. When he was only five years old, the Papaleo family moved 16 miles to a very poor neighbourhood on the east side of Hartford. They rented a couple of rooms on the fourth floor in an eight-storey apartment house on Portland Street. The rent was 40 dollars a month. It was a stinking hovel, unheated, with only one cold-water running tap, and had only one stove in the kitchen. He was the first child of Salvatore and Mary. Times were extremely harsh and very tough indeed. Mr. Papaleo worked as a labourer six days a week, working 10 or 12 hours a day for a measly few dollars. The money he received was not enough to keep them in food and clothes, especially later on when a sister, Frances, came along, and a younger brother, Nicholas. Mrs. Papaleo fed the family on spaghetti most nights, with no meat.

Little Gugliemo did any kind of menial jobs which earned money, he ran errands, delivered newspapers and swept the pavements for local shop keepers. He would do anything to help the family budget. His family was poor, very poor. Everyone had to pitch in and help bring money into the household.

Middletown was a multi racial community with black, white, Italian, Irish, Jewish, Polish, German and Chinese. As a skinny nine-year-old kid in this kind of troublesome environment, young Papaleo became proficient at shining shoes on Main Street. Yet he was frightened and indeed, terrified; there was a reason for this unhappy circumstance. The bigger, rougher kids used to lie in wait for him, then beat him up and steal his hard-earned money. If he saw them first, he would run. If he saw an open door he would dash into the house, any house and slam the door behind him. One day a neighbour having watched the youngster running away and hiding said to him later: "Every time I see you, somebody is punching you or banging your head against the wall. Why don't you go down to the gym and learn how to fight?"

Young Papaleo started shining shoes to help the family finances. After school, he would go downtown and try and find a little corner in which to work. Eventually, he landed the corner of Anne and Asylum Streets, which was one of the best spots in the city. But he had a great deal of trouble before he made it his own. He was just a scrawny little lad and the other kids had no trouble running him off. When the big guys picked on him, he would run. One night Mr. Papaleo was looking down onto the street below from his upstairs window, he saw his son Gugliemo taking a severe beating from a much bigger boy. He was upset, but what disturbed Mr. Papaleo more than watching his son getting hurt was that Gugliemo did not attempt to fight back. He allowed this bigger lad to overwhelm him, never throwing a punch back in anger. After the skirmish had ended, Mr. Papaleo called his son into the house and took him into the basement of their home. "Why you no fight back?" asked the stern-looking father in his broken English accent. The fretful youngster tried to explain his fear to his father, but he could not find the right words. "I want that you make me proud of you. I want you to fight back, no matter how big or tough those kids are, You must fight them back hard, you understand? You have to go back out and settle it. Don't bring your fights home. Don't let anybody hit you without you fight back." Mr. Papaleo concluded.

Young Gugliemo wanted to make his father proud of him more than anything. Italian fathers were known to be very strict with their children. The father was head of the household and as such had to be obeyed in all circumstances. It was said that Mr. Papaleo had been an amateur boxer and he was a keen follower of the game. When he was old enough, Gugliemo accompanied his father to the local tournaments and developed a liking for the sport.

Mrs. Papaleo, upset at seeing her son come home regularly with a black eye or a bloody nose, decided to do something about the situation and enlisted him at the Charter Oak Gym where he could learn how to box and defend himself. But after a few sessions in the gym, a gruff-voiced trainer told Gugliemo he was much too young and far too little to become a boxer. Telling the lad to go home because he would get hurt in the gym, looking directly at the 12 year-old baby-faced youngster standing in front of him he added: "Come back when you're bigger and older." The bright-eyed youngster looked appealingly at the coach who went on to explain boxing was a tough sport, and he looked more like an altar boy than a fighter, advising him to play baseball or try something easier. With that the coach closed the door on master Papaleo. The youngster though, was not put off by these petty remarks, well meaning though they were. He was determined and committed to become a somebody through boxing. This would not be the first rejection the lad would receive from the officials at the Charter Oak Gym. It was obvious they had never encountered a youngster as keen or determined as Papaleo. He was finally accepted as a member in 1937 at the age of 14. If only those well-meaning coaches had possessed the foresight to recognise the glittering diamond they had in their midst, they would have welcomed the diminutive youngster with open arms. He proved in time to be their greatest member!

One day while he was having a street fight, a man watched and later told Gugliemo that instead of getting lumps knocked out of him for nothing, he should box amateur and then he would get seven dollars for getting the same lumps. Upon hearing this information, young Papaleo was more determined than ever to box. Armed with an old-pair of boxing gloves which someone had given him, he marched the three blocks from his home to the Charter Oak Gym and demanded he be allowed in the gym, and demanded they teach him how to box and learn how to look after himself.

Many years later Pep, explaining how he stopped being scared and running away from other kids as a youngster, said: "One day a kid came along while I was shining shoes on my corner. 'Scram, it's my corner now,' said the kid. I decided I couldn't keep running, so I decided to stand and fight. "The hell it is," I replied. "He left but he said: 'I'll be back.' "A few minutes later he came back with his cousin, a great big boy who must have been a head taller than me. He grabbed me by the shirt and wheeled me around the corner to an empty car lot. We fought like pigs for 20 minutes. The blood was spurting out of my nose and my stomach felt like it was coming apart, but, somehow or other, I hung on, and the kid finally said: 'That's it, I quit.' After that, nobody ever bothered me again."

In the gymnasium the youngster still had some of the terror of the streets in him. He was scared every time he put on the gloves. He didn't want to get hurt and he had to find a way to avoid it. His early beginnings in boxing saw him get knocked down nine or ten times a day, but he learned because he was so determined. In his neighbourhood it was tough to be small. Those bigger kids would corner him in some back alley and whip the daylights out of him. "Being knocked down in a gym was nothing compared to those alley beatings," he remarked many years later.

After a few months of training and learning the tricks of the boxing trade, young Papaleo started to develop a beautiful silky loose and relaxed style. He was nicely balanced, with lightning speed and razor-sharp reflexes, along with a wonderful left jab. His consummate boxing skill captivated older fighters who were starting to notice him, and began to watch his workouts with a great deal of interest. Gugliemo was always asking older fighters questions about boxing. He wanted to know everything about the boxing business inside out. A few of the old-timers who were regulars in the gym started to tell the Charter Oak coaches about how highly they rated the youngster. He was like a little bag of bones and had the looks of a choirboy, said one of the old-time fighters. What really impressed people though, was that for a kid, and a novice at that, he had great co-ordination and balance. He was a 'natural,' but he practised and practised and never stopped practising. After a while he was really dazzling and the way he avoided getting punched was a thing of sheer brilliance. He seemed to learn so quickly.

Papaleo was a beaver for training and would box with any fighter in the gym in order to improve his skill and ring awareness. He was becoming a student of the fistic arts, studying every aspect of the sport from top to bottom.

After watching some of the Charter Oak boxers winning watches and trophies in local amateur tournaments, Gugliemo decided he wanted some of these prizes for his mother's sideboard, not to mention the seven dollars which would help towards the family budget. Some of the amateur tournaments around the Hartford area were held at a venue named the Du-Well Athletic Club in Norwich, a somewhat appropriate name for a boxing arena but many up-and-coming young fighters started their boxing careers there. It was packed to capacity for every tournament and it was not long before little Gugielmo was booked to make his first appearance. With no television, live amateur boxing shows were very popular and always well supported in the Connecticut area.

On many occasions during the season boxing teams from Canada and New York would travel to box at the DU-WELL A.C. With interest at fever pitch, fans had to scramble for their tickets. The visiting teams were good and they usually included a number of national champions or Golden Gloves winners in their line up. Many outstanding fighters were on view and full value for money fights were a top priority.

In 1938, aged 15, and weighing around 89 pounds, Gugliemo had his first amateur bout. Boxing in majestic fashion and showing skill beyond his tender years, he won his first contest clearly. The audience gave him a standing ovation. His amateur career went like a dream from the beginning and he won his next 20 bouts to finish as Connecticut flyweight champion. Papaleo, who had boxed on a number of occasions around the Connecticut area, started to gain a reputation as well as picking up valuable experience. He was very popular with the fans who loved his smooth brand of boxing. His brilliant hit-and-hop-it style drew the spectators wherever he appeared. He was a slick mover between the ropes, making his opponents miss by inches as they punched thin air. Usually the opposition he faced was much older than himself, they were mature hard-nosed sluggers or brawlers who showed no mercy whatsoever to any opponent, no matter what the circumstances were. But Papaleo, the baby-faced youngster, had these kind of fighters floundering around the ring as they tried in vain to land haymakers on his chin.

At this time, young Papaleo also had a full-time job working in a wallpaper plant, lugging rolls of paper around for $13 a week. He was the dutiful son, helping to keep the family finances in order because his father was ill and working only occasionally. Though he knew he had a duty to help his family, he really just wanted to box and intended to eventually make boxing his full-time profession. Night and day he thought of nothing else but boxing and he would read the sports pages and every boxing magazine, and dreamed of the day his name would appear on the pages.

Amateur boxing in America in those tough times was completely different from the amateur set-up in England at the same period. It was as different as night and day. For example, in England and in most other countries a lad of 15 would not be allowed to compete in a contest against an opponent who was over 12 months older than himself, or more than five pounds heavier. In America, though, a youngster could face a boxer of open age at any time in his amateur career and the weight difference was also usually forgotten. It was also a well known fact that many so-called amateurs who boxed during those times were in fact fully fledged professionals using aliases to fool the amateur officials. This happened a great deal, especially in the American armed services, particularly when these men were posted overseas. Many professional fighters decided not to mention their occupations when they were conscripted, this was done in order to avoid certain duties and to get into the service boxing team where they would receive special perks and privileges.

Another difference between the American amateur boxers and his counterpart in England was that after their amateur contest the boxer would receive a watch as his prize for taking part in the contest. The fighter would then go into the organiser's office, hand the watch back and receive a certain amount of dollars depending on how important he was to the organising club. Strictly speaking, these lads were really professionals. This was an accepted part of the American system since conditions were so poor.

On one occasion after boxing twice on the same night on a local amateur tournament up in Crystal Lake, Papaleo handed back his two watches and was given 50 dollars. It was a huge amount of money to the youngster-more than he had ever seen before! His parents, though knowing their son was training at the Charter Oak gym, were still unaware he was boxing in "bootleg" tournaments, so he stashed the money in his shoe. But guilt overcame him as he knew such a large amount of cash would help his family considerably. However, he fancied buying a sports jacket which he had seen in a store window, so he left 10 dollars in his shoe and handed the remaining 40 dollars to his mother. Mrs. Papaleo was alarmed at the sight of so much money. A devout Roman Catholic, she asked her son: "Where did you get all this money from?" The lad explained he had fought twice on the same night and received it as his purse. Mr. Papaleo was working at that time for only a paltry 15 dollars a week at the WPA. When he came home his wife confronted him and told her husband about the 40 dollars, thinking their son had gained this money by doing some criminal deed. Mrs. Papaleo demanded the father question Gugliemo straight away. Calling his son into a side room of their home, the stern-looking father demanded to know just where and how Gugliemo had got all this money. The explanation from the young Papaleo was simple and his father accepted it with relief. The 10 dollars which he was hiding in his shoe was almost burning a hole in his conscience. Mr. Papaleo was so pleased with his son that he gave him two dollars to spend! Then he told his lad: "If you boxed twice last week and got 40 dollars, try and fight twice a week from now on."

The reason Mr. Papaleo had been unaware of his son's ring exploits on the amateur circuit, was because his son had boxed under the name of..."Willie Pep." The choice of this name would be a source of anger and bitterness within the family over the coming years with his father. The reason for this was because Italian fathers take great pride in their family names and traditions they uphold their customs religiously. The name change came purely by accident. During one of his earlier amateur contest the ring announcer could not get his tongue around Gugliemo Papaleo while making his ring introductions. The youngster was called "Peppy" at school and in the neighbourhood, so the announcer shortened it to simply "Willie Pep." And with this name a true boxing legend was born.

Mr. Papaleo though, did not like the family name being changed, but as long as his son was bringing home 40 dollars then, Willie Pep it remained.

Over the decades millions of people from all over the world would come to respect and admire this pseudonym. This name, undoubtedly, stood as an advert for the "Noble Art Of Self Defence." Willie Pep was to become the greatest boxer who ever laced on a pair of boxing gloves. There may well have been far more dangerous knockout punchers than Pep, that is not in dispute. But there was none who could claim to be smarter inside the ring than wee Willie. This man, who just by stepping through the ring ropes, brought nothing but class to a very brutal sport.

In 1938, Pep became the Connecticut State amateur flyweight champion, he and his family were overjoyed because he was now beginning to become a "somebody." This would be the first of many honours to come his way through the brilliant use of his immaculate boxing skills. The following year he was crowned the State bantamweight king. Amateur boxing officials and Hartford fans drooled over his undoubted talent. Even at such a tender age, he was graceful and smooth in his movement. Pep was a study of every move in the boxing text books. He became one of the all-time greats of amateur boxing in the New England vicinity, beside being the hottest attraction, with sellout crowds attending his contests, he was topping amateur cards all over the state and organisers were delighted at the gates the youngster was drawing to their tournaments.

One day, while training in the Charter Oak gym, he was asked to spar with a bigger and much heavier fighter who had a fight lined up and needed some sterner gym work. Though only 16, Pep willingly agreed, but instead of a gentle sparring session, it turned out to be an all-out brawl. One of the old-time fighters who was watching the action was dismayed at the youngster getting himself involved in such a fierce punch-up. Later, he pulled Pep to one side and quietly told him never to fight like that again. Explaining, that with his speed and reflexes he didn't need to fight that way and added that he should never take punches that he could avoid. With Pep's ability and talent there was no need to fight in that manner. Always remember, the old-timer added, "hit them and don't let them hit you." Pep heeded this wise old man's advice to the letter. Especially when the fellow added: "Son, when you're in the ring, imagine a cop is chasing you ready to bust your skull with his night-stick. (truncheon). Don't get caught and don't get hit. That way you will last longer than the majority of fighters. And you'll end up with all your marbles (brains) intact, and you sure won't get hurt." Those remarks became Pep's philosophy throughout his entire career. He was featherweight champion of the world for nine years, which was longer than any other champion in the division's history and he was still boxing when he was well into his 40s. The human body can only take so much punishment, but Pep is living proof elusive boxers last longer than big punchers. This became his simple explanation to people who asked about his longevity. Pep studied the ways of the artful ones in the gym, the ones who could land a punch, get away, move in again, out and around and make use of the full dimensions of the ring. Other fighters had trouble nailing him with a punch. With a mind as agile as his body, he noted the tricks they knew and copied them and made up plenty of his own.

In his early days at the Charter Oak gym, Pep learned a great deal about ringcraft from a couple of fighters, Red Guggino and Jimmy Leto, who also trained at the gym. Leto was a good body-puncher and he tried to make one out of Pep, but he wasn't good at it, Jimmy was smart, he told the youngster to stick to his own style of boxing and showed him some moves.

Pep's amateur boxing record was one to be proud of. He took part in 66 bouts, winning 63 and losing only three. Pep told me he could not remember every one of his amateur opponents, but he vividly remembers one of his three defeats in particular. In fact, he will never forget this bout for as long as he lives. It took place on 3 December, 1938. It was at a tournament being staged in Norwich, which of course was in the Hartford area. All the tickets had been sold two weeks before the event, because the Salem Crescent A.C. from New York City were appearing as the opposition. This club, with big George Gainsford as their chief coach, always brought top class fighters with them and many were Golden Gloves champions.

Pep recalls the event: "I got on the scales to weigh-in for this tournament and the needle stopped at my weight, 105 pounds. (This was with my overcoat on). I didn't know who I was due to box and as I got off the scale, a tall, sleek, black kid jumps on and tips the beam at 126 pounds spot on. This fellow looked full of confidence and he was very imposing. I pitied the kid who was going to oppose him, but this coloured guy looked straight at me and winked. I turned to the man who was acting as my manager, a guy I called 'Buster,' and said: "who's fighting him?" "My manager was a very brave man. 'You;' he replied without batting an eye. I couldn't believe it. The other guy was over 20 pounds heavier than me. My manager says to me: 'Don't worry, you will beat him. This kid is nothing, besides, if he was any good he wouldn't be fighting you would he?.' Now, that's confidence for you."

The bout went ahead and money obviously changed hands between all concerned. We can assume that with a full house eager for action the amateur officials came to a compromise with Pep's manager. Pep continued: "I fought him, or, at least I shared a ring with him. He was introduced to the crowd as Ray Roberts. What a lovely boxer this guy was, and his punches were like dynamite when they landed. He had an abundance of class, and like I said boy could he punch! He had a punch like the kick of a mule. He put me down in the first round with a wicked left hook. After sampling that blow I ran like a dog. He couldn't catch me again. It was more like a track meeting than a boxing contest. Of course I had no right to be in the same ring as this fighter. And no right giving away 20 pounds."

The true identity of Ray Roberts was later discovered to be none other than the fabulous, flamboyant, Ray Robinson, who was the open-class Golden Gloves featherweight champion and who would later add the "Sugar" to his name. Incidentally, Robinson was not his correct name either; it was "Walker Smith," but Sugar Ray Robinson sounded better. After defeating Pep, Robinson was making his way back to the changing room when he passed Willie's father. "Your boy is good, he has the makings of a champion," he told Mr. Papaleo.

After he lost to Robinson, Willie's parents, who originally didn't like the idea of him becoming a fighter, used to tell him to go to a trade school and learn to become a mechanic. But Pep won 20 more contests in a row until he was beaten by a great little fighter named Angelo Podano. Podano got shot and seriously wounded during the war, but for this incident he would have become a world-class fighter. Altogether, as an amateur Pep only lost three fights. His other loss was to Earl Roys.

In those bleak, tough days of the 1930's and 1940's many fighters had themselves a manager. Pep was to comment frequently about his manager, known to him simply as 'Buster.' "He was the bravest man in the world when it was someone else getting into the ring, said Willie.

At this time Pep was trying to learn how to box. His first manager was Pete Merrone and his trainer was Mushy Salow. At first they tried to make a puncher out of him, but he was too skinny and he used to get shellacked. Then he started to box and soon found he could handle himself with the best of them, without getting tired. In all the time he was an amateur he didn't think he ever got a bloody nose. In fact, Willie seldom got hit at all. To give you an idea of what kind of a boxer he was, he fought a very good fighter named Georgie Stone five times. The first time Willie took away Stone's amateur flyweight title. All in all, Pep defeated Stone five times and he never once got hit with a punch. The last time they fought Pep floored him. Georgie picked himself up and said: "I've had enough. No more fighting you."

Pep was getting better and smarter with each contest. He put on brilliant displays of ring craft. He was, as Tina Turner would sing on her smash hit recording many years later: "Simply The Best." He was also diligent about his conditioning, religiously doing his roadwork, hail, rain or snow, he could be seen pounding the roads around his home. He knew that even with his God-given talent he still needed to be in tip-top shape. There were no short-cuts, and no easy way of training. It had to be done and done correctly. Failure to adhere to this strict code of preparation only invited heartbreak and disaster. In the gym, he spent hours going over certain moves and correcting his mistakes. He would shadow box in front of mirrors using his imagination and talking to himself, making believe he was facing murderous knockout punchers who were intent on annihilating him. He would check, and double check his footwork, because realising he was so slight and frail he knew how vital it was to have sound mobility. He was able to move about the ring not only gracefully, but also with the minimum of fuss.

He also used the big mirror to work on his head movement. Not because he was vain, but to check he was slipping punches to within a fraction of an inch. Young Pep was indeed striving to become a perfectionist. And how well this dedication to the smallest detail would pay dividends in the coming years. He moved about the ring as if he was gliding over a ring full of eggs, so light and dainty was his footwork. Fred Astaire had nothing on him when it came to speedy movement in the tightest of space. He could zig-zag in mid movement which often resulted in his opponents being sent the wrong way then, after sending his frustrated opponents off balance and leaving them unguarded, he would score points by clever counter punching. With his nifty style of boxing Pep would have been a sensation in the 1940 Olympic Games and a near certainty to win a gold medal, but the games were of course cancelled due to the outbreak of the war.

Boxing changed dramatically in America during the 1930's through to the 1960s compared to most other countries throughout the world. Most of the American fighters were basically in the ring with the sole intention of knocking out their opponents as quickly as possible. These men were aggressive sluggers. They were mean tough hungry fighters who took no prisoners. They were all striving to become "names" in the fight jungle, in order to achieve glory and with it, financial security for themselves and their families. They seemed to be a different breed and ilk compared to the boxers in England. "They have fellows in the States, sweeping out their gyms who could beat our British champions," was a well known saying around the English boxing establishment during those times. Pep was to rise above these man-eating tigers in those tough, rough and harsh times and his star would shine bigger and brighter than any other. He became a craftsman of his profession like no other boxer before or since. Though only 17, he had been fighting as an amateur for two years, and was now bored with the amateur boxing scene. When somebody told him he could get 20 dollars a fight if he turned professional, he decided that was what he wanted to do. There were dozens of would-be managers making him offers, but Pep was a very special talent, and as such, needed the right kind of management team.

Lou Viscusi and Bill Gore
Lou Viscusi was a very knowledgeable and well-connected fight manager, known throughout the boxing world simply as "Mr Lou," though Pep

always referred to his manager as just Lou. Viscusi was born and raised in Tampa, Florida. He was already a boxing manger at 19 when he and his fighter, Jimmy Leto, arrived in Hartford at the same time as the Great Depression in 1929. He was known as "Mr. Promoter" around the New England area during the 1930s and 1940s, because he dabbled in wrestling, ice shows, circuses and semi-professional football, though boxing was always his first love. He managed several good class fighters throughout the years and also managed three world champions. Willie Pep was his first. After Pep, Viscusi took Joe "Old-Bones" Brown to the world lightweight title and then Bob Foster to the light-heavyweight crown. Mr Lou, also manouvered the likes of Roy Harris and Tony Licata, into world championships. When it came to moving fighters into championship class, Viscusi, an Orson Wells lookalike, had no equal.

He had a charming nature and was a very loyal and trusted friend. He was from the "old school" where a man's word was his bond. Viscusi was a man any aspiring boxer needed as his manager. Mr. Lou, was famed as a man who never wrote a letter in his life, preferring to do all his negotiations over the telephone no matter if it was morning, noon or night. The average person could live quite comfortable on Mr. Lou's telephone bill for a year. He was a soft-spoken, smooth operator and one of the most powerful men in boxing during Pep's career. It was openly said he had the right connections with the underworld, which prevailed in big-time boxing during the thirties through to the sixties. Viscusi was mentioned frequently during the infamous Senator Kefauver hearings held in Washington, in which the Senator was holding various investigations into the running of boxing.

Dan Parker, a famed sports writer who was feared for his scathing and critical straight-from-the-shoulder, no-holds barred journalism, headlined his column in the New York Mirror in January 1962. "Viscusi, Carbo Front, Gives Up As Houston Promoter." The forthright Parker wrote: "Lou Viscusi, henchman of Frankie Carbo, who has operated in open violation of the boxing rules, in the dual role of promoter and manager of boxers, for the past four years in Houston and other Texas cities, announced recently he had disposed of his holdings in the Texas Boxing Enterprises." Parker's article was a scathing attack upon the various boxing commissions for allowing irregularities to take place despite the Kefauver hearings. Though Parker stated quite clearly that Viscusi himself had no police record or was involved in any criminal activities whatsoever. He said, however, that Mr. Lou was one of Frankie Carbo's front men. It must be stressed though that Viscusi, according to the article did not think the exposure of his connection with the underworld boss of boxing ever hurt is standing. Whatever the rights or wrongs of the Carbo affair, Lou Viscusi, was a great manager and his record proves it.

Discussing his manager many years later, Pep said: "I had to share my purse with Viscusi fifty-fifty. It wasn't like that at first. The contract stated I would get two thirds and Lou would get one third. Expenses would come off the top. But there was some small lettering which stated that should I become a champion the split would go to fifty-fifty. Being a world champion seemed somewhat far away at that time. He was a good manager, though, and he treated me fairly."

It was a fact that Viscusi insisted from the beginning that Pep should take out two annuities. The managers sincerity was proven to Bill Lee, the Hartford Courant, sports writer. Mr. Lee was present when Viscusi asked the president of a Hartford insurance company to become Pep's legal guardian at the time Willie was a world champion and started earning big money. The invitation was declined, but Willie did invest in two annuities. But over the years one of the annuities diminished as Pep kept persistently borrowing. The other he still kept going and was able to draw on it when he reached the age of 39. In Viscusi and Gore, Pep had the best brains possible. These two were hard-nosed professionals through and through. But they both cared for their fighter. And that is the number one priority for a good team relationship. Gore did the training and teaching while Viscusi did all the matchmaking. Both men never questioned what the other was doing because they both respected each other's ability as being good at what he was doing. In all the years they were together, Viscusi, never once told Pep how to fight or interfered with his training in any way. "Lou just booked my fights and did all the negotiations, he left all the training, coaching and corner work to Bill Gore, there was never any friction between us, it was a wonderful arrangement and we worked like a team," said Pep.

Bill Gore was a native of Providence Rhode Island, a tall, scholarly-looking man who seemed to have been born with a thatch of white hair, he was quiet, honest, loyal, dependable, a deep thinker and educated in the ways of the life of his fighters. He was already a boxing trainer of repute when he teamed up with Viscusi in 1940. Gore had trained Melio Bettina, the world light-heavyweight champion and briefly coached Mike McTigue, another former light-heavyweight title holder, beside many other top-class boxers before teaching and conditioning Willie Pep to become the featherweight champion of the world. After Pep, Gore trained world champions, Joe Brown and Bob Foster. Altogether Gore worked in 29 corners in which his man was going for a world championship, these included Roy Harris, Cleveland Williams, Manuel Gonzalez and many others. He took fighters all over the world.

It is difficult to avoid sounding too effusive when talking about Pep's coach and trainer. But Bill Gore was an exceptional man, a true teacher, dedicated to passing on his knowledge, wisdom and experience to his boxers. He read widely in the pursuit of knowledge on boxing but, what was more important, he had the insight and skill to transmit that knowledge in a simple usable form to the men under his care and guidance and knew when it was most needed. Under Bill Gore's tutelage, Pep flourished and showed rapid improvement in his technique, and elevated his dream of becoming a world champion into the realms of possibility. Bill quickly stressed the need for specialisation if Pep was to reach his goal and become a champion. He had to train, and not just for a specific contest, but be prepared for all eventualities which he would encounter in the future. Gore was already mapping out his plans for Pep's assault on boxing's highest pinnacle. There is no question that Gore was instrumental in the development of Pep's immaculate boxing skills and polishing the brightest star in the boxing firmament. These two blended together splendidly with superb results. The two characters brightened the darkest smoke-filled arena's on the boxing circuit and at times brought a smile to a sometimes too serious sport. It does not matter one iota how individually brilliant a boxer might be. He still needs a cool head, and a knowledgeable coach to help bring the best out of him. Gore became Pep's mentor as well as his coach and how well these two "gelled" together is there in hard facts in the record books.

Gore was not obsessed with trying to prove himself through Willie Pep. He had already proved himself with many other champions. His main aim was to help Pep fulfil his full potential. Bill was a tough task master, pulling no punches, always straight talking and, at other times, showing the depths of emotion required in his total involvement in coaching boxers. Bill Gore demanded isolated intensity which he maintained was the requirement for success. He did not leave much room for negotiation. He questioned Pep about his aspirations in boxing. Gore was a perfectionist. He disliked the wild-swingers and brawlers who relied on brute strength, and who just waded forward throwing uneducated punches with not the slightest idea where they would land instead of using their brains to make openings to exploit to their advantage. He liked his boxer to be smartly turned out in the ring. He did not like them to have long hair, but this was purely on practical grounds, because he did not like his boxer fighting with hair flopping into his eyes. He believed the boxer had to give himself the best chance he could by operating in a contest and, if he couldn't see properly, then he was giving the opposition an advantage.

Talking to a reporter in the early days of their relationship Gore said: "It was my privilege and honour to help Willie Pep. He was a trainer's delight, because he listened and acted upon the advice he was given. He made things simple. But it took hours and hours to perfect his style and smooth movements. From the beginning he had ring savvy and a toughness which belittled his size. It makes no difference how knowledgeable or brilliant any trainer might be. It is the guy sat on the stool between rounds who makes a trainer look world class. Believe me, it's the fighter that matters. It is his success which makes or breaks a trainer."

Gore was not the type who wore fancy designer track-suits while working in the gym or the ring, like so many modern day trainers are fond of wearing. In the gym, he would be found wearing just his vest or an old white cardigan while putting Willie through his training routine. As we enter the middle 1990s, trainers are more like conditioners than teachers of boxers. This type of trainer is needed of course, but the fighter needs to learn his profession from the teachers of the boxing arts and sciences. Gore was a throwback to when boxing gyms possessed "teachers" who taught their charges all about the science of boxing.

The Little Things
Standing on the ring apron watching Pep work on his technique while training under Gore's supervision was both edifying and a chastening experience. The trainer's eyes rarely leave his pupil. The longer you observed Gore at work the more obvious it became that he had mastered all the arts of making a world champion run smoothly and successfully. Motivation, man-management, incentive, they are all ingredients of his

formula. 'Do the simple things' he would tell Willie in that quiet but firm manner of his. 'Concentrate on doing the little things well.' Had he been from New York, or based in the "Big Apple," Gore would have been talked about as the greatest trainer ever, or certainly on the lines of Ray Arcel, Charley Goldman, Jack Blackburn, and others of that ilk. But it never bothered him unduly what anyone thought about him. "He was a boxer's trainer," said Pep. By that statement Willie meant that for boxers who relied on skill and finesse, Bill Gore was the ideal trainer for them. He loved scientific boxers. Another feature about Gore was his reliability. He never missed a training session nor was he late. He epitomised the differences which exist between the best and the ordinary coaches. He would never force Pep to train. Rather he would encourage and work on the technicalities with him.

There was a third member of the training team; Johnny Datro, a young trainer from Hartford was also a great asset and whom Gore thought very highly of though not much was heard about him.

Speaking to writer Jimmy Breslin, about Willie Pep in later life, Gore would give a little smile as if the mere mention of Pep's name had switched on happy memories and he said: "I started him off in the gym. Show him something and bingo! He learns it for life! I remember once I showed him how to spin a man. What you do is spin him and take the step past him and come out behind him. 'I don't know,' said Willie, 'I just can't get it right.' That was the first day. So he went back into the gym in the afternoons. He kept practicing for days, too. After that he could do it like second nature. Imagine that? He learns a move that nobody in the business can do today. And this kid learns it in a few days."

Gore said Pep was a hyperactive fellow who couldn't sit down for a minute. Journalists said Willie lost a lot of his money gambling. But Gore didn't know anything about that, but what he could tell everyone for certain was that though Willie Pep might well have been a heavy gambler on the horses and dice, he never once gambled on any fight. Gore, did not mean by actually putting money on his fights. No, he meant Pep would not gamble whether it was right or wrong to fight a fighter a certain way. He was confident enough to beat them with his ability and skill, yes, he never took a gamble on winning. He was certain he would be declared the winner on his own merits.

Bill Lee, remembers Lou Viscusi had been keeping an eye on young

Pep's amateur achievements and showed a keen interest when the brilliant youngster expressed a desire to leave the amateur ranks. Mr. Lou had watched Pep on many occasions and was impressed, Willie had arranged to meet Viscusi in a local Hartford gym to discuss a contract. But he became ill and was rushed to hospital suffering with appendicitus. Viscusi visited Willie in hospital, though he couldn't have been very impressed as he looked at the skinny little kid, practically lost in a great big hospital bed. He looked anything but a fledgling fighter. Mr. Lou looked him up and down a couple of times and then said in a deep voice: "Do you really want to be a fighter, kid?" "That's all I want to be," replied Pep. "Then I'll help you out," said Viscusi. When Pep recovered from the appendicitis, he went to the gym to meet Viscusi. Bill Gore was in the room as Pep discussed his contract with Mr. Lou. Bill Murray, who was a very good fighter of that period was topping a local bill and Gore was training him. Viscusi told Pep he would have his first professional contest on the undercard to the Murray fight. He wanted Gore to take a close look at Pep and give his opinion of Willie's potential.

When Gore left the gym, Viscusi looked hard at the youngster and asked him a pointed question: "Willie, do you really want to learn how to box?" "Yes, I do," replied Pep. "I want to learn everything there is about boxing, inside out, because I want to become a world champion." Mr. Lou smiled at him and added: "Good, that's what I wanted to hear you say. Do yourself a big favour, listen, learn, and do everything Bill Gore tells you and I promise you that you'll never regret it. You will become a world champion, and a great one. Gore is a wonderful teacher, he will show you things about boxing which you never knew existed. I have worked closely with this man for years. Bill is a person who you can bet your last dollar on. Listen and learn what he preaches."

Having decided to make boxing his livelihood, Pep soon learned that if he were to fulfil his new-found ambition, he would have to have more in his repertoire than a left jab, a right cross and a left hook. Gore and his new pupil were talking about the change from amateur boxing to the professional side of the business when the trainer told Willie to meet him the following morning at six o' clock in the cafeteria on Asylum Street. Willie had never got up that early before to train, but he was so excited about working with a real professional that he was up way before six. He went over to the cafeteria and Gore was sitting with Bill Murray. Pep noticed

Murray was eating ham and eggs, with coffee. Gore asked Willie to have something to eat. "No", said Pep, explaining that he never ate before running. Gore took the two boxers to Keany Park, where they commenced their run. They would run at a jog, sprint, loosen up. Willie found he was having trouble keeping up with Murray. After about an hour of this, he was absolutely exhausted. After the run was completed, Gore told Pep to meet them about eleven 'o' clock in the cafeteria. When he got there at eleven, Murray was eating a snack. Gore asked Willie to have something to eat but was told that he had already eaten at home after the roadwork. When they went to the gym Pep sparred with Murray and took a walloping. This went on for three or four days, meeting in the cafeteria, roadwork, then the gym. The youngster found he was tired out and was having trouble holding his own while sparring with Murray. Finally, he began to take tea and toast at the cafeteria with them. Then he began to eat like Murray and he found he was getting stronger. Soon Billy Murray couldn't hold him in the gym, a few months later, Murray told Gore, "This kid is fantastic."

The point was Gore had not told Pep a thing. He just indicated that he had been training wrong by having him work with Murray. From then on, Willie Pep trained Bill Gore's way. (Bill Murray was killed on active service during the war.)

Making His Professional Debut

In 1940, when Pep made his professional debut, there was a much bigger battle taking place in Europe with dark grey clouds of forebodence hanging in the air and many lives being lost. Ultimately the world was at war. It was shocking and sport in Britain and Europe had taken a back seat. But in America boxing was booming and in its heyday. Television had not yet made its mark on the sport, but just about every town in the United States of any size had weekly boxing shows. Top stars could be seen performing in the small towns as well as the major venues.

The featherweight champion, or the National Boxing Association version of the title was held by Petey Scalzo. Billy Conn, who is remembered for giving Joe Louis one of his hardest championship fights, was the light-heavyweight champion of the world. Lou Ambers was the lightweight king. Henry Armstrong the welterweight holder.

Those "Good Old Days" meant busy boxers, large crowds and the ticket price was right. While Pep was preparing to make his debut, onlookers in the gym would look on in amazement as he was going through his workout, startled by the simple and easy way in which he would evade punches from his sparring partners. Watching him train was a thing of beauty, he was so majestic and graceful in everything he did but Willie never took liberties with the other less gifted boxers engaged to help him prepare. To him and Gore, his sparring partners were there strictly in order for him to practice his skills and polish up his movements in preparation for the night when it mattered most of all, the fight itself. Gore remarked to a fan: "He's only a youngster, but he's fabulous!" He practised his boxing technique until he became an expert. Then he would practice some more. Never satisfied until he had everything working to perfection, Pep really was breathtaking in everything he did between the ropes. He was not a devastating hitter by any means, but he was sharp, precise and very accurate. He dominated opponents with his perfect and efficient jab, which was like a trombone. When meeting the many bull-like opponents over the coming years, he performed like a matador, tormenting and frustrating them. He had also built up tremendous reserves of stamina which served him well.

Talking to a young reporter one day about his early childhood, Pep related a little incident which had a great bearing on the way he boxed throughout his career. It happened when he was 14! He had had enough of running away from bullies in his tough Hartford neighbourhood. These kids had made his life miserable. Coming home from school, two young thugs chased after young Pep, and in desperation the spindle-legged little kid raced ahead of his two beefy pursuers. This was getting to be a regular after-school game, chasing the skinny youngster, who ran so fast and scared so easily.

This time they caught him after Willie sped into a blind alley, the two young hoodlums closed in, eager for the sport that was to come. For an instant their prey, standing barely five-feet and less than a hundred-pounds cowered, the two bullies were about to show their victim no mercy what so ever. When they received the shock of their lives. A very surprising thing happened. The two kids were head and shoulders bigger than Willie. They were just about to give him a working over, as one of them was about to biff him, by sheer instinct, Pep smashed out with a quick left. His fist went like an arrow straight into the bully's mouth, then a straight right came out of nowhere and the thug landed on the cement on his backside. The other bully, mouth gaping, stared at little Pep in wonder and then Willie let fly with his two fists. He really lashed into him before he could raise his hands. The bigger lad gasped, then ran out of the alley. Moaning and spitting blood, his beaten companion scuttled after him. Willie could never forget the look of astonishment, and the shock which registered on their faces. The two bullies were surprised by Pep's action. Willie ran like the wind as fast as his little legs could carry him, but he would never forget the look of sheer disbelief on those fellows faces. They were completely dumb struck, startled and bewildered by his instant reaction towards them.

This was the beginning of a legend. Pep had had enough of running. He had decided to fight back. Expecting to be beaten, he was astonished to discover, suddenly, the hidden powers and blinding speed which undermined the genius that was to make the name of Willie Pep a synonym for fighting mastery. It was to last for 29 years. It grew and glittered and he wore it like a suit of armour. The way he had licked these two young thugs, who outweighed him by about 50 pounds, was the method with which he would put to devastating effect during his 241 professional contests many years later. Indeed, many of his opponents would feel just as those young thugs had felt after their short, but painful confrontation at the hands of Pep.

On 3 July, 1940, Willie made his professional debut in Hartford, clearly outpointing James McGovern over four pulsating rounds. He received 50 dollars for his first contest. He took it home and gave it to his father. Mr. Papaleo was pleased and suggested his son had better stay a fighter. After all, 50 dollars was more than all the family earned in a week. This was the start of a ten year reign which would never be bettered, only a fluke defeat and a draw marred his otherwise perfect record in his first 134 professional fights, becoming a boxing legend in the process. He would break records at the turnstiles and draw record crowds to his performances. He would travel all over America and give ordinary fans the chance to watch a genuine super star of the boxing ring in action without them having to travel to the big cities. He achieved immortal feats in the ring until he lost his wife, his money and his army of followers and also his title as "King of the featherweights" when too much success went to his head. But let me not jump ahead of the story.

After his first victory Willie was on his way. Just 22 days later he gained his second victory, again by a points decision over four rounds. His opponent was a tough little fighter named Joey Marcus and once again it took place in his home town of Hartford. Willie, boxing as a bantamweight, was feeling on top of the world. He had gone from being a frightened kid into a confident happy-go-lucky youngster in just a few short years. Life seemed wonderful. Professional boxing was Pep's only source of income. He had no other occupation, having given up his job in the paper plant to concentrate on being a full-time fighter.

Before 1940 was over he would have eight more bouts, winning them all in superb style, including six stoppages. Pep was attracting big crowds around Hartford. Ten bouts in less than six months, a schedule few fighters would attempt today. Willie's first 20 professional contests were boxed mainly in and around his hometown. There were a large number of boxing venues around the Connecticut area in this period. Places such as the Hartford Auditorium, Norwich Armory, New Haven Arena, Dawbury Armory, Norwalk Armory, The Candlelite Stadium, Ocean Beach Auditorium, beside many others. It was in these halls that the up-and-coming youngster learned his trade.

Though he was a well known face throughout Connecticut, he was virtually unheard of outside his own state. "The Ring" magazine was known as the bible of boxing in those days. Managers would try their upmost to publicise their fighters in this publication, going to any lengths to get Nat Fleischer, the founder and owner, to mention their names, because once featured in the "Ring" it meant vast exposure. In turn the manager could demand a bigger purse from the promoters. Some managers were better than others at obtaining plenty of publicity. For example, Battling Siki's manager had his fighter walking down Broadway with a lion on a chain. Much later Sandy Saddler was dressed up with a Scottish kilt and proclaimed to be a Scotsman, when in fact he was a black American. There were all kind of pranks and stunts pulled by managers and publicity agents to get their fighters the right attention.

Harry Markson was head of the boxing department for Madison Square Garden for many years. In the early 1940s he was attending a dinner in Hartford, honouring a retiring Connecticut State Boxing Commissioner. Just before the speeches started, he felt a tap on his shoulder. It was Lou Viscusi. Lou whispered to Markson that he had a fine young prospect in his stable and would appreciate it very much if he, when called upon to make his speech, would say a few complimentary words about his new prospect. Markson had never heard of Willie Pep at this time. It was in Pep's early days, but Markson did oblige Viscusi and he proclaimed that Mr. Lou's young prospect had all the necessary ring attributes to take him all the way to the top of his division. "Mind you, I was proved correct wasn't I?, said Markson, adding. "He really was a wonderful boxer. Willie was a throwback to the good old days of the prize ring when scientific boxing was in its flower. There will never be another boxer like Pep. I know times have changed and all kinds of records are being broken, but I doubt very much that Willie Pep's feats will ever be bettered. He could do everything in the ring. He was a genius!"

Pep though, looked nothing like a fighter with his smooth features and raven mop of black curly hair and frail looking body, but what a joy he was to his followers once he stepped into the ring and the bell sent him into action. The crowds were transfixed watching this gifted kid. His footwork was akin to a Gene Kelly or any top class dancer. He was quite a crowd-pleaser. It was marvellous the way he could bob and weave, slip and slide, avoiding punches with ease. Pep knew full well that the fighters who he was facing would show no mercy whatsoever to an 18-year-old novice boxer. Some of the fighters from that era were ferocious sluggers who would try and knock you out in the opening seconds of a contest. In the main the type of fighters that roamed the rings in Pep's day were true craftsmen of boxing. They had to be, because there was no soft or easy build up for them. They fought whoever they were matched against otherwise there were other fighters ready to take their place. With the vast numbers of professional boxers of that period it was inevitable that good fighters would emerge from such a competitive situation. One such fighter was Charley Burley, this man never got the breaks to become a champion or make any vast amounts of money. Burley would have been a certain champion in any other era. He was absolutely brilliant at boxing and hitting. Archie Moore said of Burley that he was the hardest opponent he had ever faced. Lloyd Marshall, Holman Williams and Jimmy Bivins were other capable fighters of that period who could quite feasibly have become champions only for the system. The world champions and the top-ten contenders were a class above the rest of the pack. That was why it was so hard to break through and gain entry into the top ten rankings. Potentionally Pep was head and shoulders above them all.

Boxing gets a terrible reputation for the damage it does to the human brain, but done the Willie Pep way it becomes an art form and acceptable. During Pep's career there were only the eight world champions, and the man in the street could name all eight champions in the eight divisions from flyweight to heavyweight. Boxers knew how to fight or they found themselves floundering and struggling to survive in the shark-infested waters of professional boxing. There were no easy rides for anyone. In those good old, bad old days, even the very best prospects learned their trade as anonymous preliminary fighters. If they made mistakes or looked less than perfect, nobody except the fans in the arena knew about it. When the time came to finally showcase them in a big fight, the boxer had already had ample opportunity to iron out the wrinkles. Pep was no exception. Today, it's different. Even moderately gifted fighters frequently appear on television or satellite, viewed by millions of people, where every flaw is scrutinised, every mistake magnified. This of course is the negative side of this system.

In the 1940's through to the 1960's, there were a lot of very capable fighters who never got anywhere or made any real money or ever got a title shot. Middleweights such as Artie Towne, Rory Calhoun, Joey Giambra, Holly Mims and George Benton, to mention just a few. In between fights, and to gain more knowledge about his chosen profession, Pep thought nothing of travelling throughout America in search of action in the numerous gyms which existed in nearly every town or city. This was one of the reasons why his improvement was so rapid. He was footloose and fancy free, happy doing something which he had dreamed of doing since he first laced on a pair of boxing gloves. He wanted to keep improving but to do so it required an open mind, which he had. In a strange gym, he had to pit his wits and skills against the gym champions. These fellows were the toughest fighters of their own gyms. Kings of their own domains. Pep was always ready to tackle these kind of fighters. Many times he would casually walk into a gym. The local managers, always on the lookout for easy touches, would offer the baby-faced kid a dollar a round to spar with their tigers. Pep duly accepted the managers invitation. Once the manager saw Willie making the local stars look foolish, through his fascinating speed and brilliance they would quickly order him out of the ring, for fear of making their fighters look inept and like raw beginners. Quickly paying him his dollar, they would enquire if he had a manager. When knowing they had no chance of signing him because he was already under contract, they would wish him well and send him on his way, shaking their heads at his flawless technique and marvelling at his aptitude. Willie had a bubbly attitude towards life, always laughing and ready for a bit of frolicking with his pals.

Pep told me: "I loved getting into the ring with the local big shot. I'd make him miss me a few times. This made them steaming wild. Then they would lose their cool. After that they were tailor-made for my brand of boxing.

I was never a one-punch knockout fighter, but I used to practice correct punching. I knew the best targets, this cut a lot of guys up badly. And I was very accurate about where I placed my shots and this would again bust guys up a great deal as well."

It is a true saying that one can never learn enough about one's chosen profession. This applies in any walk of life, be you a sportsman or a doctor, or whatever your trade and with this in mind Pep could never learn enough. This attitude remained the same throughout his boxing career. He hated to stand still. He loved the involvement of everyday boxing events. To Willie the gym was his office. That's where he perfected his skills. He would spend hours watching other fighters work-out. His total dedication to his profession would put many modern day fighters to shame.

In his second year as a professional Pep had 22 contests, winning them all in breathtaking style. He made certain those 22 contests were bouts of skill, his brain prevailing over his opponent's brawn. In every respect, he never took risks, ever. The opposition was nearly always of a high quality. In the main they were knockout sluggers. They seemed to be in abundance in his day. Pep traded on his guile, agility and craft. He was, even at his tender age, arguably the most accomplished ring general ever produced by America. He was a master tactician whose lack of a real knockout wallop appeared to be his only flaw. In some of those 22 bouts he would tie his opponents in knots with his outstanding and clever feints and smart footwork. His defensive technique was good enough to nullify their power. The boxing connoisseurs loved his reassuring presence; a reaffirmation of craftsmanship in an era dominated by sluggers in two much of a hurry to learn the nuances of their profession. Even this early in his career he was receiving accolades such as: "Pep of the slick moves...He has perfect balance." He treated every opponent's punch as a personal insult. He seemed so comfortable in the ring, so suited, that when he was boxing, you couldn't imagine him doing anything else. He was like the laughing cavalier in the boxing ring, moving with flair and putting a smile on boxing's usually stone face.

Many of the older fighters regarded Pep as nothing more than a young upstart, but he had learned his lessons well. With his beautiful loose, relaxed style, moving side to side, never standing still or flat footed, he would leave his opponents frustrated and totally bewildered. Pep got off to a fast start as a professional. He won his first 22 fights in a row, all of them in the Connecticut area, and most of them four rounders. A place they loved him was at Holyoke, Massschusetts. He fought there a lot, one night he boxed a rough, tough fellow named Ruby Garcia from Puerto Rico. Pep was the 3-1 underdog, but he won that fight. The fans and the newspapers said it was one of the greatest fights in the history of the Valley Arena. (Pep beat Garcia twice more, the third occasion was on 12 December, 1941 in a four rounder at Madison Square Garden. That was his Garden debut).

On 16 July 1941, Willie faced the toughest task of his 22 fight career when he fought tough-looking, experienced Irish Jimmy Gilligan of Buffalo, at the Bulkely Stadium in Hartford. The main event was between Marty Servo, who was unbeaten in 43 bouts and New York's Bobby Britton, the son of Jack Britton the former welterweight champion. (In 1946 Servo would beat Freddie Cochrane for the world welterweight title, knocking him out in four rounds and would retire because of an injury without ever defending the crown.)

The crowd were anticipating a cracking contest between Pep and Gilligan, Willie had been spectacular so far in his brief pro career and performed artistically in many of his contests. He boxed beautifully to outpoint Gilligan, winning all eight rounds. When I visited his home in 1994, Willie recalled an amusing incident which happened around the 1941 period. He was only a four round fighter and only getting small purses. Things were going well for him but he was beginning to get restless. Being young and impulsive he wanted recognition and bigger purses. Viscusi didn't seem to be moving him. Pep was boxing four and six round bouts and there was not much money in those kind of fights. One day, in October 1941, Willie and three friends decided to run away. They were all dissatisfied with their lives for one reason or another. One lad wanted to be an actor, so they decided to go to California. Another one, Jasper, owned a car, a 1936 Ford convertible. They pooled their money together and found they had twenty-five dollars between them. They made it to California in five days and five nights. Stopping on the road to buy a loaf of bread and eat it on the way. One day the car hit a rabbit. The lads got out, and skinned it and cooked it. All of them agreed it tasted awful. They finally made it to Los Angeles, the car was by now clapped out. And on the remaining 15 dollars, Willie and his chums took a room at the New Grant Hotel. They got a double bed and a twin. At bed time they would flip a coin each night to see who got what.

The following day Pep went to the local gym on Main Street offering his services as a sparring partner in order to earn some much needed money. He met a trainer, Al Lang, who said he'd like to see Willie box. Some of the managers and trainers looked at the puny-looking youngster and shook their heads. "Kid, you will get yourself killed in here. Go back home," he was told. Persistently Pep pressed forward until he was told to get stripped. Finally one particular manager said to him: ""Okay, kid, you can box with my guy. I'll pay you a dollar a round. Put the gloves on and spar with him," pointing to a swarthy-looking well-built fighter. When they got into the ring everyone in the gym stopped punching the bags and speed balls or whatever they were doing in order to watch this sparring session. There was a sudden hush about the place. After going three brisk rounds at breathtaking speed, the manager called "enough." Lang and everyone in the gym was suitably impressed with Pep's almost flawless technique and toughness. Lang had of course like everyone else in that gym thought Willie would get anihilated but Pep had no intention of standing flat-footed and slugging it out with anyone, least of all the fighter he was sparring with. Willie took his three dollars and he and friends headed for the nearest restaurant. He went back to that gym every day for a week. The three dollars he earned for sparring was the only money the four friends had between them. It was their food money. On the last day of sparring as Pep was changing into his gym clothes, Lang asked him if he knew who he had been sparring with all that week?' Willie told him he had not got a clue, Lang looked surprised and said in a slow drawl..."Manuel Ortiz, that's who you've been sparring with, and he couldn't lay a glove on you. Kid, you're some fighter." (Ortiz would win the world bantamweight title less than a year later). Lang was so impressed by Pep's displays with the teak-tough hard-punching Ortiz that he booked Willie for a contest in the American Legion Stadium in Hollywood. The Hartford kid was the four round opening contest. The stadium was packed to capacity. Phil Silvers (Bilko) and Betty Grable were sitting ringside. Pep won his fight easy and he was supposed to get 50 dollars, but he owed Lang 15 dollars. Then some man who was acting as a manager took his cut, Willie finished with only ten dollars he was absolutely disgusted as well as broke, so he wired home for some money. He and Jasper went back to Hartford by bus. The other two lads stayed on the coast.

Although a slugger and brawler, the late but great Rocky Marciano was a great admirer of Willie Pep's special brand of boxing. Rocky openly admitted he was in awe of his idol, making no secret of his admiration for the "Will-'o-'the-Wisp," as sports writers had begun calling the Hartford wonder boy. Marciano's style of fighting was as far removed from the velvet touches of Pep as one could ever imagine, but this did not stop the "Twentieth Century Caveman," as that doyen of boxing reporters, Peter Wilson called Marciano, from appreciating the amazing, delicate and refined boxing ability and ring savvy of Pep.

1942 was Pep's third year in the professional ranks and it would be another fantastic year for the youngster who had now moved up to the featherweight class. He was a growing lad and though he dearly wanted to box for the bantamweight championship, time was running out for him in that division. He could no longer struggle to hold the bantamweight poundage. Willie had 24 contests, and would go on to achieve immortality and a place in ring history in this momentous year. The quality of some of the 24 opponents he faced set the seal for the rest of his career. And mark him down as a prospect of the highest order. A closer look at some of these opponents shows the true brilliance of the up-and-coming Hartford prospect. Though Pep was making a huge impression around the New England area, he was totally disregarded by critical New York reporters until after his baptism of fire on 24 February of 1942, at Foot Guard Hall, Hartford, (the venue where he made his professional debut) when he faced his toughest task in "Whistling" Willie Roach, a rugged and dangerous black fighter from Wilmington, Delaware. In this contest, Pep did a masterful job of execution on the cagey tough-as-nails Roach who could soak up punishment all night long and still throw punches in retaliation. The Hartford youngster boxed with more vision and skill than he had ever displayed in any previous contest and his rapier like punches were sheer perfection. Pep must have delivered between 80 and 90 punches in every one of the eight totally absorbing rounds, but could not floor the game Roach. In a momentous clash, the Delaware scrapper kept stalking and boring in with his head every minute in an attempt to force Pep into a corner or against the ropes to deliver his own power-packed left hooks. But Willie kept his chin tucked onto his chest, ducked, and skipped around the ring, parried intended knockout blows with nonchalance and boxed majestically, never allowing the Wilmington boy to get set.

Roach could never find Pep standing still long enough for him to land two successive punches. The sharpshooting Hartford lad made his foe miss repeatedly then poured rapid-fire counter punches to head and body with such eye-catching accuracy that he won seven of the eight rounds. The capacity crowd were rooting from the first sound of the opening bell, so exciting was this encounter but wondered how any man could withstand such a beating without going to the canvas. Pep received a rousing ovation at the conclusion of the bout, his thirty-seventh professional victory. Roach, though thoroughly beaten, was also given a tremendous hand for his ability to extend Pep and bring out in the Hartford kid skill not even his close followers knew he possessed. Roach was a very dangerous fighter and would go on to prove to be one of boxing's uncrowned champions.

Spider Sensationally Demolished

Pep's 39th contest saw him fill the new Hartford Auditorium for the first headline fight held there. It was estimated 4,000 fans were inside with the same number outside. With all the seats in this converted car barn occupied and much of the standing room filled by late comers, general manager Frank Dubinsky made a brief welcome speech and introduced Melio Bettina, the former world light-heavyweight champion who had been trained by Bill Gore, and the famous rodeo star Hoot Gibson. Though Pep's fight against Willie Roach was considered by the boxing writers as his best to date, his bout with John "Spider" Armstrong of Toronto surpassed even that, and he was even more impressive and spectacular. Willie, giving the appearance of being stronger than ever before, floored the tough Canadian twice in the first round for counts of nine and came very close to ending matters then and there. But Armstrong came back aggressively after each count and in round two he nearly caused a shock when he staggered the local idol with a perfectly placed left hook. This was a barnstorming bout with the fans ecstatic with excitement. The third saw the hard-punching Spider connect on Pep's chin with three bristling right handers. Pep took the blows without any signs of distress.

The crafty Canadian fighter was forcing the fight and the Hartford lad changed tactics. In round four the speed of Pep's punches sent Armstrong down near the ropes for another nine count before climbing dizzily to his feet. He tried to duck and weave out of trouble before Willie showed no mercy and dispatched a crunching right cross on his chin. The lantern-jawed Canadian hit the floor with a resounding thud and his head hit the ring boards. Game as they come, Spider tried valiantly to beat the count but was finally counted out by referee Joe Curry. Though this was a convincing victory, Spider was Pep's best and most experienced opponent and left the large crowd completely satisfied the Hartford youngster was ready to meet the leading world featherweight contenders. By the virtue of this clean knockout over a respected fighter, Willie showed he was improving with every contest. There had never been any doubts about his speed and boxing skill, but against Armstrong he displayed a teeth-rattling wallop against a genuine "name" fighter.

The two victories over Roach and Armstrong were impressive and brought Pep much needed national acclaim but the manner in which he handled former world champion, Joey Archibald, made the fans and boxing officials really sit up and take him seriously. Joey Archibald of Providence, Rhode Island, had won his world featherweight championship (albeit the New York version) in 1938. Beating Mike Belloise on points in New York, he successfully defended the title twice before losing it to Henry Jeffra in May 1940. Archibald regained his championship a year later by beating Jeffra in a rematch, only to lose it yet again to one of the most dynamic punching featherweights boxing had seen for many years, the devastating knockout sensation Alberto "Chalky" Wright, by a knockout in the 11th round in September 1941.

In June 1942, in an open-air tournament in the Bulkeley Baseball Stadium in front of 5,500 spectators the former champion was selected to test out the Hartford sensation. The newspapers predicted a close contest and stated in no uncertain terms Archibald would test Pep to his very limits. But Pep gave another beautiful display of ring science as he won all eight rounds on referee Louis (Kid) Kaplan's score card. Kaplan, a former champion in the featherweight division, was astounded at the easy way the youngster handled the cagey Archibald. Joey was still in possession of his ring generalship and he needed it in order to keep himself from being stopped by the flailing fist of the up-and-coming prospect. This was a contest of styles between two technically skillful boxers. It must be stressed the former champion's ducking and clutching tactics spoilt the fight from being a classic. Willie had to do all the leading and in doing so he boxed like a future champion. Archibald for all his ring knowledge managed to connect with only three solid punches. The local man's blinding speed saw him pile up an insurmountable margin and won with plenty to spare. Only Joey's savvy saved him from getting beaten inside the distance. Boxing officials were flabbergasted at the manner in which Willie easily defeated his vastly experienced opponent. (The various record books show this as a ten round contest, but it was in fact only an eight rounder. They did fight a ten rounder four months later, with Pep easily outpointing Archibald again).

New England Champion

After his easy victory against Archibald, manager Lou Viscusi decided the time was right for his young prodigy to box for the New England featherweight championship. The champion was lanky Abe Denner of Boston who had won the crown by flattening the highly regarded Sal Bartolo, who also hailed from Boston. He had made one successful defence of his title when he outpointed New Haven's Snooks Lacey over the 15 round distance. Viscusi had selected another vastly experienced campaigner for his young prodigy to challenge. This would be the first occasion Willie would be called upon to travel more than eight rounds. The champion had fought far more seasoned opponents and fought several 10, 12 and 15 round contests. Beside having the edge in experience, Denner had the advantage in height and reach. Being unusually tall for a featherweight, at 5ft 9ins, he was three-inches taller than Pep plus had a reach of 70 inches compared to Willie's 67. The reason Viscusi took this fight for his young prospect was that Willie had been rapidly improving with each contest and was looking sensational in the gym. The manager intended bringing Willie along slowly, but the manner of the kids victories was forcing Viscusi to re-think his plans.

The Bulkeley Baseball Stadium was the venue for this encounter and over 6,000 fans were seated for an eventful occasion. The Boston fighter looked menacing as he entered the ring. What followed was a scintillating and scientific display from the challenger which had the enthralled spectators spellbound as they saw Pep win ten of the 12 rounds on referee, Lou Bogash's scorecard, with the other two rounds even. Willie's blinding speed had the champion totally bemused from start to finish and his rapier punching inflicted a nasty cut under his left eye. There were no knockdowns and it was much too one-sided to be exciting, but it was a good, interesting scrap nevertheless. Denner, though he was unable to nail the darting Hartford kid with a solid punch, tried hard and stood up manfully to Pep's fire. The dethroned champion was never in serious danger, although he was staggered and knocked off balance a dozen times.

The manner of Pep's victory over the Boston brawler was brilliance personified. The home town crowd applauded both fighters long and loud as State Athletic Commissioner, Frank S. Coskey, presented the new champion with the New England championship belt which had been donated by the Ring Magazine. He then cracked the inner circle of the boxing establishment with a smashing victory over Pedro Hernandez, who was generally regarded as the world's number two ranked featherweight. The masterful way he had dealt with these well-established fighters in such breathtaking fashion was very impressive indeed. Bill Gore told close friends that in these contests Willie had complete control over his opponents. He was perfection said the trainer, further stating Willie was very strong-minded for a youngster. "He knows he has 30, 40, or more minutes in the ring, and he quickly assesses the opposition, then will settle down and do whatever is necessary to secure a victory," concluded Gore.

Bill Lee, the Hartford Courant journalist said: "Pep spent the entire 22 rounds against Denner and Hernandez tantalising them, but doing it all with absolute majesty and grace." Pep's progress since his first professional contest at Foot Guard Hall, in 1940, had been phenomonal. This fellow was not your stereotyped boxer, that last word, with it's implication on monotony, terrified him. He was a boxer of boundless energy.

The way some sporting stars appear these days, they are a law unto themselves, a breed apart, untouched by everyday obligations; and the way some of them behave, the ordinary fan can be forgiven for getting this inflated opinion of his hero. He would, however, very quickly change his mind if he could have spent just a short time behind the scenes at Willie Pep's training headquarters. Self-importance, exaggerated self-esteem, arrogance and conceit were not qualities likely to be found in Willie Pep.

Ray Arcel was in the 1940's already a well-respected trainer of world champions and top contenders, and he would continue to be instrumental in developing many more champions up to the 1980's. Ray fondly recalled the first time he saw Pep. "I had been hearing good things about Willie

Pep. But you must remember in those days there was several top fighters in each division who were quite capable of becoming champions given the opportunity. But I must admit Pep was really something special.

He made boxing look so simple. He was quick-not just physically, but quick up here (he tapped his temple). Willie saw things, and did things in a split-second. He was only five foot six and, his arms and legs were like matchsticks, but pure genius every inch of it. Mind you, he had a great teacher in Bill Gore. The secret is having a great fighter and a great trainer working together. Willie Pep and Bill Gore were exceptional, what a combination."

Poison Ivy

Boxing meant everything to young Pep, he lived and breathed nothing but boxing, when he wasn't fighting or training he was an avid film fan and loved going to the cinema, and there was no shortage of picture houses around the Hartford area.

It was quite obvious how advanced Pep had become in just a short time in the professional ranks. Besides beating the likes of former champion Joey Archibald, he was taking on and beating other well established fighters who in any other era would have become world champions themselves. Though things were progressing well he once again became restless in the summer of 1942, mainly because he thought his stablemate the more experienced Bobby "Poison" Ivy, also a featherweight, was getting all the publicity and the big purses. Willie left Hartford and moved to New York. There he met a well-known fight manager, Dewey Fragetta, and he took Pep to the Pioneer Gym, saw him box and was very impressed by what the youngster displayed. When Viscusi found out where Pep was he phoned and told Fragetta to send Willie back to Hartford immediately. When Willie arrived back home, Mr Lou, looking perplexed said to him: "Goddam it, all right, I'll move you up in class."

Though only a featherweight, "Poison" Ivy was the New England lightweight champion at the time. It was no secret there was friction and an element of "needle" between Willie and Ivy. Bobby was responsible for giving the younger Pep some wicked gym beatings when Willie was only an amateur and climbing the fistic ladder. Pep had never forgotten Ivy's liberty taking and vowed to pay the more experienced fighter back with interest.

Pep told me about his feud with Ivy, and said: "Bobby Ivy, was a stablemate of mine. He seemed to be getting all the attention and all the good fights and big purses. He was a main-eventer and I was the preliminary boy. Everything around the gym and in Hartford was Ivy this and Ivy that. I said to Lou: 'What's the matter with me? I ain't got poison Ivy.' I never really got along very well with Ivy. The truth is, he used to hammer the living daylights out of me in the gym."

In the early days, before Bill Gore took over Pep's training full-time, Willie had a fellow named Lenny Merullo trying to teach him how to box. Merullo had trained Bat Battalino, the old featherweight champion. Battalino was a bullish type of fighter who would just walk in and punch. Merullo tried to teach Pep the same way, but Willie was not a puncher and he knew it. Ivy just held him in contempt. While trying to be a puncher, Pep would try and mix it with Bobby Ivy in the gym and the older fighter would just cream Willie. Ivy was a lot stronger and a real good puncher. Pep badly wanted to get even with the more experienced fighter. He finally got his big chance after he had won another string of fights. The fight with his bitter rival further sealed Pep as a boxer to be reckoned with. The promoter, Ed Hurley, had thought about waiting awhile before matching these two local fighters, chiefly because of the risk to Pep's spotless fistic reputation. But the growth of the war effort convinced him that if Pep and Ivy didn't fight that summer, they may never get the chance to fight.

At this point Pep was unbeaten in 47 bouts, and was only a few steps away from recognition as the outstanding contender for Chalky Wright's featherweight title. Pep's New England title was not at stake against "Poison" Ivy, because the match was made at 128lbs. Ivy was 23, but a veteran of five years ring campaigning during which he had fought the toughest men in the feather and lightweight divisions. Although his record included some 14 defeats, Ivy had a big advantage over Pep in the matter of experience. Bobby also possessed a devastating left hook, particularly when he whipped this punch under his opponents rib-cage. This was the punch, Ivy's many followers said, which would take the starch out the spindly-legged Pep and slow him down to a walk. Ivy was ranked sixth and Pep was ninth in the Ring Magazine ratings in the featherweight division. Excitement in the Connecticut area for this showdown encounter was at fever pitch. There was nothing (and still is) like a fight between two local fighters to whet the fans appetite and start the cash registers ringing. It was an open-air tournament and Hurley was praying for fair weather. Extra stewards and police would be in attendance. They did not want a repetition of the Pep v Hernandez fight scenes, where there was crushing and confusion in the crowd. The ring had been pitched between the pitcher's box and second base to enable fans at the ends of the grandstand and in the bleachers to get a better view of the action.

Though it was quite obvious Pep and Ivy disliked each other, there was no childish mudslinging and back-stabbing, no character assassinations, with two fighters shamelessly digging dirt on each other, a prevalent malaise of modern day boxing hype. If we are not careful boxing will end up like wrestling but the point 'is' boxing is for real.

The fight was held on 1 September, 1942, in Hartford at the Bulkely Stadium. There were over 9,000 spectators inside the stadium and they paid $27,000, the third largest gate in the history of Hartford boxing. The atmosphere was tremendous, it was a really big occasion for Hartford boxing fans. The noise was so loud hardly anybody could hear the introductions. All Hartford's celebrities were at the ringside. The announcer George Dunn introduced Kid Kaplan and Bat Battalino, Mayor Thomas J. Spellacy, and Lieutenant Commander Alfred F. Rice. While this was going on Ivy looked calm and cool with a smirk on his face. Pep couldn't wait for the introductions to end and the bell to ring so he could get into action. He was confident, razor-sharp and he wanted this fight more than any other. It was as they say: "Pay Back Time" and Willie fully intended paying "Poison" Ivy back with interest. Pep was the underdog. But he certainly didn't fight like the underdog. The first five rounds passed quickly and Willie had the bout well under control, making it look easy.

Then Ivy got him in a corner and, remembering what always happened to him in their gym sessions. Willie must have thought "here it comes, he's going to deck me." Bobby stuck his fist into Pep's stomach, all the way in, but it did not seem to hurt the younger boxer. Ivy did it again and Willie still didn't show any sign of discomfort. Then he knew he was stronger than "Poison" Ivy, and that he was there for the taking. After boxing his way into the lead with crisp counter-punches, and displaying his remarkable defensive technique, and with the huge crowd roaring for each fighter, Pep moved up a couple of gears and set his man up near the end of the ninth round, giving Ivy a terrific shellacking and then knocked him out in one-minute and thirty-seconds of the round. Having not lost a round, it was his 48th straight victory. From then on, he really moved up the boxing ladder. The next day, Willie became a house owner. It was a lovely white painted, two-family residence at 27-29 Standish Street. Willie bought it from the previous owner Mr. W. A. Leonard. Getting back to the Ivy fight, it must be realised what an amazing feat of controlled skillful fighting it was as Pep won every round of what turned out to be a one-sided affair. He gave his home town rival a thorough beating. Only Petey Scalzo and Richie Lemos had previously stopped the teak-tough Ivy and these two fighters were former world champions.

Bill Lee remarked after the fight: "Pep beat Ivy with one punch. A crisp left jab. He started using it in the first round and kept giving Ivy a face full of it for nine more. Every time Ivy got ready to deliver his famed left hook to the body, Pep would step in and jab him off balance. One round was much the same as another. Pep boxed with cold-blooded caution until he unleashed his heavy fire in the ninth. Ironically, it was a left hook to the body late in this round that spelled doom for the game little Ivy! Willie drove the punch below his rivals ribs, the punch doubled him up and took the wind out of him. Referee, Lou Bogash of Bridgeport, guided Ivy to his stool after halting the fight."

Dan Florio, Ivy's cornerman and who trained Jersey Joe Walcott, climbed back into the ring after his fighter was led to the changing rooms and did a bit of measuring. "This ring was rather large, and it suited Pep. My guy likes a smaller ring," he told the press after the contest.

William Newell a respected sports journalist wrote in the Hartford Courant:

"It was like the man said. Pep beat Ivy with one punch, a beautiful straight left jab, he started it in the first round and kept giving him this punch throughout the fight. It was legalised murder."

Though Pep had now gained a reputation all across the States as a scientific practitioner of the noble-art, the tough-talking New York fight fans were still not fully convinced he was as good as his perfect record of forty-eight professional victories made him out to be. Up to this point Pep had fought only twice in the "Big Apple," but won the two bouts in style. He had beaten Ruby Garcia on his first appearance and four weeks later had outpointed Sammy Parrota, again over four rounds.

Main Event At The Garden

Pep's next fight after beating Bobby Ivy, was his first main event at Madison Square Garden. His opponent was Frankie Franconeri of Bayonne, New Jersey. Willie knocked him out in the first round. Even the sceptical New York boxing writers were suitably impressed with this result. Dan Parker (Parker, was a famed boxing reporter from New York) wrote in the New York Daily Mirror after that fight: "Pep showed everything an outstanding fighter should have, dazzling speed, super boxing ability, unusual punching power, a cool head and a fighting heart." The fight with Franconeri was a scorcher for the brief time it lasted. Willie put his glittering ability on display before a critical Madison Square Garden audience and left them gasping with his performance. knocking the highly rated Bayonne fighter bowlegged in the first minute of the fight, he finished him off 67 seconds later, referee Arthur Donovan stopping the massacre. Franconeri had previously given Charley "Lulu" Costantino, the number one ranked contender for the world featherweight title a hectic fight.

In Willie's dressing room immediately after the demolition of the New Jersey fighter, he was besieged by newspapermen looking for additional material on America's new wonder boxer. In Pep's day a champion or top-ten contender had to box opponents the fans demanded or risk being frozen out, because the boxing followers would not buy a ticket to watch top-rated fighters in easy matches. The promoters knew the turnstiles wouldn't click if they didn't come up with the fights the public demanded, so they made the best fights. Let's face facts, 20,000 people are not going to attend a boxing tournament to watch the mis-matches and one round blow-outs which are prevalent in modern day boxing. The current problems are due mainly to television demands. This then was the solid foundation from which Pep built his challenge for world honours. He boxed every opponent his manager selected for him. He ducked nobody, fighting them all. The slick movers, the rough, tough bangers and the knockout merchants, black fighters, white fighters were all faced. Any nationality would be tackled, it never bothered him in the least. Anybody and everybody who fancied their chances, or who stood in his way to gaining a world championship were accommodated. Viscusi was pushing Pep's claims for a title fight, but he was receiving the brush-off from certain influential officials. Pep had run up a record of 49 victories in just two years. He deserved a title chance. What a contrast with today's "world" champions!

Bill Gore seemed to sum up Pep perfectly when he said: "Willie has plenty of confidence." The cagey old trainer enlarged his statement: "Yes, he has plenty of self-belief. And we all need plenty of that. Willie has it in abundance. You can see it pouring out of him. Even in training he has the confidence to try different moves or attempt certain punches, some people say it's cockiness and arrogance, but take it from me it's an ability to believe in his skills and to overcome any unforeseen circumstances. He does things right, and when he's fit and sharp nobody can touch him. Confidence, it's in all of us you know, deep, deep down it's there. It wins wars, gets politicians elected helps students to pass their exams, teachers to teach, surgeons to perform operations successfully. We all need confidence in any walk of life, to cross a busy street you need confidence. Some of us have none, some a little, some not enough, some too much. But Willie Pep has the right amount."

When Lou Viscusi announced his young fighter's next opponent was none other than the formidable world featherweight champion, Alberto "Chalky" Wright, it was obvious the cunning manager considered Willie was more than capable of looking after himself. "Willie's apprenticeship is over," Mr. Lou told the press. "We have groomed him for this championship challenge. Sure, Wright is a mature fighter and a very strong puncher, his speciality being his left hook which has won him a lot of fights. But Willie is a bit special, I've no worries about him facing Chalky Wright," the manager concluded.

Wright, a black man, was born in Durango, Mexico in 1912. A professional for many years and rated one of the hardest knockout punchers the featherweight division had seen for the past 30 years, he also had one of the best jobs outside of boxing he was Mae West's chauffeur. The sexy Hollywood screen beauty had taken a liking to the fun-loving Mexican many years before and employed him. But now as world champion, people drove him around, opened his doors, tipped their caps and called him sir. English fans had been impressed by Wright's brand of box/fighting while he was over in this country as "Homicide" Henry Armstrong's chief sparring partner. Fighting in front of a full-house at Liverpool Stadium, Wright stopped Dan McAllister of Belfast in five rounds. A few weeks later he again packed the Stadium when he sensationally flattened the highly regarded Kid Tanner of British Guiana in seven rounds in what was described in the British press as an "All Black" battle. Chalky had won the world championship in 1941 when he savagely knocked out Joey Archibald in the 11th round in Washington, D.C. Wright was exciting to watch and he successfully defended his title twice before putting it on the line against the 20-year-old "Will-'o'-the-Wisp." He knocked out Henry Jeffra in 10 rounds, and outpointed the tough Charlie Costantino over 15 rounds.

Known as a happy-go-lucky sort of character outside the ring, it was no secret he was very friendly with many well known gangsters of that period and was also very popular with many of Hollywood's movie stars who would regularly attend his fights. Many times promoters would match him with much heavier opponents, whom he would sensationally knock out. It was nothing for Chalky to take on fully-fledged welterweights in the gym and flatten them with a single punch. He could hit, there was no doubting that. He was a real wild, exciting character in every respect. This then was the champion that Pep had to defeat before he could call himself a world champion. What a formidable task! Chalky told the press conference for his fight against Pep that he could speak two languages Mexican and American. "Are you really a Mexican, Chalky?" he was asked by a nosy reporter. "Do I look like one," he laughingly replied. His father had been a regular soldier in the United States cavalry. He had jumped the border into Mexico and married the granddaughter of a slave who had escaped from Georgia. The father left home when Chalky was a mere baby, and was hardly remembered by young Wright. The boy grew up in Los Angeles, learning much that is not found in any books, though books were never of paramount interest. He found flaws even in a classic book like Nat Fleischer's Ring record book, which listed only 125 fights for him while he maintained that he had taken part in at least 300!

Harry Markson was doing the publicity work for promoter, Mike Jacobs, and Markson said: "Chalky was a publicity man's dream. He was funny, very witty and always had gorgeous women hanging around, no doubt because of his Hollywood connections. He lost thousands of dollars on gambling with dice. The horses were much too slow for him. 'You have too wait to long to find out the result,' he told me when I asked him if he ever bet on horse racing. What a fighter and what a character."

It was Eddie Walker, Wright's manager, who was responsible for getting

Willie the fight. Pep was enjoying fantastic success, not having lost a fight in over three crowded years as a professional, and he had appeared on the undercard on three of Mike Jacobs' tournament at Madison Square Garden, winning two four-round preliminaries and, on his third appearance practically shattered Frankie Franconeri in one round. But Mike, the shrewdest and most knowledgeable of all promoters, somehow failed to be impressed, and in his quest for a challenger for Chalky, never so much as considered Pep. Then one October day in 1942, Eddie Walker dropped into Jacobs' office in the Brill Building, headquarters of the Twentieth Century Sporting Club. "I got a guy for you, Mike", he said. "Who?" responded Jacobs. "Willie Pep" said Walker. "Nah" Mike said "He wouldn't draw a nickel" added the promoter. "Ask your matchmaker," Walker suggested. Mike called in his man, Nat Rogers, and asked him what he thought of Pep. "He's the hottest thing in Connecticut", Nat said. "They'll go to see him wherever he fights," he added. Walker then knew that he had Jacobs' attention.

"Listen Mike," Walker said. "I had Chalky fighting in Hartford and New Haven just a little while ago, and all we heard about was Willie Pep. He's idolised up there. They think he can beat Chalky, I don't, but if they do and they will pay to see him try it, he's for me. Thousands will come down from New England, you'll have a sell-out. Make the match".

And so the match was made and Jacobs' wasn't disappointed with the crowd which was 19,521, and the gate receipts of $71,868,70 were a record for an indoor featherweight championship fight. The last big gate between the smaller fighters was when Tony Canzoneri outpointed Benny Bass in 1928, and they drew $63,656 at the box-office. The crowd was swelled considerably by the fans who came in from Connecticut.

In this period, Mike Jacob's was undoubtedly the world's leading and most powerful boxing promoter. A peculiar looking fellow, he had a bald head and ill-fitting false teeth which he continually gnashed while talking. One might be forgiven for wondering why Jacobs did not rate Pep as a drawing card? Well quite simply, Uncle Mike, as he was called by everyone in boxing circles, knew very little about fighters other than say Joe Louis who was his biggest attraction, Henry Armstrong and perhaps Sugar Ray Robinson. He relied on his matchmaker and other people around him who were more steeped in boxing knowledge. However, it must be said he certainly knew how to promote a boxing tournament. Jacobs was purely a businessman, and was one of the canniest operators ever to enter boxing, which he did by accident. He was unique in the respect that he promoted with his own money. He drove a hard bargain, but one had to understand his background. Jacobs had had to battle for anything he received. As a skinny Jewish lad, he grew up in an Irish neighbourhood in New York, which was tough enough. He was a hustler from his early days, selling newspapers and fruit around the streets, he sold tickets on summer excursion steamboats, and became a ticket broker for all the big events in and around New York. He was not afraid to try anything if he thought he could make money. In the 1920s he had helped Tex Rickard, the famous promoter who built the old Madison Square Garden. The Hearst trio of journalist, Damon Runyon, Ed Frayne and Bill Farnsworth were behind Jacobs in the beginning, using him as the "front" man. This was because of their "feud" with Jimmy Johnston who was in charge of Madison Square Garden. The three newspapermen were part of the powerful William Randolph Hearst newspaper organisation, (Hearst was the first newspaper owner to publish a separate sports section), which put on two charity boxing tournaments a year, an indoor Christmas fund card and in the summer an outdoor Milk Fund carnival. This arrangement had been going on for a number of years. While he was alive and boss of the Garden Tex Rickard helped the organisation with the shows. But when Johnston took charge, things changed and the newspapermen found the flamboyant Johnston hard to deal with. They needed someone who could help them...Enter uncle Mike!

Within a short space of time the four men formed the Twentieth Century Club, and promoted their own tournaments in opposition to Johnston and Madison Square Garden. For obvious reasons the journalists could not be seen to be involved with the running of the promotions, though they certainly gave it plenty of publicity. Jacobs finally broke Madison Square Garden's powerful monopoly on boxing and the heavyweight picture when he signed Joe Louis to a promotional contract. Jimmy Johnston had approached the Louis management offering them a deal, but because Louis was black, Johnston was more than a little disdainful toward him believing that the public would not pay money to watch a black fighter topping promotions at Madison Square Garden and other major venues. Whereas the colour of a man's skin did not bother Jacobs in the slightest, what concerned him was could he make money with the fighter? In Louis, Uncle Mike had the biggest sporting star in years.

It was a bitterly cold, damp November night in 1942 as the spectators packed into Madison Square Garden. The atmosphere was tense, the noise absolutely deafening. Those present were about to witness one of the greatest exhibitions of boxing ever seen between two little men. It was unknown for anyone other than heavyweights, or certain middleweights, to draw such large audiences. Though he was extremely popular and a murderous puncher, in New York Chalky Wright had no pulling power whatsoever. He was not a great ticket attraction. In comparison, the good-looking Pep was highly popular indeed. It was mainly down to him that nearly 20,000 people paid record gate receipts for a featherweight championship contest. Willie was to receive $12,000 from the live gate and $400 from the television rights.

How ironic then that Connecticut, Pep's home state, was a National Boxing Association supporter, and as such recognised Jackie Wilson as the world featherweight champion! (Later attempts were made to match Wilson with Pep in order to unify the title, but by the time they eventually fought, Wilson had lost his version of the championship to Jackie Callura). Many Hartford fans were disgusted with their boxing official's refusal to recognise their home based fighter as the true champion. For his part Pep could not have cared less about the boxing politics. He knew Chalky Wright was the only genuine world featherweight king. Pep, talking to reporters before the contest, said: "People don't appreciate Chalky Wright as much as they ought to. Here is a man who fought for twelve years before he got a chance to fight for the world title. And, I've got mine after less than three years as a professional."

On the eve of the fight, Willie had spent a very restless night in his hotel room. Usually when in New York he would be bright-eyed and bushy-tailed, but not on this occasion. The room was quiet, no friends were allowed to visit him until after the fight. He attempted to sleep but kept tossing and turning. He tried hard not to think about what lay ahead of him in 24 hours time, but the more he tried his mind kept running forward to when he would be facing the world champion. He looked into the bathroom mirror of his hotel room and wondered what the hell he was doing fighting a fellow who had rendered the majority of his opponents unconscious. Quickly, Willie tried to think of something else. His thoughts went to the morning papers which one writer stated he had a "touch of genius" and he would be installed as the favourite. He paced the room, and heard one of his helpers talking in the next room."If Willie is worried at all he shows no sign of it since we arrived in New York," the man said. Well perhaps that was the way he looked to outsiders. But inside, things were different. He got back into bed and tried to close his eyes and his mind and find some relief in sleep but the neon signs were flickering on and off. The city was beginning to glitter and glow it was full of vitality. Soon, he dozed off into a deep sleep – tomorrow couldn't come fast enough.

At ringside the air was heavy with expensive perfume and cigar smoke. The ringside was full of celebrities from sport and showbusiness and the usual sprinkling of politicians. This was the Garden, the dream Willie had dreamed since first lacing on the gloves. He was centre stage now, the bright lights, beautiful ladies wearing sparkling diamonds and other assortment of jewellry; photographers with their flashlights popping. Down below in his dressing room Willie was perspiring, the tension in the small room was suffocating. He jumped off the rubbing table and did some light shadow boxing, then a sharp knock on the door followed by a loud voice calling. "You're up" sent a quiver through his body. He was scared and he fought to overcome it as he put on his dressing gown and in a few short minutes this former shoe-shine from the wrong side of the tracks; this kid with less than three years experience; this youngster who was not even of legal age to box for 15 rounds, was heading for his moment of truth.

This was Pep's first 15-round bout and he boxed accordingly, he displayed magnificent defensive skill throughout the contest. The early rounds saw Willie box scientifically, using a stiff left jab which found Wright's face time after time. It was like a trip-hammer bang, bang, bang, finding it's target every time. Pep bounced around the ring as though he were riding an invisible pogo stick but, now and then, he paused long enough to pile up a sufficient number of points to win the rounds. "When I saw Chalky square off at the beginning of the fight I said to myself: 'This old-man is going to be a cinch for my jab.' I popped him... his head wasn't there. He was really cute. It wasn't long before I realised that he was slipping my jabs. Not just by moving his head but by inching that pivot foot so that what I was aiming at was moving inches at a time. But once I compensated, and sussed him out I was alright," said Pep.

Boxing with flair way above his limited experience, Pep had his supporters applauding long and loud. Chalky was looking for the one big punch which would terminate the bout quickly. He was trying to nail the elusive foe in front of him, but Pep was like a shadow, and so fleet-footed.

Wright, for all his vast experience, couldn't get anywhere near his challenger, let alone land a decent punch on him. The big question the fans were asking was could the kid avoid the dynamic punches of the champion for the remainder of the 15 torrid rounds? Pep's speed and footwork were really amazing. He was scoring points, then smoothly moving backwards, then forwards, to his left, then sliding over to his right, pivoting on his left foot, ducking, bobbing and weaving, slipping and sliding out of danger to the sheer delight of the neutral fans who were in raptures. Wright was going like a steam engine trying to nail Pep with a right hand should he falter for a moment. A majority of the New York fight fans were expecting fireworks, and they were less than impressed by the challenger's constant movement, they wanted red-blooded action, toe-to-toe confrontation. But to the boxing connoisseur this was a fascinating encounter. The "Wisp" was keeping the contest at long range, spinning Chalky off balance whenever he got set to throw his bombs.

Between rounds, Bill Gore pounded the strategy into his boxer's head for the rest of the fight: "Stab and move," then the usually mild-mannered trainer added."If you do anything else, I'll hit you over the head with the stool." Pep did exactly what he was told. He never allowed the champion to penetrate his immaculate defence with a solid punch. It can't be emphasised enough what a truly dangerous puncher Wright was. He was always looking to score a spectacular knockout which he had achieved so many times in the past. His legs were all gnarled-looking, sort of what you'd see on an old tree, and he stood with his feet wide apart. That's all wrong, according to the boxing instruction manual. His arms looked frail and skinny, except around the muscle parts, and he held them low. That is also wrong, according to the book. He seemed to put all his weight on his back foot and he gave the impression that he was sitting in a rocking chair, though he was standing up naturally. One important thing, though, his lead leg, the left, was a pivot. He didn't go one step with his right without moving first to get a new lineup of direction. He was a cunning fighter. But the young challenger, by back-pedalling round the ring with Wright in hot pursuit and throwing punches desperately in the hopes of catching his speedy opponent, Pep was making the champion miss and tiring him out. But Willie did more than merely keep out of trouble. He was hitting Chalky with straight punches, while never standing still long enough for the champion to connect on him.

There were nearly 5,000 fans from Hartford in the crowd, and their voices could be heard above the rest of the din. The bout was a crackerjack with Pep boxing beautifully, before slowing down to pace himself for the full distance. In the seventh round Wright began to roar, he sensed the kid was feeling the pace and tried to impose his authority. He sliced a nasty gash under Pep's left eye in the eighth round, but though the blood dripped slowly, it never bothered the youngster in the least. Back in the corner at the start of the ninth, Chalky looked like a little old man of the ring. He claimed he was 32 years-old, but he was obviously at least five years older. During the interval after the eighth round, Bill Gore told Willie to move up a gear or two and stretch the champion to the limit instructions which Pep followed to perfection. Wright was an excellent ring mechanic but he never got a real good shot at Pep. One ringside wag said: "Chalky thought the kid was flagging a little and tried to go to town on him, but he never got any further than the suburbs." In the ninth round, while ducking one of the champion's wild swings, another follow up right cross caught Pep on top of his head. And on his own admission, Willie had a very hard head. He was dazed but managed to keep upright and out of further danger, but he felt dizzy for a few rounds after the punch landed. Just imagine what might have happened had that right hand from Chalky been bang on target? Every punch Wright landed was worth ten of Pep's, but he was made to miss so often that his scoring punches were almost negligible, where as Willie's fast, accurate jabs, which rarely missed their target, saw his score mounting higher the further the contest went.

With the neutrals in the crowd yelling for Chalky to surge forward and land with his big guns, the championship match became more intense and with the Hartford supporters rooting for their man the Garden roof was nearly lifted with the volume of noise from the fans who were by now standing up on their seats shouting the two boxers home. At the commencement of the bout, Pep had been installed as the favourite at odds of 10-to-11. The left jab of the challenger was in Wright's face at every opportunity. Roared on by his followers, Pep started to leave the old champion gasping to keep up the pace, but it wasn't that the older man ran out of gas, it was more that the kid seemed to get faster and fresher and more confident and less taut. There is no doubt that early in the contest Pep looked as if he was petrified at the mammoth size of the crowd and the yells from his fans with an occasional thought to the experience of the flat-nosed fighter facing him across the ring. As the contest wore on, it became quite clear the only way the little title holder could retain his crown was by way of a knockout. And he needed the Hartford lad to stand still, which he of course would not do.

There was no palpable difference in their weights, with Pep coming in at 125 and one half-pounds, (8st-13-and-a-half-pounds) and the champion tipping the scale at a quarter of a pound more than his challenger.

There were many boxing experts who claimed before the fight started, that the weight had weakened Willie, who they claimed usually weighed 130 (9st-4lbs). But he showed that he was as strong as an ox in the last stretch of the bout. When announcer Harry Balogh raised Pep's hand as the new world champion, Jimmie Walker, author of New York's boxing law, rose spontaneously clapping and cheering Pep for his brilliance. The weapon which won the title for Pep was immaculate use of his left jab. This largely foiled the plan Wright had prepared, which was to bang away at Pep's slender frame in the hope of weakening him and leaving him open for the knockout. Two judges scored 11 out of 15 rounds to Pep, and the referee had him the victor by ten clear rounds. Wright had nothing to be ashamed of, he had tried his best and had no complaints about the decision.

The lasting image of that time will always be Pep, slim as a reed, holding aloft his arms in a token of victory in Madison Square Gaeden. It was a moment the boy from Hartford became the golden icon of the Forties. The celebrations which had begun in the ring continued in the dressing room and then spilled out onto the streets and nightclubs and all the way back to Hartford on the trains and coaches and in the cars. Pep went out on the town, he called in at Toots Shor's, The Paramount and The Copa, stayed at the Ritz and celebrated with Joe DiMaggio and Frank Sinatra and bandleader, Harry James. He had a ball, dancing the night away..

After the fight in Chalky's dressing room, a disdainful reporter said to the former champion: "I wouldn't want to win the big one the way Pep did, running all the time." Looking completely exhausted Wright replied: "I would. If I was a young fellow like him, fighting an old fellow like me, I would fight just the way he did. I hope the kid will give me a return as soon as possible." Willie would go through his entire boxing career with this love-hate relationship with certain members of the press, especially those hard-to-please New York scribes. Some loved his silky smooth skills, while others wanted to see him stand flat-footed and do a bit of slugging. For his part, Pep had no intention of slugging with anyone, certainly nobody as dangerous as

Chalky Wright. Willie would fight his own way, whether reporters were pleased or not. They, he reasoned, were not taking any blows.

Many boxing purists, though, were delighted at his victory. It made a change for them to witness rare boxing moves at a fast pace. American boxing was infested at that time with an abundance of all-out tough, aggressive brawlers whose sole intention was to render their opponents into total oblivion.

Talking to a reporter from Hartford about his title victory, Pep said: "Lord above, what an awesome puncher Wright is. There was no way I was going to stand toe to toe with that guy. He would have taken my head clean off my shoulders. It was a desperately hard fight for me all the way. Knowing that one wrong move on my part and he was going to wallop me. He caught me on top of my head in the eighth or ninth, and for a few rounds after that I didn't know where I was. That punch shook me up, it put respect in me. That respect saved me in the end. I did miles of roadwork in preparation for this opportunity, I left nothing to chance. Bill Gore told me to move, move, and keep moving. I followed his instructions to the letter. I figured it out that no knockout shots were going to nail me. I went in for left hooks off the jab. They were the ones he couldn't get away from and they caught the officials eyes."

Thousands lined the streets and roads of Hartford when the new world champion received a civic reception from officials of his home town. He was feted everywhere he went, invited here, there and everywhere. Being only a young man he never took things seriously. He certainly did not understand the importance of what he had achieved and what it meant to be a world champion. He was now a world celebrity. Sadly it all went to his head. In the ring he was having no trouble at all, but outside the ring Willie would have problems adjusting to life in the fast lane.

The first thing Willie did when he received his purse money a few days later, (which was a little over $6,000 plus the $400 from the television rights. Because of their fifty-fifty split, Viscusi also received $6,000), was to buy his mother and father their own home. It was a big white house in a nice neighbourhood, it cost him $18,000.

They were overjoyed and delighted at what their son had done for them. Winning this title was something his mother had prayed for at her local church. Life was one big ball to the youngster and he soon fell for the hard luck stories from people. None of his money from the championship went into his bank account. He became blase about the value of money, and he lent money to anyone who gave him a hard luck tale. Willie dressed in the most expensive clothes and he bought a Chevy for $900. All the publicity and sudden fame turned his head. There were plenty of well-wishers at the Pep household. They talked with pride about how little Willie had shined shoes, sold newspapers, did anything to survive, before making it in the boxing business. How ironic that on the day Willie received his purse money and was declared in the Hartford Courant newspaper as the kid who had it all; wonderful talent, a world title, fame, fortune, glory and a lifetime before him to spend it. A short story appeared in the same paper which was headlined: "Joe Louis Has Real Financial Problems," the story told of the millions of dollars Louis had won, and taxes which he owed, bad investments and obligations to his managers and promoters. There was a cold, stark warning here for the new champion. But Willie wasn't listening. The optimism and innocence of youth had just been replenished.

Pep credits boxing with saving him from a life of Hell, and God only knows what would have been in store for this youngster. "Boxing was my vehicle out of unpromising surroundings," said the new champion. Frequently, though, sportsmen lose their aims and driving motivation once they reach the top of their profession and slowly head downhill. This was not going to be allowed to happen to Willie Pep. Less than three weeks after becoming the world champion, he was back in the ring knocking out Jose Aponte Torres in seven rounds in Washington, D.C, then stopping Joey Silva in the ninth round in a contest staged in Jacksonville. Both were non-title bouts, but he was cashing in on being the new world champion. He was in brilliant form for both contests.

A Married Man
Three weeks after becoming the youngest world featherweight champion this century, Willie got married. The new champion was booked to fight a ten round non-title affair in Washington, against a tough Puerto Rican based in New York, Joe Aponte Torres. Before leaving Hartford with his entourage, he went to St. Patrick's church rectory while the priest performed the marriage ceremony. He was 20 years old and his bride, Mary Woodcock, of Hungerford Street, Hartford, was a year older. After the service the young couple kissed goodbye and Willie was on his travels to Washington.

Many years later while discussing his early life with a journalist, Pep said quite candidly: "I never went looking for girls in my life; I was in the limelight, so they came looking for me. They married me for my name and my money." Talking about his first wife, he added, "I loved that little girl, but I wasn't ready for marriage. She wanted for us to get married sooner, but I told her I couldn't get married until I became a world champion, never expecting to fight for the title so soon. But I kept my promise and we got hitched after I beat Chalky Wright." The marriage only lasted four years, but it produced two beautiful children, a girl and a boy. "That's the only thing I wouldn't change," said Pep. "I was in the service for two of our four years together, maybe that's where the trouble started, it certainly didn't help. And with me training and travelling all over the place, it takes a toll on a wife who likes to go out and have fun. She left me. It cost me thirteen thousand dollars to settle the divorce but I kept custody of the kids." It was a rocky marriage from the beginning. The easy money and the adulation which was heaped on the young Pep had certainly changed him. He soon became involved in a domestic triangle which came to the official attention of the Hartford police. Later in the Hartford Superior Court, Mary told Judge Alcorn, Willie beat her when she objected to the late nights and some of the company he was keeping. It was a peculiar affair, Judge Alcorn granted Mrs. Pep a divorce but gave custody of the children to Willie. Mary told the court she was satisfied the children were in good care from Willie's parents. Willie's mother, having raised her own brood, now brought up her own son's two children. "My mother was terrific. She had raised her own family and started out all over again with my two kids," said Pep. (When his first wife remarried, Willie agreed to let their daughter, Mary, return to her mother, though his son, Billy, stayed with him and his parents.)

It was Bill Corum, a sportscaster and a sportswriter for the then New York Journal newspaper, who gave Pep the tag: "Will-o-the-Wisp" after his brilliant boxing exhibition when winning the crown from Wright. When asked by some reporters about his school achievements and why he hadn't gone to college, Pep replied: "I was not interested enough in my academic progress while at school. I needed to help my family. Anyhow, from the age of 15, everything was geared to boxing for me. College doesn't help once you climb into that ring, you've got to know how to box, you've got to be in tip-top shape and you've got to have the will to win." Over the coming years Pep would dance in the world spotlight, and the world cheered. Admired by millions, he would drink with Frank Sinatra and become a close friend, dine at Toot Shor's, have winter holidays in Florida and beat everyone Viscusi put in front of him.

New York Writers Still Cynical

It was Pep's fifth visit to New York which saw the cynical boxing scribes finally mark him down in their note books as something "special." If Willie disappointed some New York critics when winning the title, he showed them he could fight as well as box when he made his next appearance in New York. The young featherweight king was matched in a ten round over-the-weight contest against Allie Stolz, a fierce two-handed battler, in Madison Square Garden in January 1943. Fight fans were rubbing their hands in anticipation of this contest. Stolz, they said, would show if the Hartford champion was the genuine article or just another flashy mover. This tough little fellow, Stolz, was highly regarded by the New York fight fraternity, they loved his all-action style of fighting. Though it was only 29 January, 1943, Pep had already fought twice that month. He had easily outpointed Vince Dell'Orto in New Orleans, while Billy Speary had been soundly thrashed in Hartford, both contests going the ten round distance.

Allie Stolz was a fully-fledged lightweight, and a very highly-rated contender for the world title in that division. In May 1942, eight months before meeting Pep, Stolz had lost a closely fought 15-round decision against Sammy Angott when he challenged for Angott's world lightweight title. Allie was bitterly upset at being left out of the forthcoming lightweight elimination tournament which was about to be staged around this time. His exclusion was boxing politics at work. Meeting the current world featherweight champion would be his way of telling the organisers to go and chase themselves. Stolz had fought many times in New York and the critics loved his blood and guts approach to fighting, in fact they rated him very highly indeed. The New Jersy fighter thanked "Uncle" Mike Jacobs, the promoter, for giving him this opportunity against Willie Pep.

A boxer in those times who could not punch had to be something extra special in order to get anywhere in the tough world of professional boxing. Watching fighters who could not punch was not the fight followers idea of fistic entertainment, give them a puncher every time. But Willie was indeed extra special. He could probably have been described as a classic boxer/puncher on the same lines as boxers of a later vintage such has Eder Jofre, Wilfredo Gomez and Prince Naseem. Though basically a boxer, Pep could hit with power. One had only to ask any of the 22 opponents who had failed to go the distance with him at this period of his career to verify this fact. He never relied on brute strength, he scored his knockouts with a high degree of technique instead of raw power.

At the noon weigh-in, Willie was 127-three-quarter pounds, while Stolz came in at 133-half-pounds. It was another bumper gate at Madison Square Garden with 19,088 paying fans jammed into the famous old arena in anticipation of seeing a classic and exciting confrontation between, the bull-dog type of fighter, Allie Stolz, and the artistic Willie Pep, a boxer who put perfect tactics and a high degree of skill before anything else. There was a fantastic buzz about the Garden as the fans were electrified from the first bell as Pep joined issue, and gave the crowd an exhibition of superb box-fighting, showing speed and fighting spirit which acclaimed him master of every phase of the game. Whatever illusions Stolz may have entertained about re-entering the lightweight championship hunt, they were shattered forever after the one-sided drubbing he received from Pep through 10 speedy rounds of blazing boxing action. Pep did everything but knock out the New York favourite. In fact, near the end of the second round, to the consternation of most onlookers, including some of his own adherents, he floored the gritty Stolz cleanly with a left hook delivered with such precision that Allie staggered erect only to be saved by the sound of the bell to end the round. So bewildered was Stolz that he walked into Pep's corner! In the third session, Pep hammered his rival from pillar to post after taking a foul left hook from Stolz. Both fighters ended up suffering from cuts, Allie was damaged over his left eye, while Willie also had a slight nick under his left.

For most of this one-sided contest, Pep's versatility and ringcraft had his rival absolutely bewildered. He belaboured his opponent, giving him a boxing lesson. Sitting at ringside were many shrewd boxing observers who later claimed Pep made it all look too easy for it to be described as a tough fight. Stolz's vaunted cleverness was totally discounted, as was his supposedly superior hitting power, his established ring generalship, and his weight advantage of almost six pounds. Pep proved himself a little perpetual-motion boxing machine. Willie was absolutely phenomenal, showing great resolve in a passionate atmosphere. At the end of round six, jarred and groggy from taking the champion's blinding punches, Stolz again headed for the wrong corner only to be restrained by the referee, so bemused and dazed was he. After ten rounds of sheer perfection from Pep, there was no doubt about who the winner was. The unanimous decision in favour of the Hartford boxer by referee Billy Cavanaugh and judges Bill Healy and Charley Draycott was merely a formality. No other verdict was possible. In fact, Stolz won only one round, the eighth. For the rest, Pep simply overwhelmed his highly touted rival.

Changing his tactics from the start, Willie went straight on the attack, and ceased his tireless assault only in brief interludes. Bill Gore told reporters that Pep's technical ability and temperament was excellent. "You saw all the years of practice in this victory. He was fantastic," said the trainer of Pep. Mike Jacobs was delighted with the vast turnout of spectators. Once again the legions of Pep's supporters had travelled down from Hartford, but the hard-to-please New Yorkers were also taking to Pep now. The gate receipts came to $65,989. Interestingly, the show's last bout featured another youngster who was destined to become one of the all-time greats of the lightweight division, none other than Ike Williams, who won a points victory over Jersey Moore. Williams was brilliant, while also showing glimpses of why he would go on to become a boxing hall of famer.

The newspapers were full of praise for Pep's performance against a recognised, creditable fighter in Stolz. James P. Dawson, a veteran boxing writer for the New York Times, wrote: "Willie Pep the Hartford gladiator was a miniature Billy Conn, against Allie Stolz. It was a wonderful battle and the huge crowd were rewarded, for it was one of the most exciting bouts of recent years, albeit Pep alone made it so. With startling ease this amazing little champion, Pep, won his 59th fight. He certainly made his critics and doubters sit up and award him the respect and acclaim his victory deserved. Pep blasted away the suspicion he had been lucky when beating Chalky Wright."

The critics claimed Wright had suffered from an off-night when dropping his title to the Hartford youngster a few weeks previous, but when Willie hammered the daylights out of the very respected Stolz in front of Allie's own faithful supporters, they could see that here was a scientifically brilliant ring tactician, who once again proved brain over brawn is a surefire winning technique.

Talking about these important early career fights, Pep said: "The big fight writers weren't too convinced about me yet, and I didn't really blame them, but I convinced them after I beat Allie Stolz. For this fight, Bill Gore got me to reverse the strategy we used on Wright. 'Be the boss from the start,' said Bill. 'Move away from his power (which was Stolz's left hook to the liver) and feint him when he starts to press.' I did exactly that and Stolz won only one of the ten rounds. Afterwards, Casewell Adams of the Herald-Tribune wrote: 'Pep operated on Stolz as deftly as a Park Avenue surgeon with a golden scalpel.'"

Bitter Taste Of Initial Defeat

Lou Viscusi made his first bad move when he accepted an offer from Mike Jacobs for Pep to top a Madison Square Garden bill. Willie was riding high after his tremendous showing against Allie Stolz a couple of months previously. Jacobs offered Sammy Angott as Willie's opponent. Six months earlier Angott had relinquished the world's lightweight title. It was an absurd match in every respect, Pep had nothing to gain by winning unless it was to establish himself as a challenger for the lightweight crown. Willie had built up an immaculate record, winning his first 62 professional contests, so you can be certain then his first defeat will remain memorable and boxing affectionados would remember the name of the boxer who inflicted the first loss on the undefeated pugilists unblemished record. Since dethroning Chalky Wright, Pep had won eight bouts easily, giving boxing fans a shot in the arm with his brilliant scientific displays in the ring.

    A married man now, Pep had been kept busy, not only in the ring, but enjoying himself socially, visiting the race tracks and night spots. He was a celebrity and very much in demand. Everything in Pep's garden was rosy. He was the darling of the fight-crowds during this period. He would spend hundreds of dollars on his wardrobe alone. He maintained that as a world champion he also had to look the part. Willie went to the best tailors for his custom made suits. The clothes fad had really started after his seventh professional contest. On the day of the bout he had bought himself a new suit and on the night he won his fight. Every time he fought after that he would wear his "lucky" suit. A close friend, Charley Green, who attended all Pep's fights would cajole him about his suit. Pep was that busy preening himself that he didn't seem to understand the importance of his upcoming fight against a very tough and awkward opponent, Sammy Angott, who was referred by members of the cynical New York press as the "Clutcher" for obvious reasons. Five months before boxing Pep, Angott's manager, Charlie Jones, who came from Louisville, explained to the New York Boxing Commission his fighter had relinquished the world lightweight title and announced his retirement from boxing as the undefeated champion of the world. The real reason was not being revealed, though Angott claimed it was due to his delicate and frail hands.

The Wisp v The Beau

The dynamic Beau Jack was recognised and regarded as the true lightweight king. Jack was a massive crowd-pleaser and fight followers loved his non-stop type of action. There was never a dull moment when he fought. The truth of the matter was that Mike Jacobs wanted to feature Jack against the chirpy, bouncy fresh-faced kid, the Will-'o-'the-Wisp, for the world lightweight crown at Madison Square Garden. He envisaged another sell-out crowd and they reasoned what an attraction it would be for the paying public. The Garden officials knew both Pep and Jack were fantastic attractions. Willie at first denied he was planning an attempt to gain the lightweight title, claiming his up-coming bout against Angott was just another fight for him and gave him pocket money. However, the newspapers were buying none of this, and printed stories that Pep was planning to go for the heavier title and Angott would just become an asterisk in sports history.

Sammy Angott though, was fighting for his credibility, besides his future. He had retired, he claimed, because he was fed up and upset he wasn't receiving his fair dues. The big money he was promised, never seemed to reach his bank account and he was suffering with his very delicate hands. He had found himself a job in a defence factory, but decided to give boxing another shot after he had been promised he would make some big money. Angott, therefore, was out to show the boxing public he had perhaps been a little too hasty in announcing his retirement. And what better man to come back against than the sensational 20-year-old wonder kid, the current featherweight champion, who was a heavy betting favourite. Pep, it seems, had made the big mistake of not taking Angott seriously enough. "When I beat Sammy Angott, this will pave the way for me to box Beau Jack for the undisputed lightweight championship of the world," said Pep. Little or nothing had been written about what a victory over the new world featherweight champion would mean for the awkward and tough ex-lightweight king.

The Pep versus Angott bout had originally been scheduled for 15 rounds, but speculation became so rife that the winner would claim the vacant crown, the contest was cut down to ten rounds. This took it out of the championship class, thus preventing the winner claiming his just rewards. The New York Boxing Commission feared Pep more than Angott, simply because he was the big attraction and would obviously have all the newspaper support on his side if he were to win. In those days the Commissions feared the wrath of the newspapers, who held a great deal of power and sway in what went on in the boxing circles, but Pep once again explained to everyone concerned he was not interested in the heavier title, stating he just wanted to keep busy, the bout with Angott was a money-spinner for him and that, he claimed, was the bottom line. Of course nobody took his protestations seriously. They knew a second title would make Willie the biggest single attraction in boxing at that time. The newspapers said a victory over Angott, who was 28, was just a formality for the dancing master from Hartford. Sammy, from Italian heritage, was born on 17 January 1915, in Pennsylvania. His real name was Engotti, not Angott. He turned professional in 1935 and by 1939 he had fought 59 times with only eight defeats and two draws. He was not an exciting fighter in any way, lacking a knockout wallop and certainly not regarded as a craftsman of the ring. He depended on his durability and clutching style of fighting to win his contests. From a boxing purist's point of view, Sammy could stink out any arena, he had no crowd appeal and was poison at the box-office. For all this, Angott beat the likes of Jackie Wilson, Aldo Spoldi, Petey Sarron, Freddie Miller, Bob Montgomery and Allie Stoltz. All well-known names of that period. Then in 1940 he became lightweight champion.

On the evening of 19 March, 1943 there were between 18,000 and 20,000 fans packed into Madison Square Garden to see if Pep could extend his unbeaten string of victories. There seemed no limits to what this kid could achieve. As a victim for Pep, Angott had excellent credentials, because though never regarded as a "great" pugilist, he was known as a spoiler, and a teak tough, willing type of fighter, who, in his 90 previous fights had only taken the count six times. These were the days when a boxer could fight once a week. Most boxing pundits envisaged ten very tough rounds with the speedy Pep emerging victorious, but what a shock everybody received, especially Pep! Straight from the opening bell, Angott looked and performed like a world champion. He was strong, fearless and positive in everything he did. He looked better in this fight than he had ever looked before. Sammy had never punched with such venom. He was inspired, and Pep would be the first to agree because for the first five rounds he simply could not get going. He had no rhythm, and Angott was beating him to the punch, using his own consummate boxing skills. Pep who was nearly seven pounds above his championship weight, looked sluggish in his movements. Trainer Bill Gore gave his boxer a good talking to at the end of the fifth round. From the sixth round Pep changed tactics and became a pursuer as he stormed forward looking for a knockout.

This is where the tough reputation of Angott came into its own. Pep tried everything he knew to bring the bout to a close, but the cagey ex-champion tucked his chin into his shoulder and rode out the storm with the large crowd roaring both boxers into a frenzy of excitement. Could the "Will-'o-'the-Wisp" pull the fight out of the fire? He was outboxing his man. Had the distance been over 12 or 15 rounds, then there is no doubt the younger Pep would have pulled back the points which he dropped in the first five. He could possibly have gone on to cause a stoppage, but it was not to be. The crowd were quite happy and delighted with the absorbing contest they were witnessing, plus they received full value for money. The fight went the scheduled ten round distance and Angott held on to win a close, split decision. Pep was shocked he had not been declared the winner. The crowd were not very happy either, but Willie did not seem to move into top gear until it was much too late and he only had himself to blame. There were many fans, plus a large number of newspaper scribes, who firmly believed though not at his fluent best, Pep still did more than enough clean hitting and attacking to gain the decision. It seemed Willie had underestimated his opponent and not bothered to open up with both hands until it was much too late.

Later in his dressing room, Willie took his favourite suit of it's hanger and handed it to his pal, Charley Green. "Here you are, Shyki, (the name Green was known has to his friends). You always wanted it, I've only wore it about 50 odd times, it's brand new but it's yours. To tell the you the truth, I thought I beat Angott," said Pep after the fight. "But he got the verdict from the ring officials. He beat me by using psychology. Sammy was one the craftiest fighter I ever faced. Many sportswriters called Angott a wrestler. Maybe he did rassle me around some. I don't alibi and the loss is in the record book."

When Pep went down to the weigh-in Angott walked straight up to him and said: "Hello Willie, how do you do?" Willie was surprised by Sammy's friendliness toward him. "I always knew you'd be the champion," Sammy added. What a nice man this is, Willie told Lou Viscusi. "I said to myself. I'll take it easy. He's got a wife and two kids, and he's a nice fellow," said Pep. In the first round Pep was not hitting Angott at all. When the two fighters got into a clinch Angott said to him: "When you gonna start fightin, kid? C'mon, kid, let's fight." This kind of behaviour went on for five rounds before Pep could pull himself together. The former lightweight king took the play away from the current featherweight champion. Sammy had terrible balance for a top class fighter. Pep came away from this fight with an understanding of how a fellow who looked so sloppy could do smart things. More than that, here was a man who bounced around like he would tip over. He didn't. He would come up with punches from different angles. Willie could not get away from many of them.

"When I finally puzzled him out, I realised he had been going side-to-side on me, the left foot sliding out fast when we went that way, the right doing the same thing when he went right. The moves were no accident. He learned to do it in the gym. I know, because he told me later. I hurt him a few times and was coming fast at the end but it wasn't enough. He won the decision 5-4-1 from the referee and one judge, and another judge gave it to him 6-4. Most fight experts thought I won," said Pep.

To prove what a durable opponent Angott was, seven months after gaining victory over the young featherweight king, Sammy regained his old lightweight championship when he outpointed Luther "Slugger" White over 15 rounds at the Hollywood Legion Stadium. He first won the title in May 1941 when he beat Davey Day over 15 rounds in Louisville. This was for the National Boxing Association version. He gained universal recognition a few months later when he outpointed Lew Jenkins over 15 rounds.

Time was running out for him, though. He lost his title in March 1944, in Hollywood, when he dropped his crown on points to Juan Zurita. Angott's professional record showed him as having 125 bouts, with only 23 losses, and holding a version of the lightweight championship on three occasions. Sammy hardly received the credit he fully deserved for being the first boxer to beat Pep in 135 bouts, though he himself considered this victory as one of the greatest of his career. Further proof of Angott's awkwardness and durability can be seen in the fact that he fought Henry Armstrong, losing a close ten round decision and drew with Beau Jack. He also had a stoppage victory over Ike Williams, though Ike later gained revenge by beating Sammy twice. He also fought Sugar Ray Robinson on three occasions and though losing all three bouts, he took this wonderful champion the distance each time and Robinson himself, thought Sammy was a really tough fighter. Angott retired in 1950. He lived in Canton Ohio, with his wife, Evelyn,he had three children, a son and two daughters. After a long illness Sammy died of a heart attack in Cleveland in October 1980.

The featherweight king seemed to be the one person who did praise Sammy, saying: "He was one hell of a fighter. He beat me. Yes, it was very close, but the record books show he won. I was upset and disappointed straight after we fought, but I have no complaints." Willie was enjoying life to the full. He was living it up for all it was worth, one day sitting in a bar, the juke box was blaring a popular recording of "The Moonlight Gambler" Willie, turned to a friend and said: "That song reminds me a great deal of myself." They both laughed. The champion recalled a very embarrassing incident when he was arrested along with 27 others for taking part in a cheap crap game down by the river bank in Hartford. "It was a pure fluke I was at the scene," said Willie. It seems after arriving back in Hartford after one of his fights out of town he originally went looking for some friends and was told they were in the woods. Off he went looking for them, when he found his pals they were deep into a game and the betting was heavy. As Pep was watching the players gamble, the police raided the spot and the champion was placed under arrest. As he stood in the police court the judge, named Cornelius A. Moylan, remarked: "Willie, I'm ashamed of you. This is disgraceful. Not long ago my little boy was pleased to get your autograph. You have a moral obligation to the countless young folk who have made you their idol. When my son heard about your arrest he felt hurt and so do I. You must set some sort of example to the generation of young Americans to whom you are a hero." The world champion hung his head in shame. He was fined twenty-five dollars. He paid the fine straight away, but this minor incident cost him a great deal of respect and adulation. He would sadly, never be allowed to forget this visit to the courtroom. Willie's gambling exploits had been described out of all proportion. One well known Hartford resident and a gambler himself remarked: "Listen, I've seen this kid gambling a lot. He lost a lot of times, but I saw him win as often as he lost." Adding: "And I'll tell you this, he lost more money on dames than he ever did gambling."

The sights and sounds and the tingling excitement of the race track thrilled Willie. He loved going to the track on race day, seeing the colours, the speed of the thoroughbreds, were undeniable attractions. The man born to be king of the featherweights immediately fell in love with the sport of kings. And Pep admits all these years later the buzz he had about racing as a young fighter is just as intense today. During his boxing days he found it so relaxing away from the pressures of big-time boxing.

The Golden Era

For countless boxing fans the Golden era of boxing was from 1940 to 1950. There was Joe Louis, Ezzard Charles and Jersey Joe Walcott in the heavyweight division; at light-heavyweight, Gus Lesnevich and Freddie Mills ruled the roost, while at middleweight Zale, Graziano, Cerdan and LaMotta were the kings. There was only one outstanding champion at welterweight, but what a champion he was the charismatic, flamboyant one and only...Sugar Ray Robinson, who even in this company was so impressive he was already being hailed, even by his few critics, as the greatest fighter of his time. At lightweight, there was a pair who would stand out in any age in Beau Jack and Ike Williams, and obviously Pep and Saddler were part and parcel of these glorious times. Manuel Ortiz was the standout bantamweight king and Jackie Paterson was the flyweight with thunder in his fists.

Between April 1943 and December 1944, Pep had fought 19 times, winning them all, and defending his title twice in the process. His management had him boxing all over the States against all types of opponents. There were rumours circulating about Willie's love of the night spots and gambling while failing to show the dedication required. He was friendly with sports figures such as Duke Snider, Joe DiMaggio, Ted Williams and "Hammering" Hank Greenberg, and other fighters and sporting and show-business celebrities. He would visit the night spots with them and have some fun. These fellows were real heroes to their fans. But once he was ordered to commence training, that was it as far as socialising was concerned. Bill Gore heard the whispers but dismissed them as nonsense, but he told Viscusi: "Keep him busy, that's the only way he will learn his trade. Get him fights against anybody, anywhere. Let him meet every type of fighter and then just watch this kid improve. He needs experience to go along with his world class ability." Viscusi certainly heeded the wise old trainer's advice, and kept his young boxer active. When Willie was not fighting in competitive bouts, he would be drilled in the gym by Gore. He would work on his moves and different techniques always in perpetual retreat. He was a phenomenal warrior.

In April 1943 Mr Lou accepted an offer for Willie to box Jackie Wilson in an eagerly awaited 12 round non-title clash. It was a match many writers had been suggesting in their columns. For quite some time Wilson was born in Arkansas, America in 1911. A coffee-coloured, smooth-boxing and hard-punching fighter who gave everything he had in all his ring battles. He was regarded by insiders as one of the hardest fighters in the featherweight division in those palmy days. Wilson had a fast left jab, and could box beautifully when the need arose. British fans got a first hand view of Jackie when he campaigned on our shores during the late 1930s. Jackie Wilson won his world featherweight title (the National Boxing Association version) in 1941 in Los Angeles when he outscored Richie Lemos over 12 bristling rounds. Successfully defending his crown against the same person only four weeks later, in January 1943 again in Los Angeles, Wilson lost his championship when he dropped a points decision to Jackie Callura in Rhode Island. He failed to regain it when he lost a decision again to the smart Callura in March 1943. Now here he was, just a few weeks later, fighting Pep.

Gore had no worries about who Pep was matched against. He was confident this young man was one of the "Special" breed, an athlete who nature throws into our mists perhaps once or twice in a lifetime. Many boxing scribes from the 1940s have been loud in their acclaim for Pep's skills. Though they were not slow to point out his lack of punching power and this was true to a point but only because he was constantly on the move. It was 26 April, 1943 in Pittsburgh when the Hartford whizz kid and Wilson, the Leechburg stylist, were scheduled to cross gloves, at the Gardens. Pep had trained at Ketchell's gymnasium on the South side of the city. The champion had looked brilliant in his workouts and said he did not want to get caught napping against the local favourite.

Asked by local reporter Jimmy Miller if he knew much about Wilson, Pep replied: "Wilson is a 'cutie' and a fast-moving boxer with a good jab." Then Willie emphasised the three things he wished to complete as soon as he possibly could. He, along with Wilson, was awaiting his call-up papers any day: "I would like to box Jackie Callura of Canada, who is the holder of the N.B.A. version of the featherweight crown, just to clear up the muddled situation. Secondly, I would like to tangle again with Sammy Angott, who handed me my first defeat. Then I will be ready to enter the services to help fight those Nazis." Wilson who began his professional career in 1931, had trained hard for this big chance to break back into the championship league. He completed his preparations at the Centre Avenue Y.M.C.A. Jackie had boxed dozens of rounds against fast-moving Ossie Harris, Billy Bates, Ray Ferris and an assortment of local fighters. He was confident of winning and realised that victory over Pep would put him back among the top ten featherweights.

Another local scribe, Eddie Beacher, wrote: "With both principals keeping one ear cocked for the bugle call which will send them marching off to war, this twelve-round whirl between featherweight king Pep and the battle-scarred Former NBA king, Pittsburgh's Jackie Wilson, can hardly serve as little more than a warm-up for a bigger fight (The War). Both battlers were recently classified 1-A and will be climbing into khaki to join the married men's brigade in Uncle Sam's service any day now when their respective draft board's care to knock on their door. Still, both fighters would like nothing better than to pass out of the fight picture in style. For Wilson in particular, this bout means a great deal. In normal circumstances, it would very well be the most important fight of his 13-year career. Jackie, you know, has licked many a champion in his time, from Ireland to Australia, but with all his victories and world travels, the happy-go-lucky black fighter failed to find the pot of gold at the end of the rainbow." Beachler indicated should the 33 year old former champion lose to Pep and fail to use his advantage in experience, craftiness and whole-hearted determination to stay in boxing's top class, then Wilson would be well advised to retire from active fighting and concentrate on his farm in Leechburg and await the call from his draft board. When Pep fought Wilson it was a humdinger of a contest.

Willie was still smarting over his first ever professional loss to Sammy Agnott a couple of months previously, though it must be said, the defeat had not robbed him of any confidence. He had fought three times since that shock defeat and had looked brisk when decisioning Bobby McIntire in Detroit. Then he outscored the teak-tough Sal Bartolo in Bartolo's home city of Boston, the first of their three epic fight series. Then the Hartford wonder kid defeated Angel Aviles in Tampa, Florida. Once the bell rang for the Pep versus Wilson clash the champion boxed superbly. The crowd were treated to a contest of skill, crisp hitting, ring science and bravery. They thoroughly enjoyed every second of this absorbing battle between two wonderful ring practitioners. Pep outpointed Wilson in a storming battle of wits. Once again he boxed brilliantly, his speed as always, giving Wilson problems. This was like the vast majority of this young champion's previous contests, full of class and boxing ability, plenty of everything which made boxing an exciting spectator sport. The majestic way Pep handled Wilson made his sceptics sit up and take a fresh look at his credentials.

Watching Pep in action was like going to the theatre, to watch a best-selling play or a musical which had received rave reviews and broken all box-office records. Yes, he was that brilliant! It was suggested by a boxing journalist of those times there were two reasons why boxing followers went in their droves to watch Pep's ring performances. They wanted to see if what they had heard and read about this frail "Baby-Faced" wizard of the ring was true. Could he really defy logic and avoid getting hit by fighters who had awesome reputations for taking heads of shoulders with their knockout bombs? Was he really a true ring artist? Could he really make these ferocious knockout destroyers look foolish? It was also similar to watching someone walk across Niagra Falls, with the crowd holding its breath and wondering. "Will he Fall?" Pep walked this kind of tightrope every time he entered the ring. He had the fight audiences in suspense and asking themselves the question. "Will he get hit tonight?" Time after time he emerged virtually unmarked. Pep was a thinking boxer of the highest order. Willie must have danced, skipped and run hundreds of miles during the contest against Wilson, feinting and drawing the strong-punching Wilson's leads then countering him superbly to score points before hopping out of danger. He hardly lost a round, so immaculate was his display. Wilson wanted a toe-to-toe confrontation, a shoot-out to the finish. He wanted Pep to stop moving and trade punches with him. But Gore advised his boxer to keep doing what they had planned. And what a wonderful exhibition the little Hartford man put on. Viscusi speaking after the contest said: "It was brilliant. I just sat on the stool, and enjoyed this spectacle of the sweet science which Willie was performing. He was like a surgeon performing a delicate operation, it was marvellous. You have to remember Willie is just a kid, but he gives classical exhibitions of boxing in every fight. Believe me, I've seen all the so-called great fighters throughout history, but they couldn't hold a candle to this kid when it came down to ring perfection. The fans preferred a contest of skills, than watching two fighters just slugging it out." The world featherweight champion put his faith and conviction in his own remarkable self-belief, in his boxing technique and his speed. There were no complaints from Wilson when the decision was announced. Pep had used this 12 rounder to hone himself for his forthcoming championship encounter against former victim, Sal Bartolo.

There was a sad ending for Jackie Wilson who died in 1966. He had been ill for quite some time and been a patient for 15 years in the Torrance State Hospital in Leechburg. After beating Wilson, Pep told reporters about his love of horse racing, "If I hadn't become a boxer I would certainly have been a jockey. I loved horses. There were about six or seven tracks around a 120 mile radius of Connecticut, it was easy for me to visit a track." Willie admitted he had lost large amounts of money gambling. Many people were asking, where on earth were his advisors and his family to help and advise him not to be foolish by throwing away his money on these vices? Well, certainly Gore and Viscusi did try and advise Willie to put his cash away in the bank. In fact, as outlined in a previous chapter, Viscusi opened a pension fund in which Pep would not be able to draw upon until well into his thirties. In later years Willie invested money into a Chilean oil field which cost him thousands of dollars when it went bust. He also owned some night clubs; two in Florida and one in New York, but Willie was let down badly by his business partner on each occasion. His judgement again let him down when he purchased a tavern in Hartford. He put his father in charge but Mr. Papaleo snr was no business man, and it turned out to be a complete financial disaster, costing Pep in the region of 15,000 dollars. His mother and father pleaded for their famous son to try and save his money for that well-known rainy day, but it was all to no avail. Willie was too busy enjoying himself to pay attention to their well intentioned advice. If he would have invested his money sensibly, at least he then would have had something to fall back on as he got older and into the veteran stage of his career. A good solid pension scheme would have been another good investment which he should have considered. But sometimes the fighter is his own worst enemy, and it becomes hard work making these lads understand the big money does not keep pouring into their bank accounts.

Sadly, it's a true fact of life that very few boxers end up wealthy people. In fact, most finish up penniless! In Pep's day things were a lot different. Boxing was mainly controlled by the thugs and gangsters of gangland. And the fighter might never know what his real purse was. It would have been divided into many portions, with the fighter receiving only what the thugs thought he should get. This of course did not happen in Pep's case. Viscusi was a well connected and established manager who looked after his fighters' welfare and interest. In all probability Pep would only meet his manager while in training or just prior to one of his bouts then briefly after the contest. When they divided his purse money, they would go their separate ways until the next fight. What Willie did with his money was up to him.

"I can't live his life for him," was, and still is, a well-known saying of boxing managers. Professional boxing is littered with heartbreaking stories, many of them from former world champions who earned huge amounts of money before finishing flat-broke. Joe Louis springs to mind. Sugar Ray Robinson was another example. He vowed boxing would never have to hold any benefits for him when he finally retired, but sadly he finished up penniless. Ike Williams, Randy Turpin, Ken Buchanan, Jose Napoles and Panama Al Brown all made the same mistakes. The list is endless. One would expect boxers would learn from the plight of past champions, but sadly, they don't. It still happens. They never believe that it can happen to them.

It was soon back to business for Pep. He had another robust and dangerous challenger to attend to in Boston. The squat, smart-moving and highly regarded Sal Bartolo on 8 June, 1943. The champion had been kept busy, boxing in many States, gaining new admirers and he was of course now a married man. His wife though was left behind with his parents while Willie was out on the road fighting or in training camp. She was never allowed to travel with her husband while he was fighting in the various towns and cities. Managers and trainers would never allow wives near their husbands during preparations for an important contest, nor would they even agree to any 'phone calls from the fighter's loved ones for fear that the spouse would relay bad news, thus upsetting his preparations for the upcoming business. Pep, though, in the main was not hard to train. He was a fitness fanatic, doing his roadwork and regularly attending his gym sessions. The amazing thing about him was his thirst for learning. He would practice new moves continuously while most fighters, once they have achieved their goal, lose the thirst for advancement. Right from the beginning, Pep decided he was going to be a big star and if it took hard training to achieve this, then so be it. He vowed to give his preparation everything he had.

After his convincing victory against Jackie Wilson, Pep found himself preparing to tackle the little Bostonian, Salvotore (Sal) Bartolo. This was a return contest they had fought three months previously in Boston and gone ten pulsating rounds. Pep had gained a very close, but clear-cut points victory. The Boston fighter's management team had demanded a quick return bout with the featherweight championship at stake this time. They claimed the extra five rounds would suit their stronger fighter. They were also convinced, like a great many more people in the boxing business, the champion was having a struggle to maintain his weight.

Contracts were signed and the match was made for Boston. The venue or the surroundings did not bother Willie in the slightest. He was quite willing to box any opponent Lou Viscusi selected for him, and it certainly never worried him if he had to box in his opponents territory. His only concern was that his purse money was secure. This was not bravado on Pep's part.

He believed wholeheartedly in his own ability to outbox anyone he was matched with. It was the supreme confidence which only a very special breed of boxer possessed. After being classed 1-A in the selective service, Pep was expecting his call-up papers to arrive at any time. The champion was only 20 and in ordinary times could have expected a long, fruitful earning power expectancy in the ring, but circumstances in Europe had changed all that, and the prospect of his early induction into the army had made him eager to fight as often as he could with his title at stake. Pep wanted to carry his championship into the service with him, and whether he did was up to the 24-year-old Bartolo of East Boston. This was the first outdoor fight in Boston in many years. There was speculation of a 25,000 turnout of fans to watch these two New England fighters swap blows. Bartolo himself was classed 3-A by the selective service, but was expecting to be reclassified, so both fighters were preparing to swap their boxing gloves for service rifles. This was Willie's first championship defence. Bartolo was making his first championship bid. As a campaigner for the title, he had engaged in more fights than Pep whose rise to the throne was one of the most rapid in featherweight history.

If long and faithful service merits reward, then Bartolo was ripe to realise the ambition of all fighters to win the championship of his class. The East Boston man had campaigned for almost seven years as an amateur and professional, and had only a few defeats chalked up against him. In contrast, Pep had been fighting for only three years as a professional. He had fought his first main event bout 16 months previously, scoring a four-round knockout over Joey Rivers. From that time on, his success had been uninterrupted in the featherweight ranks, and not until he elected to go out of his class to meet Sammy Angott, the former lightweight king, was his string of 65 straight victories broken. Pep not only established a record run of victories while winging his way to the top of the 126-pound division, but his drawing power had put him in a class all by himself. When he won the title from Chalky Wright, the receipts were nearly $72,000. His meeting with Angott drew $70,000, and his first fight with Bartolo, which was a non-title fight, attracted gate receipts of $39,000, the biggest ever for a featherweight contest in the city of Boston. Thus the young man who first fought for a stake of fifty dollars had earned nearly $300,000 for various promoters in half a dozen recent bouts.

Co-promoters Jack O'Brien and Eddie Mack, contended loudly that the Pep-Bartolo championship clash would produce the first $100,000 gate in New England history. This seemed an exaggeration. They were depending on a beautiful summer night, the venue was at Braves Field, Boston. The local newspaper reporters were high in their praise for their fighter, this of course was based on his excellent display in his ten round clash with the young champion a few months previously. "Off his showing that night, Bartolo seemed to have an excellent chance to slide home the winner," said W.A. Hamilton, a Boston reporter.

This would be the first time the swarthy Boston fighter had ever gone the 15-round distance, and those extra five rounds had spelt defeat for many of Pep's opponents. Bartolo was a forward moving warrior who used both fists effectively. He was a dangerous right-hand counter hitter and he invited aggressiveness on the part of his opponents in order to nail them with his smashing right-hand punch. Sal furnished a sample of his soporific hitting in his first meeting with the champion when he staggered Pep with a terrific right-hander to the jaw. It was noticeable, however, that "Barty" never came close to scoring with a similar punch for the rest of the contest, and while he fought niftily enough to keep pace with the champion, he lost by a margin of one point.

That was close enough for him and his hundreds of admirers to believe his bid for Pep's title would result in the native son bringing Boston its first world featherweight champion.

Out of his last ten contests before facing Pep for the championship, Bartolo had won nine. Some well-known scalps hung from his belt; Willie Roach was stopped in six rounds and Joey Archibald and Pedro Hernandez were both clearly outpointed over ten rounds. These were good victories for the Boston fighter, because all three were well-known fighters who were highly ranked in the world top ten of the featherweight division. Though it must be said that the champion had also defeated the same three fighters. This contest between Pep and Bartolo was a natural. Their first fight in the Boston Garden was a sizzler. The two antagonists had tangled in what was expected to be another routine victory for the amazing Pep. On that occasion, in the sixth round, Bartolo, a purely local product, and considered a stiff puncher for his size, suddenly detonated a left hook. This power-packed wallop was followed with a sizzling right cross, and saw the supposedly unbeatable Pep start wandering in dizzy fashion down Queer street as if looking for a lamp post. Bartolo didn't finish him that night, but stated before the title fight: "Just give me another opportunity. You will see me flatten Pep, believe me, I'll knock him out."

"I underestimated Bartolo the first time we fought," said Pep. His exact quotation being: "I thought I had a chump. I wasn't sufficiently careful, got tagged. Bartolo won't be able to hit me with a handful of ice-cream salt. He is supposed to be a big puncher, but remember the old slogan, he can't hit what he can't see." As Pep jigged down the aisle to the ring, he wore a bright red ring robe with a blue collar and white bands on the sleeve and pocket. Bartolo wore a brown dressing gown; so brown it almost looked like suede. For the battle, Pep wore a champion's purple trunks trimmed with blue binding. Bartolo's were red and black. As a contest for a world championship, this confrontation was no thriller, but it was an interesting bout with Pep providing most of the entertainment. Once again, his boxing skill was all that could be desired. He was flashy, alert, quick off the mark with his punches, and his defence was first-class. Once he had the measure of his challenger, Willie boxed like the champion he was. Bartolo, who had been expertly coached by New York's Ray Arcel, who also acted as chief cornerman, was aggressive up to this point, and his best rounds were undoubtedly the second, sixth, seventh and ninth when he made an impressive showing. He won two of these by small margins while the others were even. In these rounds the challenger showed scant regard for Pep's reputation. He wanted to trade blows and quite a number of his rights to the jaw found their target and brought him glory.

In the remaining rounds, the champion was the complete master and there was never any doubt as to who would emerge as the winner. As the fight progressed Willie got better and faster. His punches landed effectively throughout the whole of the bout. This was by no means one of his toughest battles, yet it wasn't a one-sided affair either. Pep turned back Bartolo's championship bid because he was a supreme performer. He had learned his lessons from the mistakes he made in their first bout. The anvil-chinned and sting-fisted champion had everything firmly under control. The fight was fast but futile, the tempo was rapid, the action animated. Pep was too fast, he knew too much, his punches were too swift, he had too much class for the challenger. Bartolo tried hard, the crowd were hollering for him throughout the 15 rounds. Even Mayor Tobin, in a handsome grey Homburg, was rooting audibly from ringside. And, Police Commissioner Joe Timilty, in a new grey skimmer, featuring a jaunty red feather, was another ringsider who was shouting advice to the Boston fighter and it was good advice too.

Sal was much too cautious and at times, too bewildered, as his opponent outsped him, outpunched him, outgeneralled and outscored him. The bout went the distance at a fast pace, but there were no knockdowns, no truly staggering blows, and although the champion's left nostril dripped blood through the later rounds and Bartolo's left eye was slightly strawberried from the middle stages of the bout, there was no outstanding evidence of wear and tear. It was just a fast boxing lesson delivered by a cool little artist who was too smart and much too fast for the East Boston fighter. The crowd were spellbound by Pep's artistry for most of the fight. Cheering occasionally when their man delivered a good punch, and roaring briefly in the 13th when a quick jerk of Pep's pinioned left threw Bartolo flat on his back. But, barring a faint back drop of boos when the unanimous decision was rendered to the champion, when referee Johnny Martin lifted the hand of Pep it was quiet indeed. The crowd clearly voted with the referee and judges. Bartolo though, was far from disgraced. In fact, he fought a hard and willing battle. But Pep was in a different league to him. The ultimate round was fast and both men were slugging at the finish.

The contest was expected to reach the proportions of 25,000 to 30,000 and to contribute some $75,000 for a Boston record, but it drew only 14,000 for a gross of $46,984,30. At least half the ringside seats were filled with New York boxing writers. The fight had the full championship trappings. The National Boxing Association Commission insisted their fighter, a young Canadian from Hamilton, Ontario, called Jackie Callura was the rightful world's featherweight champion. The Hartford flash, however, was generally considered authentic in states where the big rings are, or were, and he looked sufficiently authentic on this pulpit on this particular evening. Pep was the legitimate world featherweight champion, of that there was no doubt.

Nat Fleischer, editor and owner of the Ring magazine said: "If Abe Greene and his colleagues of the National Boxing Association adhered to the principles of boxing instead of playing politics with the game, they would come forth like true sportsmen and give the Connecticut lad his just due." They would concede what the world already knows, Willie Pep is the legitimate holder of the world featherweight crown. If Abe and his championship committee had been present in Boston the night Willie took Sal Bartolo apart with plenty to spare, they would no longer withhold recognition from the boy who won the title the hard way in the ring against the real champion, Chalky Wright. Since that battle seven months ago, Pep has lost only one fight, that to Sammy Angott, an overweight match, and in his only defence of the crown, he showed Bartolo why he is deserving of the honours being withheld from him by Messers. Greene and his N.B.A. committee. Any boxing commissions to the contrary, there is only one featherweight champion, and his name is Willie Pep. He is the class of the division and Bartolo can testify to that."

Pep, who was guaranteed a purse of $30,000 for his evening's work, was undoubtedly the winner in two ways. The Boston challenger was getting a percentage, the sponsoring Boston Boxing Association did not exactly get wealthy. It was thought the promoters lost money on the tournament. On reflection, the way Pep handled such a potentially dangerous opponent as Bartolo was impressive. He had completely defused by his clever boxing technique, and nullified a tough, rough, hard-punching, well-respected and highly thought of contender. In the process, he made Bartolo look like a beginner and the 15 round contest look so easy and one-sided.

Manuel Ortiz

After successfully defending his title against Sal Bartolo in June 1943, Pep went into the United States Navy. He might have been a fighting machine in the ring, but certainly not in the service as he was soon to find out. Willie got called up for induction in June 1943. The local draft boards in Hartford had been getting hundreds of calls and letters and they all said the same thing. "My son's in the Army, why isn't Willie Pep?" Well, Pep tried to explain that he was supporting his mother, father, son, sister and her husband. He was also having trouble with his ears at this time. His local doctor signed a certificate stating he had "perforated eardrums." However, Willie went down to the draft board and passed all the tests with flying colours except for his ears. Four or five doctors took his charts and went into a huddle. While the army medical staff were discussing Pep's case, a top ranking Navy officer, a lieutenant Commander, approached the champion and said: "Willie, why don't you join the Navy? You could be an inspiration for our men. It's far better than the other services. We'll get you on the boxing team, maybe we can get you as a boxing instructor. The Navy needs high profile world stars like you"

Pep was suitably impressed by what the Commander had told him, but said a few years later: "It sounded fine to me, so I joined the Navy. What a terrible mistake." At the time of Pep's impending induction both Viscusi and Gore, expressed doubts Willie would pass the physical examination. They said he always had trouble with his ears of a nature that made swimming an uncomfortable experience. They revealed when taking showers Pep was careful to avoid letting water trickle into his ear. "He used to wear a bathing cap in the shower," said Bill Gore. It was thought Pep's ear trouble flared up again when he tried to meet the swimming requirements in the physical instructor's school at Bainbridge. "Scores of boxers have been discharged from the service because of punctured ear-drums," said Viscusi. None-the-less, Pep was now in the United States Navy. After doing his boot training at Sampson, New York, the Navy officials wanted Willie to go as a hospital apprentice. "Me, a hospital apprentice!", he said, "no sir." So they made him the water boy for the football team. Mal Stevens, the former boxing commissioner of New York, was the head coach. For four months they had Pep in OGU. Out-Going Unit. He boxed two exhibitions to earn himself a couple of weekend passes.

No matter how hard he tried he just could not adjust to life in the Navy. He thought that because of who he was, a world champion, everybody seemed to be making things awkward and difficult for him. "I didn't know anything about left face, right face, left flank, right flank, all that stuff," he said. Pep's petty officer was a strict disciplinarian. One day he said to Willie: "Just because you're Willie Pep, don't think I give a damn." The commander of the unit was a good officer but didn't like boxing either. So Pep began to fool about and was given KP in the kitchen for answering the chief back. He was now totally disgusted and disenchanted with the Navy. There he was, a famous world champion, he had offered his services as a boxer, but the commanding officer didn't seem to want to use him in this role. He could have done a great deal of good for the Navy if they had given him the opportunity. In frustration Willie finally went to see the chaplain. Requesting that he help him get a posting elsewhere. "Let them do something with me. I'd rather go over seas on one of those boats than hang around doing nothing here," Pep said.

A few days later Pep found himself on his way to Bainbridge, Maryland, a physical instruction school. That was a rough life. He had to get up at five o' clock in the morning, and run around the camp a few times. He didn't like that at all. If he had been training for a fight, it would have been different. His ear then began giving him trouble, it began to run, and he went to sick bay. "I don't know how they figured they could cure my ears by putting me in the psycho ward," said Pep talking a few years later about his experience in the Navy. "But that's where they put me. If you had a bad back they put you in the nut ward."

There were a couple of other well-known athletes in the same ward as Pep. A well-known tennis star and a ballplayer (who shall remain nameless). They would do nothing all day but play cards. The second day Willie was in the hospital, Lieutenant Commander Wright came to see him and told the world champion he was going to get discharged. Willie was overjoyed at this news but he had to wait a further ninety days for his discharge papers to come through, spending it in the company of mentally sick patients. It was quite an ordeal. There were all kinds of sick people on the ward, one big strong fellow used to get violent headaches and go berserk. He would bend the brass bars on the bed, he was really strong and aggressive. One day Doctor Wright asked this man why he was causing damage to the bed? The man told the doctor he was very sorry for the damage he had done and proceeded to bend the bars back into shape. The Doctor looked startled and turning to Pep he whispered: "This kid's got to go." The man used to have violent fits. Once he started walking toward Pep. Willie was slightly concerned and started talking to him soft and fast. "What you doing? It's me, your old buddy, Willie Pep," he said. Finally the man must have recognised him because he stopped short. Ninety days of things like that was enough for anyone to stomach. Willie said he felt like he was going to be stuck there forever. But his discharge papers finally came through and the Navy shook hands with the champion and let him go home.

Headline News

After serving only nine months Pep was honourably discharged from the Navy. This of course made headline news in the Hartford newspapers, with photographs and stories about why he was released from active service so quickly. Many people were very sceptical and far from happy about his sudden discharge. The champion received a great deal of adverse criticism concerning his release from the Navy. But compared to other sportsmen, Pep had a rough deal during his time in the services. Other well-known boxers like Joe Louis, Billy Conn, and Sugar Ray Robinson for example, were doing a public relations service for the Army, by boxing exhibitions on all the army camps. By a strange coincidence Pep's discharge came the day before Lou Viscusi had to report for his induction physical. Mr Lou, was one of a group which had to report to New Haven for his test. Also in the group was Jimmy Leto, the former outstanding welterweight and one of Viscusi's first signings, the man who taught Pep many of the tricks he employed in the ring. Viscusi was not expected to pass his examination because of poor health. (As this book was in process in 1997, my inquiries lead me to believe Viscusi is still alive).

Another strange occurance concerning the draft at that time was the case of Maurice (Lefty) LaChance (LaChance would be one of Pep's latter opponents) and his manager, Sam Michael. Shortly after LaChance had been honourably discharged from the Marine Corps for medical reasons, his manager, who was 38, passed all the requirements and was inducted into the Army. He left LaChance in charge of Viscusi and Gore. After his discharge and all the upsets, Pep started fighting in earnest again. Gore though, was shocked when Pep commenced training and he found Willie was over the lightweight limit. Having his first contest for nearly ten months in his home town of Hartford, Pep soundly outpointed Leo Francis over ten brisk rounds on 4 April, 1944. Willie donated the whole of his purse to the Red Cross Fund. He showed little signs of any ring rust whatsoever. Two weeks later he was in New Heaven, showing his brilliance with another win over sneaky Harold "Snooks" Lacey. Willie was making up for lost time on the fight circuit. For the Lacey bout, Willie had reduced his weight to just a couple of pounds over the featherweight limit. Twelve days later, in Philadelphia, he outscored Jackie Leamus, again, over the ten round route.

His weight now was just half a pound over the championship poundage. His fourth consecutive ten rounder since his discharge from the Navy was gained against Frankie Rubino in Chicago. These four bouts helped to get the world title-holder fit and razor sharp. Pep was still highly popular wherever he fought. While he was sharpening his tools on these good class opponents he was also earning good money which was well needed after his long lay-off. He fought in Buffalo where he trounced Joey Bagnato in two rounds before scoring another ten round decision over Julie Kogon, in Hartford.

Plans were being hatched by Viscusi to match Pep against the current world bantamweight champion, Manuel Ortiz. This would be a big money-spinner for the featherweight king. Fans were eager to watch this match-up between two current world champions from different weight divisions.

They would, of course, meet at catchweights, (a weight in between the two division weight limits) but before this match came into fruition, Pep met a tarter in the tough and durable Willie Joyce in Chicago. Joyce was a real slick boxer and a very smart mover indeed. A top-ten contender, he also possessed a beautiful jab and was a master in the art of feinting. Before meeting Pep, Joyce had just beaten the "great" Henry Armstrong and was eager to cross gloves with the world champion even though their fight was not for Pep's title. What a tough battle he gave Pep. It was without doubt one of Willie's hardest encounters ever. Pep had to outjab his opponent to gain a tough ten round decision. When Willie would feint and try to hit Joyce, the crafty Joyce just feinted him right back. It was a mighty tough ten rounds for the young champion who had to work over-time on his ringcraft and left-jabbing. Joyce was a real cute boxer and what made this bout more amazing was that it took place only ten days before Pep was scheduled to box Ortiz in Boston. Some warm-up fight! Taking seven tough fights before a big-money contest against a current world champion would be unheard of today. But that is what Pep put himself through in 1944. Champions and top contenders fought regularly in those days and against stiff competition. There were also further negotiations taking place for the champion to defend his world crown against the man from whom he took it, Chalky Wright. Madison Square Garden were talking to Viscusi about this return confrontation.

Manuel Ortiz fancied upsetting the odds by beating the youngster who he had paid a dollar a round to act as his sparring partner a few years before. The bantamweight champion's connections were demanding this bout should be for Pep's world featherweight title. For his part, Pep could not have cared less what was at stake against the taller Ortiz. He left all arrangements with Viscusi. He was sharp and ready for a big test. He had got himself in remarkable condition through those tough and demanding seven bouts leading up to this meeting with the highly respected bantamweight king. Ortiz was an idol among the Mexican fans who turned out in droves to see him fight. With boxing becoming more popular worldwide he began to travel, defending his crown against David Kui Kong Young in Honolulu and Tirso del Rosario in Manila. In between these bouts he was stopped on a cut-eye by Manny Ortega in El Passo, Texas. This was the only time in his long distinguished career he failed to finish a fight. On a visit to Europe he boxed and lost to Ronnie Clayton, the British featherweight champion in Manchester, England, in 1949 and beat Jackie Patterson in Scotland, 23 days later Theo Medina in France. In May 1950 he travelled to South Africa and lost his his title to Vic Toweel. But by then he was well into his thirties and having trouble making the weight, though Toweel boxed brilliantly to become South Africa's first ever world champion at any weight.

Ortiz should have hung up his gloves after losing to Toweel, but like far too many champions he kept going. He did retire in 1951 only to return to ring action in 1953. On 10 December, 1955 he lost on points to Enrique Esquedo in Mexico City and quit for good at the age of 39. The strong aggressive Ortiz lost only 28 of 128 professional fights. However, during the period of his peak years, from 1940 to 1946, he lost only three of 62 fights. He fought no less than eleven world champions, and his total of 49 knockouts was topped only by two previous bantam champions, Panama Al Brown with 57 and Charles LeDoux with 79. Ortiz defended his title successfully 15 times during his first term as champion and added four more after regaining the crown. Had he not been called up to serve in the army he may have made many more defences. His eight title successes in one year is a record for his division. Only Henry Armstrong beat him in the number of defences in one year, Armstrong defended his welterweight title 11 times in 1939. His total of 19 defences is only second to Joe Louis' 25 defences of his heavyweight crown. He was installed into the "Boxing Hall of Fame" in later years, but Ortiz is the forgotten man of the bantamweight division.

In some pre-fight publicity, Manuel's manager recalling the occasion Pep and Ortiz sparred with each other in Los Angeles, said: "My Guy boxed with Pep, I gave him three dollars a day. He wasn't worth the three dollars then, and he ain't worth it now." What a statement to make. And what a difference in money from the measly three dollars he received for sparring with Ortiz a few short years previously, to the $20,000 he was receiving to tackle Ortiz now. But on 17 July, 1944 Ortiz was at his peak and ready to beat the reigning world featherweight king. The bout between these two superbly matched ringmen was held at Braves Field, Boston. There was a gate of over 10,000 paying spectators and Pep was at his most majestic. Ortiz had successfully defended his title ten times prior to his meeting Pep, and was considered at that time to be the greatest bantamweight champion ever. Pep weighed nine stone 1¼ lbs, while his Mexican rival was a quarter of a pound lighter. The contest was absorbing and certainly one for the connoisseurs. Ortiz waged an aggressive struggle, but his efforts seldom made even the slightest impression on the more skillful Pep. Like the majority of fighters who faced Pep, the bantamweight champion seemed intent on scoring a knockout right from the outset. When Ortiz rushed, Pep usually fired two or three lightning lefts before spinning him of balance. Ortiz's best rounds were the second, sixth and eighth when he managed to catch Willie resting, and he would flay away with a body attack. What a wonderful advert for boxing this contest was turning out to be. It was a memorable, thrilling and artistic confrontation.

It was a thoughtful, intelligent battle with brilliant moves and counter moves with Pep's superior boxing craftsmanship standing out brightly. The Hartford Italian's educated left hand, which deflected most of Ortiz' bull-like rushes, earned him seven of the ten rounds. While awarding Pep seven of the ten rounds, referee Johnny Martin also gave Pep a total of 98 points for 92 to Ortiz. The score cards of Judges Jimmy McCarron and Joe Blumsack also credited Pep with 98 points with 94 and 91 respectively for the Mexican.

Pep was truly magnificent. He boxed for the purists in the ring and he always aimed for one thing, to please. At a reception after the fight, Willie was recalling his early days in the fight game as a 17-year-old. He explained it was perfectly true, he had sparred several rounds with Ortiz in the Main Street Gym in Los Angeles and had indeed, received a dollar for each round he endured. But emphasised Willie: "I used those sessions to learn as much as I could from this wonderful fighter." The two champions had nothing but respect for each other and remained close friends until Ortiz's death a few years later. After his thrilling victory over the bantamweight king, Pep did not have much time for celebrations, because less than three weeks later he was back in action, taking on another toughie in the highly-touted Lulu Constantino. This fight took place at the Municipal Stadium in Waterbury with a crowd of over 9,000. It resulted in another ten rounds points victory for the champion. Pep was not only winning his contests, he was also winning nearly ever round of these non-title fights so brilliantly was he performing.

The return match with the still very dangerous Chalky Wright had been arranged, and Willie once again raised eyebrows by taking on and defeating two highly regarded fighters in preparation for his world championship defence. In the first of these two contests he outscored Joey Peralta over ten rounds in Springfield, boxing brilliantly in the process of winning every round. His feinting and footwork in this bout delighted the crowd. Then ten days before facing the fierce-punching Wright, he knocked out Charley Cabey Lewis in eight rounds in front of his home town supporters. Lewis was certainly no easy task, he was one of those fighters of that period who was quite capable of beating anybody on any given night. For example, in November 1947, he flattened a young rising New York prospect, a fighter named James Carter in seven rounds. Three years later, this same Carter won the world lightweight championship when he demolished Ike Williams over 14 rounds. Carter would eventually go down as one of the all-time great lightweight champions. That showed the pedigree of Charley Cabey Lewis.

Pep's Speed His Greatest Asset

In September 1944, Dennis "Dinny" McMahon was sat talking to reporters in a Hartford restaurant. McMahon was the well respected Chief Inspector of the State Athletic Commission, but was better known as the manager of Louis (Kid) Kaplan, the former featherweight champion. McMahon was asked by the journalists for his views on Willie Pep, his immediate plans and prospects, and as the manager of a legendary world featherweight champion, what was his opinion on Willie Pep has a fighter? The scribes were obviously out for a story and knowing it was rare indeed for a former manager of a past champion in the same weight division and also from the same area, to be gushing in his praise for a current title-holder. McMahon though, liked Pep's style and said Pep was going to box in Montreal after he defended his title against Chalkey Wright. Willie was booked for a ten round non-title fight against a fighter he had beaten previously named Jackie Leamus of Philadelphia.

"Pep will beat him again. It's just another spirited workout for the champion and some extra pocket money," McMahon told the reporters. Then he commented on how well managed Pep was, praising Lou Viscusi and adding: "Lou has more elaborate plans for Willie. The kid loves boxing and will fight every week if allowed. Let me tell you something, Pep is a great, great boxer. He's the fastest boxer that ever stepped into a pair of boxing shoes. I have never seen anyone who could run, glide and dance like Pep. My guy, Kaplan used to outmaul 'em. Battalino (another former featherweight champion from the area) would outslug 'em. Pep, however, is lightning fast, but he throws a variety of jabs and hooks to keep an opponent either off-balance or on the defensive. He's smart enough to outbox the maulers and sluggers and he rarely takes punishment. The boxing equipment he has will keep Pep going a long time. Like I've said, his speed is his asset." Pressed by the journalists about how Pep would fare in his forthcoming title defence against Wright, McMahon replied: "Chalky Wright has two authoritative hands but they are nothing more than threats against a speed-demon like Pep. Like in baseball you can't hit the ball if you can't see it. I visualise Willie being around a long, long time. If he doesn't get careless, and continues to keep in tip-top shape and listens to the artful advice of Bill Gore, he'll have no worries. Pep is a real champion"

"Is he as good as the past champions though?" he was asked. Dropping his eyelids and looking in deep thought, Dinny exclaimed: "Yes, Willie Pep is one of the truly great champions, a great, great boxer. They'll never forget little Willie, I assure you"

There was an interesting little story when old-timers discuss Chalky Wright's abilities as a world champion one interesting topic they seemed to forget was Eddie Mead who originally managed him along with Henry Armstrong, virtually gave his contract to his associate, Eddie Walker. One day, Mead, told Walker that Chalky was nothing more than a sparring partner and would never amount to much. "I don't want the guy. I can't use him," he said. Wright at the time was travelling everywhere with Armstrong acting as his companion and sparring partner. He was having a wonderful time. At the time of the transfer, Chalky was getting old as lighter weight fighters go. But instead of being upset by Eddie Mead's snub it galvanised his career, it was just the tonic he desperately needed and he was determined to show Mead what a mistake he had made when he unloaded him as excess baggage. "Eddie Mead, couldn't see the potential in Chalky Wright," exclaimed a reporter. Over the ensuing years Wright proved he most certainly wasn't second-hand talent.

The Return With Chalky

Mike Jacobs was expecting a crowd in excess of 15,000 to attend Madison Square Garden, New York on 19 September, 1944, for the long awaited return contest between Pep and the veteran former title-holder, the tough, crashing, bashing Alberto Chalky Wright, who never stopped trying to knock his opponents senseless. This was an eagerly awaited showdown between the ex-champion and the young current crown bearer. The fans and the reporters had been clamouring for this return fight. Wright was always a very popular fighter giving value for money, and was hardly ever in a dull fight. His popularity had not diminished despite the loss of his title to the Hartford boxer. Chalky could outpunch the best fighters in the featherweight and lightweight divisions and had fought them all. He had been thirsting for revenge against the 22 year-old champion ever since losing in their first fight. Wright felt well capable of turning the tables and regaining his title. This contest had all the makings of another brilliant boxing confrontation, between a brilliant boxer in Pep and the brutal puncher in Wright.

Both boxers had trained diligently and were as fit as fiddles. They were raring to fight. A couple of days before the bout, Pep was made a slight betting favourite at odds of 5 to 9 to defeat Wright. But on the day of the battle the champion had moved to a 2 to 7 favourite to win. In training the young champion was reminded by his trainer Bill Gore to continue where he had left off the last time they had fought. Pep told me while preparing for this fight, Bill Gore had implored him to move and circle in all directions, making Wright tire himself out while trying to nail Willie. And to make certain he made Wright miss by giving him plenty of head movement and most of all, keeping him off balance at all times because then Chalky could not get set to throw his potent left-hook. The left-hook was Chalky's favourite weapon and he certainly knew how to deliver this blow to perfection.

Mike Jacobs was giving this return bout the big publicity build up. The newspapers and magazines were full of reports on how the two gladiators were preparing and there was also daily radio coverage. Pep knew what to expect from the former title holder, who, besides being a dangerous hitter, was also a proud warrior who could be relied on to keep going all-out for the full 15 rounds. Taking a break from training, Pep mentioned the punch he had taken from Wright during their first fight which had hit him on top of his head: "He caught me with a punch and I was in a trance for a few rounds. I was determined I was not going to get punched like that again, so I put more emphasis on speed." Pep was known as one of the quickest boxers ever to grace the roped square. He could run faster backwards than most fighters could achieve running forward. While running he would move backwards and sideways then break into a graceful sprint. The champion was a familiar figure running in the local parks in the early mornings just as he is today at 73 years of age.

During his sparring workouts it was like watching a game of chess. You could almost hear his brain working out the moves in advance. Many champions and top fighters who employed sparring partners, would try and knock these poor fellows into oblivion by throwing murderous wallops with the sole intention of stretching them flat out on the canvas. Many trainers swear that by doing this it helps to make their fighters "meaner" and more "spiteful." They maintain it gets their fighter ready for the actual fight. That is open to question of course, but Pep would use his hired sparring partners with courtesy and respect. For him, they were helping him to tune up for the night of the contest, nothing more. Willie obviously knew he was much better than his sparring partners, that's why he was a world champion. So, he reasoned, why take liberties with them? This was his answer to reporters who questioned him as to why he hardly ever opened up on his hired help. "I only need them to get me sharp, in shape and ready for the big night, which is the night where I know that I'll have to pull everything out. I don't want to go stale before the fight, because that is usually what happens to fighters who have "wars" in the gym. Many boxers leave their fight in the training ring by having far too many gymnasium battles. That is not my style," said Pep. As a boxing coach myself I have discovered through trial and error that too much hard sparring leading up to a contest does take the edge off a boxer's performance, resulting in staleness or the boxer being "burnt-out." Bill Gore made sure the sparring which Pep did under his supervision was educational and nothing more.

There was a crowd of 15,433 who paid gate receipts of $66,740. Mike Jacobs was once again delighted at this huge turn out. As usual there were quite a few thousand fans down from Hartford to support their champion. Wright drew his usual hordes of celebrities because of his connections with movie star Mae West. At the weigh-in, the challenger hit the scales at 125-one-half pounds. The champion came in at 125-one-quarter-pounds. The fight was not as thrilling or as exciting as their first contest two years previously. It was not one of Pep's better performances by a long way. Willie started the first round by bouncing a terrific right hand punch off Wright's head. Then it was fascinating to watch Pep switch from orthodox to southpaw and back again, punishing the veteran with two-handed blows. The second was won by the game Los Angeles-based fighter when he caught Pep in the face with light left hands. The champion, though, rode the punches and as a result, the blows lost their sting. It was all Pep in the third stanza when he was moving as if on electric heels, flicking out his left jab and repeatedly knocking Chalky's head back on his shoulders. This was beautiful boxing skill on the retreat, vintage Pep. From the fourth through to the seventh round Wright looked like causing a massive upset. He caught the champion repeatedly with power packed right crosses to the head. Standing flat-footed to gain more power for his shots Wright was moving after Pep in an all-out effort to finish the fight and take the crown back to Hollywood. It was all Chalky and the large crowd sensing that there might well be an upset on the cards, were cheering wildly for the 33 year-old former king. Pep seemed unable to offer anything in return.

In the eighth round though, the tide began to turn in the champion's favour. He had solved the problem of the ex-champion's right hands, and got his brilliant footwork moving with swift gracefulness. Pep went back to his plan of long range boxing which did not please the neutral fans but Pep was now starting to dictate the pattern again and he fought this way for the remainder of the 15 rounds. At the conclusion of the fight Pep had won very clearly indeed. It was by a unanimous decision, but he was far from impressive. He beat Wright mainly because of his educated left jab and a very sturdy pair of legs which generally kept him out of trouble and away from his opponent's heavy blows. Chalky tried to make a fight of it but Pep knew exactly what he wanted to do and proceeded to do it. Willie's left jab was working overtime round after round as Wright advanced. The champion would bang that straight left jab into the challengers face, then, hop out of danger.

The crowd were disappointed at the fight. When it came to in-fighting Pep would have none of it. He would not fight at close-quarters, with the still powerful former champion. Whenever Wright took the action into close-quarters, Pep would grab hold of him in a tight bulldog grip and would hold on until the referee, Frank Fullam, pulled him off. Despite all this, the world champion won handily. Chalky when standing flat-footed was obviously the heavier puncher but he landed so few blows compared to the countless left jabs from the champion, that he was well outpointed.

Pep took a literary bashing from the media for his somewhat lethargic showing. He had won with something to spare. It was no bad feat to box below par, yet still win convincingly in a world championship contest against a very strong and dangerous fighter such as Wright, who had only been stopped twice during his 14 year professional career. One of these defeats was at the hands of Henry Armstrong. Talking after the fight to Bill Lee, the Hartford Courant sports writer and other journalists Pep said: "What chance had I got of trying to knock this guy out? My aim was not to try and flatten him. My only concern was to retain my championship. Chalky didn't like the way I fought him. But, that's too bad. After he nailed me a few times I began to move like lightning." After being made to miss repeatedly, Chalky became extremely annoyed at one stage during their fight and growled at Pep: "Stand still and fight."

Pep continued: "When he shouted that, I hit him with a cracking jab straight in the middle of his face and I replied: 'Do you think I want to get killed.' I know it wasn't a great fight for the fans and I'm sorry about that. But, I say it again, this guy could really punch. There was no way that I was going to take any kind of risks against him. I kept boxing my own way which was to win and stay out of danger. Bill Gore kept urging me to use my speed and keep hitting and moving. I was glad to heed his wisdom and advice. It was a very tough fight but the only damage I received was a little nick on my cheek."

The Garden fans wanted to see fireworks and toe-to-toe slugging with plenty of excitement. What they got was 15 rounds of magnificent counter boxing from the young world champion. Gore, annoyed at the criticism of his boxer, told several reporters after the fight: "I doubt if any other boxer could have been so dazzling. Willie showed everybody what boxing could achieve as a fine art. Don't forget, Wright was no stiff. Boxing is the name of the game and this was a remarkable exhibition of superb ringcraft. Willie's demonstration of boxing against Wright was a thing of beauty." "I sat in our corner and I was entranced by Willie's scientific boxing. He displayed the 'Manly Art of Self-Defence.' Pep is the greatest fighter I have ever trained. He has everything, including class!"

As previously stated, the Madison Square Garden boxing fans loved knockouts and red-blooded action. They didn't get what they hoped for with the Pep versus Wright match. But in the semi-final bout their knockout wishes were granted. Billy Arnold, the new knockout sensation who hailed from the city of brotherly love, Philadelphia, was featured in a slugfest with Joe Bennett, whom he knocked out in the first round. Arnold at a latter date would fight the "dead-end" kid himself Rocky Graziano, in a sensational fight before losing by a knockout to the future world middleweight king. Less than a month after beating Wright, Pep, once again startled the boxing establishment by going over the border to Canada and handing out a ten round boxing lesson to old foe, Jackie Leamus in Montreal. Less than three weeks after his victory over Leamus, Pep was involved in another return contest, this time it was Charley Cabey Lewis, the tough little black fighter, who he outpointed in Hartford in a further ten rounds of first class boxing.

This amazing little champion ended the year of 1944 with two further ten round victories, beating Pedro Hernandez whom he had defeated previously and who was at one time a top-rated contender, Pep easily outscored him. Hernandez was a tough and determined fighter and the Washington fans loved every second of this absorbing contest. Boxing followers from all over the states were flocking to watch this busy and sweet moving champion wherever he appeared. In December, Pep concluded a very successful year in which he had fought 16 times, winning the lot in majestic fashion and also defending his championship into the bargain. It was on 5 December in Cleveland that he scored his hat-trick of victories over his old rival, Chalky Wright. This was another bristling ten round bout, a non-title affair in which the artful boxer, Pep, won every one of the ten rounds convincingly by boxing beautifully to the delight of the fans. Chalky was still not satisfied with his showing against Pep. After the contest the former world featherweight king laughingly said: "If Mr Pep would just stand still for a second and give me a chance to nail him, I would be a very happy man indeed. I just know that if I hit him then I'll knock him out." It was quite clear by now that Chalky's best fighting days were well and truly behind him. Yet, he would still not accept that in Pep, he had met his master.

"Immaculate Skill From Will-'o-The-Wisp"
There were a great many boxing writers who strongly fancied the tough and sturdy little Bronx featherweight, Phil Terranova, to upset the Hartford featherweight champion Willie Pep, and a fight between these two outstanding featherweights was duly arranged for Pep's world crown at Madison Square Garden, on 19 February, 1945. It was Pep's last fight as a civilian. Despite his medical discharge from the navy he was expected to be drafted into the army at any time. Terranova was a former world featherweight king himself. He became the National Boxing Association version of the featherweight champion when he beat Jackie Callura, in August 1943, scoring a resounding eight round knockout. The contest was staged in New Orleans. The robust Bronx fighter gave Callura a return bout with the title at stake and this was to be his only successful defence. Once again the fight was in New Orleans, but this time he did a quicker job on his opponent, finishing the Canadian fighter in six rounds. Phil then lost his crown to Pep's old rival, the East Boston fighter Sal Bartolo, over the 15 round distance. This bout took place in March 1944, in Boston. Bartolo gave Terranova a re-match two months after taking his title, once again soundly defeating the Bronx boxer on points over 15 rounds.

This second encounter was once again held in Boston. The Pep-Terranova match was the first championship bout of 1945 to be held in Madison Square Garden. It was also one of the few championship matches available given the demands of the war being what they were that year. The Hartford maestro had fought twice leading up to this championship clash against Terranova. He had scored two resounding ten round points victories over Ralph Walton and old his rival, Willie Roache. Pep arrived in New York a couple of days before his battle with the Bronx man. He had completed his rigorous training schedule in his home town of Hartford. He had also undergone his pre-fight medical by Dr William Walker, the state Atheletic Commission Physician. The doctor found Pep to be in tip-top condition, a fantastic and remarkable physical specimen, said the doctor. Everything else was found to be satisfactory after his full examination of the champion. Pep went back to his hotel and was resting and setting out his battle plan with trainer Gore. They were both satisfied he was well prepared, having run miles while completing his roadwork in preparation for this forthcoming challenge. Both men knew the ever popular Terranova would have the majority of the crowd cheering for him even though there was a large selection of Pep's own supporters travelling down to New York from Hartford as usual. There was no doubt in Pep's mind about the eventual outcome of the bout, but he was expecting one of his toughest and hardest confrontations against the challenger. Willie also knew the Bronx-Italian was the harder puncher, and could also withstand a punch without going to pieces.

Phil felt pretty confident he would set a precedent in this fracas for the world championship contest. No boxer in history had ever won and lost an N.B.A. title and come back to win recognition anew as a world champion. Terranova had done his training stint in manager Bobby Gleason's New York gymnasium. He sent word out through the press that he was ready and willing to beat the champion. "This is the most important scrap of my career. I have had a long career in the ring, but I am physically and mentally ready. There will be only one winner, and it won't be Willie Pep, I can assure you," said the challenger.

Terranova was a chubby walk in style of fighter who just threw punches hoping they landed where he intended them to land. The distance of 15 rounds held no fears for him. He could box quite splendidly into the bargain. But knowing the fight crowds thirst for excitement he had become more a fighter than a skillful boxer, which meant he was a hard opponent for anyone to face in the ring. He was also a very proud man, as tough and courageous as they come. He feared nobody. The champion was placed as the early betting favourite to win, despite reports his boxing form had deteriorated since his stint in the American Navy.

Promoter Mike Jacobs had been expecting a crowd of 14,000 plus. He was charging the following. Ringside $12 other prices were reserved seats $10, $8, $6, $4, $3 and $2, 50. General admission was $1,50. Matchmaker,

Nat Rogers had put together a really terrific undercard. Disappointingly for Jacobs there were only 10,247 paying spectators in the Garden on the night of this eagerly awaited fight of the champions, though one was by now an ex-champion of course. The officials were referee Arthur Donovan, the two judges were Marty Monroe and Tom Guilfoyle. Speculation was rife on the boxing grapevine that the challenger was planning to go straight out and nail Pep and knock the champion out of his stride in the hope of forcing Willie to slug it out with him toe-to-toe. The Garden crowd was excited and looking forward to a terrific all-action brawl. There was also gossip during the rounds that the champion's mind was on other things, because after this contest he was going to be inducted into the armed services. Pep had also been involved in a real barnstormer of a battle only two weeks earlier, when he had outpointed the slick-moving Willie Roache.

"Was Pep on the slide?" Reporters and fans were asking the same question. This of course was utter nonsense. There were even some well-known boxing scribes who claimed Pep was a miniature, modified Harry Greb, a silly assessment. Nothing of course could have been further from the truth. The styles of both Greb and Pep were poles apart. Willie was a shining light and an example in this sometimes brutal sport of prize-fighting, where pure physical strength seemed to be all that was required. In short, Pep was a fistic genius!

The bout against Terranova was one of Pep's finest boxing performances in his 87 professional contests thus far. For this magnificent showing against the durable Terranova, Willie put on the equivalent of an "Oscar" performance. It was a boxing connoisseur's delight to watch this spectacle of the "Sweet Science," executed in such a magnificent manner by the brilliant champion. The crowd agreed Pep displayed a marvellous exhibition of beautiful and classy controlled boxing, which his hometown supporters had been witnessing for the past few years, indeed, ever since he took up the noble art at an early age. Boxing like a master and handling himself with an assurance seldom seen in American boxing circles, he gave the stout-hearted, tough, rough, eager and willing but painfully inadequate little Bronxite a boxing lesson which he would never forget. Pep outboxed, outfoxed and outhit Terranova all through the 15 rounds of controlled ringmanship. Boxing in this manner, the champion was a revelation. There were no wild swings from the educated fists of Pep. No blind rushes into trouble from him. He was the finished product, supreme and masterful, cool and calculating in the art of hit-and-get-away-without-getting-hit style of fighting. He was truly magnificent.

It was a fantastic demonstration of boxing science which was a joy for the fans to witness. Of course Phil Terranova accentuated the beauty of the Hartford boxers performance because the Bronx lad was a slugger on this occasion and showed no signs or pretence at boxing skills. The challenger seemed to have one thought on his mind, and that was to knock Pep out. This kind of thinking suited the titleholder and he revelled in the style of all-out aggressiveness from Terranova. The challenger tried to jab in an effort to prize open the tile holder's defence, but his forte was punching and he relished fighting at close quarters. Pep was more than aware it was on the inside where the Bronx fighter wanted to fight, and so he took appropriate action, making sure he kept boxing from a safe distance and not letting Terranova fight his kind of fight. Hence there was hardly any close quarter exchanges, and the challenger achieved nothing. At one point Pep stood still and avoided every punch terranova threw at him by the use of head feints and slipping the blows.

The onlookers who appreciated boxing class at its highest, they had the thrill and pleasure of watching this spindly legged boxer named Willie Pep, out think, out manoeuvre and out guess his rival at practically every turn of this absorbing contest. The ex-champion became so desperate as the bout wore on that he more than once tried hard to grab the champion's left arm and pull him close for a full blooded body assault. But he had no success with this ploy. Phil looked dejected when this plan of attack failed.

Terranova's best round was the fourth, he caught Pep with a long left hook to the side of the jaw. This punch shook Pep down to his heels. The challenger swung everything at the featherweight kingpin in an effort to bring him down. He rushed at Pep with great fury and tried to follow up his advantage throwing left and rights to both head and body. This was the kind of action the challenger wanted, this was his kind of fight. But Pep coolly grabbed Terranova's arms and held on for all he was worth until his head cleared. This would be the only round Terranova looked like he could score a knockout. In fact, it was the only round which he clearly was the better fighter. In every other round he received a lesson in how skillful boxing should be displayed. Phil absorbed a severe beating which was a painful setback to his championship hopes. Pep hit his opponent with every punch in the boxing manual. Left-jabs blinded the Bronx tough guy, hooks and straight right hands dismayed the challenger and put a stop to his rushes for round after round. Uppercuts lifted his head upwards and body shots rained down onto his chubby unprotected midsection. Then there was the lovely little step over to the side when the Bronx hard man would rush at Pep in a blinding rage, but which was woefully futile with his attack. There were no knockdowns, though, in the sixth round after falling off balance from throwing some punches, Pep touched the canvas with his gloves. Then in the tenth round after throwing a left jab to the challenger's body he slipped to his knee. However, these were the nearest approaches to a knockdown that the battle held. During this contest, Pep gave a beautiful demonstration in the art of feinting. It was a sight to behold, sheer brilliance. Terranova was a sucker for these feints from the champion. There were many occasions throughout this title showdown when the challenger would drive Pep into a corner, only for Willie to turn him out into the ropes. Terranova showed all his pent-up fury at being made to look like a second rater, compared to the immaculate silky smooth boxing skills of this brilliant champion. It was in these moments the fantastic ability of Pep came out like a glowing star in a clear night sky. Pep would feint his bewildered opponent, then bang him and straight into the ropes would go Terranova. Several times Pep did the feint and had Phil slipping and sprawling through the ropes, making him look foolish to say the least. This was true craftsmanship of the highest order. And how the crowd applauded every move. He was using foot and shoulder feints which had Terranova plunging into the ropes. It was beautiful to watch and majestic in its application.

The Garden fans were spellbound by the fleet-footed title holder. It was a unanimous decision in favour of the flashy and flamboyant champion. It was a mere formality really, because the crowd and Terranova's corner crew knew Pep was a clear and outright winner long before the official announcement was made. The three ring officials gave the award to Pep when the final bell rang in the 15th round. The only surprise with their decision was the very conservative scoring. In a mild way, it was complimentary to Terranova. The referee scored ten rounds to the champion with two rounds even and three rounds to the plucky challenger. Judge Monroe gave Pep ten rounds and five for Phil, which was generally considered flattering to the Bronx fighter. Monroe's scorecard brought forth a stream of booing, whistling and cat-calls from the audience. They suggested Monroe must have been watching some other fight. There was no way the game

Bronx fighter had won five minutes of this classic contest, let alone five rounds. Judge Guilfoyle was much nearer the mark giving Pep 12 rounds with Terranova only two, and one even round.

The weights were given as Pep at 124-three-quarter-pounds while the challenger scaled 125lbs. The boxing writers voted Pep the overwhelming winner, giving the ex-champion only one winning round, the fourth. One New York paper said: "In the other 14 rounds after his big attack in the fourth round he could have "A" for effort, but, was minus on execution." It was said Terranova failed in his attempt to win Pep's title because he could not get the champion to box at close range and this was mainly true. Yet, the wonderful exhibition of every skill in the boxing book was the biggest factor. Pep boxed on a different planet than his foe. He was never off his toes. If you liked your boxing as an art form carried out at top speed then without a doubt this battle was for you. It had everything one could wish to see in a boxing contest. Good punching, beautiful feinting, toughness, will-power, courage and brilliant footwork. It was a typical Matador versus the Bull scenario enjoyed by the crowd. If boxing fans today could be entertained with contests such has this one, then they would flock to arenas in their droves.

There was a very interesting fight on the bottom of this world championship bill. A certain Joe Saddler from Harlem scored a one round stoppage in 23. This was Saddler's 26th professional fight, of which he had won 23, lost two and drawn one, scoring 12 by the short route. A few days later, Sugar Ray Robinson would tackle arch rival, Jake LaMotta for the third time. Those were the days when fight followers could watch "real" world-class fighters. What would this kind of contest bring today? It would be regarded as a "Super-Fight" of the highest order.

On 14 March, 1945, Pep was inducted into the United States Army. He had a very peculiar service record. After his short stint in the Navy for which he was honourably discharged in January, 1944, many people had complained to the authorities that the world champion should be in uniform again and so the official draft board sent for Pep and within days he was back in uniform, this time as a soldier. Explaining why he was called up again and discussing his Army career Willie said: "This was the time when the newspapers were making all that stink about athletes who can play professional sports ought to be in the service. I went for induction again. The ear didn't make any difference this time. So I told them I wanted to go back in the Navy. I figured I knew all the ropes by now. But it turned out the Navy didn't want me. I had to go into the Army instead. They sent me to Fort Devens in Massachusetts to await assignment."

On his first day Willie earned the distinction of becoming the only soldier in the history of Fort Devens to go AWOL (Absent without leave) while waiting to be assigned. Everybody was sitting around the barracks drinking. Pep remarked: "I never saw so many lushes." Then a sergeant ordered Willie to get a bucket and wash all the windows. He started to do as he had been told but all of a sudden, something came over him. He felt like he was being singled out because of who he was. He put the bucket down, got into his dress uniform and walked right out through the gate. Not a soul asked him for a pass or anything. Willie went straight home to Hartford. When his father saw him he said: "What the hell are you doing home so soon?" Pep explained what happened. His father was extremely angry and demanded Willie get back to camp as soon as possible. Lou Viscusi drove Pep back. But Willie went back reluctantly, Mr. Lou tried to reason with his young champion. Viscusi told Pep he should not disgrace his family, and reminded him that he was the featherweight champion of the world.

When they got to the camp, the captain of the gate asked Pep for his pass. "I'm AWOL," Willie replied. "What happened," asked the officer. "I don't know," said Pep. Willie tried to explain to the officer he had just walked out of camp claiming he must have had a lapse of memory. "I don't remember a thing (which was a lot of baloney; I would have kept going to China at the time)," said Pep. The officer was really angry with Willie. But he did not want it to get out that a man had gone AWOL, so he gave Pep 30 days in the brig. Willie's ear started troubling him again, and he was sent to a military hospital and spent a week on a ward. One day the doctor came up to him and told Willie they were going to send him home. A few days later the same doctor called to see Willie again but told him that the top brass had refused to discharge him, but told Willie he would not be posted overseas. Pep was then sent to the Cushing Hospital in Framingham, Massachusetts, to act as a military policeman. There were four policemen at Cushing. They had routine duty like taking the mentally sick patients to the hospital mess for their meals.

They gave Willie a gun, too, although he had never learned how to fire one. He never had it out of his holster until his friend, Shikey Greenberg, came to visit him. Greenberg was never called up for service because he had flat feet. Willie told his friend that the army had made a soldier out of him. He pulled the gun out of the holster and pointed it at Shikey, who let out a scream. Willie told his friend not to worry, the first chamber was always empty. Then he pointed the gun into the dirt and pulled the trigger. Boom! It went off. Shikey yelled. "What are you trying to do. Kill me?" He was real scared. So was Willie, because they were real bullets. Fortunately, before he had chance to kill himself, his discharge came through. He was finally a civilian once more, and he didn't think the Marines would bother to take him into their service.

When he went into the service he had 6,000 in the bank. When he got home, his money was all gone. Pep discovered his wife had been doing quite a bit of spending. That was when he checked up on her. She was even selling the furniture in their apartment, and Willie had bought her the best furniture money could buy. One day when he got home he found a man in the house waving a 50 dollar bill in the air. "Who should I give it to," he said. "What's it for," Willie asked.

"It's for a chair I bought." "Give it to me," Pep hollered. That was the only money he ever got from of all the furniture which he had bought with money from his fights. Willie and his wife finally got divorced and his wife was awarded a $12,500 settlement. His lawyer's fees came to another $3,000. But the judge awarded Pep the custody of the two children, Willie junior, and Mary. Willie was delighted about that. He adored his two youngsters. One old time fighter when discussing Pep's generosity said: "Willie, was the easiest touch in the world. He fell for any old hard-luck story." "I saw from first hand experience his generosity in handing out his hard earned money. He was a great guy, but foolish with his money. He thought he could keep earning big purses and he was a big spender."

It was October before Pep fought again. He beat Paulie Jackson in Hartford, winning an eight round clear-cut points decision. The champion wanted to make up for lost time while he was in the services. He also needed to replenish his bank account which was considerable low after his marriage break up. After beating Jackson, Willie squeezed in four more extremely tough contests before 1945 closed out. There is an interesting little story connected to one of the four fights which highlights Pep's supreme ability against some of his opponents. Booked to box in Lewiston, Maine on 5 December, 1945, Pep faced Cannonball Harold Gibson, a local fighter in the town's city hall building. It was probably one of the few isolated cases in which a newspaperman directly influenced the result of a contest. Bob Zaiman, a reporter from Hartford, had a cosy spot in which to view the champion's contest. It was soon obvious the Cannonball kid was no match for the sleek Pep and after three minutes it became apparent Willie could put his opponent down for the full count whenever he felt like it. As the third round got underway Pep was giving his usual masterful exhibition of class and skill, Zaiman was absorbed in the proceedings when he felt a tap on his shoulder and turned to see it was Viscusi, "What do you think?" asked Pep's manager in a whisper. "Willie can flatten this guy in the next round. Do you think I ought to have him hold back and get the full ten rounds under his belt?" The reporter took a quick look around the packed hall before answering. The fans in this northern outpost, seldom got to see a champion of any description in action, let alone a super pugalist like Pep. They were enjoying his artistry despite the one-sideness of the contest. "Let it go the limit," Zaiman told Viscusi. And so, Pep allowed Cannonball Gibson to last the entire ten rounds. But he administered a beating to the young local fighter.

When the final bell sounded, Gibson could hardly see through his swollen eyes, his lips were twice their normal size, his nose was like a raw piece of meat and his ribs were sore and tender from the constant pounding they took. The audience stood and cheered Pep loudly as he left the ring, and Bob Zaiman felt quite proud of himself for permitting them to see the world champion in all his glory rather than a quick finish. But it would have a sickening effect on the reporter later that night.

As was customary after a Pep contest, Willie, Gore, Viscusi and who ever else was in their party would visit a restaurant for a meal before retiring for their sleep. Lewiston is a small town and there was only one decent restaurant open for business at such a late hour. Zaiman was talking with Pep at the dining table while awaiting their food to be prepared. Sat directly facing Pep on the opposite table was Gibson and his handlers. Willie could not help but see the victim of his night's work. It was not a pleasant sight. Willie stopped talking and looked at his plate but every few minutes he would steal a glance at Gibson who was having difficulty eating his food because of his swollen lips. Suddenly Pep leaped to his feet. "Let's get out of here," he said and quickly rushed out of the door. The others anxiously followed him into the street, they had not even started their meal. "What's wrong," Zainman asked the champion. "I want to go back to Hartford right now," said an obviously distressed Pep. Everyone prevailed upon him telling him to eat first and get some sleep. "Gee whiz, Willie," said the reporter. "It's an eight hour drive back to Hartford and we're all dog tired. Let's go back to the hotel and sleep for a couple of hours. We'll all feel better in the morning." Pep would not listen. He insisted on driving back immediately and the others had no choice but travel back with him. He was ashamed of the merciless beating he had administered on Gibson and wanted to get away as quickly as possible from Lewiston.

Later, Viscusi told the reporter that if Pep had scored an early knockout, he would have had a meal and spent the night in his hotel room and they would have all had a comfortable and restful drive back to Hartford.

A few days later, Bill Gore talking to some friends said: "You know, this kid is unbelievable, he really is. He is so advanced in skill over his opponents that most of his fights are considered one-sided. He makes potentionally tough fights look relatively easy, he doesn't just win the fight, he wins practically every round." Some reporters asked Gore, why Willie did not score more knockouts. "He could, you know," said the trainer. "Yes, if he wanted, he could stiffen a lot of those guys he's fighting" No doubt thinking of his last victim, Gore did not state that many times Pep purposely carried fighters in order to give the crowd a show. Gore, added: "Willie punches from the balls of his feet, he puts plenty of swivel into his hip movement and he punches from the shoulder. But, geez, what a lovely little boxer. He's without a doubt the best I've ever trained. I can't see me getting another guy like Willie again in my lifetime. He's a one off!"

In his last bout of the year he was held to a surprising draw by the then little known black fighter, Jimmy McAllister, this contest being staged in Baltimore. There has since been all kinds of allegations concerning this fight. It was rumoured there was some kind of betting coup taking place, but no conclusive evidence to back up these very malicious accusations against Pep has ever been produced.

Fighter Of The Year
The year ended on a good note though, when it was announced Willie Had been named 'Fighter Of the Year' by The Ring magazine. In strong competition, Willie beat fighters such has Ike Williams, Bob Montgomery, Sugar Ray Robinson, Gus Lesnevich, Tony Zale and many more. "His influence on boxing was splendid, his patriotism could not be questioned," the magazine said. Surprisingly, the top lightweights for this year were,

number one; Chalky Wright, (who had won six fights, with one loss and a no contest), number two; Allie Stoltz, a former Pep victim and in third spot was Willie Joyce another fighter whom Pep had convincingly beaten. This gives the reader some idea of the quality of Willie's opposition.

Revenge Over McAllister

A substitute was given his big chance to gain renown and revenge at Madison Square Garden on 1st of March, 1946, when Jimmy McAllister, a Baltimore fighter, was set to engage the featherweight champion of the world, Willie Pep. Although the fight was scheduled for ten rounds, and Pep's title was not at stake, the opportunity was still a big one for the little known McAllister. The Baltimore scrapper had moved into this clash with Pep through a set of circumstances, one of his own making and the other over which he had no control. On 1st of December, 1945, in his home town, McAllister had fought a ten round draw with the champion, and that was that. Little was thought then of the outcome, despite the fact that it was the first draw for Pep in his professional career which at that point embraced 94 contests.

Jimmy McAllister was not a well known boxing star in the sport's firmament. But on that fateful night in December, 1945, this small, tough, sturdy black fighter threw a spanner in the works of Pep's boxing career, and he shocked the boxing world. McAllister's name would be enshrined in the boxing record books forever. It would prove to be the one and only draw on Pep's marvellous boxing record. The boxing scribes maintained the Baltimore fighter, boxing in front of his hometown supporters had just been lucky, and he had caught Pep on a rare off night. They would soon gloss over this failure by Pep to stop this comparative tyro. It was also pointed out by reporters that the champion had taken the match much too lightly.

Another big factor they said, was the fact Pep had lost his sharpness which had been dulled by his army service. However, McAllister was another one of those extremely tough and fearless fighters who seemed to be in abundance in those days. The Baltimore scrapper was more than capable of giving any fighter fits, and who, on any given night, would more than likely cause trouble for any champion. The Madison Square Garden matchmaker had certainly not selected an easy opponent for Pep when opposing this fellow in the Garden ring. This return encounter only came about because the scheduled contest between the featherweight king and Sal Bartolo had been cancelled when Bartolo had pulled out through illness.

Mike Jacobs who was the president of the powerful and influential Twentieth Century Sporting Club. (Jacobs, masterminded Joe Louis's rise to the top of the heavyweight division as well as helping Sugar Ray Robinson and other well-known stars of the thirties and forties) was set to promote Pep against the tough East Boston fighter Bartolo in a unification showdown. (Bartolo, being the National Boxing Association featherweight champion). This much awaited championship confrontation was originally set for 1st March, 1946, at Madison Square Garden, but the Boston fighter fell a knockout victim to the dreaded influenza bug which spoiled both the plans and the proposed fight. Bartolo had to pull out of the meeting with Pep just a week before they were due to fight each other. On hearing the news, Jacobs was hopping mad and his badly fitting false teeth almost fell out of his mouth. He thought about cancelling the whole tournament, when Bartolo had to withdraw, but his matchmaker, Nat Rogers prevailed and explained to Jacobs that there was really no need to cancel the tournament. He convinced his boss he had the perfect solution to all their problems. Rogers was a very shrewd matchmaker who was steeped in boxing politics. Rogers also knew the fight crowd would be intrigued by the match which he was about to suggest to his boss.

"Mike, why don't you match Pep with the only guy to hold him to a draw Jimmy McAllister?" said Rogers.

But Jacobs got the name of McAllister confused. He thought Rogers was talking about Jimmy McLarnin the old welterweight champion. Once Nat explained Jimmy McAllister was a tearaway featherweight scrapper from Baltimore and what's more a negro. (McLarnin, the former welterweight champion was white) and it was not the old welterweight champion, Jacobs became more interested. Rogers had met his emergency and solved their problem head on. "This kid McAllister is the only fighter who has had a draw with Pep. And don't forget, Willie has had over ninety fights. He is a hell of a fighter. We will do well at the gate for this return encounter. Trust me," said the elegant Rogers to a worried Jacobs, finally convincing the promoter to go full steam ahead with the promotion.

But Rogers assessment of McAllister's fighting ability did not convince the boxing pricemakers. These people made Pep an overwhelming betting favourite to defeat the Baltimore slugger with the odds at 1 to 4. Pep would be cheered on by a large delegation of loyal fans from his home town of Hartford. This of course was a non-title contest. Jacobs was thrilled and was seen rubbing his hands in glee at the turn out for this fight. There was an amazing crowd of 19,914, in Madison Square Garden, who paid $63,987, to watch these two gladiators go at it hammer and-tongs. Pep hit the scales at 129-one-half-pound, with the confident McAllister tipping them at 128 dead.

The fans were roaring from the first bell, but it was the clever Baltimore fighter who looked like a world champion as he clearly won the opening round by out-boxing and out-punching the strangely lethargic Pep. Little Jimmy was ready to mix the action from the start. He chased the featherweight king catching him with two-handed salvos and which saw the Hartford ring artist on his back foot. McAllister was also punching hard to Pep's body, but making sure he didn't get caught by the champion's counter punches. The crowd were full of admiration and marvelled at the Baltimore fighters confidence, his zest for fighting and the dismissive way he was treating the world champion. Jimmy was the master at long range boxing which was Pep's strong point during that first session. He sparkled with the use of long left leads followed by a snappy short right cross which surprisingly found its target time and time again. He was hooking and then switching to a solid jab which was catching Pep every time. The champion was very quiet and seemed subdued. He didn't look in the mood to fight. Yes, McAllister was having things all his own way and, frankly, he made the champion look like a novice. "What's wrong with Pep?" everyone seemed to be asking as the first round ended and both fighters returned to their corners.

"Willie, get your feet moving and use your left hand. Start boxing this guy, pull yourself together," Gore pleaded in a calm manner as he ministered to the champion during the one minute rest period.

What was wrong with Willie? Was he disappointed this was not the original proposed championship match against Sal Bartolo? It was suggested by many insiders Pep had prepared for the style of Bartolo and, when he pulled out, Willie lost some of his drive and motivation. Whatever the reason he would certainly have to pull himself together and very quickly indeed, as Gore had told him, because the plucky McAllister was up off his stool before the bell rang to start the second round, ready to continue his domination of the champion.

A huge upset looked on the cards as the second round saw the Baltimore fighter commanding the proceedings where he had left off in the first round, though Pep did try and throw some punches at his lively opponent. But these blows were way off the intended target, plus McAllister was avoiding them with ease. Jimmy was firing rapid-fire punches at the slow-footed Pep. The neutrals in the large crowd were yelling and cheering as these punches found their mark once again. But the signs were that McAllister was getting over confident and this was to prove his downfall. Boxers like Pep are a special breed, they could be going through a bad patch like the champion was facing in this contest, then bang! Everything changes round with one piece of magic.

McAllister was making the fatal mistake of becoming much too cocky and taking unnecessary risks. His left jabbing had bothered Pep throughout the opening round, but where he made his mistake was in thinking that what he could achieve with his left hand, he could also do with his right cross. He became arrogant after catching the champion with a long right cross to the head McAllister tried another right hand, which proved to be his downfall. Pep rode this blow, and when the punch had spent its force the Hartford boxer struck back like a viper's tongue, returned a terrific power-packed right cross which landed flush on the onrushing Baltimore fighter's jaw, making him blink in astonishment. This was where the class and pure ringmanship which set Pep apart from other fighters came into its own. In the short time it took Jimmy to blink his eyes, Pep had delivered another crisp right hand which was more powerful than the first punch a few seconds before. This last punch though, was fired at McAllister's heart. The punch was bang on target, like a missile. This blow forced the game Baltimore battler to bend over, the wind knocked completely out of his well-conditioned body. He was like a limp rag doll on a rainy day. Before the champion could throw another punch, McAllister fell face first to the canvas, then very slowly rolled over onto his back. He remained in that position while the referee, Mr Jack Burns, counted him out. The time was two minutes and forty-four seconds of the second round. McAllister was knocked cold, his moment of glory gone forever!

He had tried hard, and indeed, was having the better of the exchanges for almost two-rounds against the best pound-for-pound boxer in the world. He also had the glory of having forced Pep to a draw just three months earlier. Afterwards he was totally bewildered and couldn't understand how Pep, who was having such a bad patch, could suddenly delve into his bag of tricks and come up with the winning formula.

It was a massive crowd for this contest considering no title was at stake. It emphasised once again the vast drawing power of Willie Pep. The fans loved to watch the smooth brand of pure boxing skill from the wisp, and that was the reason they turned out in their droves to support him. Pep had now avenged the only draw on his record and completed the job by scoring a clear, clean cut knockout. McAllister received plenty of offers for fights on the strength of his two exciting fights against Pep.

A little footnote to the Pep-Bartolo proposed contest which should be recorded. Bartolo appeared before the New York State Athletic Commission the day before the Pep versus McAllister confrontation. He handed the commission three letters from three doctors, attesting to his recent illness which had forced him to withdraw from his bout with Pep. The reason for his attendance in front of the commission was because there had been several rumours suggesting Bartolo was not as sick as he claimed he was, but for reasons known only to himself and his camp, he did not want to go through with the sanctioned Pep fight. This was why the New York State Athletic Commission requested he appear before them, and also insisted on medical proof!

The commission accepted the letters from the doctors and did not impose any penalty on the Boston man. However, the board retained Bartolo's forfeit of $1,000. This would be returned to him when he fulfiled his contract to box Pep. Mike Jacobs was of course impressed with the large turnout for the Hartford boxer's latest contest. But he was angry and extremely annoyed at the circumstances leading up to the pull-out by Bartolo. He intended staging the Pep-Bartolo match later in the year. Jacobs knew this match-up between these two wonderful little fighters was a sure fire sell-out in the making and would draw a big crowd at Madison Square Garden.

Jacobs told the press: "Sal Bartolo was examined by Dr. William Walker of the New York commission staff. Dri Walker declared he could not find anything wrong with Bartolo."

The Boston fighter had claimed he could not train because of a heavy cold. Lou Schiro, the manager of Bartolo, told Jacobs he could not be expected to order the boy to go through with the Pep contest if the boxer was not in top shape. Eddie Eagan, chairman of the New York commission, and Abe Greene, president of the National Boxing Association, had agreed to accept his explanation.

Three weeks after disposing of the frisky McAllister, Pep went to Kansas City for another return fight, against former world champion Jackie Wilson, whom he soundly beat on points over ten rounds. Two weeks later, after his defeat of Wilson, Pep flattened Georgie Knox in three rounds in Providence. Four more winning contests followed before he defended his featherweight crown in the "needle" match with Bartolo.

Willie's One-Hundredth Professional Victory

Willie Pep was in pursuit of personal excellence throughout his entire boxing career. He knew commitment and self control were the keys to obtaining excellence. While training for his forthcoming title defence against Sal Bartolo, a reporter from the Boxing and Wrestling magazine asked Bill Gore. "How important is fighting to Willie." Without blinking an eye, the trainer replied. "Believe me when I tell you, that boxing is the most important thing in his whole life." Enlarging further on the question Gore continued. "Boxing is a tough business. It's like a long hard road. There are numerous obstacles to overcome and barriers to cross. Becoming as highly skilled a fighter as a Willie Pep, in this highly competitive minefield of world class boxing, demands total commitment and sacrifice. He has this in abundance."

Making the featherweight limit though, was becoming a bit of a problem for Willie. Two days before he was due to cross gloves with his old rival, Boston's tough, Sal Bartolo, in a unification showdown on 7 June, 1946, he was visited in his Hartford training quarters by the State examining physician, Dr William H. Walker. Dr. Walker, had been asked by the New York State Athletic Commission to visit Pep's training camp and run the rule over him. "Willie Pep is in excellent condition," said Dr Walker, the physician, who was accompanied to Pep's headquarters by commissioner

John Christenson, and Twentieth Century Sporting Club matchmaker, Nat Rogers. The three officials watched Willie training. The champion was working out in a full length woollen top and trunks, also two thick sweaters. This of course caused speculation in the press about Pep's problem in making the featherweight poundage.

Customarily, he would be found making the prescribed 9-stone as much as a week prior to a championship match. There was no question he was having a struggle, but remember, this was the first occasion for more than 16 months he was required to get down to the featherweight limit. The Hartford fans though were worried and sceptical about his fighting form, having watched their man in training and going through serious routine stages in which he had been compelled to reduce his poundage drastically. Pep told his admirers: "Don't worry. I'm very confident I shall become the undisputed world champion. I will establish I'm the one and only featherweight king. I'm punching harder than ever, training has gone well."

He was in a frisky mood and looked unconcerned by the speculation about his weight problem. Adding to the champion's sentiments, Gore said: "This is a message to all Pep's fans, – don't worry about his weight. Believe me, he's in great condition," Continuing, the crafty old trainer said: "Willie is quite capable of performing such 'unbelievable' feats in the ring that fans often wonder if this skill was within the capacity of 'other' fighters, like Bartolo,? They seem to forget that there is only one Willie Pep!"

Word had filtered back to Willie's camp that his opponent, Sal Bartolo, was in tremendous form and banging out an assortment of sparring partners at Stillman's Gym in New York City. "That's great," laughed Pep when being told this information. "There should be no excuses from him after the fight. Because I'm going to beat him."

The Pep camp usually arrived at their destination a couple of days before his scheduled fight in order to rest and relax, but on this occasion he was still going through his paces in Hartford the day prior to his fight with the Boston slugger. It surprised onlookers that he went through such a strenuous session. He even assembled his sparring partners and proceeded to box eight brisk rounds with them. Bill Gore explained this was done in order for Willie to reach his peak for the fight. On this occasion the reason for such a session was because Willie just wanted to make certain his weight was in check. Pep's routine just prior to such an important contest is not unusual, though it obviously alarmed his supporters to see the champion boxing eight rounds. Many coaches believe that if their boxer feels he needs this kind of workout, then they let him do it. The day before he boxed Jack Dempsey the first time, Gene Tunney did a similar thing. And just hours before he was to box a 35 round contest, Muhammed Ali lined up his sparring partners and proceeded to engage in a full dress rehearsal for his actual contest. Many boxers feel much better mentally for having such a strenuous session.

At the noon weigh-in on the day of their third contest, the 23-year-old Pep registered 126-lbs, (dispelling any fears about his weight problem~ while the spirited, 29-year-old Bartolo scaled 125-one-half-pounds. The vast crowd at the weighing in ceremony sensed this fight had all the hallmarks of something sensational. The fact that if the Hartford boxer won, it would be his 100th professional victory may have had something to do with it. Tickets were hard to obtain and New York was buzzing more than usual.

Bartolo had won the National Boxing Association version of the featherweight crown in March 1944 after outpointing Phil Terranova, who was of course a former victim of Pep's. He had successfully defended his title on three occasions, outpointing Terranova again and then Willie Roach, who had been thrashed by the Hartford champion. Then Sal beat another Pep victim, Spider Armstrong, knocking him out in six storming rounds. It had been a political move calling Bartolo the N.B.A. featherweight champion. Every boxing follower plus every organisation in the boxing world considered Pep was the rightful king of the featherweight division because after all, he had taken the title from the recognised champion Chalky Wright. Pep was without doubt the class of the featherweight division, which had been clouded in confusion since "Hammering" Henry Armstrong surrendered the crown back in 1937. Speculation was high that the fans attending Madison Square Garden on the night of 7 June, 1946, were in for a feast of red hot boxing excitement.

The referee was Ruby Goldstein, and the judges were Artie Schwartz and Marty Monroe. Pep was the betting favourite as he entered the ring at odds of 5-to-13 in front of over 12,000 fans. It was a clammy sort of atmosphere in the Garden, and the first two rounds were quite tame, with Pep moving behind his left jab and tying up the Boston man once they came to close quarters. He was constantly dancing out of harms way. Bartolo was chugging forward doing his upmost to rough up the champion, but Willie would clinch, then having been broken up by the referee, he would be up on his toes again. Pep was scoring points and skipping away.

Both seemed very respectful of each others ability. After throwing several right hands at Sal's chin, Pep would then frustrate every Bartolo effort.

They traded left hooks in the third. Bartolo caught Pep with a solidly thrown right to the body, but the Hartford boy came back with a short left hook followed by a right cross which stunned his rival. This was certainly Pep's round, as was the following session. Willie was countering brilliantly as Sal seemed intent on rushing forward, only to be frustrated by the elusiveness of Pep. In another rush during the fifth round, Bartolo caught his opponent on the ropes and scored with a volley of head and body punches, but here again, Pep showed his artistry as he slipped, twisted, turned, ducked, bobbed and weaved out of danger. This was the challenger's round, but to say he was the aggressor is a misuse of the word. The class of the champion stood out like a lighthouse on a foggy November night.

The Boston fighter was much too respectful of his rival coming into the sixth round. The fans were expecting more fireworks from him to back up his workouts in Stillman's gym. Urged on by the crowd he surged forward and both fighters traded blows until the noise reached a crescendo. This was what the spectators wanted, but it wasn't what Bill Gore wanted.

"Box," "Box," "Box," he urged his man.

Pep had a slight edge in the seventh which was rather a tame three minutes. Gore had urged his boxer to use his right uppercut as the Boston fighter was stooping as he came lumbering forward. In the eighth, Pep threw this punch, which proved the best blow up till then. He drove it through Sal's shaky defence driving his head back on his shoulders, Bartolo was dazed and hurt badly, but managed to hold on for his life. The ninth was was won decisively by the champion who was by now in full flow. He had the plucky challenger's nose bleeding profusely as he chased him around the ring cracking him with combinations of hurtful punches. Pep continued his mastery in the 10th with a punching bombardment of hooks, right hand smashes and uppercuts which saw Bartolo having no idea of how to contain him. By the 11th round, Willie had the scent of victory in his nostrils and once more he connected with a solid right uppercut. This was a power-packed shot and the impact had Bartolo staggering around the ring. The champion was going all out to win in style with no disputes or arguments whatsoever. He was the one and only true world champion and he wanted to hear no more nonsense about who was the rightful one was.

Pep's home town supporters were imploring him to go all out in pursuit of a knockout. The Garden was a bedlam of screaming, cheering spectators. The nose was vibrating around the arena. Willie was boxing with a swagger which only the great champions possess in abundance. There was only going to be one universally recognised world champion when this contest was over, and it was odds on that it would not be a fellow named Sal Bartolo. In Pep's corner before the 12th round bell sounded Bill Gore spoke quietly but firmly to his charge: "This guy is a sucker for that uppercut, he's dipping his head forward when he attacks, wait, let him lead then counter him with the uppercut."

The steady battering Pep had dished out to his challenger was clearly taking effect. It had lowered the brave Bostonian's fighting moral, weakened his physical resistance and softened up the Bay for the coup which came with blazing unexpectedness. Willie opened up with a couple of jolting left and right hooks to the jaw, blows similar to countless others he had landed with earlier. During a brief lull, Pep swung forward and delivered two crisp, right hand blows, one of them was a devastating short uppercut which had all his weight behind it. This punch landed flush on Bartolo's chin like a bomb, and toppled Willie's perennial challenger and stretching him out cold. He was counted out by referee Goldstein as he was in a prone position, trying to gamely rise from the canvas amid a din from the thousands of delirious fans who seemed electrified by the dramatic conclusion. The champion departed from the ring amid rousing cheering and clapping with his title claims established beyond dispute.

Bartolo was removed from the ring and taken to Saint Clares Hospital, by order of Dr Vincent Nardiello, who expressed a certainty that the Boston boxer had suffered a fractured jaw on the left side. Later, X-rays revealed a fracture of the lower left maxillary bone. Dr Nardiello announced Bartolo would undergo an operation to wire the jaw, which would remain like this for four weeks.

"It was not the final knockout blows which caused the jawbone to be broken. But a terrific right uppercut which Pep connected with on my guy's jaw in the ninth round. it was this blow which brought about my fighter's downfall. This was the first knockout or knockdown Sal has ever suffered, although he was the victim of a technical knockout in a fight with Abe Denner, at Boston in 1940 when the participants head's collided," said Bartolo's manager.

What a way to win his 100th contest, a truly amazing piece of ring history, which will never be equalled. Willie became the undisputed featherweight king and in advancing himself to this exalted position he proved once again he was the best featherweight since the peak days of Henry Armstrong. The critical New York press were universal in their praise that Pep had gone through eleven rounds of superb boxing, handling the rugged, determined challenger almost as he willed, before finally knocking out the respected little battler for his most decisive triumph. Pep had demolished the roughest, toughest, and most respected featherweight in the world, with a brilliant and astounding performance which had not only the press in raptures but also the boxing followers who were drooling at the mouth such was the boxing wizardry they had seen. Willie Pep was like a breath of fresh air for American boxing. He was a sensation the way he boxed being so loose and relaxed in his movements and so accurate with the delivery of his punches. He had beaten the brave Bartolo by totally outclassing him in every phase of the game.

A few weeks after his victory over Bartolo, rumours were circulating that Willie was once again acting like a playboy, and courting the fairer sex more than a young athlete in his position should. Various gossip mongers claimed he was shirking his training duties and running about all over the place. Bill Gore, Pep's wise, old trainer once again denied this talk. He met Pep in private and explained the malicious scandal mongering. "The way you talk now Willie, is the way you will talk when you finish fighting," he told Pep. "If you keep paying attention to what I'm telling you then you'll be alright. You can enjoy yourself to a certain extent. Just remember Willie, this boxing business is tough and very mean, you are a star one minute and a bum the next." Continuing his theme, Gore looked directly into Pep's eyes and said: "I have seen hundreds of talented kids who could, and should have been champions. But they never achieved anything of note. I'll tell you why. They were playboys, no moral fibre, hardly a scrap of dedication, very little self-respect or control, no character and very little temperament. In short, they wanted the easy life, they had ability but didn't want to work at achieving anything worth while. Son, you have everything, don't throw it away, keep your discipline and you'll keep your brains."

Gore was a brilliant teacher and corner man, respected by everyone, he was in total charge of the training camp. He knew he had an easy job preparing Willie for his fights. He said on many occasions that a genius like Pep comes along only once in a lifetime. A boxer such as a Willie Pep, was the equivalent of scooping the pools and the lottery. The tall, elegant coach was confident of whoever Pep fought, he knew Willie could look after himself in any company, even in the gym where the man-eating, hungry fighters roamed trying to make a few dollars sparring. "I just stick his mouthpiece in and sit on the stairs and marvel at his unique defence," he concluded.

The Phantom Of Minneapolis

25 July, 1946, will be forever etched and enshrined in the memory of boxing followers everywhere, especially those living in Minneapolis. It was another stop on the Willie Pep boxing road show, his contest against Jackie Graves will be remembered as the brilliant champion's finest three minutes of his entire career. Pep was booked to meet Graves, a tough, hard-hitting southpaw from the State of Austin, a sleepy little town in Minneapolis. It was a non-title contest and the bout was to be staged at the Mill City Auditorium. You might well wonder what was so special about this particular contest. This was not a glorious battle with the likes of Archibald, Wright, Bartolo, Ortiz or Saddler. Those were the big paydays involving the world press, the hero worshippers, the headlines and the glitz and glamour. Apart from being a very useful brawler, Graves, known as "The Austin Atom," was one of those awkward southpaws who tended to make things very difficult for any fighter. He tended to raise his performance against established world ranked fighters like Pep. Graves was well known as a fighter who would not hide when the going got tough. In fact, he thrived in those situations. This bout against the world featherweight champion was a dream come true for the local fighter.

Two years previously, Graves and his manager Len Kelly, along with promoter Tony Stecher, were sitting at ringside in Chicago when Pep fought

Willie Joyce. Graves, who had launched his professional career only five months earlier in 1944, was eager to see Pep in action. "I may fight Pep one day and would like to get a line on him," Graves told Kelly and Stecher. "Anyway, I should learn something about boxing from watching a great champion like Willie Pep in action." Earlier that afternoon Eddie Metrie, a Milwaukee manager, asked Graves, Kelly and Stecher if they would like to meet the champion. The trio jumped at the opportunity of meeting Pep. After the introductions, Metrie said to the Pep camp: "This boy Graves is a pretty good featherweight. He looks like he might go places with experience. Maybe, you can make some money with him some day."

Although Pep and Viscusi had never heard of Graves up to that moment, they were very gracious to the Minnesota youngster and his friends. "We'll keep him in mind," Viscusi told Stecher. "If he whips some good boys and looks like he rates a match with Willie, we'll give him a chance." "Yeah, I've been hearing a lot of nice things about you, Jackie," said Pep as he shook hands with Graves. "Keep on winning kid, and maybe we can make a few bucks together sometime. I'll be pulling for you to win every time except when you fight me," added Willie with a grin.

"Thanks for being so nice to me," replied Graves. "I hope I can earn a match with you in the future."

With that, Graves and his friends wished Pep good luck against Joyce and made their departure. Pep and Viscusi probably forgot all about Graves after Willie defeated Joyce and returned back to Hartford, but Pep made an indelible impression on Graves. The Austin Atom made up his mind that night to do everything possible to earn a match with the champion. Graves gained the right to the Pep fight by whipping top-notchers like Harry Jeffra, Jackie Wilson, Charley Cabey Lewis, Tony Olivera, Louis Castillo and Baby Gonzales. The Pep versus Graves contest was a fight the fans of the Northwest had dreamed about for years, it was the most important bout in Minneapolis since the famous battle between Sammy Mandell, lightweight champion, and Billy Petrolle, the "Fargo Express," in the same arena in 1928. The Pep-Graves bout would set a new record for gate receipts (for boxing) in Minneapolis as it would draw $39,000, which represented a full capacity. As Pep said in Chicago, he and Graves would "make a few bucks together." Willie's share, after Federal taxes were deducted, would be approximately $10,000. Graves' share was $7,000.

Graves really fancied his chance to lick the "Wisp" in front of his hometown fans. He had got himself in really sparkling shape by training at the Lake Shore Acres, a summer camp which was located at Mille-Lac Lake, up in Minnesota's tall pine country, 100 miles north of the Twin Cities. He was tanned, as sharp as a tack and quietly told his friends that he thought he could upset Pep. "Chance a few dollars on me," he told them.

The big New York reporters wrote Graves was no stiff (a term used to describe a no-hoper). He drew big money in the Twin Cities, was a former national Golden Gloves champion and a rarity among smaller scrappers being a solid southpaw hitter. Rival stables shied away from fighting him as it was tough enough to fight a southpaw, but better still to avoid a knockout puncher from the hated, unorthodox stance. Before meeting Pep, Graves had fought in 39 professional contests of which he had lost only two, and those were by close points decisions. He had 20 knockouts to his credit, proof that he could bang with the best of them. He was a very dangerous foe for any featherweight to tangle with.

Places like Minneapolis did not get to see many world champions performing live. They were pleased and delighted to welcome Pep and his party. The venue was a complete sell-out within days of tickets going on sale. Everyone was after tickets. This was a big event for the locals. Pep was the attraction, of that, there was no doubt. Though the locals waged plenty of bets on their man Graves, they respected Pep, but they fancied Graves' robust style of sheer all-out aggression might prove the classy champion's undoing. After all, the fight held an obvious threat to Pep because he had only faced two southpaws previously. In Graves, they claimed, Pep had never met a fighter who could dish out more punishment.

It was bedlam outside the arena. With not a spare ticket available anywhere. Even the black-market spives had sold up early. There was an electrifying excitement hanging in the air. While staying in Minneapolis Pep set up quarters in the old Nichllet ball park. A couple of days before fighting Graves, Pep gave an interview to Don Riley, a respected sportswriter, who was also doing the commentary of the Pep versus Graves fight for radio station WHIN. Willie was giving his opinions about horse racing, dogs, women and dice, his favourite hobbies. When Riley asked the champion: "Willie, how come you don't knock out more guys?" Pep grinned, "Just a habit I guess. Going the distance keeps me in good shape. I don't need so much training. And besides, I don't want to bust my hands up."

The question was then asked: "Could you ever win a fight by not throwing a single punch? Just by moving around?"

"That's very interesting," Willie admitted. "I suppose if a guy banged up his hands he might fake it, if he could move real fast."

Later, Pep and Riley were fooling around and striking up little wagers on how the forthcoming fight with Graves would develop. What round would it end? Silly things like that. The champion was bored and just fooling around with this kind of talk, but he was warned Graves was certainly no pushover. He could fight.

"Tell you what. Let's try and find out: If we're both around when the third round starts, I won't throw a punch at Graves throughout the entire three minute round. And I bet you I'll win the round," Willie told a startled and surprised Riley. Riley smiled, and replied: "Not even you could get away with that. Certainly not against a determined, destructive-puncher like Graves, who I can assure you will be looking to knock you out for every second of every round the fight lasts." With that Pep broke out in a melon-sized grin. "Just wait until round three," he added. It was a hot, sultry night in Minneapolis, and boxing history hung heavy in the air in the Auditorium. The Pep versus Graves ten round non-title fight had all the tensions of a Yankee Stadium heavyweight scrap. Sat in their seats, spectators were about to witness one of the few truly immortal performances in the whole of a boxer's history. The heat was unbearable at ringside as Pep made his way down the aisle towards the ring. Stopping as he reached Riley, who was sitting ringside and with his earphones on: "Let's have some fun tonight Don. Remember, I won't throw a single punch in the third round and see how they score it," he told the astonished reporter. Riley blurted out what the champion had told him over the airways of America. This was the cocky, confident Pep who could get away with amazing feats. He was that good.

As the Master of Ceremonies made the usual introductions, the square-jawed Austin assassin, Graves, looked exceptionally powerful and well-muscled. When he shed his white terry cloth robe, the shoulders looked more like a middleweight's. He looked ten pounds heavier than the fragile looking Pep. As the bell rang to start the contest, the fans started shouting and making a din. It was a very exciting opening with plenty of honest endeavour from the home town hero and with class from the Hartford boxing maestro. Pep not only beat Jackie with lead rights, he got his left jab over Graves pawing right. He scorched Jackie in the opening round, moving gracefully from side to side with the grace of a doe and the speed of an Olympian. "You could not hear yourself think, the noise was so intense and deafening," remarked Riley. Graves charged Pep all over the ring, looking dangerous with those wild southpaw swings which were aimed like missiles toward the slender world champion's head. Pep was bouncing on the balls of his feet. Ever on the move, jabbing the bewildered Graves' head back on his shoulders every time he made him miss, which was often. But the local hero cheered to the echo by the fans, would not be subdued. He kept charging forward. Graves had fought many times, but he had never before come face to face with such blinding hand and foot speed. He was getting hit with a steady tattoo of left jabs and hooks. He had no answer to the amazing little boxer in front of him. The champion's punches were rattling off his head and body like machine gun bullets. "I knew he was fast, but never dreamed that he was this fast," a breathless Graves told his cornermen. Willie had the bout under firm control. He was slowly draining all the strength and power from the gutsy local hero. For the first two rounds Pep gave Graves a boxing lesson.

As the third round started, Graves moved after Pep like a dangerous, wounded tiger. Stalking his tormentor, the champion feinted with his head, shoulders, feet, gloves, even his backside. Then he feinted jabs. The sellout crowd were on their feet beseeching Graves to land a punch. Any kind of punch, but sadly for them, he was hitting nothing but the night air. The fans were now admiring the artistry of a superb boxing champion, but praying for a miracle to happen. This was supposed to be the big showdown, for Graves, but instead, the taller Minneapolis fighter with the uniquely-upright style found that his blasting punches were not landing on target. Pep cheekily turned southpaw mimicking Graves' style of fighting, but Pep's southpaw jabs were purposely missing their intended target. Jackie tried everything he knew. He tried rushing Pep into corners, but the featherweight king spun him around and was dictating the contest from the outside. He was laughing at the local fighter every time he made him miss which was every time he threw a punch. The champion danced, ducked, bobbed and weaved. He would be in front then at the back of his flustered opponent. Pep continued his humiliation of Graves for the rest of the third round doing everything without firing one single punch!

Three minutes in the ring is long enough, but three minutes using only defence might as well be a lifetime. Think of any modern fighters who were considered elusive, like Sugar Ray Leonard, who's speed enabled him to frustrate many good fighters, but he never remained punchless for more than a few seconds at a stretch. The "Great" Muhammad Ali had his rope-a-dope, but even he uncovered to throw a punch at his opponent every few seconds. To go a full three minutes without offense requires a unique level of skill and brilliance. Pep had it in abundance!

As this round progressed Graves was becoming wild and resorted to throwing desperate haymakers. He was totally befuddled and frustrated, he could do nothing about Pep's, to use a modern theory tactic of "switch-hitting" whereby the champion regularly and smoothly switched from southpaw to orthodox and back again. At the screams of his supporters, Graves pitched forward again, but Pep was not there. He left his calling card-head and shoulder feints, shuffles etc. For a full three minutes Pep moved, taunted, twirled and tied up this fearsome slugger, but never threw one single punch. This was the most amazing display of brilliant defensive boxing skills ever witnessed. So adroit, so cunning, so subtle that the 8,000 roaring excited fans did not notice the world titleholder's tactics were completely without attack. On this performance Willie Pep transcended anything and everything that had ever been seen before in a boxing ring. Riley sat transfixed in his commentary position shaking his head at such a masterful display. He had never seen a performance to get anywhere near what Pep had just given, but this was vintage Pep. He walked a tightrope in every bout where he had to pit his slender body against teak tough brawlers every time he stepped into a ring. He had to pit his wits against his opponents' brawn. This is what attracted thousands of fans to his fights. These contests were spectacles, works of art, masterpieces to be treasured for ever. All through the fight the fans saw ability and skill which they could have only dreamed about seeing in person. Pep was like a phantom-the-phantom of Minneapolis.

The end of the bout came in the eighth round. It was clean and merciful as only a skilled craftsman could achieve. Pep ripped Graves' strong body with a withering combination of blows thrown from all sort of incredible angles. His hands were so fast that they were mere blurs and flashes. He was too much for the game but outclassed fighter from Austin who had given his body and soul in a fruitless effort to beat his master. Body punches finally brought a swift halt to the one-sided contest. The referee mercifully dived in to rescue Graves as he was bent over and hurt badly from hooks to the liver area. "He was so fast, I could not see the punches coming at me. They seemed to come from everywhere," Graves was muttering to the referee as he was helped back to his corner. This was what the public had paid their hard-earned money to watch...Class! Brave Jackie had not once throughout the bout taken a backward step. But, in Pep he met a man from a different league. Graves' aggression counted for nothing, because nearly all Pep's contests were against similar aggressive style of fighters. Yes, the fans saw that velvet touch of class. Pep rose to the top like cream. He was the nearest thing to perfection one could watch in the ring. When the three judges handed in their scorecards for checking with the local boxing commission officials, all three had Pep the outright winner of the third round. It was not even close, yet he had not thrown a punch in anger of any description. None seemed to care or notice he never fired a shot. (Fortunately, the ESPN punchcounter machine, used today by television companies to provide statistics, was not at ringside!)

"No other boxer in ring history could have equalled that masterful display of scientific boxing. That was true greatness. And Willie Pep is the greatest," said one of the judges to reporters at the reception. Riley viewed Pep's audacity as blasphemy and anticipated doom for him when the champion had first told him what he was going to try and do in that round. Pep was probably the only fighter defensively skilled enough to even consider trying it, let alone pull it off. Riley concluded it would have been comparable to Jesse Owens winning the Olympics with a broken ankle. "That was greatness, Willie Pep was the greatest," he said.

Muhammad Ali, when he was in his prime in the Sixties, was another brilliant boxer who seemed blessed with blinding speed, especially for a heavyweight. But he could never box with the same flair as Pep when at his peak. Sugar Ray Robinson looked awesome when he let his combinations fly like greased lightning, but as great as he was, Robinson never could box in the manner of Pep. There were a great many "super champions," but none could match the artistry of little Pep. And this kind of showing, like his performance against Graves, was not a "one-off" fight. Certainly not, this was how Pep performed in every contest. It must have been a magnificent feeling for Bill Gore, knowing he had such a talented boxer as Pep to guide. Most trainers try their hardest to avoid knockout punchers, but Gore never had the slightest doubts about whoever faced his charge because he was confident Pep could find the solution. Willie was at times like an optical illusion. Always up on his toes, body limp and loose with a slight bend of the knees, he sometimes looked totally disinterested, but that's when his sharp brain was doing its job. He was out-thinking his foes, looking for his next counter. There are many fighters who are good at making their opponents miss, but they don't capitalise on what they have just done. Not Pep, he would make them miss, then hit them back as hard as he could.

Fighters like Graves often made the mistake of watching Pep and thinking: "If I put pressure on this guy, he won't be able to keep moving around the ring like that for ten or 15 rounds. And, the law of averages states I must surely connect with my punches sometime throughout those rounds," but Pep was gifted and exceptional in every sense. The target which they aimed at was just not there to be punched. After a few minutes of hitting emptiness they soon learned the harsh reality they were facing somebody, the like of which they had never encountered before.

It was Pep's eyes that would flash at the merest sign of weakness or uncertainty in his opponents. He saw it in an instant and used it to his advantage. He would wrongfoot the opposition and disarm his intended aggressor. Though he was a laughing cavalier type of person, with his easy-come-easy-go attitude to life, Willie was no shrinking violet glorying in his tremendous achievements of winning a world title at 20 and running an amazing record of successes. Pep was an overwhelmingly generous man, touchingly loyal to his family and friends and especially to Viscusi and Gore. But when it came to boxing, he was on a completely different wavelength. He was comfortable in himself because he knew he was talented and highly successful once he put those gloves on. Possessing a "frightening ego" which he kept under wraps very carefully, he would never boast about what he was going to do to an opponent, or what he had achieved. So relaxed when chatting to reporters, as if it was the most natural thing for him to do, he was never the slightest bit boastful when asked about his boxing exploits. Willie would never put an intended opponent down in print or verbally. He would have a bit of fun as he did with Don Riley about not throwing a punch in the third round of his bout with Jackie Graves, but he would always praise other fighters no matter what they might say about him. He firmly believed he had the ability to beat any other fighter.

Riley became a believer after watching Pep's magic in 1946. He maintained those three minutes of defensive brilliance were the greatest three minutes of skill ever displayed in a boxing ring. "Willie Pep was the greatest fighter of all-time. He was boxing's finest defensive tactician. He was the consummate defensive fighter, one who possessed equal mastery of footwork, parrying, blocking, slipping and every other defensive trick," he said.

For some boxers, one special fight will be the highlight of their career. For others more accomplished, a series of fights against a particularly bitter foe will define their place. But Willie Pep was not just a good fighter with an good career, nor an outstanding fighter with an outstanding career. Indeed, he was an unbelievable fighter who crafted an impossible fighter who crafted an impossible career.

Airplane Disaster

After his phenomenal victory over Graves, it was soon back to business for the champion. Boxing in various places, he showed his refined skills to eagerly awaiting customers. He had a further five bouts before the end of 1946. He won in nonchalant style when knocking out Doll Rafferty, a notoriously slow starter who fought in a lackadaisical manner, in six and Walter Kolby in five rounds apiece. Then he added crafty southpaw, Maurice "Lefty" LaChance, a fully-fledged lightweight, to his stoppage record when he flattened him in the third round. Paulie Jackson took him the ten round distance before losing on points, then it was Thomas Beato's turn to feel Pep's power as he went out in the second. Then in his final contest of the year he was matched against old foe, Chalky Wright, who he blasted out in three torrid rounds. This was another non-title fight and Chalky was looking like an old man by this time, the accumulation of far too many tough ring battles.

After the fight Chalky walked into Willie's dressing room, rubbing his chin he smiled. "Hey, boy," said Wright. "You finally learned how to punch. That's it, I've had enough of you. I give up. You're some fighter, boy." Willie smiled and embraced the former champion, thanking him for his sentiments.

When Chalky disappeared, Pep turned to Bill Gore and said: "Learned how to punch! I knocked out an old man. I took no pleasure or satisfaction from this victory. He was a terrific champion and a swell guy." Then adding wryly: "What a banger, he was ferocious. I should know, because I felt the wind as his punches whistled past my jaw. Was I relieved to see the back of him." Many years later, after having over 200 professional contests, Pep always spoke admiringly and with respect whenever Chalky Wright's name was mentioned. Many of the marvellous moves which Pep demonstrated better than anyone else in the world, were learned in those four absorbing fights with Wright. Willie was heartbroken a few years after their final meeting, when he learned Chalky had been found dead in a bathtub, in his mother's Los Angeles apartment. The news dispatches gave Wright's age as 45 at the time of his death. This was as it appeared in Nat Fleischer's record book, but Nat only had Chalky's word for that.

At this period the war in Europe had ended and things on the sporting scene were quickly getting back to normal. Everyone felt happy and relieved the bombing and killing had ceased. For most folk sport was their outlet and a way for them to relax and to forget the rigours of that terrible battle in Europe. Boxing fans in England had suffered through all the hostilities during the terrible conflict. They started reading the sporting newspapers which had sparse publishing throughout the period of war hostilities. They were hearing rave reports on the wireless and in the various boxing publications concerning Willie Pep.

At this time, British fans were connoisseurs of boxing and boxers, and they appreciated the craftsmanship of the boxers, not for them the slambang, charge-forward style of fighting so prevalent in modern boxing. Pep's style of boxing would be truly appreciated and everyone was in total agreement that Willie would be a sensation in a British ring. The fans would flock to see him performing his superior skills and his wide repertoire of moves and dazzling speed of hand and foot. The two biggest boxing stars of this time in America were "The Brown Bomber" himself, Joe Louis, and Sugar Ray Robinson.

In his home town of Hartford, Willie was a hero and his boxing wizardy appreciated, but for some reason he had never been given the credit he deserved by the American fans. Perhaps it was because his victories had become so monotonous they were almost being taken for granted. Whatever the reason for the lack of recognition in other parts of the states, the experts were all in agreement that he ranked as one of the greatest men to ever perform in his division, and well worthy of being compared with Louis and Robinson.

Jack Solomons, known as "Jolly" Jack for his smiling disposition, was Great Britain's premier promoter. He knew a boxer of Pep's calibre would draw huge crowds if he was matched against one of our own champions. And who better to cross gloves with the American than our own boxing technician, a man known affectionately as "Nella," but who's correct name was Nelson (Nel) Tarleton. (Named after the great sea lord, Admiral Nelson). Solomons was intent on bringing the world's best fighters to England to oppose our fistic stars, and hurried negotiations were started between Solomons and Lou Viscusi for Pep to display his talents in a British ring. Viscusi, was very receptive to "Jolly" Jack's terms, stating it would be a championship bout. The venue was arranged, terms agreed, and fans were waiting with baited breath for the date to be announced.

Tarleton was a hero on Merseyside. He filled Anfield, the home of Liverpool Football Club, and every other venue in Liverpool when he appeared. Nel was talked about in the same breath as Jim Driscoll, the "Peerless" Welsh wonder. He boxed with only one lung, the after effects of tuberculosis when only a youngster. He was a brilliant boxing master who won two Lord Lonsdale belts outright while successfully defending his British featherweight title. His remarkable defensive capabilities saw him through 143 professional bouts without ever being knocked out or stopped. "Nella" an impeccable boxer, with his slicked back hair which was parted in the middle, Edwardian style. He had beaten Al Phillips, the "Aldagate Tiger" against all the odds to keep his title and second Lord Lonsdale belt. Though by now a veteran, Nel was very popular and could still attract large crowds to his fights.

Solomons was wringing his hands in glee and also in anticipation of what Pep versus Tarleton would draw at the gate. This was a match between two of the cleverest boxers to ever lace on the gloves. But as time went on it looked like everybody's hopes would be dashed. Norman Hurst, Britain's busiest boxing writer, had tracked down Lou Viscusi through the help of Transatlantic Telephone Services. The purpose of Hurst's call was to find out the true facts. The husky voice of Viscusi came over the air loud and clear. Lou explained Pep's position regarding his swollen ankle and stating he had to go through with two fights already arranged, one in Milwaukee and another in Cuba against Miguel Acevedo for a purse of

$10,000 with Ring editor, Nat Fleischer acting as the referee. It was Fleischer who had arranged the Cuba contest.

"I can not let these people down," commented Viscusi. "Willie is really looking forward to crossing gloves with Britain's grand old master. They tell me Tarleton knows all the tricks in the game. It should be a terrific fight."

However, the impression Hurst received was that after Pep's injured ankle was better, he would be obliged to go through with his other arrangements and the contest against Tarleton would definitely not take place after all. Another offer from England was also on the table for Viscusi. Jack Harding, the manager of the new National Sporting Club, offered Pep $50,000 guaranteed for two fights in England. Al Phillips would be his first opponent and Cliff Anderson the second. There would also be a percentage of the gate as a bonus if the figures warrant it. Boxers of Pep's ability were far from plentiful and offers were pouring in for his services. The proposed Pep-Tarleton fight never materialised, and not long afterwards Tarleton retired from active boxing. The best money though was offered for an over-the-weight match in Manila. Jes Cortes, through the Ring magazine said they would pay Willie $30,000 with three round-trip tickets to defend his title against Little Dado or Dado Marino of Hawaii, again with Fleischer acting as the referee. But unfortunately for Pep's bank account, none of these proposed contests came to fruition for reasons beyond his control.

Pep and a few of his friends, who were also his sparring partners and stablemates, Johnny Cesario and Nick Stato, had spent an enjoyable New Year in Florida. Willie had been in light training in Miami preparing for two important fights which were scheduled for early in the New Year. While sparring he was troubled by an ankle injury which forced the postponement of scheduled ring appearances in Cuba and London. After a few days though, the ankle had responded to treatment and was apparently fully healed. Willie had taken part in 18 contests the previous year 1946, and had also unified the world featherweight title by knocking out Sal Bartolo. He was feeling on top of the world. His future was bright, and he was loving every minute, enjoying being the world champion. Viscusi and Gore were also in Florida. Both maintained homes in Tampa. Gore was himself recovering from a recent illness, but was preparing to get back into the gym with Pep. Viscusi and Gore had planned to motor down to Miami where the manager was going to complete the business arrangements for the postponed fight in Havana, and make arrangements for the big money-spinning bout against England's Nel Tarleton in London. Gore was to check on Pep's fitness and set up a training camp.

In a phone conversation from Miami, Pep told his manager he intended flying back to Hartford alone and spend a short time with his family before returning to Florida and embarking on the intensive phase of preparations for the approaching fights. Viscusi agreed to Pep's plans. With that settled, Willie went to the Miami airport and tried to book a seat on one of the scheduled airlines. There were no seats available that evening. He could have gone back to his hotel and waited until the next day for a space on a scheduled flight, but he wanted to get home as quickly as possible, see his family, and then head back to Miami for serious training. Willie recalled somebody having said that there were some unscheduled airlines which ran flights to New York out of the same airport. He made enquiries and discovered he could board a Nationwide Air Transport Services Inc plane within an hour or two. He duly booked his ticket. Capable of sleeping almost anywhere and at any time, he quickly drifted off almost as soon as he was fastened into his safety belt. The plane flew north without incident until it began running low on fuel and hit bad weather, a snow storm among other hazards, in the vicinity of Philadelphia. The New York bound aeroplane tried to make an emergency landing at an airport about 45 miles south of Philadelphia which during the war had been used as a training base for fighter pilots. Unfortunately it failed to locate this field and the plane ran into trouble in the blinding snow. Looking for an airport in southern New Jersey, it crashed into tree tops of a densely wooded area, scattering its human cargo among the branches and snowdrifts. The co-pilot and four people were killed and many injured.

On that fateful Sunday night there were three other plane crashes in America. The weather of snow, sleet and rain was atrocious and it affected a wide area extending as far as 250 miles around New York City. Pep recalls the events: "I got on a non-scheduled pick-up plane. The date was 8 January, 1947. The plane was supposed to leave at eight 'o' clock that night. It didn't start until twelve. It was a two-motor job with twenty one passengers, and it was scheduled to make two stops. We started off, and before we knew it, it was snowing. We were supposed to land in Newark, but we couldn't. So we landed in Midvale, New Jersey, in the woods! They tell me the plane came down and hit two trees and broke right in half. I wouldn't know. One of the few things I remember about the trip is that I was in the last seat and the snow was coming in on me. I told the stewardess and she said to sit in the front. She took my seat and she got out without a scratch. Before the crash, we were told to tie ourselves down. When I woke up my back and legs were killing me and people all around me were moaning and hollering. Pretty soon some workers who had cut their way through the woods put us in the back of a truck and took us to the hospital, those of us who were still alive. Actually, by some miracle, only five people died, but almost everybody was badly hurt. I was in awful pain, but sick as I was, I had the presence of mind to throw out a dirty book somebody had given me before we left Miami."

The rescuers who hurried to the scene of the crash hastily bundled up the survivors and rushed them to a hospital in Millville, New Jersey for treatment. The usual investigation began. An alert reporter checked the list of the injured. The names meant nothing to him. Then he ran across an entry that seemed somehow familiar, it read: "William Papaleo, of 27 Standish Street, Hartford., Connecticut." He read it again. Then he rushed for the telephone and rang his newspaper and the press wires. The flash was relayed to all front pages and covered the sports pages in America. William Papaleo was unfamiliar if you did not know the name he used in the boxing ring, but Willie Pep was a champion, the featherweight champion of the world. That was different. The various survivors had graphic stories to tell, as they discussed the tragedy and their individual ordeals, but none were more dramatic than that related by the slight Italian boy from Hartford.

"The first I knew of the crash was when I woke up and found I was lying on a stretcher inside the plane with the State police standing by and telling the other passengers to remain calm until more help arrived," said Pep. Following a complete medical examination including x-rays during the next day, attending physician, Dr. Howard Branin told Pep: "You're lucky to be alive." "I like to be alive," answered Pep, and then a short pause, "but my back really hurts." At Willie's bedside within hours of him entering the hospital, were his wife Mary and his 19 year-old sister, Frances, who had travelled by train, while Pep's father, Salvotore, had travelled by car shortly after news of the crash had reached Hartford. Viscusi also arrived within a day or so of the accident. Once at the hospital, Viscusi was like a mother-hen. He told the hordes of waiting reporters:

"The only thing I care about is that he'll be all right. He's only 24. He has a full life ahead of him". It was obvious that Mr Lou, after seeing the state of Willie must have thought this was the end of his career. Talking more, Viscusi added: "Say, if he quits the ring right now, they'll never forget him. Featherweight champion of the world two months after his 20th birthday, which was 26 months after he turned professional, 62 fights in a row from the start before he lost one (to Sammy Angott)." Viscusi was lost in a reverie of beloved statistics.

The Millville hospital where Pep received treatment was deluged with phone calls regarding Pep's condition, especially from young fight fans. In view of the large number of enquiries, the hospital announced that, as a special concession on the following Tuesday, a number of youngsters would be allowed to visit the world champion. The state policemen who assisted in rescuing Pep were also among his many visitors. It was with considerable relief that boxing fans learned Pep's injuries consisted only of a broken leg and some minor bruises, but they received a shock when they found out Pep's damage included several cracked vertebrae as well. Heads began to shake. Pep was through, he was finished it was assumed, but they had not figured on Pep himself. If they had stopped to think about this great-hearted little fighter's past history, they would not have written him off so easily.

"Being asleep probably saved my life. I had not taken off the safety belt and when the jar woke me. I was still tied to the seat and that cushioned the crash for me," commented Willie. This was the second harrowing air experience Pep had been through. A little over a year before, on the first leg of a plane trip from Hartford to St. Louis with Viscusi and Gore, fog prevented the plane from landing and the pilot had to circle the area for a considerable period before an emergency landing in Philadelphia. On that occasion, the trip was continued by train, and the group arrived in St. Louis on the afternoon of a scheduled fight.

One newspaper told it's readers that while only 15 years old, the burden of feeding his family fell squarely on his young shoulders, because, stated the reporter, his father was incurably ill. No one knew, and probably no one cared he said, that Pep's sensational winning streak had been inspired by the fight he was making for his family. Willie was being written off by many scribes. He was, after all, severely injured. (Many knowledgeable boxing pundits maintained that after the crash Pep was never the same boxer. They claimed he was never as fast as he was before the accident and that he lost a little something from his boxing ability. This is hardly surprising when you consider the injuries he sustained). While some reporters were visiting Willie in hospital, they were giving each other the look which meant they thought Pep's fighting career had come to its sorrowful end. Willie, looking at them and sensing their thoughts, told them from his bed: "I'll fight again. Why not?" But when he tried to move to expand his thoughts he winced with pain. "You guys don't believe me. Who'll bet I won't fight again? You know I'm a guy who gambles. I'll give you something to think about. I'll lay the price I win this one. Any takers?" Considering themselves indulgently generous, the writers said nothing. Privately they later agreed that it was 100 to 1 he'd never put on a glove again.

A few months later these same newspapermen were covering a fight in St. Nick's, a minor-league New York fight club. By way of making conversation, one of the writers said to the promoter: "What do you hear about Pep?" An expression of surprise came over the promoter's face. "Didn't you see him?" he said. "Willie's over there" and he pointed to a row in the back of the ringside, sat, crutches and all. He got somebody to drive him down." The reporters located Pep. At first glance, he looked as if his clothes were inflated like a balloon. Actually he was wearing a cast from ankles to chest, which of hinged at the waist so he could bend, and alongside was a pair of crutches. "Don't ask me, I don't feel any better than I look. But how long can you stay at home doing nothing? Besides, I've been trying to shadow box."

"I'll make a prediction," one reporter said to the others later that night. "You'll hear that Pep is back in training in the next few weeks."

Bill Gore, talking to some reporters a few years later, said: "When the ambulance men got to Willie, they recognised who he was immediately. And as they looked at his condition he was lying face down in the snow. He could not move. They said how sorry they were but his fighting days looked to be well and truly over because of his severe injuries. These men did not know or indeed understand the fighting spirit of this brave little champion. It was diagnosed in the hospital that he had multiple injuries. His fifth and sixth vertebrae in his back were broken. His left leg was also broken. He had casts on his chest and leg for six months and cuts to his head and face plus he was shook up a great deal."

Willie lost a massive insurance claim which would have set him up financially for the rest of his life. He could have sat back and left his lawyers to do his fighting for him in the courtrooms of America, but because he was young and impetuous and wanted to get back into the ring as quickly as possible, he decided to take his own action. One day while lying in his hospital bed, Pep asked the doctor how long it would be before he could start training again. The doctor looked down at Willie with sorrowful eyes. Willie, who was still in his chest and leg casts, quizzed the doctor further about what he had just asked him. The doctor replied: "Oh, in a few months. You will be here for quite some time yet. Don't worry about boxing again." Within days of this conversation with this doctor, Pep ordered the cast to be removed from his body. The medics pleaded with the champion not to be hasty, but Pep would have none of it, so off it came. When he came out of the hospital, a reporter meeting him on the steps had asked: "Is this the end, Willie?" "I guess so," answered Pep. "You mean you're not going to fight again?" Pep looked annoyed at the reporter and said: "Who said anything about that? It means I'm cutting out air travel from now on."

Many years later, recalling his stay in hospital after the plane crash Willie waxed lyrical about Lou Viscusi's help. "When I was in hospital after the plane crash in 1947, I didn't have a cent to pay my medical bills. Lou paid for everything. He was a great guy. After my fights he would pay me the exact amount of money I was due. He would give me the statement in black and white."

Willie started doing roadwork, then slowly working out in the gym with the utmost care. Onlookers were stunned by his fierce determination to get back into the ring. Viscusi could not believe his eyes after watching his champion sparring in his Hartford gym. Willie worked under the supervision of Bill Gore. Reporters were asking Mr Lou when or if this meant Pep would resume boxing, Lou was cautious with his reply. "We've got to get a good look at him to really tell. So far, I'm thrilled just to see him in the gym." Of course, just being in the gym didn't satisfy Pep. Almost daily he stepped up the amount of exercise and the vigour of it. To Gore's protests, he'd say: "Be a sport, let me take a chance, what have we got to lose?"

The inevitable day eventually arrived, the day when Willie persuaded his handlers to permit him to spar. Word of the event spread through Hartford and that afternoon the little gym was jammed, alive with talk and bristling with tension. Even Pep appeared excited as he changed into his training gear...inner doubts troubled him for the first time. "Am I pushing this a little too fast?" Is my leg going to take my full weight when I step back? "Suppose I make a fast turn, is my hip going to give way?" Up in the ring a sparring partner waited as Willie stepped in to a round of applause as spontaneous as it was genuine. The cheering warmed him like a fire on a cold autumn day. Now he was glad to be taking the gamble. The crowd were hoping Willie could make it too. The bell rang and both fighters put their hands up. Pep got up on his toes and fired a jab..."not bad," he caught himself saying. The sparring partner banged a left hook toward Willie's head. In a flash Pep was under the swing...he didn't know that he still had the reflexes. After a few rounds of sparring lightly, the action speeded up and it got more intensified and Pep delivered a crisp, short left hook of his own which caught his sparring partner and rocked him to his toes. The spectators whistled, and stamped. An amazed Lou Viscusi wig-wagged to Pep and shouted. "Ok Willie, enough for the first day."

After a few sessions of sparring with a varied assortment of fighters, Pep was declared ready for competitive ring action. Gus Browne, a veteran Hartford matchmaker, was an old hand at sizing up fighters in the gym. He said that in his opinion Willie was much slower in his sparring sessions. But, he added: "Willie, is punching much better than previously. And, he shows no ill effects from the plane crash." Browne continued. "I can't see his back is giving him any trouble. He has just about been in every possible position since he started his come back in the gym, and nothing has happened so I guess the vertebrae injury isn't giving him any problem. The broken leg seems to have slowed him down some, but like I said he's punching much crisper. Willie has been around a long time and he knows how to look after himself in sparring and in competitive fights."

Bill Lee in the Hartford Courant wrote: "Nobody knows for sure whether the badly injured Pep is wholly recovered. It will take a few fights to prove that. Nobody need have any illusions about the merits of his fight against Victor Flores, the Mexican featherweight champion, who dished out the first defeat inflicted upon Dennis Pat Brady a local prospect. Flores gave Pep a stiff workout a year ago, though Willie was far superior. But nobody expected Viscusi would throw Pep in against strong opposition in his first fight back after the plane crash. Though, Flores has enough stature and experience to test Pep under the circumstances."

Pep once again amazed the world of boxing. In fact the whole sports world was electrified by the announcement that the world champion was going back into action in a tough ten rounder with a hard-punching Puerto Rican fighter named Victor Flores. Pep's weight was 130lbs (9st-4lbs). The contest took place in front of a capacity crowd of 4,184, at the Hartford Auditorium's outdoor arena on 17 June, 1947, just six months after his plane crash. The referee was former featherweight champion Louis (Kid) Kaplan, who gave the amazing Pep all ten rounds and tallied 50 points for the champion and 33 for Flores. However, there was a fright in round four. After a collision of heads, Willie was gashed severely and a pro-Flores referee might have stopped the contest. But this referee was a solid Hartford loyalist and paid the cut little mind. Pep's corner eventually got the bleeding under control and Willie boxed on to win a merited decision. He decked Flores for a count of seven in round five and floored him again for a brief count in the seventh.

After the contest, Kaplan told the press: "Pep was unbelievable. This was near perfection."

But Willie was not satisfied with his sharpness and his timing. Always the perfectionist, he vowed that with every fight he would improve greatly. "I found out I could still fight because this kid Flores was very, very tough. You had better believe it," said Pep after the contest.

What Willie Pep did after his long, eroding absence from boxing was miraculous. Three Hartford doctors who were looking after Pep when recovering from his injuries, Dr. A.W. Brannon, Dr. John W. Larrabee and Dr. Maurice M. Pike, were sat at the ringside, and were at first startled by what they were witnessing. It seemed like a miracle had happened. Then they complimented themselves on doing such a wonderful recovery job on Pep. Willie just smiled at the medical experts, then got on with his career. He didn't smile though at what followed months later regarding his insurance claim for what he suffered in the crash. Also sat at ringside were three officials from the insurance company Pep was suing. They looked at each other and got up and left.

He fought 11 times from June until the end of the year, his reflexes were bad at first, his timing was off, his hitting was feeble, but he got better and better and from there on the improvement was steady and rapid. The morning after the fight against Flores, managers and promoters from all over the world were scouring their newspapers for the result, seeking to find out how Pep had done and how he had performed. Speculation was rife that, despite Willie's impressive gym workouts, his leg which had been broken in the crash would cause him great anxiety. His speed of foot as everyone one knew was extraordinary to say the least. And it was this the sceptics suggested which would hamper his progress. It was true that of the many injuries he sustained, the leg was somewhat slower to respond. Viscusi, though, was pleased with his champion's solid performance and said it was planned for Pep to have the fight go the ten round duration in order to test Willie to his full capabilities. A few days after the contest, Mr. Lou, had Pep medically examined by a team of doctors to see if everything was clear and progress to bigger things could be planned.

Bill Lee said Pep, though still not 25, for a few months, had showed signs of slowing down before the accident. But Mr. Lee, maintained Willie had already matured as a boxer and had become a better puncher for the change. "Willie could afford to slow down considerably more and he still could outspeed the top featherweights doing business today," he said. Warming to the observation Mr. Lee added: "Pep throws more accurate punches in a round than most fighters toss in a month. Pep fought 18 times in 1946. Few need reminding he won them all, but a significant point is that he won more by knockouts than by decision. Willie starched 11 of his opponents before the maximum time and outpointed the other seven. Pep stopped George Knox in March in Providence but Knox froze. The knockout over Bartolo followed. Then Jackie Graves was punched full of holes. Pep's next knockout was a lot more impressive. This was when he stopped Doll Rafferty, a well-considered lightweight, in the latters home city of Milwaukee. Walter Kolby, who sparred with the champion as he prepared for Graves, thought he could do well in a proper contest. It was arranged for Buffalo, Kolby, a southpaw, was stretched out early. When he finished Lefty LaChance in three in Hartford, Pep registered his sixth straight stoppage. After stowing a petrified Thomas Beato in two rounds in a bout in Waterbury, the featherweight champion rounded out his 1946 campaign by beating old rival Chalky Wright. Thus the winner of 108 out of 110 fights had begun to develop as a puncher, having knocked out eight of his nine most recent opponents."

It had been less than eight months since Willie had miraculously escaped from the aircrash, and after his comeback victory over Victor Flores in June, Willie had engaged in a further five contests getting sharper with each bout. Lou Viscusi decided his champion was now ready to defend his championship in a really competitive match and the challenger he chose was the number-one contender, Jock Leslie, a highly rated fighter and a ferocious puncher. The fight was to be staged at the Atwood Stadium, in Leslie's home town of Flint, Michigan, on 22 August 1947. Local promoter Tom Cussans had bid highly to bring this world featherweight championship match to the Michigan state. It was thought by many experts that Flint was not big enough to stage a world championship, so the city's gratitude was rained upon the young promoter who took the chance, plus the risk, and he did a splendid job. He was determined to stage this eagerly-awaited match and he brought nothing but praise and prestige to the city. Cussans was a character. He had gone into the American army as a plain GI private and wound up a major. He showed the same courage in backing this world title bout as he had done on the battlefields of Italy, where he had been wounded a number of times and for which he received many decorations.

Boxing was going through a bad time, though, with the press speculating about the gangster element which was reputed to be infesting the sport. There had been grand jury investigations, films about the racketeers who gave boxing its bad reputation, so it was a pleasure and like a breath of fresh air to watch how the boxing fans of this state came out in their whole hearted support for the city's first ever world championship contest between Pep and Leslie. It seemed unbelievable to the fans that Pep could be boxing so soon after the crash and also at top level, but the hope of the Leslie camp was Pep was now ready to be taken.

There were over 10,000 spectators packed into the Atwood Stadium and the gate drew $62, 525, 50. These fans were privileged to witness a contest which was the equal of anything staged at Madison Square Garden or any other venue in the year of 1947. The referee was Charley Rosen. Leslie gave it a good try, but in Pep he was facing a superb world champion. The challenger put up a sturdy battle, but nothing he displayed was sufficient to offset the terrific form of the champion who boxed like a well-oiled machine. He was as mobile and clever as before his pre-accident days. When Pep entered the ring the fans were uncertain about his true fighting condition. They were openly asking how much the crash had really taken out of him? Well the answer was not long in coming. He gave a flashy performance, as good as anyone would care to see. He was blocking punches, dancing around the ring avoiding Jock's heavy blows, boxing to the manner born. His left jab was constantly in the Flint fighter's face. Leslie kept his hands up high at all times. It was something similar to Floyd Patterson's peekaboo style and he punched with a raspness and a viciousness which had accounted for many of his victims. Pep was ducking and slipping these knockout drops with a nonchalant contempt. Because Jock's chin was well protected by his high guard, Pep decided to dig his punches to the body which had a devastating effect on Leslie. It took all the steam out of him and paved the way for effective head and jaw punches which resulted in his defeat.

Jock's best round was the second when the crowd were on their feet after the local man fired a crisp, accurate left hook onto the titleholder's jaw. Pep seemed to lose control for a brief second as his knees brushed the canvas, but he was upright and back to his boxing before a count could be started. Before the round ended Jock connected with a solid right cross bang on the champion's chin, it staggered him again. Pep was not fully recovered from the effects of that blow when the third round started. The experienced Flint fighter came out throwing vicious two-handed punches, which caught the champion by surprise but did not in any way phase him. Jock went all out for a knockout. The "Wisp" though, kept moving and boxing on the retreat. Leslie was awarded the second and third rounds by the officials, but these would be the only rounds he would gain. From there on in he was only briefly to enjoy any further success, because Pep moved into a much higher gear. Willie smoothly moved way out in front. His boxing was on a much higher level than his challenger. He would pick punches out of the air, throw rapid fire left jabs which rocked the gritty Leslie's head back and then unexpectedly let snappy right uppercuts hit the courageous local man flush under the chin.

The general consensus of the boxing scribes was that Pep had won every round clearly. The large gathering was noisy in their admiration of Pep's ring savvy. He hit the local boxer from every conceivable angle and tied up Jock in the clinches. In every aspect of boxing he had proved his supremacy over the Flint man. Pep was brilliant. Even though the home town fans were rooting for Leslie, they could not help but admire Pep's silky style. As the contest reached the eighth round, Willie began to gather more speed. He rained combination punches at the incredibly game Leslie's head and body. He danced around his challenger, who still kept charging forward without any restraint, but would get peppered by jabs which cut his eye and mouth. Then Pep would change the direction of his attack, and would tear into Leslie's body with a two-fisted flurry. This body assault jarred Jock from his head to his heels. This sort of attack was carried through to the 10th and 11th rounds with Jock still trying, but growing weaker by the minute.

Then came the final pay-off, a barrage of beautifully executed punches to Jock's head which were landed seconds after the bell rang to start the 12th round and put him at the mercy of the champion. He was dazed and almost went down. The champion threw a sharp right cross with a turn of the shoulder at the vital moment of impact which completed the demolition for the champ. Leslie took a count of nine and when he got to his feet referee Mr. Rosen gave him five more seconds as he kept the champion away from him, by wiping the ring dust from his gloves and asking him if he wanted to continue. The crowd booed and then away stepped the referee as Pep moved forward to finish the task. Jock tottered towards his opponent and Pep cut loose with every bit of firepower he had. Showing no mercy, he moved at his prey throwing two-handed shots to head and body. Leslie was a well beaten boxer as went down to the canvas, flat on his back. The referee could have counted him out a dozen times before the game challenger could be revived. When the gutsy Flint boxer walked to his corner, his supporters gave him a rousing reception. They stood and applauded this fine man who had tried so very hard to bring glory and honour back to his city. As for Pep, he proved without any doubt he could continue to hold his title and stay the king of his division indefinitely. He was rated, even then, among the world's best boxers in the all-time ratings.

It was Willie's first defence since he had knocked out Sal Bartolo in June, 1946 and his display had answered a lot of questions and erased a great number of doubts. Willie received every accolade for his showing against Leslie, he still had all the slick moves, the perfect balance and the way he treated every punch from Leslie as a personal insult was a sight to behold. He looked so comfortable in the ring, so suited, that when he was boxing, you couldn't imagine him doing anything else. Pep's reflexes, balance and anticipation were first class. After the contest the newspapers speculated as to who Pep should box next. They were delighted that after the plane crash, he had come back so well. He had, of course, showed snatches of weariness in the Flint battle, but his overall showing was good. He was almost back to his brilliant best.

The media suggested that Pep face Charley Riley of St. Louis, who was another tough customer and a hard-puncher who scored two sensational blast-outs over Phil Terranova in the Mound City. Another match which would was suggested and also bring the "International touch" was against Australia's British Empire featherweight champion Eddie Miller, and the British champion, Ronnie Clayton, who came from Blackpool, on the Lancashire coast, and who had just defeated Al Phillips for the British and European titles. But the boxer who they very casually added to their list was that of Joe (Sandy) Saddler, who it was reported had been conducting a successful elimination campaign against Pan-American rivals, having knocked out the champions of Mexico, Venezuela and Cuba. The New York based Saddler was not perceived as a dangerous challenger at that time, but he would play a significant role in Pep's life a little later. The fights against Saddler are dealt with in detail in later chapters of the book.

Miami Bound

On 23 July, 1947, four weeks before putting his world championship on the line against Jock Leslie, Pep had boxed a ten round warm-up contest against a sweet moving spindle-legged Cuban boxer named Humberto Sierra in-front of his enthusiastic supporters in his hometown of Hartford. The champion boxed splendidly, he needed too, because Sierra was a top-class fighter. This was Willie's sixth fight since recovering from his near fatal injuries suffered in the plane disaster. Though he was getting better with each contest, his sharpness was only slowly coming back to him, but his boxing was once again graceful and eye catching. The Sierra contest was a really good workout for the title holder. He looked and boxed immaculately and his movements were again majestic, though the tall Cuban fighter gave him some anxious moments throughout the bout.

Because of his good showing against the champion, Sierra and his connections were now demanding a return contest with the featherweight championship at stake. "I want to fight him again, but this time let us fight outside of Connecticut. Pep is like a God there," the Cuban told the press. There was of course no dispute as to who the rightful winner was in their previous bout, though, Sierra had given quite a respectful showing against the champion. But the reporters lapped up his his complaint and his remarks made good publicity. Pep of course obliged him. Most of the fight fraternity believed both Charley Riley and Sandy Saddler had stronger claims for a title shot than Sierra and many critics accused Willie of avoiding Saddler in particular. Irrespective of what anybody said the Pep camp chose the Cuban as the next challenger.

The year could be as industrious as Pep wanted it to be. The champion had started 1949 by soundly defeating Pedro Biesca over ten easy rounds in the Hartford Auditorium. Willie sprinted through each one of the ten rounds. But there was an embarrassing moment for the champion in the fourth, when he misjudged a left hook and took it flush on the side of his jaw. The blow bewildered him momentarily, and the Puerto Rican dropped him on the seat of his pants for a count of nine. Apart from this, Pep won every round clearly giving poor Biesca the mother and father of a hiding. This fight was followed six days later by Willie beating his old rival Jimmy McAllister in St. Louis, a clear-cut ten round points victory. Seven days after outclassing McAllister, Pep was fighting again, this time in Boston, beating Joey Angelo to make it three out of three all within the space of 13 days in January.

In February 1948 Willie took time out from fighting in the ring and fought a legal battle when he made a claim for 600,000 dollars (£150,000) from the American Air Line in whose plane he crashed in 1947. Willie had suffered various injuries, and his claim stated he had also suffered through worry and five months of hospital treatment. He further claimed he had lost 500,000 dollars worth of contracts.

Miami's Orange Bowl Stadium was the site selected for his sixth championship defence against Humberto Sierra. The date was 24 February, 1948. Sierra's manager, Tommy de Tardo, had been screaming blue murder in the press for his fighter to get this return engagement. He had certainly done a good job for his fighter, but this was a return contest by popular demand. Sierra was a tall, skinny boxer with an exceptionally long reach, a boxer mainly but he also possessed a fair dig in his right hand. He was something of a Sandy Saddler clone, but without Saddler's awesome power or roughness. He was a neat mover with good skills. His manager had bought his contract a couple of years previously for the paltry sum of 250 dollars. It was to prove a real bargain for Tommy de Tardo. The fight was in the open-air with a crowd of over 10,000 in attendance. This was due mainly to the vast publicity machine the promoters had employed. Having the former heavyweight champion Jack Dempsey as the guest referee also helped quite a lot. Pep and Dempsey hyped the fight for all it was worth on radio and film newsreel. And with Sierra and his manager speiling non-stop stories about what they intended to do to the champion, it whetted the public's appetite for the match.

Despite the hype from the Cuban and his connections, it turned out to be a tame contest. It was a fact the lanky Cuban had given Pep a good run for his money in their first encounter, but the importance of the occasion seemed to get to him this time around. It could have been he had not boxed in front of such a big audience, whatever the reason, he was stiff and uptight in this bout and certainly did not do himself justice.

There was another scare for the champion at the weigh-in, when he came to the scales four ounces over the championship poundage. Bill Gore took Willie into a side room and after a few minutes of fast shadow boxing followed by a good brisk rubdown with a towel Pep soon dispensed with the excess weight. He had been weighing 131 for his non-title bouts so it was no real surprise when struggling a little to make the official 126lbs. How ironic though that it should be the champion who came to the scale overweight. Viscusi and Gore had favoured Sierra over the other challengers because they had known for some time that Sierra, though fighting as a featherweight, was in fact a fully-fledged lightweight. They maintained getting Humberto down to the stipulated featherweight poundage would take the edge of the tall Cuban and weaken him.

The Miami boxing Commission Physician, Dr. McCormick, pronounced Pep to be in excellent condition after examining him. The champion was pleased and ready for action. He wanted to show Sierra and his handlers what he could do in a title match. This, incidentally, was the first world championship fight to be staged in the millionaires playground of Miami for 12 years. The newspapers billed the forthcoming championship battle as a spectacular event not to be missed. Amazing freak weather conditions hit Florida and threatened the attendance. In fact the intermittent rain nearly spoiled the whole occasion. But Pep brightened the proceedings with his excellent start to the contest. He totally outclassed his challenger in the opening round. Sensing the Cuban was not relaxed and posing no danger, he took his foot off the gas and cruised through the bout. There was some excitement in the second when the title-holder fired a rather tame left hook which caught the Cuban on the chin putting him down for a count of two. Thereafter, Humberto was darting about all around the ring not wanting to stand and punch it out with the "Wisp." The crowd did not take too kindly to this timid display from the challenger because after all, they had paid good money to watch what they thought was a competitive championship contest between these two boxers. They soon let their feelings known. The steady downpour of rain didn't help the spectators who were soaking wet after a few minutes, or the fighters who were slipping and sliding on the wet canvas. Who would have expected these kind of conditions in Florida?

The gate fell below what promoter Clarence Kantroerells, predicted although gate receipts were estimated at $75,000, more than Willie had drawn in any previous contest. His bout against Chalkey Wright, in 1942 had been his highest before the Miami encounter. This was his second championship defence in less than six months, having previously defeated Jock Leslie.

The Hartford champion came down off his toes when he found he was slipping so much on the soaking wet ring floor. He started to change his tactics and punched with more authority and precision. Sierra was feeling the sting of Pep's power punches. The Cuban made an effort and started to use a loose left jab and fancy footwork, even on this wet surface, but he was not scoring any points. When the bell for round nine sounded, Pep was out of his corner like a flash, a hail of punches were thrown at Humberto which sent him to the floor for a count of five. These blows nearly ended the fight, but on rising Sierra got on his bike and moved away. It was painfully obvious by now that for all his talk, Sierra was outclassed and no match for the champion. Referee Dempsey tried to get the challenger to try harder, but he really was outclassed. The tenth round saw Pep throw two consecutive right hands at Sierra's head, both missed because Pep seemed a trifle wild and too eager. Then, while chasing the Cuban across the ring he connected with a beautifully delivered short, crisp left hook. Sierra advanced to the ropes where he rode out the storm. But Pep had the bit between his teeth and would not be denied. A piledriver right cross smashed against the challenger's head, high up but it obviously was full of dynamite because Sierra went down as if shot. He was badly hurt and looked stunned. Dempsey did not bother with the formality of a count as Sierra lay helpless on the canvas. Only 22 seconds had elapsed of the round when the ending came. There were no arguments this time from Sierra and his manager. Pep was once again in brilliant form. His class was there to be seen in the eye of the beholder.

The crowd were especially pleased with the startling finish to the contest. They had witnessed one of boxings all-time greats in action. The fight was never a thriller because the tall Cuban's negative tactics saw to that. But just to show what a good fighter this fellow Sierra was, a few months before being demoralised by Pep in Miami, the Cuban fought the awesome Sandy Saddler, beating him soundly on points and putting the future champion on the deck for a count. This was the quality of the man Pep had soundly thrashed and outclassed.

After his successful championship defence against Sierra, Pep fought 11 more times before facing his top-contender, Sandy Saddler, in defence of his title. Some of the 11 victims were well-known names in the world of boxing. LeRoy Willis was the Detroit state lightweight champion when he faced Pep at Detroit's Olympia Stadium in May 1948. It was a boring fight for the fans with very little toe-to-toe action. Willie dictated every round and Willis' manager Dave Clark, one time light-heavyweight contender could be heard imploring his fighter to "mix it up." The champion was a clear winner. An experiment was tried out in this contest and approved. It was the use of a rubber ring mat. Commissioner John J. Hettche, indicated that this would become a permanent fixture on future tournaments staged in Michigan.

Willie stepped in and substituted for Jackie Graves who was due to top the Atwood Stadium promotion in Flint, against promising prospect Luther Burgess, who was a classy well respected fighter. Pep added Burgess to his list of victims winning a ten round decision. The Detroit boxer took a count of nine in the fifth. Afterwards, Burgess said: "Pep was a terrific boxer and a sharp puncher. A truly remarkable champion." "Willie handled Luther like a baby," said Viscusi. Luther Burgess is a well known trainer these days operating out of Detroit's famed Kronk gym.

Charley Cabey Lewis from Brooklyn was another respected tough-as-nails black fighter. Willie had fought and beaten the cagey Lewis a couple of times previously, although Cabey always made things interesting. In this their third contest at the Auditorium in Milwaukee, Pep proved conclusively to the 5,500 spectators that he was every inch a champion by the masterly way in which he won a unanimous decision. In this fight, Lewis was not only tough but also dangerous throughout the ten rounds. Some of his sharp counter punching surprised the champion and brought applause from the crowd. Matchmaker Al Fain, was delighted because this was a really good contest and the crowd were enjoying it. Pep was always in command by the virtue of his classier ringmanship. He twice floored the Brooklynite but could not keep him there for the full count. After the bout Willie was sat in his dressing room pressing an ice pack against his left eye, blood was dripping from a cut on his right ear. Looking at Bill Gore, Willie remarked: "What a tough guy that Lewis is, he always gives me a hard fight."

Chuck Burton was at one time a highly touted prospect, but he was not in the super champions class when they fought. Willie had a bad night when he fought Teddy "Red-Top" Davis on 3 August in Hartford. He got a split-decision victory which didn't go down well with the crowd. A few days later Willie obliged Davis again and trounced him, winning all ten rounds. The crowd who had jeered him, now stood and applauded him. While boxing Brooklyn's graggy campaigner, Johnny Dell, in the Waterbury Stadium in Hartford, Pep showed his compassion. After enjoying no more than a workout from Dell, the Brooklyn lad sustained a large bump over his left eye. Pep purposely avoided hitting the face. Dell was inspired and rushed the champion but all his efforts to score were futile as Willie merely threw body punches. Referee, Billy Conway stopped the one-sided affair in the 8th round. Dell fought in a similar style to Paddy DeMarco, a future opponent for Pep. These 11 contests were boxed in a swaggering, easy-come easy-go style. In beating Hunberto Sierra so convincingly, Pep looked unbeatable again. It was hard to imagine who could extend him, let alone beat him with the possible exception of Sandy Saddler. Talks were already taking place for these two fighters to clash. Pep was not worried in the slightest. He fought whoever Viscusi matched him with. He was on top of his game and the results and the manner in which they were achieved were gained in sparkling fashion.

Victory Over DeMarco

Willie Pep was never satisfied with just winning, he always desired to put on a masterful exhibition of boxing and give the spectators something to remember him for. When he was asked to fight the much avoided and heavier Paddy DeMarco, he readily agreed. DeMarco, was a squat 5 foot 6 inch terror of the ring with a nose flattened by countless punches. Known as the "Brooklyn Billy-Goat," Paddy, looked and acted the part of a fighter and was one heck of a tough nut as he proved throughout his ring career. He was capable of out-roughing, out-toughing, and out-fighting any featherweight, lightweight or welterweight of the 1950's. Many Boxing fans of this decade remember this fellow for the hectic fights he had with many of the top fighters of that particular period. He had no style to speak of and no punch worthy of mention, but he was as fierce and aggressive in the ring as an uncaged wild beast. He knew few rules and fought with every weapon at his command including his head and elbows! They put him in with the top featherweights around and, when they ran out of those, he went up against lightweights and welterweights.

DeMarco grew up during hard times in tough surroundings. Yet he served as an alter boy in his local church! He looked like a fighter from his early teens. Born in Brooklyn on 10 February, 1928, Paddy spent his childhood and teen age years in the tough Navy Yard section of New York. DeMarco began fighting in the Golden Gloves, he lost in the semi-finals, then turned professional in March 1945, winning a four-round decision over Salvatore Giglio in Jersey City. He was managed by Jimmy Dixon and Cy Crespi. All seven of his fights that first year were held in Jersey because, at 17, Paddy was too young to get a boxing licence in New York. But he wasn't too young to get the better of more experienced opponents, winning three decisions and scoring three inside-the-distance victories, while dropping just one verdict in that first year. Paddy's father was a big help to his son. DeMarco was hoping his family would not find out he was boxing, but his picture appeared in a newspaper one day. Paddy thought his father would be upset, but Mr. DeMarco said to his son: "Paddy, if boxing is what you want to do, then tell me and I'll help you all I can."

When he was old enough to qualify for a New York licence in 1946, he switched his operations back to Brooklyn. He won nine fights and lost just one during 1946. The following year he was undefeated, winning 13 bouts and facing tough opponents such has Patsy Giovanelli, Bobby Williams, Jimmy Warren, Danny Bartfield and Johnny Dell. He had won 28 out of 30 when around this time he was introduced to top contender Terry Young in a bar in Greenwich Village. Paddy told Young, who was a close friend of former world middleweight champion, Rocky Graziano, the original dead-end kid, how he was interested in becoming a top fighter like Young. Paddy recalls that instead of offering him any encouragement, Young insulted him by "slagging him off". From that moment, DeMarco's strongest desire was to fight Young in the ring. Finally, it happened in January 1948 with DeMarco beating Terry on points in a real upset decision. They fought a rematch three months later and again DeMarco beat Young.

During his career, Paddy earned the reputation of being one of the roughest and toughest scrappers in boxing at the time. He beat the classy ring "artist" Billy Graham, who he had been anxious to fight and who he disliked a great deal. "Billy would never give me the credit due. He had a superior attitude. He was like that with other fighters too," said DeMarco. Coming up to his fight against the world featherweight champion, Pep, DeMarco had beaten Terry Young and was on top form. A tough confrontation awaited the featherweight king. This was the busiest and best time in the fight games long history, when fighters fought the best opponents every time they appeared in public.

The battle between Willie Pep and Brooklyn's Paddy DeMarco, who by this time had developed into a deadly left hooker, was another eagerly awaited contest which the fight trade were drooling over, and which turned out to be a classic. These two fighters fought at Madison Square Garden in September, 1948, once again Pep was displaying his skill in the mecca of boxing simply known as the "Garden." This place was like a second home for Pep because he had fought there on several occasions. "I'm looking forward to boxing Paddy DeMarco, he has a reputation for being a tough and hard-punching fighter who certainly comes to fight. I know the fans love his style of fighting and our two styles should bring out the best in each other. It should be a wonderful contest for the fans," said Pep when the match was signed and sealed. This was another ten round non-title fight, because DeMarco was a fully-fledged top-rated lightweight contender. Mike Jacobs and his Twentieth Century Sporting Club were once again the promoters. Jacobs was relishing the takings from this humdinger of a fight. This match, between the supreme boxing champion and the 20 year-old all-action slugger, was expected to draw a big gate. This would be Pep's first contest in New York for almost two years, his last appearance being in June 1946 when he stopped Sal Bartolo. These non-title fights were usually big money spinners for all concerned. The New York press built up the gate by churning out endless stories about the forthcoming matchup, and about the two fighters themselves. Mike Jacobs was delighted. It all helped sell tickets and that was what the boxing business was all about;-putting bums on seats. This clash between DeMarco, who could knock a mule out with his left-hook and the velvet smooth moving "Will-

'o'-the-Wisp," was a genuine clash which the punters would flock to watch. Paddy was after his 22nd consecutive triumph. He had an overall record of 34 professional bouts going into this match with Pep, of which he had won 32 since turning to the professional ranks in 1945. Pep was taking part in his 134th ring battle of which he had lost only one. Willie had completed all his training for the DeMarco fight in his home town of Hartford. Reports indicated he was boxing faster and better than ever before. Onlookers were thrilled to watch this "Artful Dodger" going through his paces. "I know that in DeMarco, I'm facing a tremendously tough guy who takes four or five punches in order to get his own shot on target. I know he can bang, I respect his ability as a fighter Paddy is feared throughout the boxing world for his durability and his tough reputation. My game is boxing. And believe me, that is what I fully intend doing when we meet," said the champion. Willie seemed to be working extra hard in training on his left jabbing. He was moving gracefully against his two tough sparring partners. In fact, local reports were indicating the champion was looking absolutely brilliant in his gym workouts. This made him a slight betting favourite going into the fight.

The Brooklyn fighter had based his training camp at the same site Joe Louis and Sugar Ray Robinson had previously used with great success, Greenwood Lake, New Jersey. And from the reports coming out of the camp, DeMarco was hooking trees down with his left and looking mean and menacing flattening his sparring mates like skittles. DeMarco's chief sparring partner was Charley Noel who told the press: "Paddy is very sharp and punching like a middleweight. Pep is in for a torrid night, don't be surprised if Paddy stops Pep."

On the night of the fight, DeMarco was indeed a very hot prospect, a great favourite with the fight followers. But he was about to face a far superior ringman. This fight drew nearly 10,000 spectators into the Garden, which brought in $29,869, in gate receipts. Pep had been made a 1 to 2 betting favourite by the time the two fighters entered the ring. DeMarco was very confident he would emerge the victor and humble Pep into the process. From the opening bell, DeMarco rushed at the champion in an effort to knock him out of his stride. Pep showed caution and remained up on his toes and out of range. In the second session, the Brooklyn fighter rushed wildly at Willie and virtually shoved him through the ring ropes. Willie got back into the ring and proceeded to punch Paddy about the head with both fists. The crowd cheered wildly at this action. The champion though, was on the floor again in the third round, but it was only a slip, he had the better of the round by the use of his smarter boxing. In the fourth, the champion took another accidental tumble and also absorbed a bit of a body beating as DeMarco was raging and swinging punches with a reckless disdain. The fans were enjoying the confrontation. They were right behind the rough, unschooled Brooklyn youngster who was using every trick in the book and many which were not even in it, in his futile attempt to score over the experienced titleholder. DeMarco showed no end of willingness. He rushed at Pep constantly and threw punches from every angle. The greater part of his blows, though, were easily avoided. When they got to close quarters Paddy mauled, shoved and tugged away repeatedly, seeking to hit Pep on the chin and body, though he wasn't particular where his blows landed. From the fifth through to the seventh Pep managed to muffle his whirlwind opponent, but DeMarco forced his way forward and took the eighth and the ninth with the use of his big right hands to the champion's head. One punch opened a cut beside the Hartford man's right eye. Against these wild tactics Pep could do little except return two-handed fire, with the result that there was a considerable amount of inside rough stuff that made for a great deal of furious action, which again delighted the spectators. Pep's greatest strength was ring "savvy" which enabled him to make DeMarco flounder at times and miss wildly with his intended punches.

While there were no knockdowns, each fighter was on the floor several times as the result of slips or shoves. The world champion landed the hardest and more stinging blows throughout the whole of the contest, these being straight right hands to the body which slowed Paddy down a great deal. Pep also switched this punch to DeMarco's face, only a boxer of Pep's calibre could get away with throwing this blow as a lead. Yet he used this move many times throughout the bout. Willie used these stinging body shots to the ever advancing Brooklyn brawler. These punches, though not devastating, had the desired effect and slowed the younger man down. Cheered on by the crowd, Paddy was winging his powerful punches toward the fleet-footed featherweight king. In reality, this was his only hope of winning. Pep was in a few classes higher than the gutsy lightweight contender and his beautiful boxing skills made certain DeMarco did little more than try! Everyone in Madison Square Garden knew who the winner was going to be. In fairness to DeMarco, he tried everything he could but he was out of his league with Pep, and he had no answer to the champion's cleverness and majestic brand of boxing. The featherweight champion won the final session and regained the upper-hand scoring with his own rights to Paddy's head. These punches lacked crispness and knockout power, but still stung and rocked DeMarco's head back time and time again making him look confused and weary.

The balloting in Pep's favour was unanimous. Referee Arthur Donovan voting five rounds for Pep, three for DeMarco and two rounds even. Judge Joe Agnelio calling it eight and two for the champion, while judge Charley Rosen scoring it six for Pep, three for Paddy and one even. Most New York observers had it seven to three in favour of the Hartford man. When the decision was announced DeMarco was visibly displeased, as were his seconds. Why they thought he had won, though, was a complete mystery, since Pep was clearly his superior through most of the ten rounds in this tough contest. Pep scaled 128-and-one-quarter-pounds, while DeMarco was 133-one-half-pounds. In this fight, Pep showed other students of boxing the correct method of how to counter a dynamic left-hooker like the Brooklyn banger. Willie demonstrated the art of keeping a left-hooker quiet by constantly keeping DeMarco off balance by the constant use of his own quick left jabbing. Pep held his right glove at the side of his face to guard against any stray blows which might have got through his defence. When he made Paddy miss, the champion would then counter with his right cross, or his left jab. It was beautiful to watch the manner of this boxing master going through the motions. He made it looked so easy with his loose style of boxing.

"Paddy kept throwing those big left hooks. He always believed one of these punches would connect on my chin. That's why I licked him clearly. A guy feels foolish when he misses and is jabbed off balance. I kept doing this to him, that's how I handled DeMarco. He was a really rough and tough kind of guy to fight, without a doubt, this was one of my hardest fights ever," said Pep after the fight.

"I'm very disappointed. I gave it my best shot, this guy is faster than I realised. What a great, great boxer he is though!" said DeMarco. After his victory over DeMarco, Pep went on to much more success and bigger events. But what happened to DeMarco after his loss to Pep? Well after the Pep fight, Paddy fought Billy Graham. In 1949, he was stopped by Sandy

Saddler in nine rounds after a real slugfest, the first knockout suffered by DeMarco in nearly 50 fights. Talking about Saddler, Paddy said: "Saddler was one of the strongest fighters I ever met in my whole career. And boy could he punch."

Except for the Saddler loss, he had won nine and drew one that year. In 1950, Paddy won ten and lost one fight, beating brilliant fighters such as Orlando Zulueta, a classy Cuban, plus Dennis Pat Brady, Kid Dussart and Young Junior. His only defeat was against a fighter who he had previously beaten, Teddy "Red-Top" Davis. (Pep had defeated Davis twice in succession just prior to boxing DeMarco). In 1951, he was undefeated winning eight contests. His biggest feat was his revenge victory on points over Sandy Saddler-Saddler was of course, the featherweight champion at the time. Toward the end of 1951, he again defeated Saddler on points.

In 1954, Paddy became the lightweight champion of the world, outboxing and outbrawling James Carter. This was his peak, and with hindsight it shows what a wonderful scalp Pep had on his belt when he clearly outboxed DeMarco. But sadly in the return fight against Carter, DeMarco was saved by the referee in the 15th and final round after giving the former champion a gritty run for his money. Paddy was weakened by a virus. Paddy beat well-known fighters like Arthur King, Enrique Bolanos, Eddie Chavez, Henry Davis, Armand Savoie and Ralph Dupas. But sadly after Carter beat him it all downhill for the quiet but likable Brooklyn fighter. In 1959, Paddy retired from boxing leaving a record of 102 professional fights, winning 75, losing 24 times, with three draws. His victories were honestly earned. In later years Paddy worked as a dealer at Caesars Palace in Las Vagas. Paddy was a wonderful advert for his family and boxing. A gentle and quiet person, but what a terror between those ropes!

The Shock

When boxing people get together and start talking about the great fights and wonderfully nostalgic encounters which they remember, when the talk gets around to what a great boxer Willie Pep was, straightaway somebody comes right back and mentions Sandy Saddler. These two wonderful champions are bonded together like Dempsey-Tunney, Louis-Conn, Ali-Frazier, Leonard-Hearns and other rivalries which have flourished throughout the history of the fight game. In the case of Pep and Saddler, this is most unfair to these two all-time greats. Both had far too many memorable events throughout their careers to be recognised merely because of the four wars they had against each other. However, what exactly happened?

There was no question in the minds of boxing followers that when Pep faced the tall, skinny, long-legged black fighter, Joseph Benjamin Sandy Saddler, known as Sandy Saddler, for the first time, on 29 October, 1948, he had most definitely taken his challenger much too lightly. Willie himself had certainly not envisaged how tough and dangerous this stringbean of a fighter out of the slums of Harlem would prove to be. If anything, Willie was guilty of overconfidence and he was about to learn a sharp, painful, and humiliating lesson beside paying a very heavy penalty. He was a 1 to 3 betting favourite going into their first championship contest. There is every possibility the champion had not trained as hard or as diligently as he should have done for this bout. He was feeling quite secure about the outcome.

Six months before meeting Saddler, Pep had knocked out Humberto Sierra. Sierra had beaten Saddler on points. The Cuban paid a visit to Pep's training camp and after exchanging the usual pleasantries he told the champion: "You will beat this guy with ease. No problem at all. I beat him easily, you have too much class for him. Willie, I'm telling you it's a cinch, believe me." Pep had also knocked out Jock Leslie, who had scored a stoppage victory over Saddler. Although this defeat happened early in Saddler's career, Willie had soundly defeated another fighter who held a victory over Saddler, Phil Terranova. On this basis, he was more than confident of defeating the fearsome-punching Saddler. He had boxed dozens of hard punchers in the past, and beaten them with simplicity and ease. So he reasoned, Saddler was just another tough kid who had a powerful punch, and he would deal with him in the same manner as the previous opposition, seemed to be Pep's mode of thinking while preparing for their fight.

Charley Johnston had been waging a long and loud campaign for his fighter to box for the title. Meeting Viscusi by chance in a New York restaurant one evening, The two managers had a long conversation. It was a game of verbal chess. Johnston pressed Mr. Lou further. "You want a shot at the championship?" Viscusi said. "Then you pay for it. We'll cut up the 60 per cent, 50-10." Viscusi also obtained a return contest for the title in the event Pep should lose the first contest. Johnston was visibly upset at Viscusi's take-it-or-leave it offer, but bit his lip and accepted the deal. This was the main cause of the friction between the two camps. Viscusi had done a good deal for Pep, he surely could not be criticised for this. But Saddler and his manager, were bitter and very angry and extremely annoyed with Viscusi and Pep. Because Saddler had to guarantee the champion's high purse demands in order to obtain this championship chance. Sandy, it was reported, was fighting for his expenses only, receiving no purse money. He was just boxing for the privilege of contesting the world championship. Was it any wonder a feud later developed between both camps.

The crowd in Madison Square Garden were totally unprepared for what they were about to witness, and were shocked and stunned by what they saw...but not as bewildered as Pep was on this night! From the first bell,

Saddler marched forward and totally ignored the champion's lightning fast punches. The intenseness showed on his expressionless poker face. There was no doubt the challenger had come to bury the champion if need be, and take the world featherweight crown back to Harlem. In the first minute a whip like jab hit the champion's nose like a trip-hammer, and blood oozed immediately. Sandy Saddler was remorseless, like a threshing machine out of control. Stalking, his prey all the time, he virtually mugged the champion. In the second round the long-armed challenger opened up a cut under Pep's right eye, nearly knocking him out in the process. Willie was saved by the bell after Saddler unleashed a whistling left hook which caught the Hartford fighter flush on the chin. The power of this punch was awesome and made ringsiders grimace. The third round was worse still for the champion, who could not get into this fight. It was Saddler all the way. Punching in flurries he would not be contained. Pep was already paying a heavy toll for underestimating his challenger. Letting fly with three murderous left uppercuts which hit their target with ferocity, he pinned Pep into a corner and he unleashed another powerfully driven uppercut. The bemused champion hit the canvas with a loud bang. Groggy, but rising to his feet as the referee tolled nine, he was tottering and badly hurt. The fight would have been stopped today. Pep could not believe what was taking place. Saddler was like a tiger which had tasted blood and would not let go of its prey. He moved with swiftness and agility. A booming right cross smacked Pep on his unprotected face, and down went the featherweight king once more.

What was happening? The crowd, looking at each other seemed to be asking. Pep's crown was being ripped from his regal head. They could not believe what they were witnessing in front of their very eyes. Willie was badly shaken and just made it to his feet when the bell sounded and came to his rescue. But this was to be only a brief lull. In the fourth and fatal round the bewildered and soon to be ex-champion tried desperately to clutch his tormentor's left arm, all to no avail. It was the left hook from the Harlem whiplash which was causing Pep all the damage. Pep held on for dear life while Saddler was snarling and pushing Pep away trying to deliver the pay off punch. Another dazzling left uppercut hit home, sending water from Pep's head. This was the punch which should have flattened the champion, but, amazingly he didn't go down from this blow. But a few seconds later it was finished, all over. A left hook spelt the end of his championship reign. Gamely he tried to regain his feet before the referee reached the count-out. But it was too late, his title was gone.

The critics could not believe what had happened. The jubilant new champion told waiting reporters in his dressing room after the fight. "I knocked him stoned. I really laid him out. You could have counted fifty over him. Pal, I'm telling you. He was a very clever boxer though. I had always admired him." His manager, Charley Johnston was also beaming and shouting out. "Ten per cent, a lousy ten per cent, but we got something for it, didn't we?"

In Pep's changing room, he dressed rather quickly and silently. Reporters found him loath to answer their questions."This time I got nailed," was all he would say. Going into this fight, Pep had fought 136 times and had never been knocked out before, a magnificent record. But all his past accomplishments were in tatters at that very moment. All sorts of excuses were put forward for this shocking blemish on his record. "He's burned out from having too many hard fights," said one reporter. "He took this guy too lightly. Wait until they fight again," said another "He never trained hard enough," was another comment. But there were a lot worse things said about Pep's demise at the hands of Saddler, who, it must be stressed, hardly rated as the new featherweight sensation. He was described as hardly more than a decent brawler by the hard-nosed New York boxing scribes who could be cruel at the best of times.

Quotes such has "Fix" and "In The Bag," were banded about New York after the fight. Bill Lee, a veteran boxing sportswriter for the Hartford Courant, and who had watched Pep's progress from a scrawny amateur into a majestic world champion and had followed his career closely, believed Willie was guilty of no more than underestimating Saddler. "Willie beat a few guys who had scored victories over Saddler and stupidly assumed if they could beat him, then it was no more than a formality for he himself to emerge victorious," said Lee.

As the days flew by millions of excuses were doled out. Not once though did Pep make any excuses, nor did he comment on the vicious lies going the rounds. It angered him but he took it without replying. The nature of the man had not changed. In all the years he never felt it was his privilege to correct, or attempt to correct, criticism others had about him, how ever wrong he felt they were. "I got caught cold. I started out by feinting as I usually do to get the feeling for him. But he surprised me by just ignoring my feints and walking right in on me," he said.

Lou Viscusi was more shocked than most, he thought his fighter was a racing certainty to beat Saddler. "Willie fought these type of guys all the time, he never had any kind of problem before I really can't understand what happened here. I am completely bewildered," he remarked. When asked his thoughts on the fix allegations, Mr. Lou, scowled and said bluntly: "If these people know anything was wrong about the fight, why don't they speak up and give evidence? They can't, so it's all speculation and rumours." Ironically, it was Viscusi who helped get Saddler started in the fight business. "Bill Johnston was his first manager, he phoned and asked if I could get some fights for a kid he had signed named Benjamin Joe Sandy Saddler. Now I didn't know if he was pulling my leg or not. But as a favour to Bill I agreed. Johnston had tried a publicity stunt by dressing Saddler in a Black-Watch Scottish kilt and a little beret on his head. The dour-faced Saddler didn't think it was funny, but went along with it. After I gave Saddler his first pro fight, I forgot all about him. Then I got another call from Bill Johnston asking if I could use his kid Saddler again, but in a six-rounder. We remember him as a tall, ungainly skinny black kid and he gets knocked out by Jock Leslie. Now that's all we know about the kid around here. We forgot all about him," said Viscusi.

The truth was that Johnston had no need to use any gimmicks in order to publicise Sandy. The man could fight and punch. Talking further on the subject of Saddler. Viscusi said: "The next thing I remember about Saddler is Charley Johnston is now managing him, and in fairness, "the kids moving more now. He was getting fights all over the place. He began looking like a good, solid fighter but nothing special. Charley had him fighting in Detroit, Boston, New Orleans, Caracas, Jamaica and Cuba. Now I look at the listings and Saddler is rated as the number-one-contender. How do you like that?" Viscusi, warming to the subject, continued: "Nobody around Connecticut will believe it. Then Saddler fights Humberto Sierra in Minneapolis, and Sierra knocks him down and wins a split decision. Not long before that, Willie had handled Sierra like a baby. Charley gets hold of me and says: 'My guy is the number one contender now. What are you going to do?' So we make the match with Saddler. Everyone is saying easy fight, you'll have no trouble with him. I matched Saddler with a guy named Bobby Thompson in Hartford, which is Pep's home town. This was in order to show what he could do at a higher level, and also build up the

WILLIE Pep, Hartford, Conn.
Winner of

Conn. Flyweight Championship	1938
New England Featherweight Championship	1942
World's Featherweight Championship	1942
Los Angeles Times, "fighter of Year"	1944
The Ring, "Fighter of the Year"	1945
Hall of Fame	1963

*To Brian Hughes
Your the Greatest
Best always
Willie Pep*

WILLIE PEP
World's Featherweight Champion 1942—1951

"Fighting Feather" — By Pap

Willie PEP has Connecticut boxing fans excited as they haven't been since the days of Kid Kaplan and Bat Battalino

What's holding you up?

A clever boxer and a solid hitter, he has won 48 bouts in a row

Some day you'll be a great fighter like Bat

His dad had him watch boxers in training as a child

Just about my size!!

Willie has his eye on the featherweight crown

Wide World Features

The 9 years old Willie Pep showing style and gracefulness.

'The master and the pupil' Bill Gore, Pep's coach, gives Willie a massage prior to one of his early fights.

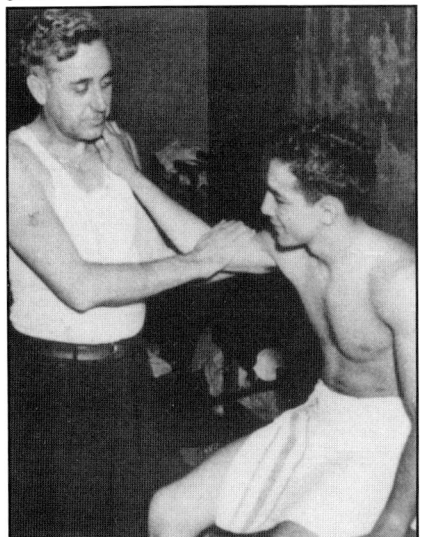

'I'm in the navy now' - Pep on home leave.

Three old friends meet backstage at the Loew's Theatre in Norwich, Connecticut in 1949. Willie Pep, Father George Donahue (Boxing Commissioner) and Frank Sinatra (Willie's friend and one of his staunchest fans).

Pep pictured with the man who was by his side throughout his glorious ring career, manager Lou Viscusi.

Pep's father Salvatore Papaleo fostered his son's early interest in boxing by taking him to watch local hero Battling Battalino training.

Pep hits the speedball while preparing to fight arch-rival Sandy Saddler for the forth time in 1951.

Tale of the tape. The first meeting between deadly rivals!

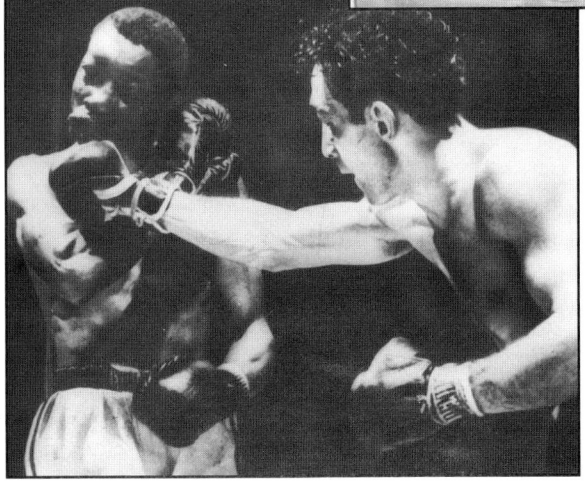

Willie Pep drives a hard right to the mouth of Sandy Saddler in their second fight which saw the Hartford wizard Regan his crown.

Willie Pep gets some attention on his damaged eyes from the doctor.

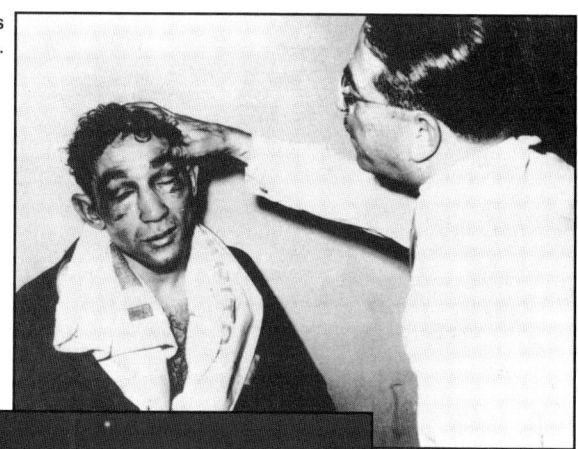

Willie Pep leaps off the canvas to tag featherweight champion Sandy Saddler of New York with a left in the first round of their fifteen round title bout at Madison Square Garden - 11th February 1949. Pep regained title he lost to Saddler in the same ring last year.

You could have continued the fight, said many critics after Willie Pep lost his featherweight title to Sandy Saddler in their third torrid battle.

backs Chalkie Wright onto Ropes in a fifteen round title bout New York City. Pep won on points - 20th November 1942.

Which way did he go? Ray Famechon, French featherweight seems to be asking as champion, Willie Pep ties him in knots.

Willie Pep's brilliant and accurate left jab snapped Ray Famechon's head back, and helped the champion defeat his tough, durable challenger.

Willie Pep cuddles his third wife Cynthia Rhodes.

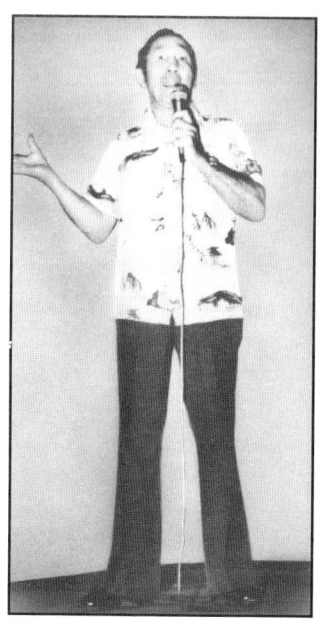

Willie Pep in 1995, doing his spot of after dinner speaking.

Doreen and Brian Meadows make a presentation to Willie Pep in 1992.

gate for a Saddler-Pep fight. The truth of the matter was, quite simply, Saddler did not look in any way impressive when beating Thompson. Willie, Bill Gore and myself were sat ringside."

It was a fact the boxing writers in those days had a big say in who boxed who, with promoters paying great attention to what these fellows wrote in their columns. They were saying after watching Saddler disappoint against Thompson, Willie had nothing to worry about, and should lose no sleep at the prospect of facing the skinny New Yorker. One scribe wrote in his newspaper: "Why this is unbelievable. I ought to go out and bet my money on Trueman to lick Dewey next week." This was the reaction to Saddler's win in Hartford. Of course, this kind of publicity killed any chance of matching Pep with Saddler within the coming weeks as Viscusi had planned.

The danger signs were there for all the Pep camp to see. Just prior to facing the champion, Saddler had fought a main-event in the New Haven Arena against Willie Roache. Roache absorbed a brutal beating for three storming rounds. He was a mess, with cuts inside his mouth and bruised and bleeding from eye wounds when referee Hughie Devlin rescued him. Now Pep had fought Roache twice, winning two ten round decisions. Roache was certainly nobody's push-over. He could both box and punch and for a long time he was a top-ten rated contender, taking on the world's top feather and lightweights. In stopping Roache so ruthlessly and clinically, Saddler had gained a psychological advantage over Pep. It was assumed such a creditable victory over a common opponent would ring the alarm bells in the Pep camp. But sadly this was not the case. What made Saddler's knockout win over Roache more remarkable, was that he achieved it just thirteen days before facing the world champion in Madison Square Garden! Can you imagine that happening today?   On the face of it Viscusi was perhaps a little lax in the preparations for his champion facing Saddler. It looked like a case of not giving enough respect to a very dangerous challenger. Though to be fair, Viscusi was not alone in neglecting the talented spider-legged Saddler. Hardly anybody in New York took much notice of him coming through the rankings. That was, until he became the number one contender for Pep's title. Even when the match with Pep was sealed, reporters did not blink an eye. They believed, like the Pep camp, this challenge was a foregone conclusion.

After winning the title, Saddler gave unstinting praise and credit for his sensational victory to his close friend, the crafty master of defence, ancient Archie Moore-the Old Mongoose as he was often called. There will never be another boxer like Moore, his record is almost unbelievable. He won 199 of 234 officially recorded professional contests and took part in many more which were not listed in any record books. He registered 145 knockouts and boxed for nearly 30 years. He was a beautiful box/fighter, who had been cruelly sidetracked out of fighting for the middleweight title, and was being shunted and avoided for the light-heavyweight championship because of boxing politics. He would become undisputed champion a couple of years later when he was almost 40 years-old, holding the title until he was 48. He took part in his last professional contest at the ripe old age of 53! "I owe my victory over Pep to Archie Moore, I am grateful indeed. He came up to my training camp for six weeks, and we worked on moves and plans to bring about Pep's downfall. It was fascinating; we practised moves and counter moves," Saddler told the press. In their training headquarters, Moore preached to his young disciple, Saddler, day and night. "Don't let Pep get any leverage. Keep right on top of this guy. He is very clever indeed, you have to deny him this asset he has of leverage or he will outbox you," he told his pal. Adding: "This was undoubtedly the most important fight of Sandy's life. And I'm glad I helped him achieve his victory. Like me, he has come up through the ranks the hard way. He's a lot better than what people give him credit for. He will be a good champion." Moore had a plan of action which he wanted Sandy to follow to instructions. Saddler was his willing pupil, taking in everything the old maestro told him. It was a marvellous sight watching these two craftsmen of the ring working out their plan of action. Archie would wear the big gloves and enter the ring and box with Sandy, stopping only to instruct his pupil. Moore was an expert at planning moves and counter moves. If the Pep camp wanted to pin the blame for his defeat on anyone, then they need not look any further than the "Old Mongoose" himself, Archie Moore.

The shock result was still being discussed world-wide. Inquests were taking place concerning Pep's unexpected defeat. Then, there were the malicious rumours still doing the rounds. The scandal mongers claimed there was some kind of "fix." They also said there was big money riding on the result and if Pep lost, then the betting boys would make a fortune. These ugly reports were so strong that Eddie Eagan, the New York Commissioner, warned both men at the weigh-in that the eyes and ears of the world were focused on Madison Square Garden that night. "I am holding you both responsible to uphold the good name of boxing," he told both fighters. "There are rumours of a 'fix' before every important fight but we don't pay any attention to them. You are two honest athletes fighting in a great championship match you will represent boxing tonight I'm asking both of you for an honest fight," Eagan concluded. "Don't worry about me," answered Pep. "I will be there to win." Saddler said nothing. He gave his answer in the ring later that night. He won so conclusively that he blew the rumours wide open.

The critics savaged Willie much more than Saddler had done during their fight. "When he went down in the third, he made a meal of it by getting slowly to his feet," said one critic. There were accusations flying thick and fast. The main bone of contention centred around the fact Pep and Saddler had a signed contract for a return bout. And this, they claimed, was why Pep took the easy way out. This was foolish talk and these sort of scurrilous allegations go on in every sport when the favourite is beaten. There were a few boxing writers who were downright rude and unfair in their reporting of the Pep-Saddler fight. Pep was guilty of no more than taking Saddler much too lightly, over-confidence which bordered on stupidity, nothing more. There were certainly no sinister motives. If Pep did take the "easy" way out as many newspaper journalists had suggested, then he certainly picked a tough way to get beaten. Think about this. In the very first minute he was bleeding profusely from the nose, in the second round Pep was rocked several times and absorbed terrific body punishment from Saddler. In the third he received a cut under his right eye and just escaped being knocked out as the bell sounded. He also took three furious left uppercuts which were delivered full blast from Saddler as he was trapped in a corner. These blows nearly separated his head from his body. He also got another cut eye and ran straight into another uppercut which put him down. Up at nine, Saddler knew he was on the right trail. He moved after Pep and a two-handed barrage put the champion on the floor again. Willie just made it to his feet before the count reached ten. He was still wobbly when the bell saved him. In the fourth round, another Saddler uppercut smashed into him, yet, amazingly he remained upright. But not for long, because a crashing left hook to the side of his unprotected jaw with all the power delivered from Saddler caught Pep flush and down he went again. He was vainly trying to get to his feet when the referee counted ten and out! Pep took unmerciful punishment during the four rounds this fight lasted. His face was a sorry mess of cuts, welts, bruises and swellings. So this was an easy way out?

Pep was broken-hearted at the manner of his defeat. For a few days after their fight he was inconsolable, refusing to meet or speak to anyone. Gone was the happy-go-lucky little fellow who hardly ever stayed moody for long periods. He relived those four horrible rounds a million or more times, squirming on every occasion. In his quieter moments he plotted his revenge over Saddler. Sammy Greenberg, his friend, got himself another new suit because like after his defeat by Angott bought a brand new expensive suit, but after the Saddler loss he refused to wear the suit again. So, Greenberg acquired another outfit for his wardrobe. Another broken-hearted fellow was Louis (Kid) Kaplan, one of Pep's staunchest admirers. A couple of days after the Pep versus Saddler battle, Kaplan, announced that he was no longer connected with the restaurant which bore his name. Rumour had it that the former featherweight champion had lost his interest in the restaurant after betting heavily on the fight!

Viscusi was still in shock a few days later, and when speaking to Bill Lee, he said: "I really am sorry I ever let that Cuban guy, Sierra, into Willie's training camp. Because he kept filling Willie's head up with how easy Saddler would be. I feel Willie started to believe all this bull Sierra was telling him, and he got lax with his preparations. There was an attitude about Willie which was wrong, I put this down to the fact he was feeling confident, so I left things alone."

Another one of Pep's staunchest fans, was a fellow who lived in Hartford. This man used to attend every one of Willie's fights and he would film them on a hand-held camera. But for the first Saddler fight he sent his tickets back, thinking this was going to be an easy task for Pep. Viscusi remarked: "I'm sorry he didn't film this fight, because we could have watched where Willie went wrong. I don't have to tell you how shocked we all still are with the result."

The Ring magazine editor, Nat Fleischer wrote: "Despite cry of a "fix" which permeated the air for two days prior to the contest, the bout was honestly fought. There could be no doubt about that. It was Sandy's flaying fists, powerful blows such as have enabled him to put to sleep the champions of many countries, that brought about the downfall of the best featherweight the division had in two decades."

Just before ending this chapter I would briefly like to mention the return fight clause which caused so much trouble and drew plenty of criticism in the first Pep versus Saddler confrontation. It was a practice which was very prevalent in world title contests during the 1940s through to the 1960s. Every champion before signing to defend his title would have a return fight clause written into his contract. It caused a great deal of wild speculation in the press and from fans. It was rumoured that more than one champion knowing they had a return bout firmly secured deliberately didn't go all out when defending their crown against certain opponents and as a consequence dropped their championships. But in the guaranteed return fight the former champion looking a remarkably different proposition, regained their laurels.

This return fight practice was unfair and needed stamping out for the simple reason that, there was nothing good about it so far as the sport itself was concerned. Ring editor, Nat Fleischer, was an outspoken critic of the return fight clause and wrote a rivetting article about this issue in one of his magazines. It was about this period that Lou Viscusi added Del Flanagan to his stable. Mr. Lou paid fifteen-hundred dollars to Earl Kane, a genial Irish manager from St. Paul, who had looked after the affairs of the speedy Flanagan from the time the young St. Paul lightweight attended the De LaSalle High School. Kane, who was having health problems, figured Viscusi could move Del up the ladder a lot faster than he could. Hence the switch. Flanagan proved a pretty useful boxer and helped Willie Pep get ready for a number of important fights. Willie liked the St. Paul youngster and was a regular spectator when Del was boxing.

Preparing For Saddler

After the shock of losing his championship, Willie took a short break away from the rigours of boxing and training. He relaxed himself by visiting the race-tracks during the daytime, and frequenting the nightclubs. Deep down though, Willie was thirsting for revenge over Sandy Saddler. Though he had been ordered to relax and enjoy himself by Viscusi and Gore, he could not get the terrible events of his humiliation at the fists of Saddler erased from his mind. It was the manner in which he had allowed Saddler to virtually mug him which was the cause of his frustration and sorrow. Pep fretted over this knockout loss. No matter how many tracks he visited or how jazzy the night spots appeared, he just could not get the defeat out of his system. The only thing which would ease his mind was when Viscusi gave him a definite date for the return contest with Saddler. Mr. Lou was having discussions with the International Boxing Club officials, and a deal was near completion. The proposed date for the return bout was set for 11 February, 1949. Madison Square Garden was going to be the setting for this return fight for the featherweight championship. Where else could such a compelling fight be staged but at the Mecca of big-time boxing?

Once the final details were settled and the contracts signed and sealed, Pep felt much more relaxed and happy. Talking to close friends, the former champion said: "I won't make the same mistakes which I made last time.

I'm determined to win my title back. Things will be different, I know the size of the task awaiting me. I also know what kind of sacrifices I have to make to gain success and my revenge. I am prepared to give everything physically and mentally whatever the cost to me personally." There was a steeliness about his whole attitude toward Saddler and the upcoming battle. Talking more about their previous fight Willie declared: "I know what I did wrong last time I fought Saddler. That wasn't the real Willie Pep, I can assure you. Put your money on me to regain my title."

Pep had fought once since his loss to Saddler. He beat Hermie Freeman in Boston in the first, putting on a masterful exhibition of first-class boxing, swiftly moving in and out. He showed no ill effects from his tousling at the fists of Saddler. The fans applauded his display with a great deal of enthusiasm. Willie wanted to see the 1948 calender shredded for obvious reasons.

In January 1949, Boxing around Hartford was in the doldrums. After Willie's knockout defeat by Sandy Saddler, it seemed like a cloud of depression had descended over the state. Boxing activity in and around Hartford was near zero, and the chances of improvement were not looking too bright. Three stalwarts kept the flag flying. Jimmy "Gaspipe" Vaccola and Joe Brady, were staging tournaments in Bridgeport. Gus Browne was staging fights in Hartford while George Sheppard promoted in New Haven. But all three promoters were finding it difficult. One of the reasons for the lack of interest was because a large majority of Connecticut citizens were factory workers and many shops were working only part-time so they were carefully how they spent their money and this blighted attendances at the boxing shows. It was said Willie Pep would bring about a revival should he beat Saddler in their return.

To keep sharp and ready for Saddler, Pep boxed another ten rounder. He outboxed Teddy "Red-Top" Davis, who was from Brooklyn, winning a points decision. The fight was held in St. Louis. Amazingly, this fight took place just three short weeks prior to meeting Sandy Saddler. He drew 4,869 fans through the turnstiles. But it was a dull and uninteresting bout, because the fans wanted aggression and fireworks. After getting a small cut over his eye, Pep understandably was not about to take any risks with the Saddler fight so near and boxed accordingly.

In his gym workouts while preparing for the return match, there was a new intensity about everything he did. He had discarded over confidence for a cautious respect. He listened intently to the instructions of Bill Gore.

Training with a burning desire for revenge and vengeance, he wanted his pride back. When out doing his early morning roadwork, there was a little extra zest and vigour behind every step he took. Every breath he breathed reminded him of Sandy Saddler. Banished were those foolish "hangers on" who filled his head with silly notions and ideas this forthcoming fight would be "easy"! He had a bevy of sparring partners helping to sharpen him up in readiness for Saddler. Dennis (Pat) Brady, Miquel Acevedo, Del Flanagan, Charley (Cabey) Lewis, Jackie Weber, Ray Edwards, Billy Kearns, and Tommy Bazzano. Bill Gore had done a masterful job in preparing the Hartford boxer for the upcoming fight. After watching Willie breeze through eight rounds of sparring, while boxing magnificently against the two toughest sparring partners, Gore eliminated the final scheduled boxing drill planned for the next day. He did not want Willie peaking to soon. There was just four days before the championship match. Now the job was to bring Willie to the scales at 126 pounds or less and still have him strong at the opening bell. At 12-30 Gore put his man on the scales and the beam was 126 on the nose. All that was needed now to make it a flawless job of training was to have Pep strong enough for come what may. It was no longer news he was physically and mentally ready for the toughest 15 rounds he would ever have to fight. The little Hartford boxer was fiercely determined not to underestimate the new champion the second time around. His training programme had made certain that he was in tip-top condition. No distractions whatsoever were allowed to interfere with his preparations, no stone would be left unturned this time. Pep's rigorous training schedule was completed two days before he was due to step through the Madison Square Garden ropes to face his tormentor, Sandy Saddler. He had done all his training in Hartford.

"Willie, is ready. This is the most important fight of his life. I have never seen him so determined. He firmly believes he has the beating of Saddler on Friday night and I also share that view," said Gore.

Trimmed down to 128lbs after weeks of concentrated work-outs, Pep limited his final session to a few warm-up exercises and a little bag punching. He left immediately for New York where he would remain until after the fight. Lou Viscusi talking on the radio, said: "This is a fight Willie has got to win. Saddler is the only fighter to hold a knockout victory over him, and the only featherweight to beat him. His matchless record of 135 victories in 138 pro fights seems to have been forgotten by those New York critics."

There was not a single metropolitan boxing writer who picked Pep to regain his title. Most of the fight experts who hung around Jacob's Beach inclined toward the champion too. They all spoke about Pep in the past tense. "He was the greatest featherweight in ring history," said one scribe. "But, Saddler's youth and Pep's loss of speed combine to give the champ the edge."

Bill Lee, the sports editor for the Hartford Courant, was firmly behind the Hartford challenger. He stood alone in picking Willie to win. In his article about the fight, he wrote: "Willie Pep reaches the zero hour of his long career on Friday night at ten o'clock, or a few minutes thereafter. The wispy Hartford boxing master, long regarded as one of the all-time greats of his class, faces Saddler again, this time in the unfamiliar role of challenger. This fight has the boxing business by the ears from one end of the country to the other, but the tempo is highest in Hartford where it may be the biggest local sports story in the memory of the oldest inhabitant."

Special trains loaded with Hartford fight fans were taking only a part of the huge crowd from every section of Connecticut who would see first hand the biggest fight in which Pep had ever taken part in. Those who were going by special train, regular trains and by automobile would be a meagre percentage of the unaccounted and uncharged thousands who would hear the battle by radio and see it on television. In the 136 fights he had in nine years of professional boxing, Pep didn't have more than three hard tussles. Most he had won by himself. The only split verdict in a fight won by Pep came in the first of three bouts with Sal Bartolo. Subsequently, Willie defended his crown twice against Bartolo, going 15 rounds without losing a round the first time and knocking Bartolo out the second time. The crushing defeat on Willie's record by the savage Saddler left everyone aghast. Most Hartford fans, and many in other cities, regarded Saddler as just another opponent for the stylish champion. This time they wanted to see the man who knocked out the great Willie Pep. Some expected to see Saddler do it again while many others were ready to tear the roof off Madison Square Garden if their home town favourite wiped the Saddler deficit off the books and regained the featherweight championship.

Mr. Lee went on to say the fight critics in New York thought it was a certainty Saddler would retain his title, because Pep was all washed up, he had lost his wonderful leg speed and reflex action. "They don't think he can escape the lethal punching of Saddler, a crunching left hooker who had knocked out 61 opponents in 99 fights, which was the best finishing record ever compiled by a featherweight champion, even going as far back as George Dixon and Terry McGovern. If the fight mob is right, and Pep is indeed over the hill physically, then Willie will be belted out again. But this writer, for one, does not believe Pep is through, and if this view is correct the result on Friday may be as big a shock as Pep's knockout in their first meeting," wrote Lee.

There are three factors governing the downfall of any fighter. These are age, the amount of punishment soaked up and behaviour outside the ring. Pep was only 26 years old, and other things being equal, Willie should have been in his prime. He had taken less punishment than any fighter in living memory. Pep had not lived a Spartan life over the previous three years, but he had not transgressed as seriously as the malicious gossip would have it. Pep himself put it this way: "Sure, I've been in a few jackpots, but I haven't done half of what people say I'm guilty of doing." Going back for a brief moment to the first Saddler fight. Willie was in perfectly good physical shape. But mentally, he was totally unprepared and seemed to have taken Sandy much too cheaply. "I grew too big for my britches," he said. To many easy fights had left Willie without the necessary sharpness to combat a fighter of Saddler's ability. Make no mistake about it. Saddler could fight. He was perhaps the heaviest puncher the featherweight division had known since Terry McGovern's time. Moreover, he was the tallest man ever to win the title with a reach to go with his extra-ordinary height. But he wasn't just a stringbean who could be blown down by a good gust of wind. Saddler was more than the tallest featherweight champion on record. He may well have been the strongest ever to wear the diadem of his class. There is not the slightest disposition in Pep's camp to underrate Saddler. He was well equipped, magnificently conditioned and perfectly instructed when he faced Pep in October. His savage aggressiveness was precisely the style calculated to give Pep trouble and when it found Willie unprepared, it was unbeatable. But Pep was now ready for the fight of his life. Keen, sharp and respectful, the little former champion would pit his matchless boxing ability, ring generalship and superior experience against the heavier punching and greater reach of the long-armed Saddler. Supporting this theory were some of Pep's previous fights. He wasn't ready for Jimmy McAllister the first time and was nailed with enough punches to enable the officials to reach a draw verdict.

However, much as it may not have been justified, it went into the books as the only draw in Pep's unprecedented record. When they fought again, Pep knocked McAllister out in two rounds. The first time Willie faced Red Top Davis the mood was wrong and Davis made it a comparatively hard fight. The second time Pep was mentally sharp and the result was that Davis didn't come close to winning a single round. The first time Pep boxed Sal Bartolo the fight was close and Willie was knocked down and badly hurt. The next two contests were not even fights.

No featherweight champion had ever lost the undisputed title and won it back again, although Joey Archibald lost the National Boxing Association version of the division championship to Harry Jeffra and won it back in a later bout. Willie would be all by himself when he fights Saddler, but Hartford fans agreed it was the old Pep in there, or a reasonable facsimile, it would be more than enough to make Sandy Saddler miss punches from Eighth Avenue to 49th Street and back again, which was enough to give the Harlem man the boxing lesson of his young life and restore Pep to the top spot of the featherweight division. Saddler was a good fighter, but Pep was a great ringman and when they crossed gloves again in Madison Square Garden, he would deliver the greatest performance of his career. It was the belief of many Hartford observers that Willie Pep would win back his title and go on to greater fame and fortune than he had ever known before. Despite what New York and the rest of the world thought about Pep's chances against Saddler, the Connecticut fans were solidly behind their man and several New York betting men expressed the belief Pep might wind up as the betting favourite on their books before the first bell. Pep's entire build-up and preparations for this match were aimed at thwarting Saddler's rough-house style of brawling, and the legion of Hartford residents rooting for Willie were convinced he would hand out a boxing lesson to the champion.

Pep himself told them: "Saddler is in for a shock. He will have his hands full. That's all I can say." Like the majority of fighters, Pep was superstitious and he had abandoned all his "lucky" accessories. The bathrobe, water bucket, bottle, towel and suit which he used at all previous fights since his loss to Sammy Angott in 1943 had all been scrapped. Even his usual suite at the Hotel Lincoln had been bypassed and he was staying at the Capitol Hotel this time. Even his travel arrangements were changed. When boxing in New York previously, Pep would leave Hartford a couple of days before the contest, but this time he was arriving in New York on the day of the fight.

Saddler had been training at Summit, New Jersey. He was in fantastic shape said his manager, Charley Johnston. "Sandy is knocking his sparring partners down like ninepins. He's ready for Mr Pep again." He completed his final workout by boxing four brisk rounds against two speedy sparring partners. He weighed 128 lbs and expected no problems shedding the final two pounds. Talking to Bob Steele, the WIIC sports announcer, Saddler said: "I'll do my best, just like the last time. And I'll beat him again."

As stated earlier in this chapter, there were several special trains leaving Hartford, plus another train from Waterbury which would carry Pep's loyal fans to the fight besides the thousands who were making their way in cars and coaches. Tickets were hard to come by. The Garden was selling some $2,50 side arena seats, but every other ticket had been sold. Station WDRC announced their sportscaster, Jack Smith, would give a resume and colour story of the fight in a telephoned transcribed broadcast to those fans unlucky enough to not have a ticket. The stage was set for the showdown! On the morning of the fight, travelling by train from Hartford to New York, the Pep party were seated in their compartment. As the train neared the big city, Willie was looking through the window when Lou Viscusi said: "We've had a long ride since we've been together, Willie. And even if this is the end of it all, we've got to say it's been a good ride." Pep looked at his manager and replied: "You're right Lou, it's been a longer ride than many people expected. But I have enjoyed it."

The Greatest Night Of His Life

The night of 11 February, 1949 in New York City was wet, miserable and cold, but nothing could dampen the enthusiasm of the thousands of fans locked outside Madison Square Garden. They could not get a ticket at any price. The "sold-out" signs had gone up a couple of days before the fight. And thousands of fans were being turned away at the turnstiles on the night. Millions of people throughout the United States would be able to watch the fight live on their television sets, free of charge. Television was one of the new wonders of the world. It was reported a record number of television sets had been purchased prior to the Pep-Saddler rematch. Despite this, the true boxing followers still wanted to be present in the Garden. The fans wanted to tell their kids and grandchildren. "I was there."

Preparing for Saddler

The whole atmosphere was exciting and overwhelming. There was an air of vivid tension and electricity. Everyone was bubbling with eagerness about the prospect of watching these two all-time great ring warriors do battle. The build up for this spectacular event had been unique.

The New York newspapers must have written hundreds of articles leading up to the fight regarding the "feud" between the two fighters and their managers. In the beginning, there was never the slightest trace of the so-called bad blood which supposedly existed between the two boxers. Feuds never entered their thinking, they were professionals. It was a few boxing scribes who had fed this line to their readers. It was they who started this bad feeling which did eventually become reality. Both fighters had said many times previously "This is strictly business, nothing more." It had been almost four months since Saddler had ripped the crown from Pep's head in such fearful fashion. He was the king now, and as such deserved respect from the press. As for Pep, he wanted the title back as quickly as possible, nothing more. To him, Saddler was just another fighter who he had to defeat in order to become world champion again. It was as clear and as simple as that. No feud, no malice, no bad feeling, and no animosity. Despite all this, the publicity machine had turned this into a 100 per cent genuine "grudge" match. Of course the fact that it helped sell more tickets was the name of the game for the people concerned.

In his dressing room Pep was shadow boxing and limbering up, he felt the "fear" factor inside him. This pleased him a great deal because he had been much too casual last time they fought, and had paid the price. It was this fear feeling which had taken him to his greatest triumphs. Yes, he was now afraid again, afraid of defeat and this pumped up his adrenaline.

Madison Square Garden was the venue of legends and over 20,000 boxing fans had paid a record $87,563 to attend the fight. The previous indoor record for a featherweight title scrap was the $71,869 established in the Garden by Pep when he won the world crown from Chalkey Wright in 1942. The question on everybody's mind was: "Could Pep do it?" The fans waited with baited breath for the bell to ring for the commencement of the dual between these two truly great featherweights. There was a buzz in the air. Pep was first into the ring, he was dancing lightly on his toes as the Master of Ceremonies, Johnny Addie, was busy making his introductions. Willie was a study in concentration, confident, yet not over confident. Every fighter needs to be "feared", this helps him to rise to the occasion.

He had done all his preparation and his homework. He knew he was going to have to delve deep into his memory bank and come up with the answers which would allow him to beat this awesome punching stringbean of a fighter in the opposite corner. If he needed inspiration, however, it must have come from the ear shattering ovation he received when announcer Johnny Addie started his pre-fight introduction. Addie had barely started..."From Hartford, Connecticut" when he was drowned out as the Garden rang with the most thunderous roar any fighter had received for many a long day. This was the ovation that told Pep his home town was solidly behind him. The thousands in the Garden were cheering for the thousands sat at home, who however much they may have wavered in the past, were now rooting for their fellow townsman to bring the world championship back to Hartford. Pep was proud whenever the ring announcer would shout..."From Hartford, Connecticut. Willie Pep."

Promoter, Mike Jacobs, was again delighted at the vast turn out of fans, as Gladys Gooding, the Garden organist, played "Happy Days Are Here Again" to open the evenings entertainment. Bill Gore spoke quietly to his man: "Move, move, move and keep moving." The articulate trainer preached: "Don't stand in front of him, attack him from different angles, keep spinning him of balance, plenty of lateral movement, Willie, don't trade with this guy." Pep knew beforehand this fight was going to be physically demanding, but he had to get psychologically tuned up as well. After nine years of steady fighting at the top level, most fighters were willing to call it a career. Indeed, most have too, because more than any other boxing is a sport for youth. It was also a known fact the lighter weight fighters suffered "burn-out" syndrome much quicker than fighters from the heavier weight classes. Little did he imagine though, he was about to perform the greatest ever masterpiece of his fascinating career. He was about to box the greatest bout of all time.

In Madison Square Garden on this night, Willie Pep, manager Lou Viscusi's Eldorado in human form, would continue on the road to glory and immortality. He was as near perfection as a boxer can be and wouldn't let his loyal Hartford fans down. Saddler was shuffling about in his corner, wearing his tartan robe, looking over toward Pep with a sullen look upon his face. He was ready, he was prepared to fight until he dropped. His thoughts went back to all the dingy, flea-pit hotel rooms, his tough upbringing in Harlem, getting the rough end of the stick when it came to purse monies and his long climb to the top of the ladder. Now he had at last reached his goal. He had achieved the status of being a "somebody." After all, hadn't he beaten a living legend in Willie Pep? Yes, Sandy had toiled along a tough old road on his way to becoming world title-holder and he was not going to give his new found fame up lightly. He looked a menacing figure standing in his corner awaiting the introductions.

If you date sensational fights from the past such as Dempsey and Firpo, as most fight observers did in 1949, or Zale and Graziano or the many more great and historic ring encounters between the worlds greatest fighters from the past and into the future, then you would have to add this second meeting between Pep and Saddler alongside them. Ring the bell, ring the bloody bell, everyone seemed to be saying in unison. Many fans were already drained of emotion before a blow had been struck in anger. Anticipation was reaching fever pitch. Thomas Danza, a neighbour of Pep's, and a boxing fan recalled being present in Madison Square Garden on this eventful occasion. "The hairs on the back of my neck were standing to attention, waiting for the gong to sound," he said. Bang! the bell sounded and the fight had started. There was already a crescendo of deafening noise. Pep kept on the outside of the ever dangerous champion, moving in all directions. Pep was foxing the taller fighter, and breaking up Sandy's concentration and rhythm by keeping him off balance. The challenger was the master from the opening bell. Moving to his right, then quite suddenly stopping in mid-movement and changing direction and ducking to his left side. Bobbing and weaving, slipping and sliding, pulling his head back from Saddler's dynamic punches, he made making them go wide with split-second timing. The referee had to caution the challenger for wrestling in this first round as emotions ran high. The crowd were spell-bound as Pep landed ten rapid-fire consecutive left jabs which rocked Saddler's head back on his shoulder. The huge crowd were going frantic as Pep was majestically side-stepping in both directions, flicking out his left jab to pick up points. Shuffling and turning his dangerous opponent every time they came to close quarters, he produced vintage boxing. Willie was brilliant, quite simply brilliant, in a breathtaking manner. Bill Gore, was pleased the way his man was boxing and turning to Viscusi he remarked: "There is a zest and sharpness about Willie tonight. If he keeps this up the title is going back to Hartford."

The scowling Saddler was looking to land the knockout drops at every opportunity. He was stalking Pep like a hunter intent on its kill. But deep down, Sandy knew he was facing a much more motivated Pep than the first time they had fought. Willie was as sharp as a tack. He was in marvellous condition and ready to write a brand new chapter to his already remarkable career. Pep was using the ring immaculately and was boxing the ears of the Harlem fighter. He was scoring points whenever he made the champion miss, which was often. His main objective was not to get tagged, so he heeded Gore's instructions and did not stand and trade punches with Saddler. Pep's sheer professionalism stood out like a beacon.

In a sport with a growing reputation as a breeding ground for wild-swingers and brawlers, Willie Pep's display and his attitude on this momentous occasion restored the connoisseurs lost faith. The ex-champion was building up a useful points lead. But one can not venture out into a storm wearing all the necessary waterproof equipment, and stay totally dry. You are bound to get a little wet. And so it was with Pep in this contest. He was dominating the flow of the bout, but was damaged around the facial area. Nobody shares a ring with the likes of Sandy Saddler and does not have some marks and bruising to show for their venture. The marks of battle could visibly be seen. There was a cut under Pep's left eye.

Willie was boxing majestically, but Saddler was more than a handful to contain. The little Hartford wraith was making the best fight of his long career. He was making his previous tormentor look silly by the use of his scientific and masterful technique, feints, slips, fancy footwork. You name it, Pep was displaying it. He gained inspiration hearing the sound of his name echoing around Madison Square Garden.

Many of the press had said on many occasions that Saddler was a "dirty" fighter. This was true, of course, although Sandy maintained the reason for this was because he knew he would never receive any kind of breaks or favours from referee's or boxing officials: "I am the master of my own destiny in the ring," he had said many times. There was no doubting the fact he could look after himself in any company. He was trying to use rough-house tactics in this fight. Many outstanding featherweights and lightweights of the forties and fifties would endorse the fact Saddler was a holy terror when it came to the rough side of fighting. Very few relished the prospect of meeting this fellow in combat. If they were unlucky enough to get caught in the clinches with him, then it was sheer hell. He would wrap those long arms around his opponents head and pull them onto his favourite punch, a sweeping left hook. Not many of his opponents realised Saddler was a converted southpaw so all his considerable power was contained in his left hand. He scored the majority of his knockouts through the use of this devastating weapon.

Pep was using every ounce of his condition to keep the fight at arms length. That way Sandy could not fight on the inside as he desired. Pep was boxing immaculately. It was a pleasure for the Garden fans to watch this man's special brand of ring magic. Could "Will-'o'-the-Wisp" keep up this extraordinary pace? That was the burning question the 20,000 onlookers seemed to be asking each other. Between rounds, Bertie Briscoe, Saddler's trainer implored his man: "Put more pressure on this guy, he's slowing down. Don't allow him to lead, keep stepping in on him." Sandy obeyed his trainers command as best he could but it was difficult trying to nail the little boxing maestro in front of him. Pep would not stand still for a brief second. The referee had to administer a further warning to the former champion for "heeling" with his glove when Saddler trapped him in a corner, but Willie's tactics prevented the champion from using his heavy punches at close-quarters. What a fascinating and absorbing contest this was proving to be as the tension mounted!

The crowd were ecstatic and certainly getting their money's worth from these two fighting furies. Willie was using every trick he had learned throughout his career. He was a master of the art of "surprise." He had studied Sandy for the first four rounds and was now ready to use different attacks in order to confuse the champion. Sandy was looking for a match winning punch and his fighting zeal was awesome. Yet Willie was putting up a competent defensive barrier and using his wide repertoire of moves. He also possessed undying courage, supreme confidence and a pair of blazing fists.

Eddie Joseph, the referee, had on more than one occasion had to warn one or both principals against rule flouting. In the fifth round a right smash opened a cut under Pep's eye. The Hartford kid ignored the wound and continued to outbox his rival throughout the remainder of this session and those that followed up to the tenth. Saddler was becoming more and more desperate with each succeeding round. He was trying hard, but he just could not get a clean shot on Pep's chin. Pep, in the terminology of many old-time fight managers, had a "first-class motor." He certainly needed it on this night.

Saddler had his best chances of victory in the tenth and 14th rounds. Before going out for the tenth, Sandy was told: "Look at the scar tissue over his eyes, it's busted up. Go out and press him." The Harlemite caught his challenger with a pile driven right cross which landed flush on Pep's jaw. This was a crunching blow and the ex-champion staggered and looked ready to hit the canvas. The long-shanked champion was quick to sense he had hurt his man and now had him at his mercy. Pep was virtually out on his feet. This was when Saddler was at his most awesome, that punch had every ounce of his weight behind it. "It would have decked a donkey," said Gore. Miraculously, Willie survived the onslaught. It was here he reached down into his very soul and brought out his wonderful defensive skill. This enabled him to get through the remainder of the round without sustaining further damage. Yes, Pep was hurt and for a few brief seconds he certainly did not know where he was. Sandy tore after his man throwing those sweeping uppercuts which if just one would have connected anywhere on his rival, would have spelt the coup de grace. Yet Pep found that indomitable fighting spirit and astonishingly pulled himself together, got up on his toes and danced away to safety. At one stage Eddie Joseph, stepped in to separate them."Break clean," he shouted, "let's stay out of the clinches." The Saddler fans booed. Charley Johnston, jumped up bristling and screamed at the referee: "You're helping Pep." At the bell ending the round, Willie limped to his corner. "How do you feel?" a worried Gore inquired. "Is he too tough for you? You're the one I'm thinking about, kid." Pep, his face cut and swollen, his arms weary and feeling as if they were ready to drop from his shoulders, his legs quivering like a jelly, had no hesitation with his answer. "Bill, I'm ahead on points, it's worth the gamble of these last five rounds. I'm telling you I'll make it, believe me."

The 11th was a vital round for the Hartford fighter who showed a fighting champion's heart by leaping out of his corner and charged the newly hopeful champion against the ropes where he knocked him bow-legged with one of the fastest and most artfully accurate punching barrages he had ever thrown in his 100 or so fights. Saddler was dumbstruck. He could not believe what was happening to him. Invigorated with his determination, Pep at times made Saddler look foolish as he boxed one of the greatest rounds of his career. He was moving right, going left, jabbing like a tongue of flame, ducking, dodging, then jabbing again. Sandy was never given the chance to use his advantage from the previous round and from that point on to the conclusion of this epic confrontation, Saddler gave the appearance of being somewhat cowed and discouraged. Pep continued to box like one of the old boxing masters as he sailed through the 12th and 13th sessions without much trouble. Saddler was showing his challenger a great deal of respect now, despite the fervent pleas from Bertie Briscoe and Ned Johnston his trainers, to "Drive, drive, push him he's ready to fall down, he's shot." Upon hearing these commands, Sandy was like an infuriated animal, surging forward trying to obey his trainers instructions. But he was frustrated by Pep's caginess and he treated Willie with extreme caution. It was written in every move he made, but his big problem was that he was content to bide his time, waiting to land one of his lethal bombs. He was desperate, he knew his title was slipping away from him. His only hope was to land an explosive knockout wallop on his opponent.

The chanting and yelling from the faithful Hartford supporters was tremendous, the Garden arena was vibrating with their constant din. The 14th saw Saddler with the bit between his teeth and his ears ringing from the chastising he had received in his corner. He went all-out to separate Pep from his senses and another terrific teeth-rattling right, the hardest blow Saddler had landed with all night, found its target on Pep's chin. Looking wild-eyed, the champion then let one of his favourite left hooks fly, followed straight away by another right that brought the hearts into the mouths of five-thousand or more screeching Pep rooters. These punches once again caught Willie flush on the jaw. They shook him down to his very toe nails. It looked like the perfect knockout Saddler had been searching for all night long. The tall Harlem fighter stood back fully expecting his rival to fall. But Pep survived and with a superhuman effort he threw a two-handed barrage of counter-punches which backed up his erstwhile punisher and amazed him.

Reporters sat in their ringside seats were shaking their heads in disbelief at what they were watching. With the sell-out crowd yelling and hollering themselves hoarse, the setting was marvellous. Pep neither gave any quarter, nor asked for any. He had given Saddler a boxing lesson throughout the fight. He had electrified everyone as he pelted Sandy with every punch in the book all from incredible angles. But he saved his greatest thrill for the 15th and final round of this pulsating battle royal. Three times it seemed the pace had begun to take its toll on Pep, and Saddler would emerge with a knockout victory. But each time, Willie was equal to the emergency and came through. After weathering that jarring fire from the champion in the previous round, the Hartford veteran dug deep down into his reserve bundle of strength and energy to take the play away from the Halemite. He was less than three minutes away from regaining his cherished championship. It was a sensational exhibition of world class boxing skills which enabled him to win the round and become world featherweight king once again. As the final round was nearing its close everyone in the Garden, Pep and Saddler Fans alike, along with the neutrals, stood and clapped, cheered and hooted no more so than the thousands from Hartford who made the rafters ring with their noise. They knew Pep had won from Hartford to Harlem and back again, the announcement of the official verdict was only a formality. Nevertheless, the happy Pep legions raised the roof again when Johnny Addie made known the clinching score of the second official. Their tumultuous cheering drowned out Addie as he tried to announce the third official's score card. And they kept up the din as Pep posed for pictures, a towel drapped across his head. Then every one of the 20,000 spectators applauded each fighter as they made their way back to their dressing rooms.

Make no mistake this was the greatest ever fight of Willie Pep's life, even surpassing the night he first won the title from Chalkey Wright in 1942. So, Willie Pep, who started making boxing records early in his career, had set up another by becoming the first boxer this century to win back the world featherweight title from the man to whom he had lost it too. Saddler entered the ring the betting favourite at 7 to 5. Abe Attell, a former featherweight champion, and who described himself as a conceited fighter said of Pep: "He's the greatest featherweight since me. Did you see how he spins, feints, blocks and punches with almost incredible speed. A fighter, even a great fighter like Pep, has to get hit sometimes, but he never gets hit on purpose. He uses his noodle." Referee, Eddie Joseph said: "It was the roughest and toughest fight I have ever handled. But what a performance by Pep"

Pep left no doubt he felt Saddler had circumvented the rules in their first encounter, and for the first time in his long career the polished Papeleo boy gave out the rough treatment to an opponent. He stepped on Sandy's toes when the strong Harlem fighter tried to pull Willie into close range and belt him about the body. Saddler tried to turn this second fight into a rough-house like their first battle, and the result was a howling brawl which threatened several times to get away from the referee's control. But to his credit, Joseph stayed right on top of both fighters. Back in his dressing room the badly battered but deliriously happy Hartford man tugged his father over to the shower-room. There away from the noise of the celebrations and in complete privacy, he said: "Pop, I had to win this one, I had to make up for the last fight with this guy. I wanted to stuff all the bad publicity and negative criticism down those doubters throats."

This was Willie Pep at his best. Undoubtedly the highlight of his long career. Possessing all the nervous courage of a small pup and the speed, guile, and ability to recognise pain immediately, Pep stayed true to his instincts and gave Saddler nothing to hit. In return, Pep hit Saddler with his best shots, his combinations, and his target-bound left jab. He had won the fight of his life. As the fans headed out of the Garden making their way to the subways or the many bars littered across Broadway, they were all unified in their praise for both these magnificent fighters: "They'll never forget little Willie Pep," said an old-timer to his companion. "Only Pep could box in that style and throw punches from the kind of angles he did tonight. The guy was amazing."

The following morning while having breakfast in his hotel, Pep, was talking to a few journalist about the previous night's fight. Laughingly he told them about an incident which he said happened during the early rounds of the Saddler fight. Willie said he accidentally stepped on Saddler's toes, and instantly Sandy yelled: "Ouch!" Upon hearing this, Pep said he continued stepping on Saddler's toes at every opportunity. The journalist thought he was joking but Pep assured them it was perfectly true. Later that day, Charley Johnston, Saddler's manager, protested about this incident and also about the referee who he claimed gave his fighter all the bad breaks.

What The Papers Said

Jersey Jones, writing in the "Ring" magazine, said: "Not since Henry Armstrong and Lou Ambers staged their gruelling two-bout argument for the lightweight title back in '38 and '39 has a hotter rivalry developed in the championship ranks of the lighter weight divisions, than the current one between featherweights Willie Pep and Sandy Saddler. Pep's remarkable 15 round triumph in the furious second meeting in Madison Square Garden, after Saddler's stunning four-round knockout in their first bout, has made a third episode on of the most attractive entries on the New York fistic agenda. "The second match between Pep and Saddler was played to a complete sellout crowd including some eight-thousand of them Willie's loyal cohorts from Connecticut. And with a $10 top prevailing, it grossed $87,563, a new world record was set for a featherweight fight. Pep, the new old master, needed every trick in his vast repertoire to pull out ahead of the lanky, vicious-punching Saddler in as bitter a brawl as the Garden has housed in some time. But what Pep may miss in brawn is more than equalised by his stout fighting heart and one of the keenest brains in the ring. Darting in and out he whipped Sandy. Pep had several close calls from disaster. Saddler forced the action from the start. He never stopped stalking Pep. But coming up for the tenth round Sandy was behind on points and couldn't seem to compete with the veteran's bewildering assortment of tricks. Willie was near exhaustion in the fifteenth, weary and battered though he was, Willie was still on his feet when the final gong clanged-once more the featherweight king. It was a great fight between the world's two top feathers."

James Dawson writing in the New York Times: "I had Pep the winner by twelve rounds, giving only three to Saddler. Pep put up the greatest battle of his career. He is no believer in theory or tradition. He is champion again because of his unflagging courage."

Even Ed Van Every, a staunch Saddler fan as well as being "The Sun's" top boxing writer had to hand it to the Hartford boxer. "Willie Pep is not only the world featherweight king again, but he has earned himself a niche beside the all-time greats of his division.

Gene Ward, in "The Daily News", called it a fight with seven rounds to each fighter with one round even. But he found no quarrel with the final verdict, begrudgingly admitting Pep deserved the decision. Said Jim Jennings in "The Mirror" "Pep looked liked a human gargoyle and took a cruel beating, but won by sheer courage and masterful boxing when his cause appeared hopeless."

Bob Zailman from "The Hartford Courier" wrote: "A rare combination of brains and guts brought Willie Pep and the world featherweight championship back to Hartford yesterday. Veteran boxing writers drooled all over their Saturday morning and afternoon columns, acclaiming the 26 year-old Hartford lad as the greatest thing that had ever happened to the featherweight division and boxing in general. They praised his ring generalship and his courage. They applauded his speed and agility. They gushed about his well planned attack and they even went so far as to pat the thousands of loyal Connecticut fans on the back for their unswerving faith in their champion. "There wasn't a single scribe who didn't think Pep deserved the victory over Sandy Saddler in the epic fifteen round struggle in Madison Square Garden. One or two thought it was closer than the verdict handed down by the two judges and referee Eddie Joseph, and one ventured an opinion that it might have been a draw, but all agreed Willie Pep's performance was the most magnificent in his matchless career." These rave notices came from the typewriters of scribes who had spent weeks telling the public Willie Pep was through and would be knocked out by Saddler. They had gone to the Garden expecting to see a desperate, frightened and faded former champion make one last, futile attempt to regain his crown from a powerfully built, lethal-punching youngster. Instead, they witnessed the most thrilling exhibition of intestinal fortitude, backed by confidence, to grace a New York ring in years and perhaps history."

"There was one writer, Lester Bromber, of "World-Telegram," who made a last minute switch to Pep before the fight and he took bows all over his paper's sports pages for calling the turn on the number one "upset" of the year. It was an upset to the big town critics but to the Nutmeg fans who jammed the arena, crowded in-front of their radios, it was a victory they expected from a fighter they knew would not let them down."

Bill Corum, "The Journal-American" columnist who also doubled as a fight broadcaster, probably was most awed at the brilliant Pep performance. This is what he had to say: "It was a superlative, extraordinary performance by a superlative, extraordinary glove fighter. It was one of those down-to-the-last-gasp battles by a fellow who had to fight sometimes from memory. But when he did, he fought from a memory that was smart and cool and collected-the memory of a champion.For Willie Pep, who once did these things in a light-footed dancing breeze, had last night to reach down very deep and take hold of that thing that makes the true champion a champion always. The thing that says there is no such thing as a six-letter word meaning to lose that begins with "d" and ends with a "t". Since there was no such a word for the Signor Papaleo, who is Willie Pep, last night, he wound up being just a trifle more than 50 per cent contributor to what was. "Surely as fast and furious a fifteen round fight as two little men ever offered in the modern annals of the ring. Pep won and he won for sure. How much more could anyone have asked? Boxing has, at times, been called an art. I don't know about that. Perhaps it has been so called only by its devotees. But if it ever was an art, it was in the hands of Willie Pep last evening. And if so, in his small field, he is a Rembrandt, a Reubens. All I know is that he's a hell'uva fist fighter, and in this one fight alone, he proved it for always." Such was the lavish praise heaped upon Pep by Corum who was one of the finest and most respected journalist in America.

Joe Williams of "The World Telegram" said: There were cynics who said Pep threw the first fight, the one which saw his featherweight championship pass to Sandy Saddler. Well, last night Pep threw something else. Punches. Hundreds of them. And most of them landed on the tall, thin coloured boy who had knocked him out, taken his title and made him the object of sordid gossip. In as wonderful a fight as the bit town has seen between little fellows in many months, the Hartford Italian, sharp-beak and bush-haired, a veteran of some 140 fights at 26, fought brilliantly and dramatically to regain not only his fistic pride and position but to erase the libel against his name as a man. It looked for a while as if everybody in Connecticut was getting a bet down on the slandered slasher from Connecticut. A roar that rocked the Garden loose when Pep was introduced. This was another, more sentimental manifestation of the Nutmeggers' loyalty to their idol who had returned to vindicate himself. It was impossible to hear a word the announcer said during the introduction. That's how explosive the roar was. I watched Pep closely at this point. He stood in his corner looking down at the white canvas, tapping his wine-red gloves together, his mouth grim-set, a straight line, and it must have been an effort that he held his emotions in check. This was a salute of friendship and faith few men ever get to know, a roaring vote of confidence from the men who know him best. How could he fail? He didn't fail. He didn't. The decision was unanimous. The fight wasn't close. It was a delight to watch Pep. Fascinating, too. He exposed Saddler for what he is, potentially great, but pea green. It is not much of an exaggeration to say Pep fought flawlessly. Making a fighter miss is a great trick, the mark of the expert is the counter. Only the pros do this with malice after thought and finesse, Pep did it repeatedly last night."

"The Herald-Tribune's" capable correspondent, Jesse Abramson, said: "After the decision was announced, manager Lou Viscusi lifted his victorious fighter up in his arms. What he (Viscusi) held in his arms was a battered, bleeding fighter, his face covered with a film of blood from cuts and bruises and welts under both eyes, over his eyes and across the bridge of his nose. What Viscusi held aloft was really a brain. For Pep did it mostly with his brain. This was the old Pep or a reasonable facsimile of the old Pep.

In the early rounds his studied tactics were those of a desperate man, though brilliantly executed. Later he fought with the old Pep confidence. Early in the fight he tapped his punches, more concerned with getting away. Through the middle of the fight and in the eleventh and twelfth he hammered Saddler with authority in his blows. He could not punch with Saddler, but he nullified the champion with an artfulness, the reach, height and power of the like of which none can surpass."

Bill Lee, The Hartford Daily Courant, said: "There were people in my company on Friday afternoon who still thought me too completely sold on Willie Pep, but I didn't back down an inch. Had I done so, Pep's magnificence on Friday night would have left me slightly miserable. But by the same token, I still insist it is not an exaggeration to say in the face of the usual knockers that Willie Pep has always been the best managed and best trained fighter in the country. The job Viscusi, Gore and Johnny Datro did in Pep's corner on Friday night was wonderful. There was Willie, working with his head and then his feet and then his hands. Ducking and moving and keeping Sandy off with his jabs and confusing him. He kept Saddler off balance. Saddler was becoming desperate, he was busting Willie's face up, but he was unable to put him on the canvas. There was the Garden audience making a noise which was deafening and thousands upon thousands gathered around their television sets, a new audience being made for boxing by this great fight. Willie he's the greatest fighter ever."

"The Greatest Fight I Ever Saw," wrote Al Goldstein, in the Baltimore Sun. "With one of the most dazzling displays of boxing skill ever seen in a prize ring, little Willie Pep regained the title he lost to Sandy Saddler."

One New York paper hailed Pep as the saviour of New York boxing yet again after the magnificent victory over Saddler. "The little fellow from Hartford officially attracted 19,097 fans into Madison Square Garden. The gate of $87,565 established a new indoor record for featherweights. It was the first sell out in three years for the Garden and came just when things looked darkest for the Twentieth Century Sporting Club. But saving New York promoters from oblivion was an old trick of Pep's. In 1942 the boxing situation was desperate in New York until the clever Hartford boxer arrived on the scene, bringing his legions of followers with him and setting a record gate which stood until his recent fight. That first fight was his first title match with Chalky Wright. That success stirred up interest in the boxing game again and Mike Jacobs was back on easy street. Pep saved the day again in his first bout with Saddler. The Garden had just made a drastic change in its management in the hopes of getting out of the red and Harry Markson, who took command wanted Pep to start the ball rolling. Willie did just that with $57,000 plonked on the line to see him lose his crown. However, many observers believe the prices for Pep's latest fight were scaled too low and that all records could have been shattered if the price had been higher. Incidentally,Pep's best record in Hartford was the $26,000 for his match with Julian Kogan in 1944, and the $23,000 he drew at the gate with Bobby Ivy in 1942.

When they start telling you about George Dixon and Abe Attel and Johnny Kilbane, you tell them about Willie Pep and the night he won his title back from Sandy Saddler," said another New York writer.

Tony Stecher of Minneapolis had flown in for the fight with Dick Cullum, a boxing writer from the Minnesota Metropolis. They were overjoyed at Pep's victory. Out in Minneapolis Pep was almost as popular as he was in Hartford. After the fight they were invited to have a drink with Viscusi. When they got up to leave Stecher shook Viscusi's hand warmly. "I want you to know," he said quietly, "we are as happy about Willie's victory as you are yourselves.

This was indeed a night to remember. Everyone in the Pep camp were happy and overjoyed and they were all chattering away. Viscusi was an extremely proud man, prouder still to be the manager of such an accomplished ring wizard as little Willie Pep. And so too was trainer Bill Gore, who was gushing in his praise. Gore usually kept his opinions to himself, but on this occasion he could not stay silent when reporters questioned him. "If you go back and look at the judges scorecards you will get a clear picture of the fight. By the 11th round Willie had won eight. Sandy had to knock him out to win, and that was what made it such a fantastic fight," said a delighted Viscusi. Willie was tickled pink when he received a bundle of telegrams, one in particular made him smile. It came from Manuel Ortiz, the bantamweight champion. Four years previously Pep had given Ortiz a painful shellacking, but such was the admiration for Willie among the members of his craft that Ortiz dispatched this wire: "My best wishes for you to regain your title. I did it myself and I know that you also can do the same. Best of luck and God bless you." From the manager of the Durant Hotel in Flint, where Pep and his team stayed while training for his championship fight against Flint's fistic idol, Jock Leslie, came the message: "We at the Durant Hotel know the title will return to Hartford. We all wish you the best of luck. Give our best to Bill (Gore) and all the gang...Scott Shattuck."

Pep Receives His Belt

A few weeks later Willie was honoured by a dinner which was held in the Club Fernindando in Hartford. The speakers for this lush, gala affair were Councilman Frank Covello for Mayor Cyril Coleman; Athletic Commissioner Billy Prince; 'Dumb' Dan Morgan; and the Reverend George J. Donahue. Willie was presented with his second world featherweight championship belt by the Ring editor Nat Fleischer. Pep was at this time universally recognised as the only featherweight champion who ever regained the crown. Previously Fleischer had presented Willie with the New England championship belt and a plaque as The Ring Magazine's "Fighter of the Year" in 1945. Three other former champions were guests at this prestigious affair, Johnny Dundee, Louis "Kid" Kaplan, and Bat Battalino. Famed New York journalist Dan Parker was also sat there with Harry Markson of the Twentieth Century Sporting Club, George Klettz of the Tournament of Champions, Dennis McMahon of the State Athletic Commission, Frank S. Coskey, a former state commissioner, and over 6 other assorted guests.

While there was a lull in the proceedings, Kaplan and Battalino turned to Nat Fleischer and began discussing Pep's capabilities as a fighter. "The fans won't know how great Pep is until he's retired. We all thought certain fighters were better in our own day, but I really must say having watched this guy in action (Pep), he'd have been as big a star at any period," said Battalino. "His balance is something special. And the way he moves about the ring, well, he's so nifty, any of us fighters from my period would have had trouble nailing him with a solid punch. Kaplan smiled in agreement and commented: "They talk about ballet dancers being graceful to watch, and I agree, but Pep brings a kind of smooth movement in everything he does. "He picks punches and delivers them with zest and accuracy. Geez, he's sensational with those flurries he fires at his opponents. He can be ranked now as being amongst the finest ring men I can ever remember. Don't forget also Willie has a kind of toughness which is not visible to people who don't understand the sport."

Fleischer, who was an expert on fighters from the past and who was not known for making rash statements, was in full agreement with the two former champions and said: "He looks puny and lacking in strength in comparison to other fighters, particularly featherweights. His boxing skill is unrivalled. His place in boxing history secured. They say he's not a great knockout puncher, but I've seen him crack fighters on the chin and watched them do queer things. Yes, Willie is a great, great boxer."

Meeting The Senate

Four days after his sterling victory over Saddler, Pep was honoured by his home State officials. He was clapped and cheered from the moment he entered the Senate chamber at the State Capitol. Willie asked the Lieutenant Governor if he could say a few words. Stepping nimbly to the rostrum in the spacious Senate chamber, the new featherweight champion of the world, his face still puffy and bruised from his heroic and memorial battle with Sandy Saddler, acknowledged an unprecedented series of ceremonies in his honour with a few simple words. Clearing his throat Willie took a deep breath and began: "This is one of the great moments of my life," he said, although he seemed very nervous. "I've had a few big ones before but this rates right up there with them all." The 26-year-old Hartford lad had just heard Senator Rocco D. Pallotti's resolution, offering him the congratulations and good wishes of the state, passed by unanimous vote. He had heard the Senate chamber ring with long and lasting cheers. He had received a handsome trophy from Governor Bowles, and, although not prepared to make a speech, he suddenly asked Lieutenant Governor William T. Carroll if it was all right to say something.

There may well have been a few tears behind the dark glasses he wore to cover the wounds above and below his eyes, one couldn't be sure. But he held his head high and wanted it known that his thanks were for everyone everywhere who wished him well in his hour of triumph. "I want to say thank you to Senator Pallotti, to the Governor and to everyone," he concluded and the room rocked with applause. The entire capitol building had been agog for hours before Pep appeared. Office workers, Senators, and just plain fans crowded the lower lobby and when he entered the door the cheering was deafening. Everyone wanted to shake the hand of the courageous battler, pat him on the back or just touch him. No visiting dignitary ever received as spontaneous a greeting as the one Willie Pep received on this momentous day. He was whisked into the Governor's office in a matter of seconds where he was greeted by the chief executive. "We are all proud of you," Governor Bowles told the champion. "I listened to the fight on the radio and I think it was wonderful. I've got a little present for you here," he continued and handed Willie a huge silver trophy inscribed with the best wishes of the state and topped by a big statuette of an athlete holding a symbolic wreath of victory. "Some people asked if I posed for this trophy," the governor quipped, "but I'm afraid it wasn't me."

Pep thanked the Governor over and over again. He could think of nothing else to say. One of the Governor's secretaries rushed up to Willie. "I want to shake your hand", she said. "I think you are wonderful" I won ten dollars on you Friday night." "Let's split it", answered Willie and the crowd roared. The secretary of the State, Mrs. Winifred McDonald wanted to meet the champion and Governor Bowles arranged a swift introduction. "I just want to touch you" Mrs. McDonald said to Willie. "I want to go home tonight and tell everyone this hand touched Willie Pep." And while this was going on a jostling, eager, adulating crowd was pushing it's way through both doors, overpowering the police and officials who were trying their best to keep them out. No sooner was the champion led from the governor's office into the hall leading to the senate, than another burst of applause exploded through the building. It was a demonstration one would hardly expect in the stateliness of the capitol building. Hundred of heads peaked around corners, over railings, and through doorways for a brief glimpse at the number one sports hero of the day.

From all outward appearances, work ceased during the half hour it took to complete the ceremonies and employees became autograph seekers, shouldering their way through the throngs with their slips of paper clutched in their hands. Willie doesn't know how many times he signed his name during that half hour but he knows it was plenty. The trophy supplied at short notice by Bill Savitt, was inscribed thusly: "To Willie Pep, a great world's champion from the proud citizens of Connecticut. State Capitol. February 15, 1949." It also included an engraving of the state seal. Senator Pallotti, from whose Third District Pep and that other former champion, Bat Battalino emerged, had this to say as he introduced his resolution to the Senate: "I'm proud to be able to introduce this resolution because Willie Pep is the second man from our district to win the world's championship. Bat Battilino first honoured the city of Hartford by winning the title and I can also include Kid Kaplan, a Meriden man who held the championship and whom we can almost claim as a native of Hartford. "We of the Third District are very proud of all three champions. Willie Pep has been a great credit to boxing for the last eight years. He has regained the featherweight championship, a thing no other man in his division has ever done. We congratulate him, Lou Viscusi, Bill Gore and Johnny Datro for a magnificent job."

The resolution as read to the Senate said: "Whereas the people of

Connecticut have been thrilled by the courageous, unprecedented, comeback fight of their native son William Papeleo, known in the boxing world as Willie Pep, in recapturing the world's featherweight championship from a great adversary, Sandy Saddler, and whereas Willie Pep has written a bright, new chapter in the history of boxing and brought honour, distinction and world wide acclaim to this city and "state, and whereas both the official family and all the people of our state are duly proud of his achievement, accomplished in the face of almost unanimous opinion of sports experts that once more go down to defeat: and, be it therefore resolved that the congratulations a good wishes of the people of Connecticut be extended to Willie Pep for his matchless achievement, and spread on the records of the General Assembly and an engrossed copy of this resolution be given to Willie Pep, the greatest champion of them all."

Later in the afternoon Pep was introduced on the floor of the House of Representatives and received another tremendous round of applause. He was escorted to the House of Representatives by Simon S. Cohen, of Ellington: Martin J. Whalen, of Wolcott: Daniel J. Mahaney, Waterbury and Frank H. Pepe, from Derby. Louis (Kid) Kaplan, the man who held the same championship some two decades ago, witnessed the entire proceedings along with William J. Prince, State Athletic Commissioner and countless sports fans.

This was the highest pinnacle of achievement for the scrawny baggy pants kid from the tough, inner-city slums of Hartford's east-side. This honour would be an everlasting tribute to Pep, who by his unique fistic style of boxing skills had brought literally thousands of new boxing fans into the sport. No greater prestige could any person ask for than to be honoured by his own citizens!

I'm The Luckiest Man In The World
"One manager in a thousand is favoured if he has a guy like Willie Pep once in his lifetime," said Lou Viscusi. "I've been blessed. And I know it." Talking with some newspaper reporters in a little bar in St. Petersburg, Florida, a few weeks after Pep's dramatic winning contest against Sandy Saddler. Viscusi who had a home in Tampa, had driven down to St. Petersburg to meet the press team who were covering the baseball training camps. Mr. Lou was a shrewd cookie, always keeping on the right side of the scribes who wielded such power. Pep was also in Florida, he was an

ardent baseball fan, and had been seen in the company of the "great" Joe DiMaggio and also hanging around Al Lang Field, obtaining the autographs of the other star ball players. When told about Pep's exploits Viscusi remarked: "Yeah, Willie, is a very simple man, with simple tastes, and a love for baseball." Viscusi continued. "He's crazy about football too."

The reporters ordered another round of drinks, they knew any time spent with the knowledgeable pilot of Pep would prove interesting and worth a story for their newspapers. Mr. Lou was in full flow now. "Fighters usually want to know. 'What do I get out of this, and where do we go now, and what are you doing about that?' Willie never worries. I tell him what we are doing; he does it. He is crazy about his two kids. The boy is four and the girl six. I do not believe any other fighter spends so much time with his children. Gus Lesnevich? Well, maybe. But if you know where the Pep kids are, you know where Willie is most likely to be.

"He has been fighting a long time. Usually, when a guy has been in the ring as many years as Willie, he says: 'I have to think of retiring, and going into some kind of business.' Or maybe it's real estate, or a cocktail lounge, or just a plain saloon. Pep is a different kind of man. He knows fighting is all that a fighter knows about. He has no plans for going into Wall Street or organising a chain of stores."

The talk got around to how Sugar Ray Robinson had made a huge success of his many business ventures. Viscusi was not quite certain about the claims that Sugar Ray was a business genius. "Yeah, Ray Robinson seems to be some kind of financial wizard. Maybe he is and maybe he isn't," said a sceptical Viscusi. "Pep has no illusions about having a head for business. Fighters spend a lifetime getting some dough the hardest way, and then blow it on something they know nothing about. Not Willie," added Viscusi.

The talk got around to how long Pep would continue boxing. "Willie wants to keep on fighting as long as he's good. He loves performing in-front of big crowds and putting on a good show so the fans got their money's worth. When he loses his fistic touch, he will retire and devote himself to getting some fun out of life and bringing up his kids."

Some reporters asked: "Is he seriously thinking of quitting?" Viscusi didn't stop to draw breath. "No. Some people may think he has come to the end of his string as a champion." It was obvious the talk would get round to Sandy Saddler, and it did. Lou told them a third fight was in the pipeline for the summer. He added: "I think Willie is still Saddler's master. I know this, he will out-think Sandy any time. Now, I'm not saying Saddler is a bum. I know Sandy took the title from Willie and held it for a while. And as you know Pep took it back in that great fight." Talking about Saddler's rough style of fighting, Viscusi agreed that Sandy cuts his opponents up, but only if you let him added Lou. "I asked Willie the other day: 'What is your frank opinion of Saddler?' He replied: 'Lou, I'm convinced Saddler hit the crest of his boxing career when he took the championship from me, and that he can not be as good as that ever again.' It could be, Pep hasn't quite the right slant on Saddler. But Willie is not the kind of man who belittles any opponent."

The journalists then asked about the next fight with Saddler? For whom and where and when? Had the Pep-Viscusi combination voted to go with Joe Louis who was the figurehead for a new promotional group and break with the Twentieth Century Sporting Club and Mike Jacobs. Viscusi replied: "If you are in business, you want to make the best deal. Do you agree? Well, we will make the best deal. But, I will say frankly, I want to see Louis wind up with this match." Viscusi chuckled. "The fighters of class and their men now are in a fine situation. With the Garden-Twentieth Century set-up, for one, the Tournament of Champions for two, and now the Joe Louis enterprise, for a third. For the first time in years and years there is hot competition, keen bidding for attractions from big name sources."

Viscusi though, was annoyed at certain Twentieth Century Sporting Club officials. "Mike Jacobs always has been good to me." "I have no quarrel with or against him. I shake hands with Mike and that's a contract. But I did not like the way the Garden acted in the first Pep-Saddler fight." Lou described how he had given Saddler his chance early in his career by featuring him on his promotions in Hartford, adding that as everyone knew, Sandy was not a good attraction. "Sol Strauss wanted Pep and Saddler. Okay! I was offered $25,000 or 50 per cent. The percentage appealed. What happened? There was a deficit of $3,800. The Garden said. 'Let Charley Johnston pay you that dough.' Johnston said: 'Let the Garden make up the guarantee to $25,000. Well, I never did get the money, not up to this second and while thirty-eight hundred is not going to make us rich, well, I don't like to be booted around.

The first contract naturally called for a second match. You will remember how there was a hitch. They said we were scared of Saddler. Well the hitch was the $3,800. I have not discussed business with the Garden since the second fight. Harry Markson moved into the picture there between the first and second fights. But I have not conferred with him. Yes, the bidding is open, and I would like to see Joe Louis put up the best offer. I like Joe."

Mr. Lou stated he was not interested who promoted the next Pep-Saddler fight as long as the money was forthcoming. But it was obvious Viscusi was a man of principles and wanted the money owed to him. This talk about Pep being scared of Saddler did not affect him personally in any way, he was a damn good businessman and he wanted the money owed, then he would talk business. Speaking further about Willie, he told the keen reporters that Pep was always eager to make good in the boxing game. At the start, as a 17-year-old, he was working as a stock boy in the Hoffman Wallpaper Company. His father was ill with an ulcer or something, the family needed money urgently.

"After an illness sidelined Willie for a few months he returned to training, " Viscusi exuberated. "I took over his affairs, and what a terrific decision that was for me. I will never forget Pep's first main bout. It was in Fall River, Mass. And the prize was all of 48 dollars. The next morning Pep met me in the gym in Hartford, and said: 'Mr. Viscusi, how did I look? Do you believe I can fight?' I said: Willie, I never would have consented to manage you if I had not been sure you could fight, and fight well. 'That's all I wanted to know' Pep replied. 'From now on, it is going to be nothing but the ring for me. I have got to make good. I am quitting my job with the wallpaper company.' When you fight in everyone's backyard, you don't compile a record like Pep's unless you have it like nobody else ever had it at your weight."

Mr. Lou went on to state that Pep had never dodged anybody, and he never feared a fighter who looked good enough to merit a match with him. "Do you suppose any other fighter would have overcome what happened to Pep in that plane crash?" Viscusi asked his eager listeners. "We were due to fight in Cuba and then fly to England after that to tackle Nel Tarleton. They wrote his obituary. But look what happened? Jock Leslie flattened. That's what happened. Guts? Now, you tell me. His mental attitude today is terrific." "He believes when he wrested the title back from Saddler, he started a new career. He's always played to big houses. A big dinner which was to be given to Willie by the State of Connecticut at Hartford in a couple weeks time, started out to be a hotel affair, and pretty soon they had to switch it to the armoury because so many people wanted to be there," Viscusi laughed.

A couple of months after regaining his title, Willie travelled to Detroit with his young stablemate Del Flanagan, who was boxing at the Olympia Stadium in Detroit. The former heavyweight champion, Joe Louis, was working with James Norris and Arthur Wirtz for the International Boxing Club who were promoting the tournament. In order to give the show some added spice Willie was asked to box a four round exhibition. He readily agreed and the newspapers gave the tournament plenty of publicity. As a result, the stadium was packed with over 10,000 fans. The champion boxed briskly against Elis Ask of Finland. It was a cracking four rounds with plenty of fine boxing and sharp counter punching. The huge throng loved every minute of the four rounds. Jack Dempsey was the guest referee. Dempsey also had an interest in the smart boxing Finnish featherweight, who he was looking after while he was in America. Afterwards, Dempsey, Louis, Norris, Pep, Viscusi, Gore and Ask all had a meal and enjoyed a social gathering while also discussing future contests.

In May 1949, Willie paid a visit to St. Paul, Minnesota. Elis Ask, Jack Dempsey's protege, was topping the bill against Miguel Acevedo, a top ten contender who Willie had soundly outboxed 12 months before. The European featherweight though had had to battle hard to gain the ten round decision over Acevedo. Dempsey acted as his cornerman. Later, Dempsey and Lou Viscui, were negotiating for a proposed contest between Pep and Ask. Nothing came of the talks and all speculation ceased. It would have been a very interesting contest as Ask, who had fought in England with success was, like Pep, a wonderful boxer.

The world champion was booked to box a four round exhibition with Mel Hammond of Minneapolis. As Pep jigged down the aisle into the ring, the crowd rose and applauded him to the echo. He repaid the crowds applause by giving a vintage exhibition of the science of boxing. Hammond, a short, squat, powerfully built black fighter, chased and tried in vain to hit him but all his efforts were fruitless. Willie could have been forgiven if he had merely gone through the motions for such an unimportant event. But he was a perfectionist. He knew the fans had shelled out hard-earned cash and so he put on a show for them. The promoter, Billy Colbert, was as delighted as was his customers.

Willie took a short break from the rigour of constant training by taking part in semi-professional softball games for E.M. Loew's Theatre. This proved relaxing for the champion and when he played there was wonderful support for his team. Willie then fought twice in eight days. In the first contest in front of 3,000 spectators in the New Haven Arena, he romped through ten rounds when outpointing Luis Ramos of New York. Willie gave him a thorough going-over as he won every one of the ten rounds of referee John Cluney's scorecard. Ramos' left eye was completely closed and his face was badly bruised after getting hit with every punch in the book. It was then on to Pittsfield, where he faced Al Pennino. Once again Willie breezed through the ten rounds. Though in the ninth round, the champion received a shock when Pennino went all out for a knockout, Pep kept control and in the tenth and final round, he made Pennino pay for his audacity. Before scoring another easy ten round victory over John LaRusso in Springfield, Massachusetts, Willie acted as a guest referee in West Springfield, the occasion was an amateur tournament staged by the South End Community Centre. He proved a tremendous ambassador for boxing as he refereed all the 15 contests on the bill.

Steady Eddie Falls In Seven

After successfully regaining his championship earlier in 1949, Pep had kept himself busy. The champion seemed much more mature the second time around as a world champion. He added four more notches on his winning belt, plus taking part in three exhibition matches. The crowds were flocking to see him in action. He performed in cities such has Detroit, St. Paul, New Haven, Pittsfield and Springfield, with a final completive victory over a stocky French fighter Jean Mougin in a fight staged in Syracuse. These bouts kept Pep in the peak of condition and he was boxing sharply and giving the fans their money's worth.

While boxing in Syracuse for the Mougin contest, Willie got his first glimpse of Carmen Basilio, the future world's welter and middleweight champion, who was in action on the undercard in a featured six rounder, Basilio won in two rounds. Talking many years later about the tough-as teak Basilio with whom he became quite friendly, Pep said: "I thought Carmen showed good movement the first time I ever saw him fight. But he was basically a fighter. His roughness was his strength, though he could box quite well. He was always a tough guy, he left the impression on me he would never give up during a fight. Rocky Marciano was the hardest trainer I ever knew, but Carmen was not far behind him in this department. In his fights he never stopped walking forward and used to wear his opponents down. The human body can only take so much punishment. I remember watching Carmen fight Sugar Ray Robinson, and Basilio got hit more in one round than I would get tagged in 50 of my fights. He was a great fighter though."

Negotiations were under way for the Hartford title-holder to defend his crown against Eddie Compo in Waterbury, almost on his own doorstep. Sitting in the lounge of a city centre hotel, Willie was asked how he felt after his superb championship winning contest against Sandy Saddler. Willie smiled at the questioner. "Beating Saddler has made me appreciate what being a world champion means, said Pep. "It brought home to me how important this world championship is. When I first won the title from Chalky Wright, I was much too young to grasp what it was all about, but now I'm a little older I feel I have gained extra knowledge. What pleased me a great deal though was that the fans were happy with the fight. I know I have said it many times before, but I mean every word, beating Saddler was the greatest night of my life and my greatest ever fight."

When a boxer goes through a physically and mentally draining fight as Pep had gone through in the second Saddler contest, when he reached the highest peak of his powers and endurance, it has to take something out of him, this is only natural. But in the following fights since regaining his title Willie seemed a far better all-round boxer. He was now ready to defend his championship. Lou Viscusi knew full well that though Eddie Compo was a sound technician and a smart moving boxer who had fought some of the top featherweights around, he would not pose much of a threat to Pep.

The final signing of the Pep-Compo fight was overshadowed by newspaper reports from New York which stated Abe Greene, of the National Boxing Association, (the N.B.A.) was considering vetoing the Pep versus Compo bout. Greene had been rather caustic at times in his criticism of the New York Boxing Commission for its failure to force title holders to defend their titles against the most worthy challengers. This was boxing politics interfering once again. Connecticut, where the Pep versus Compo fight was being held was in N.B.A. territory, if Greene meant business would he insist that the forthcoming match between Pep and Compo could not be accorded championship status unless the winner agreed to fight Sandy Saddler, the number one challenger, six months later? Of course not. Connecticut, where both Pep and Compo were residents was affiliated to Commissioner Green's organisation, the N.B.A. It was possible to visualise just what the Connecticut public would make of all this political infighting if their own two boxers were denied championship status for their eagerly awaited confrontation.

Sugar Ray Robinson was allowed in N.B.A. territory to fight Jimmy Doyle, who later died of injuries suffered after he was knocked out in the eighth round by Robinson, and Chuck Taylor who he knocked out in six rounds. There were many other instances of double standards by all the ruling organisations. Sandy Saddler was also getting into the act by demanding a rematch with Pep. The New York scribes fuelled this argument for all it was worth, they were "mixing" it again for the two proud champions. Some reporters even suggested Willie was afraid of the Harlem fighter and was indeed dodging him. These kind of innuendoes hurt Pep deeply.

"I gave Pep a quick return after I took the title from him, I never kept him waiting. I deserve my chance to regain the title and Pep should stop fighting these inferior guys and face me instead. I'm ready and waiting," said Saddler in the newspapers and on a radio broadcast. Upon hearing Saddler's remarks a very angry and agitated Viscusi said: "Let them say what they want, those New York writers think they can dictate to everyone. It sells their papers, they are causing all this bad feeling and friction with their remarks. I say who Willie Pep fights and I'm in no hurry to arrange a third fight between Willie and Saddler, let them say were stalling, so what?"

Pep's manager was doing an excellent job of work for his boxer. He was getting him the best purses available without to many risks involved. The third fight between Pep and Saddler would take place when Viscusi decided, not Greene, Saddler, or the New York press. Mr. Lou knew any fight with Sandy would be another very physically, hard, demanding fight for his man, so he was in no rush. Pep for his part left all the matching and arrangements to his manager. Aside from the upcoming Pep-Compo meeting, boxing fans had other interesting topics to keep them occupied and interested. There was Joe Louis' retirement; Jake LaMotta's stoppage of the great French fighter, Marcel Cerdan; Joey Maxim's victory over Gus Lesnevich for the American light-heavyweight crown; Ezzard Charles's decision over Jersey Joe Walcott for the National Boxing Association version of the heavyweight title, and in their lighter moments, they sang such popular tunes of the day such as Mona Lisa, Mule Train, Huckle-Buck,

Bibbidi-Bobbidi-Boo, Some Enchanted Evening and Diamonds Are A Girl's Best Friend.

Enjoy Yourself-It's Later Than You Think
There was another song, however, which seemed singularly appropriate for Willie Pep, who some boxing experts felt was beginning to slip. It was Enjoy Yourself, It's Later Than You Think. As usual, Willie shrugged off such talk, he had of course heard it all before. Critics said he had not looked good since his plane accident. But he had proved them wrong, what about his most recent victory over Saddler? And he would continue to show them in the future.

Inside the Municipal Stadium in Waterbury, Connecticut, 10,722 fans braved the chilly weather and had splashed out their hard-earned cash for gate receipts of $39,931 to watch the two local boxers in this derby showdown. Pep from Hartford and his challenger, Compo, who was only 20, was from New Haven. Local fight followers were delighted at this opportunity to watch a world championship match in their home state, usually all world title fights were held in New York. They thanked Pep for defending his laurels at home.

There was a shock at the weigh-in when the champion had to make three attempts before hitting the correct poundage of 126-lbs. (9st) Compo made the weight at his first attempt, coming in at 124-one-half-pounds. Pep's efforts provided a minor sensation. Bob Mele, Compo's volatile manager, demanded the commission should immediately strip Willie of his world championship.

Confusion blighted the weighing ceremony. Pep's contract stipulated for him to make the championship weight by 12-01 p.m. At 11 o'clock that morning Willie went for a test weight check with Bill Gore and Lou Viscusi. They were more than satisfied he was within the required poundage. Pleased with himself, Willie went back to his hotel to rest and wait for the official weighing-in event. But for some unknown reason the official session did not commence until 12-30 p.m. There was a large gathering of fans who had come to support both boxers, they were making a deafening noise with their cheering, clapping and their good natured banter. Compo was on the scale first, followed by Pep who was one ounce over the championship weight. There were screams of protest from the Compo camp, with Bob Mele shrieking and threatening all kinds of action.

This of course was Mele's chance to have the spotlight focused on himself. With all the press and officials present he was in his element and milking it for all it was worth. The Pep camp though, didn't think it very funny. The champion went through some strenuous exercises and brisk shadow boxing in an effort to shed the ounce of weight. He was embarrassed at having to do this on the day of the contest.

State boxing commissioner Sam Malkan calmed Bob Mele down, no doubt explaining if the bout was not for a world title as he was insisting, the promoting organisation would be within their right to review the purse money for both fighters...End of story. After his brief workout Pep stepped back on the scale, low and behold, it registered exactly the same as the previous occasion. Whereupon, a very annoyed Pep went into another intense stint of skipping and shadow boxing and stretching exercises but with much more vigour and determination in order to shed the offending ounce. At his third attempt, he made 126-lbs spot on, the time was now 1-55 p.m. This would be the only advantage the New Haven boxer would hold over the featherweight king. Mele, when confronted by the posse of press and radio people, said he was now undecided whether to continue his protest for Pep to lose his title for not coming in at the championship weight at the designated time. Mele also said he was undecided if he would claim the $1,000 weight forfeit which Pep had guaranteed he would make the weight on time.

This championship match turned out to be one of the champion's easiest ever victories in his long and illustrious career. Eddie Compo tried valiantly, showed heart plus an abundance of willingness, but he was a poor second best to an inspired world champion on this never-to-be-forgotten night. Pep was a heavy betting favourite at 1-6, but there were few takers. Though his record was good Compo was crossing gloves with the Hartford wizard, the best skilled exponent of the noble art he would ever likely meet. The opening two rounds saw flashes of the New Haven youngster's left jab, which proved fast, but which the champion avoided without much effort by mainly stepping backwards thus rendering the blow ineffective. Compo made a bright start, but lacked power in his punches with which to trouble Pep. Willie was content to bide his time and move loosely up on his toes. When he did decide to throw punches, they were short, sharp and extremely accurate left hooks to Eddie's face. One such blow closed the challengers right eye toward the conclusion of the second round. The

Hartford warrior had shaded the first couple of rounds. By the start of the third round Eddie's eye had completely closed. He tried vainly to corner the elusive champion, but Willie would then flail away with a bombardment of two-handed blows which were majestic in their execution and had the crowd gasping with their ferocity.

The footwork of Pep was truly a sight to behold, he really displayed his whispiness as he moved away from any sign of danger at great speed, then cleverly counter-punched to Compo's head and body while on the retreat. This was artful boxing at its very best. In round four, Willie caught his foe with light punches, Compo returned fire. He was performing creditably before the featherweight king came back at him with body shots which really shook up Eddie. It looked as if the contest was all over in the fifth, when Pep whipped over two cracking left hooks which landed with a thud on Compo's jaw. These blows were followed instantly by a beautiful delivered right cross which dropped the game, and very brave, New Haven stalwart for a count of nine. Nobody in the audience would have faulted the challenger if he had stayed down after taking such fearful, full-blooded blows. However, he did beat the count, but was promptly flattened once again from more power packed right hooks and took another count of nine.

What a courageous boxer! Pep did not wish to administer any more punishment on his foe, looking directly at referee Billy Conway, in the hope he would intervene and rescue Compo. When this plea failed, rather than punch his near defenceless opponent, Willie dropped into a clinch and pulled Compo inside, deliberately refusing to punch. Pep showed his class and sportsmanship by taking it easy for the remainder of this round. In the sixth session, the titleholder seemed very reluctant to nail his challenger, and he danced his way through the round. "Can you imagine Sandy Saddler taking it easy with a challenger," one ringsider exclaimed. "Can you honestly picture Saddler or any other fighter you care to name who would go easy on any opponent in any fight," said another. But this man Pep was a different type or person from the normal fighter. Between rounds, Bill Gore and Viscusi scolded their man, pleading with him to get the job done. Pep moved out of his corner at lightning speed as the bell rang for the seventh round. He wasted little time moving after Compo while throwing wicked, rib-bending body punches. Pep was hitting his rival at will, he looked over his shoulder, (as Ike Williams had done when stopping Beau Jack in their 1948 contest) as if to ask the referee if he hadn't seen enough but the bout was allowed to continue, then switching a sharp right hand to the New Haven lad's chin, which after landing with an explosive crunch, sent him down for another count of nine. The speed of Pep's onslaught was frightening and before Compo hit the canvas, one of his cornermen was shouting loudly to the referee to stop the fight. On reaching his feet, Eddie was wobbling and with the crowd also shouting for him to act and save a game but totally outclassed boxer, Conway ended the one-sided affair.

The time of the ending was 41 seconds of the seventh round. This was a pleasing performance from the title holder, but Compo had little to recommend him as a serious threat for Pep's crown apart from an abundance of courage, though this was his first loss by stoppage. How good an opponent was Eddie Compo? Was he a worthy contender? These questions were asked before and after this championship contest and the answer was that before the fight Eddie Compo was touted as a worthy challenger and we must remember this loss to Pep was only his second defeat in 61 contests, he was rated number eight in the top ten of the featherweight division. On this basis he was indeed a credible challenger for Willie Pep.

In his dressing room Pep said: "Eddie was a game kid. I was never worried, but I twice asked the referee to stop it before he eventually did." It was a double celebration, as this was Pep's 27th birthday, what a way to celebrate! Questions were asked by the many reporters concerning his three trips to the scales in order to make the weight. It seems impossible to understand why Willie did not shed the one-ounce at his first attempt. Pep admitted after his check weigh-in earlier that morning, he satisfied himself he was inside the 126-lbs, and was mystified to be told by the boxing commissioner that he was in fact overweight. "What about your manager and trainer? Did they not scrutinise this very important issue?," he was asked. Willie explained he must have somehow, miscalculated his weight as Gore and Viscusi had also. But, as this was the first occasion he was required to reach the featherweight limit since beating Saddler six months previously, it was possible he had made a mistake.

No, he hadn't taken Compo too lightly, he emphasised. Had the previous day's newspaper reports on the death of a 25-year-old Australian boxer named Archie Kemp, who had died following his knockout defeat by Jack Hassen at the Sydney Stadium, affected him and was this the reason he had pleaded with the referee to stop his contest and save Compo taking further punishment. "Not really," relied Pep. "I never take any fighter lightly, but I knew I had Eddie beaten, and I refrained from hitting him unnecessarily. Why ruin a guy when you're winning easily?"

Taking everything into consideration, the newspaper reporters were suitably impressed with the champions showing, though this was a safe defence over a willing but outclassed opponent, with never the slightest danger. They agreed Pep had demonstrated skills above and beyond the normal expectancy from fighters. The year 1949 had been a truly amazing and eventful one in the life of Willie Pep. He had regained his world championship in a thrilling encounter which was talked about as a classic, and would go down in the folklore of boxing history as the greatest ever world championship contest at any weight. He had been a product of the 1940s and certainly 1949 would be fondly remembered by Pep himself. It was also the year his friend, Sugar Ray Robinson, had given a most dazzling boxing exhibition against the cocky, flashy, bolo-punching, Cuban-hawk, Kid Gavilan, in defence of his welterweight title. This fight, a certainty for Madison Square Garden, was driven out of New York by the powerful boxing manager's guild in their fight against the Garden's officials. The fight was eventually held in Philadelphia's Municipal Stadium, with Robinson winning.

World boxing champions are no different from the average person. Infact, they get more trouble from drunks and people who fancy making a name and reputation for themselves by telling everyone who will listen to them who they have sorted out. If his victim happens to be a world champion the story is so much better. Willie was invited to a Hartford nightclub on this particular occasion. He was accompanied by a beautiful young lady who he had known for quite some time. As the night wore on a former boyfriend of Pep's companion came over to where the couple were sitting. He was obnoxious and loud. Pep quietly asked the fellow to leave them alone. Later, he came back to their table and was shouting obscenities, then suddenly slapped the woman. Willie got to his feet and told the man he was out of order and he must leave the club. The man threw a haymaker at Willie, naturally it missed. With that, Pep slapped him, making certain it was with the open palm of his hand. The nuisances's lip was cut slightly. The police were called and arrested this chap for causing a disturbance. Taken to court the following day, he was found guilty and fined.

Pep thought that was the end of the matter, but a few days later the man filed a claim against him, claiming Willie's hands were weapons. Willie visited his lawyer who told him this could linger and would be nothing but pure aggravation and not worth fighting in court. The man was asking for a thousand dollars. "Give it him, Willie, save yourself the hassle," said the lawyer. Willie paid up plus $500 for the lawyers fees. Pep had hardly touched the fellow, he hadn't started the trouble but ended up paying out his hard-earned money. There was another occasion when Pep could have found himself in hot water. He owned a little club in Tampa, Florida. Willie was stood at the bar enjoying a laugh and a joke when a drunk became really rowdy. Pep walked over and politely asked the man to leave the premises, when all of a sudden the man pushed a 45 revolver into his stomach, screaming he was going to blow Pep to bits. Using all his charm, Willie got the fellow outside the club, but the man was absolutely drunk and demanded Willie stick his hands in the air. Just then a police patrol car passing saw the incident and apprehended the drunk. It was a frightening experience for Willie and something he never forgot for a long, long time.

Chillin' Charlie Riley

Negotiations were taking place between Lou Viscusi, boxing officials and promoters from St. Louis with a view to having Pep defend his championship in their city. The suggested challenger was local hero, "Chillin" Charley Riley. After his stunning knockout over Eddie Compo in Waterbury, Willie was in big demand. The proposed date for the title confrontation was suggested as 16 January, 1950. The final details were still being ironed out between Viscusi and the promoter, Hans Bernstein, when it was suggested by the boxing officials of St. Louis that Viscusi should first allow the champion to box a ten round non-title bout against former world bantamweight king, Harold Dade, a black fighter who was a merchant. Dade they knew well as a tough little scrapper who had previously boxed Riley. "A fight between Willie and Dade would whet the fans' appetite and make for a bigger gate when he puts his title on the line against Riley," said Mr. Bernstein. The programme would feature Riley opposing Proctor Heinold. Pep obliged the promoter and St. Louis was in for a boxing feast. Willie put on a truly vintage performance, ending the year by easily winning a ten round points decision over Dade. The former champion had given Willie very little to worry about throughout the entire fight. The champion at times humiliated Dade by the use of his classical smooth-style of phenomenal boxing while, bouncing rights and lefts off his opponent's cranium. It was indeed a masterful boxing lesson for the former world champion to receive from the current world title holder. Pep had given a flawless performance. The St. Louis boxing fans had warmed to this brand of educated boxing, they sat in astonishment at the champion's superb skills and the manner in which he achieved success over Dade. They respected Pep's special brand of magic, his quick-fire bursts of rapid punching and above all his excellent footwork.

Though one-sided, it was nevertheless an interesting contest, a rare sight for the crowd of near 17,000 to behold. What was certain, was that they liked what they had seen and would gladly come back for more. A few weeks before facing Pep, Dade had boxed brilliantly to extend Sandy Saddler the full ten round course, giving the former world champion some very anxious and worrying moments. This fellow Dade certainly knew how to look after himself alright. He was nobody's push-over, he could handle himself with the best in the bantamweight and featherweight divisions. That's what made Pep's dominance over him so interesting. But boxing against Pep he just could not fathom out how to curb or contain the elegant champion in any way.

Meanwhile, Riley won a convincing ten rounds decision over Heinold. And so it was now all systems go for the championship match between the Hartford man and his challenger. This was a fight which the St. Louis fans had been clamouring for the past two years. Pep knew Riley because he had used the tough St. Louis fighter as a sparring partner on a few occasions in the past. Riley had also worked as a paid helper to Sandy Saddler in earlier days. The newspapers were full of stories leading up to this interesting championship match. Tickets were selling briskly and it looked like being another sell-out. The New York press had wrote previously that Pep had been side tracking Charley Riley, when the fight was announced, Riley was given only an outside chance of defeating the brilliant champion by the media outside St. Louis, though he was highly regarded in his home city and plenty of wagers were staked on him to bring the title home.

The local fighter was an all-action fellow, highly popular and a chirpy character with an abundance of confidence, especially in his punching ability. Charley wanted to become rich and famous. Who better to start with than the scalp of the fighter many experts were already describing as the best ever featherweight. Pep was held in the same esteem as Joe Louis and

Sugar Ray Robinson. Charley would at least have the edge in the statistics department, except for height, where Pep had a three-inch advantage over the challenger who was 5ft 2ins. But, said one reporter, "Pep will balance the scales in nimbleness, a master's degree in boxing science, plus a good solid punch. Except for possibly Sugar Ray Robinson, Pep is considered without a rival in the art of flattening noses." Throughout boxing circles Riley was regarded as a solid professional, who had a sharp, hard and accurate right-hand wallop. He had an impressive knockout record, having floored 26 victims in his more than 50 bouts. He had won 16 fights on points and gained one draw. On the down side, he had lost seven decisions, but had been floored only twice in his career. Charley had fought all the up-and-coming prospects, plus the top-rated fighters and never been counted out by any one. These statistics though, did not really tell the true story of the fellow. He was teak-tough in every department. Every opponent who fought him had their work cut out to contain him. He was an aggressive forward, bobbing and weaving type of square-on-fighter who attacked his opponents by going directly to them. He relied a great amount on his toughness to wear his foes down. New York reporters were comparing the performances of both champion and challenger in their respective fights against Harold Dade. Riley had lost his first encounter with Dade, and in the return had managed only a draw. Many critics maintained, though, he had done more than enough to gain the verdict. However, a draw against a fighter of Dade's quality was respectable. Pep, they pointed out, gave Dade a shellacking and a sound boxing lesson into the bargain.

Interest in the fight was causing the promoters to hope for a new record in receipts. The old record stood at $52,592,50, set by the heavyweight clash between the "Brown Bomber," Joe Louis and Tony Musto in 1941. No attendance record could be set, however, because Kiel Auditorium, the sight for the Pep-Riley battle, held less than the arena, which was the site for the Primo Carnera-Chuck Wiggins fight in 1933 which drew 18,130.

Reports from both training camps were that both Pep and Riley had trained hard and diligently, both looked in good shape and in tip-top condition. Riley's chief sparring partner, Ted Roberts, told the press Charley was punching like a welterweight and Pep was in for big trouble. They were ready to go into action at the drop of a hat. There were no weight problems for either man, though Pep, in his training camp in Tampa, Florida, had been wearing heavy clothing during his workouts. "Nothing to worry about, this is not unusual. Willie likes his cream cakes," Gore told observers. Miguel Acevedo was his main sparring partner on this occasion. This would be the champion's 145th contest. He had only lost twice and had that one draw.

As the fight drew nearer, so lightly was the St. Louis fighter regarded that plans were already in progress by the International Boxing Club, who were the new big power dealers in American and world boxing circles in those times and based in New York, for Pep to defend his crown against the French champion, Ray Famechon, in Madison Square Garden, in March. Lew Burston, foreign representative for the IBC, had already left America for France the day before the Pep-Riley bout with orders to sign Ray Famechon. Burston had also been told to renew the IBC contract with London promoter, Jack Solomons, for the exchange of fighters. This was a dirty, murky business. When he heard this news, Riley was not bothered in the least. "It will be me who will be defending the title against the Frenchman. I intend to be the new champion. I'll beat Pep. Let the the IBC make their plans, but they will just have to change the names," said Riley.

He was a sparkling little fellow who just did not care what the experts or newspapers said about his chances against Pep. "I'm very confident," he added. In training Gore had been coaching Pep with the emphasis on throwing the right uppercut because of the St. Louis's fighter's tendency to rush at his opponents with a square on stance. Pep was never a great puncher, but he certainly knew how to place his blows to have the maximum effect. "I won a great number of my fights with my left jab, but on this occasion Bill advised me to make use of my uppercut, bringing the power from right foot and bending the knee more.

At the two o'clock weigh-in, Pep scaled 123 and one half pounds and Riley weighed exactly the same. The official crowd was 11,115 who paid $56,905 at the box-office for the privilege of watching this world featherweight contest – and they were not disappointed. It was an exciting and very nostalgic night for the St. Louis boxing fraternity. They waited eagerly for the first bell. The first four rounds were duelled on equal terms. Charley was doing his best to live up to his "Chillin" reputation as he tried to make full use of his awesome punching power. Pep was dancing around almost playfully just poking his jab out here, throwing it there and mixing this up with hooks and lightly thrown combination punches through the middle of the St. Louis fighter. He was elegant, skill personified, which seemed to bring out the caution in Riley. Though the local fans were rooting for their own fighter and hoping that he could win the title, they could not help but admire the Hartford man.

Pep was so loose and relaxed, but also like a coiled spring when he needed to punch and move away. Referee Harry Kessler, who was a St. Louis man, had an easy fight to control with hardly any infringements from either boxer. Riley seemed baffled as to what tactics to use against the elusive champion. It was one thing to look good while sparring with someone, as Riley had done on many occasions when helping Pep prepare for other fights, but it was a completely different situation when it came to the "real" thing, a world of difference as Riley was to find to his cost. Knowing Pep's reputation for treating his hired help lightly, it was no surprise to Gore and Viscusi to watch Charley's frustration when facing the real Pep. When the fifth got underway, Pep had been mainly fighting in flurries. Riley was backing off toward the ropes where he would squat square on, throwing wild, roundhouse punches. The local fans were baffled by their man's tactics. He seemed to lack any semblance of fistic knowledge whatsoever, and was mesmerised by Pep's feinting and his scientific boxing. Pep circled Riley, stinging him with head and body shots, Charley was becoming more and more like a novice, not knowing what to do. Willie was ever patient.

A Chilling Ending

The end came quite suddenly, after one minute and five seconds of round five of the scheduled 15 rounds. The champion fired a short left hook which landed under the challenger's heart. The power of this blow took the breath out of Riley, he gasped and his facial expression gave the game away that he was hurt badly. Within a split second, Pep had dipped his body at a right angle, putting all his weight on his right foot and drove a sledge-hammer right uppercut into the game but outclassed St. Louis fighter's face. It was an immaculately delivered punch. The crunch of glove hitting bone could be clearly heard by spectators sitting ringside. When the final blow landed, Riley spun about forty five degrees to his right and fell flat on his face as if poleaxed. He lay motionless, there were loud shrieks from the crowd and great concern for the diminutive contender. His handlers jumped into the ring and pulled his mouthpiece out. It was several minutes before Charley could walk around, even then his glassy unseeing eyes were still half shut.

This was a perfectly executed punch delivered like poetry in motion, beautiful to watch-if you were not on the receiving end of course! Pep had never at any time come to danger at the eager hands of the St. Louis slugger all through the completed four rounds. It was widely expected Riley would give the champion at least a tough workout.

"What a punch. I thought Pep set him up with a right hand body punch. Then he threw that right hand punch threw the middle of Riley's defence. That was world class, what a fantastic uppercut. It has been a long, long time since I saw a punch thrown like that and the way it connected was awesome. Pep is a brilliant world champion, one of the best I have ever seen and I have been around a long time." said referee, Harry Kessler.

Reporters were glowing in their praise for the way Pep ended this contest. Then, turning to Gore, they asked him why Riley seemed puzzled by Pep's style of boxing. "He must have boxed hundreds of rounds in the gym with your guy, surely he would have known what to expect from Pep," said a reporter. Gore explained: "I have told you guys before. There's a world of difference between sparring in the gym and an actual fight. Willie never goes flat-out with his helpers anyway. He uses them mainly to polish up his boxing, like a car mechanic fine tunes a car engine. Riley must have got the wrong impression in these gym sessions with my guy. Riley boxed with a lot of other fighters in our gym, and boy he had some wars. But he could never understand how gentle his workouts with Willie were treated. And that was his biggest mistake tonight. He took that kind of thinking into the ring and you saw the result."

The climax came so quickly there was some disagreement in the discussion of the ringside observers as to precisely how the ending was made. Was it a left hook delivered before the knockout, or, a right hand thrown to the body before that lethal punch landed. That seemed to be the argument. But of one thing everyone was in full agreement, Riley took no time at all to hit the canvas, and he stayed there long after the count reached ten and out!

The Ring magazine voted Pep "Fighter of the Month" for his demolition job on the dangerous challenger. A few months later, a St. Louis journalist was talking to Pep about the brilliant way he administered the match-winning punch against Charley Riley, who this reporter believed would never suffer a knockout defeat, certainly not from the hands of such a regarded light hitter as Pep himself. Willie smiled, then continued to explain how he achieved it. "People have been asking me about my right uppercut. Well, this is a very 'funny' punch. It's a sucker's punch. If you don't time it just right, you're the sucker because you leave yourself open to the other guy's right cross or jab. I was very fortunate with this particular punch against Charley Riley. Nobody had ever knocked Charley out before. He had fought them all, the tough, the good, top bangers, smooth boxers, and out-and-out brawlers too. He was a bobbing and weaving type of fighter, very hard to contain. But seriously, I love Charley's type of fighter. Most fighters don't like meeting guys who can flatten you if they manage to tag you. But Bill Gore taught me these kind of fighters are meat and drink for boxers such as myself. To blast you out, they've first of all got to hit you. If they can't find you, your problem is solved' he used to tell me. What he meant was that I should use my speed to keep these hard hitters away from landing their bombs on me. 'But, when you make them miss, make sure you make them pay,' Bill would also say."

On the same night Willie was dispatching Riley in St. Louis, his number one challenger, Sandy Saddler, was over in Caracas, Venezuela, flattening Paulie Jackson of Pennsylvania in less than a minute and a half. Jackson had fought Pep on three occasions going the full distance each time. A short time after the Pep-Riley fight, Irwin, a Chicago promoter was staging a tournament in which all the proceeds were being donated to the "Black Charities." Mr. Irwin's previous venture, an open-air show, had flopped dismally and he lost $25,000. His latest tournament featured Sandy Saddler against Harold Dade in a joint top of the bill with Artie Towne, Sugar Ray Robinson's stablemate who was fighting Lloyd Gibson. Mr. Irwin seems to have been badly advised in his selection of bill toppers, as only Dade was from Chicago. Why he chose to ignore the likes of John Holdman, a stiff-punching heavyweight, and Clinton Bacon, who had recently defeated Archie Moore, was a mystery. Then there was another Chicago boxer whom he could have featured and helped draw the fans, the classy Freddie Dawson, a leading lightweight oozing with class. It wasn't surprising the ticket sales were slow.

In order to boost the gate the promoter came up with a new stunt. He engaged a galaxy of six world champions to box four round exhibition bouts. He agreed to pay them $2,000 or $2,500, depending on their popularity value. The Chicago boxing fans were pleased at having the chance to witness six current world champions, albeit only boxing meaningless exhibitions. But on the night of the show only 7,200 fans turned out. Ezzard Charles, the heavyweight king punched Joe Modzele around for four rounds. Former champion, Joe Louis, acted as the guest referee, and received $3,000 for his services. Jake LaMotta, the Raging Bull, the middleweight champion, played and clowned about with his sparring partner, as did Sugar Ray Robinson, the welterweight title-holder. Bamtamweight king, Manuel Ortiz showed his trickery against Chuck Wilkerson.

The sparse crowd enjoyed the workouts, but were thrilled when Willie Pep jigged down the aisle and proceeded to exhibit his brand of boxing magic, and his four rounds against the Cuban Miguel Acevedo ended much too soon for the audience, who by their hooting and hollering clearly enjoyed the four blistering rounds and wanted to see more. Sullen-faced Ike Williams, the lightweight king, was also well received as he crossed gloves with his stablemate, Arthur King. Ike threw his bolo punch and delighted the crowd with his boxing style. It was a promoter's dream to have six current world champions on his tournament. Sadly, the venture was a fistically and financial failure. The takings were only $28,000, which was $14,000 less than was required to break even for the charities share.

A few days later the newspapers were full of stories concerning Willie's next challenger. It was reported in early February that Ray Famechon had set sail for New York, his objective being a contest with the featherweight king. Famechon was hoping to emulate Eugene Criqui and Andre Routis, both of whom won the world's featherweight title for France. Interestingly Famechon had the solid backing of all the British fans, who had come to acknowledge him as by far the best nine stone fighter in Europe. Incidentally, the Frenchman should have fought Pep five months earlier in a catch-weight contest, but the fight failed to materialise for some unknown reason. Boxing observers in England commented that if Famechon hoped to beat Pep he would have to learn to close his gloves when punching. He had a tendency to flap and cuff which was very noticeable in his last contest in England when he defeated Bernard Pugh on a ten round points decision five weeks before facing Pep.

Crudeness vs Wizardry - The French Connection

"Ring wizardry, a lost art in boxing today, enabled Willie Pep, world featherweight champion, to retain his crown in this St. Patrick's Day bout in Madison Square Garden with Ray Famechon, European title-holder, making his American debut," wrote Nat Fleischer in the Ring magazine. "It was a sad-faced, crying, bewildered and befuddled challenger who left the ring asking, "What kind of champion is this who refuses to fight and runs away?"

Fleischer was spot on when he continued: "In England such an exhibition as Pep gave would be welcomed with uproarious cheers. Recently I saw a packed house at Earl's Court raise the roof off that famous arena in acclaiming the science displayed by Joey Maxim when he defeated Freddie Mills via the knockout route to win the world light-heavyweight crown. Yet Maxim's performance failed by a wide margin to equal that of Pep in the Famechon fight. But in America we have become accustomed to jeer and boo science. What the average American fan wants to see is legalised mayhem, the slugging dock type of fighting, and that's why the majority of the 12,106 fans who paid $67,141 to see Pep and Famechon, hissed and booed when Willie's hand was raised in victory."

Many boxing observers over the years have claimed Willie Pep reached his peak the night he regained the featherweight championship in that thrilling and unforgettable fight against Sandy Saddler in 1949. But there are just as many fans who firmly believe his last successful defence of the featherweight title saw Pep at his most brilliant best. And I, along with many English boxing fans, tend to agree with their sentiments, our reasons are explained in this chapter. As a challenger, Famechon did not compare to Sandy Saddler, but it was unfair to him the manner in which the press kept drumming up the feud between Saddler and Pep. That was the fight they wanted to see more than any other. The press were starting to make this fight into World War Three. And they practically dismissed the French fighter's chances as virtually nil. This though was not the case in England, where there was a great deal of interest in the forthcoming event. Next to having one of our own fighters taking part in a world championship contest, we naturally took an interest in the fortunes of those who endeavoured to wrest a title from our American friends, who had held them all, with the exception of the flyweight for a long, long time. Of course there had been short breaks, such as the brief reign of Freddie Mills, and the odd occasions when a native of France had claimed a title for a short spell, but on the whole the Americans had had it all to themselves for the best part of the present century and any attempt to prize a title from them was an event worthy of special attention.

Raymond Famechon was a worthy contender and the pride of France since he defeated his countryman Paul Dogniaux on points for the French title in 1945. He had taken on all-comers from all parts of the globe. He had fought successfully in Paris, Maubeuge, Brussels, London, Nice, Amiens, LeMans, Nottingham, Geneva, Rome, Algiers, Manchester, Madrid and Montreal. "Have gloves will travel" seemed to be his motto. This debonair Frenchman was a great favourite in England where he beat the best featherweights Britain could offer. Ray held victories over such boxing stalwarts as Danny Webb, Ben Duffy, Al Philips, Bert Jackson, Frankie Williams, Tommy Burns, Johnny Molloy, Bernard Pugh and Ronnie Clayton, all these men were creditable fighters in Europe. The French fighter had a long and impressive record.

His losses could be counted on the fingers of one hand, his consistency had been remarkable over the years. Later, while campaigning in the U.S.A. after the Pep contest, he defeated Tony Longo and the fierce-punching Charlie Riley, Archie Devino and Pep's stalemate Glen

Flanagan. In between he had knocked out the useful Spaniard Louis de Santiago in three rounds in Madrid. In Britain, Famechon was acclaimed as a superb boxer, fast and accurate in his punching with a sound knowledge of ringcraft and footwork. Against a certain type of opponent Ray would look no fancy-dan boxer, but a sturdy, square-shouldered, robust, hustling knockout puncher. Ray demoralised his opponents with his grit, toughness and durability. He also possessed a splendid left jab, which he planned to use to telling effect against Pep. His biggest fault was a tendency to hit with the open glove, and this was a weakness that would prove his downfall against the world champion.

The American public had little doubt that their champion would beat the Frenchman. In preparation for the Famechon bout, Willie boxed twice in February. He outboxed Roy Andrews over ten rounds in Boston. A few days later he was in Florida where he was matched with New York's Jimmy Warren at Miami's Dinner Key Auditorium. There was an attendance of around 4,000 who paid over $10,000. It was a listless contest though Pep won every one of the ten rounds. He had several chances to nail the New Yorker, but seemed content to merely stroll through the bout. Afterwards the Miami Boxing Commission fined Warren 250 dollars for his inadequate display, while Pep was fined 500 dollars.

The Florida newspapers were questioning why the commission sanctioned matches that included class performers like Pep against such inferior opposition, and contests staged in Florida between Sugar Ray Robinson against Al Mobley and Rocky Graziano versus Joe Curio back to the Pep versus Famechon contest.

At first there seemed little interest in the Pep versus Famerchon fight and ticket sales were going slowly, although the upcoming championship match had economic implications in France. Coca-Cola was starting to sell worldwide, but the wine growers were up in arms because for centuries the French kids had been brought up to drink wine, and now they were drinking Coke. The agency that had the Coca-Cola account in France must have thought Famechon was a certainty to defeat Pep, and they were prematurely prepared with a case of Coke in the Frenchman's dressing room. The idea was that after he won, they would have pictures splashed on all the front pages of every newspaper throughout France of the new world champion celebrating with a Coke in his hand. A reporter related this fact to Pep who smiled, and replied: "I didn't know that."

Boastful At The Weigh-In

This kind of hype helped attract a fair-sized crowd. The champion was the betting favourite at the high closing odds of 1 to 6, and he made the figures stand up with the greatest efficiency. At the weigh-in conducted by Eddie Eagan, the New York boxing Commissioner, the champion weighed 123-3/4-lbs (8st-12-3/4lbs). Famechon came in at 125-lbs (8st-13lbs). Recalling events of this time Pep said: "Famechon was kind of fresh (boastful) at the weigh-in. Eddie Eagan was explaining our rules to him. Eagan told him he couldn't spin a man. The Frenchman just reached out and grabbed me.I figured I can't fight him here, but I'll see what I can do in the ring. I think Famechon thought I was going to get into the ring and trade punch-for-punch, maybe that's the way they fight where he comes from, but not here. He looked tremendously strong and powerful."

I was told that he was supposed to have had hundreds of amateur fights, plus sixty pro' fights. They said he had fought every style there is. Well he had not fought anyone who had my style, and unfortunately for him he was about to fight my style of boxing that evening."

The referee was Ruby Goldstein and the two judges Charley Shortell and Jack O'Sullivan. From the moment the bell rang to start the contest, Willie was up on his toes. The Frenchman came forward trying to connect with his punches on the frail, puny-looking champion. The first six rounds saw Pep breezing through his challenger's punches using a good straight left jab which he doubled and trebled, then switching right hands to Famechon's body, hardly receiving a punch in return. It looked a fight which would go the distance. The French fighter was showing himself as a game, tough opponent with plenty of spirit and proving to be an extremely strong and robust ringman. He was in the finest physical condition of his life, but it must be said on this night these were the only things in his favour. When he did manage to penetrate Pep's defence, he, exhibited a total lack of punching power, though the English and European boxers would strongly refute that statement. His hitting though, on this night, never once bothered the champion. In truth, Famechon looked very crude, or, it should be said Pep's brilliance made him look this way. When he tried to fight on the inside, his lack of knowledge was so limited that he permitted himself to get into the most grotesque poses when he attempted to match the canny and wily Pep.

Towards the end of the sixth round Willie caught the European flush on the jaw with a whipping sharp left hook which bounced of his chin. This blow sent the challenger reeling backwards across the ring. Pep was so confident his punch had knocked Famechon down, that he moved into a neutral corner turning his back. But a count was not forthcoming and in a few seconds the surprised champion found himself the target for an avalanche of Famechon blows. This was the only round in which Pep came close to scoring a knockout. For the remainder of the contest it was Willie scoring points. It followed a familiar pattern with Famechon walking forward trying hard to land his haymakers, but not getting anywhere near his target while Pep was using his snappy left jab. Ray had his moments with the 13th round being his best, but he kept trying hard and had one or two chances, but they were few and far between. It was the champion all the way. He was cruising to victory, contrived almost exclusively by the use of his immaculate left jabbing, complimented by his lightning fast footwork and his savvy at close quarters. So seldom did he use the right hand that as late as the 11th round a fan shouted from the galleries: "Hey, Willie, what did you do with your right hand. Leave it in Hartford?" Without a doubt this was a scintillating performance from Pep.

Despite some of the fans discontentment, his movements were a sight to behold. He made Famechon look like a very ordinary boxer. At times Pep was at the back of his opponent, then patting the Frenchman on his backside, side-stepping to the left, then ducking to his right. The crowd, though, still wanted to know what was wrong with his right hand? Lou Viscusi explained there were no problems at all. It did look as if Willie coasted throughout the contest, but his manager said Pep had no complaints and no injury whatsoever. He was a convincing and clear winner at the conclusion of the 15 rounds.

Was Pep in decline? This was the question asked by reporters sitting at ringside. A majority of the crowd soundly booed Pep at the finish of the bout. But so decisive was his victory that Goldstein gave the champion ten rounds with two rounds for Famechon and two even. Judge O'Sullivan scored nine rounds for the champion, three for the invader, with three even. The other official gave it to Pep by 12 rounds with only three to the game, but outclassed challenger. The general consensus amongst the press at ringside was Willie was an overwhelming winner by 12 rounds to 3.

If Pep was so brilliant in this contest against Famechon, why then was he booed and jeered? Well Nat Fleischer answered that question quite clearly. The truth of the matter was simply that the American boxing fans had begun to take these absorbing boxing displays from Pep for granted. They did not appreciate how dangerous and highly regarded the Frenchman was in Europe. There were of course the usual rumours which were being passed around by the pressmen, that Pep was avoiding a return fight with Saddler. This was most certainly not the case. The truth of the matter was that Viscusi was holding out for the money he and Willie were owed from a previous Pep-Saddler fight. That surely wasn't being frightened as the critics claimed. Mr. Lou had explained on many occasions to everybody who would listen, that as soon as he received the money owed to them, a date for the return with Saddler would be announced.

Boxing fans in England were shaking their heads in disbelief when hearing the news of Pep's easy and convincing victory over the Ray Famechon. They were amazed at the ease with which the champion had handled a fighter they had conceived as the assassin of British featherweights. And yet here in the Madison Square Garden ring, Famechon was being made to look inept and foolish and nothing more than a strong, courageous, but limited fighter. Some journalist claim this was the contest where Pep was at his brilliant best. Speedy footwork, lovely defensive skills, side-to-side movement, crisp punching from every angle, head movement which resulted in blows being evaded to within inches, lateral movement, ducking, bobbing and weaving-all were displayed in this contest.

All in all, Pep's performance once again outlined the noble art of self-defence. He was breathtaking as he made this defence of his crown one of his easiest bouts of his long and illustrious career. However, the main bone of contention was the fans dissatisfaction which seemed to be that they were unhappy the champion had failed to produce a knockout. It had to be remembered Famechon had taken part in 61 professional bouts without ever being on the canvas. This was the Frenchman's first contest on American soil, though he would in later years, campaign very successfully in the States. The general opinion, though, was that the little Hartford boxing master had reached his peak in regaining his title from Saddler and he was now on the wane. Yet for a man who was constantly fighting in major events, it was an amazing exercise in self-preservation which spoke volumes for the fighter's athleticism and his awareness. Survival against such terrifying fighters as were around in Pep's time over three minutes, has to be down to something more than just plain luck, after all he had taken part in a 150 contests and suffered only two defeats!

The morning after the fight the newspapers tore Pep to pieces for his inability to score a knockout and demanded he should now face the fearsome Saddler. They ignored the fact that Famechon had never before been stopped, knocked out or been on the floor. So why did they expect Pep to be the first boxer to knock him out? Tony Canzoneri, the former featherweight and lightweight champion of the world, was a ringside spectator for the Famechon fight. When asked for his observations, he said he had mixed feelings about the fight. He told reporters he thought Pep was very smart and clever, but added: "He's so weak. He should have flattened the French guy." Tony made some other sarcastic comments which seemed to be tinged with a touch of jealously. It was a well known fact that Canzoneri had lost millions of dollars which he earned during his fighting days, he was broke, and was now a member of a night club act which starred comedian Joey Adams. One thing was certain, Willie Pep would never have criticised another champion the way Tony Canzoneri had done about him.

Another ringside observer was Johnny Dundee, the former world featherweight king. Dundee was impressed by Willie's speed and clever feinting and his impeccable boxing throughout the entire 15 rounds. Johnny was much more specific in his assessment of the Pep versus Famechon contest and pointed out that in his opinion the Frenchman would have made it a much better fight if he had only traded left jabs with Pep instead of trying to knock out the champion. "Mind you, he couldn't do that, because he couldn't hit Pep," he said. Bill Gore shook his head when he heard what the critics were saying about his champion. "Tony Canzoneri was a great champion in his day, and equally, Willie is a great champion today. His display against Famechon was truly boxing at its best. Hit your opponent-and don't get hit back."

Talking to me in his home some 44 years after the Famechon contest Pep said: "It was my footwork which enabled me to beat Famechon. I forgot about driving the car and walked every chance I got. Let me tell you, it all paid off. You have to train just right for each fight. For example, though I did the usual amount of roadwork for every contest which was between two and four miles, incidentally I ran a few times with Rocky Marciano, he did eight or nine miles. But I emphasised it more. I didn't want to leave my strength on the road. But at the same time I had to be careful not to overdo it." Pep described Famechon, as a 'double tough' fighter, who bobbed and weaved and who walked right toward him, throwing punches all the time. Willie said the Frenchman was strong as a bull and he knew he had to keep away from him. He boxed him exactly as he and Bill Gore had planned. He flitted all around him-even at the back of him-jabbing away at every chance he saw. Famechon's trouble was that he had a big puncher's footwork, he kept coming in that's all he knew just walk straight in on Pep. Well, Willie was not about to let him take him apart, he boxed and moved all night. He felt perfect, right to the end of the 15th round. "Yet it wasn't an easy fight for me," added Pep. "I had to keep moving the whole time, in and out, from side to side...It takes a lot of practice. The idea is never get your feet tangled up. He would get set to land a punch and I would jab him then move. I will never forget it. I have never seen a fighter as frustrated as Famechon. He was punching the air. I had no intention of getting hit," he concluded.

The Coca Cola company were upset with the result. The reporter who gave Pep the story about the Coca Cola connection then went on to say he was present in Famechon's room after the bout, and said the French champion was dazed and in a world of his own and with his head down looking at the floor and muttering in French "Pep had no pride in being a world champion. I could not hit him with any punches, because I could not find him." The agency officials were like mourners at a wake, and there was a big crate of Coca Cola over in the corner, unopened.

This was Pep's last victory as world featherweight champion. It was sad and many people were predicting the demise of the "Will-'o'-the-Wisp." It was hard to understand their thinking. Here was a champion who had just beaten the European titleholder in a canter; given as fine a boxing exhibition as one could wish to see, yet he had received a hostile reception from his own countrymen.

Ruby Goldstein, one of New York's best referees and an ex-fighter himself said in a magazine article : "I won't stick my chin out and say Willie Pep is the greatest featherweight of all time. I could run into many contradictions. Johnny Kilbane, Johnny Dundee, Henry Armstrong, Kid Kaplan and Sandy Saddler were all great, too, and it's difficult to make comparisons, particularly when you get into different eras. Pep was extremely clever and fleetfooted. Talking some time later, Goldstein waxed lyrical about the Hartford boxing master and said in his opinion Pep's fight with

Ray Famechon was a cracking boxing contest. "Pep was really elusive. He moved in front of the French fighter, in the back of him, right side, left side and once or twice when Pep was against the ropes he got down so low to avoid punches that Famechon came close to falling out of the ring. The bout was one-sided, I agree. The thing that lingers with me was at the final bell, while awaiting the scores of the officials, Famechon was directly facing Pep and dancing up and down. I've seen such actions numerous times, but this seems to happen when the fight is close and each boxer is anxiously awaiting the decision. Famechon seemed to have a look of astonishment instead of anxiety. Perhaps he had never fought anyone with the style of Pep. I'm certain if he made a statement it would be: 'How do you hit a guy like this'. Pep was a speedster and a ring general, a truly magical boxer."

Lou Viscusi, talking about the disappointing turn out of fans for the fight said: "Television was the problem. All the bars in and around New York were packed with St Patrick's night celebrations, viewing the fight for nothing."

The critics were not to know of course that Famechon would go on to defeat some of their toughest featherweights, for example, less than a month after being trounced by Pep, Famechon had two fights in America where he outpointed Tony Longo in Waterbury, nine days later he outpointed Pep's old challenger, Charley Riley. He knocked out Luis de Santiago in three rounds in Madrid, before going back to the States for a further six contests of which he won five and reversing his only defeat.

In April 1953, he would come to England, where he dished out another drubbing to our champion Ronnie Clayton, stopping him after five ferocious rounds. And what about the Frenchman's absorbing, thrilling battle against the hitherto unbeaten "Black Flash" Roy Ankrah which was held on a glorious summer's evening on the Notts County Football Ground? There was no doubt that the Famechon versus Ankrah contest was the finest featherweight attraction to take place in Europe for many years. It aroused worldwide interest and was dubbed a final eliminator for the world championship. It was also regarded as one of the most thrilling bouts of 1953.

Fans stood and cheered both men all the way back to their dressing rooms after Famechon won a very close decision and put himself in line to meet the champion Sany Saddler. Famechon did eventually meet Saddler on 25 October, 1954, at the Palais de Sport in Paris. It turned out to be a complete mis-match, Saddler brutalised the Frenchman in five blood-filled rounds. The ring looked like a slaughter house and Saddler was accused of using every foul in the book as he cut the brave Famechon to ribbons.

A couple of years after the Pep versus Famechon contest, C.W. Herring, the Paris correspondent for the Boxing and Wrestling magazine, talking about the Pep versus Famechon title fight said in his opinion Famechon had been given his chance against Pep in rather peculiar circumstances. Mr. Herring claimed that the Frenchman had almost been taken from the boat on his arrival in New York and pushed into the ring with Willie without any special preparation. It should be noted however that Famechon had defeated Bernard Pugh in Liverpool on 2 February 1950, and on 17 March he fought Pep. Famechon's nephew, Johnny Fanechon, won the world featherweight title in 1969.

Pep had five more bouts before his next defence, winning them with ease. Art Llanos was flattened in two rounds in Hartford. Pep had loyal supporters who stayed with him through the good and bad times, and he loved boxing in front of them. Tough New Yorker Terry Young was the second of his five victims in another ten round contest held in Milwaukee's "New Arena." Young had fought Saddler in 1948, their fight was a battle royal and a never ending foul-ridden spectacle held in New York, both fighters were guilty of rule-breaking and having a "war" before Saddler won on a stoppage in the last round. Pep won a unanimous decision over Young, throwing the boxing manual at him. Young kept coming forward all the time, walking into repeated rapier-like left jabs followed by perfectly delivered right hands which were rocking his head back on his shoulders. In the final round, so confused with his own inability to subdue Pep, Young turned mauler and wrestler but it was to no avail. Pinky Mitchell who described himself as the former world Junior welterweight champion, commented: "The great Willie Pep left little doubt in the minds of the 6,500 fans who paid $24,636, here in Wisconsin, that he is the nation's number one fighting man, by the masterful way he in which he handled the nine-and-a-half-pound heavier Terry Young. Young an aggressive gamester was in there pitching to the final bell. The decision after a most enjoyable fight was unanimously to Pep.

Pep followed the Young victory by clearly outpointing another Saddler victim Bobby Timpson, in the Outdoor Arena in Hartford. It was an enjoyable ten round workout for the champion. Willie, as the crowd expected dominated the contest from start to finish, though in the opening session, Timpson landed a cracking right on the unsuspecting world champion's jaw. After that pep got down to work and the Youngstown, Ohio, fighter used negative spoiling tactics which certainly didn't endear him to the fans who were appreciating Willie's masterly skills. Pep was totally and majestically outclassing these fighters with such ease that anyone not knowing the true credentials of these opponents, might tend to believe they were what the American's called "bums," but this certainly was not the case.

Married Again

Flushed with his success and good publicity from the Terry Young fight, Willie started courting again, this time it was another Hartford girl, a real beauty named Delores Von Frenckell. It was love at first sight. So anxious were the couple to get married that Pep forgot that the wedding day coincided with a contest booked against Bobby Bell in Washington the same day. This brought him trouble with the Boxing Commission. After failing to turn up for the contest he was suspended until he had fulfiled his contract with the promoter. "I guess we'll have to postpone the honeymoon," Willie laughingly told his new bride. "Don't worry we'll celebrate after the fight." They held a belated wedding reception in their hotel afterwards.

It certainly was not an auspicious start to wedded bliss and Delores soon discovered her man would be rarely at home due to his boxing commitments. If the new Mrs. Pep thought her troubles were over, she was mistaken because they were just beginning. Seven days after beating Bell on points over ten rounds, her new husband packed his kit, gave her a swift kiss, and was off to Scranton for another ten round contest against one Proctor Heinold who he outscored and outclassed over the full distance. An easy workout in which he sharpened his body and reflexes. But, his reign as the world featherweight king was nearing its completion. He was about to face his outstanding contender, Sandy Saddler, in the fight the American public demanded.

A few years later, while reminiscing about three of his past wives and his bug for gambling, Willie laughed about his situation and about how much money it had cost him overall. He would lend money out to almost anybody who gave him a hard luck story. Talking about his wives he said: "I guess I was unlucky in my choice of wives. Over the years they cost me plenty. My first wife, Mary Woodcock, wanted to be a singer and she couldn't sing, he said wistfully. My second wife Delores Von Frenckell, was obsessed with dancing and wanted to become a dancer but she couldn't dance. My third wife Cynthia Rhodes, cost me nothing but peace of mind...At least she didn't want me for my money, because by that time I didn't have anything left."

Pep was being bombarded from all sides for his side-tracking of Sandy Saddler who was the obvious contender for his title. Well over 12 months had elapsed since the Hartford wizard regained his crown from the Harlem hard man. But this sort of situation was nothing new, it took place in the old days. If a leading contender was able to get a champion into the ring without waiting years he was indeed a lucky man. But unlike the old days, strict commission supervision and regulations made sure that defaulting champions toe the line usually within a six months period, whereas years previous Pep could have simply forgot all about Sandy Saddler. Another dodge which many old-time champions used to their advantage but which was completely out of order was the "colour line," it was the custom of some of the past champions immediately after winning a world title to make a public announcement that this was to be the case. Whereas in the 1940s a champion coming up with a similar dictum would be stripped of his title on the spot. Willie Pep had never refused to box any fighter his manager matched him against, no matter what colour. It was a fact that Pep fought dozens of black fighters throughout his long career. The critics of Pep and his manager didn't know of the skulduggery which had taken place apertaining to the money which was owed to him previously.

My Kidney Punches Made Him Quit

It was about this period that Pep formed a very close friendship with Rocky Marciano. They were more often than not found in each others company in Florida, enjoying themselves while sampling the good life. Willie commenced his training schedule in preparation for the Saddler return. Once in training, the two fighters would go their separate ways. No matter how much boxing followers appreciate a contest of wits and skill between two scientific exponents of boxing, what whetted the fans' appetite more than anything else was when a boxer fights a slugger, especially if the two men are of championship calibre and also, if it happens to be a grudge match. Well they were granted their wish when Willie Pep signed to defend his title against Sandy Saddler. The date was September 1950, the venue the Yankee Stadium in New York. Pep was to face the fighter who he had fought in a bitter, but thrilling 15 round battle only 18 months previously, arch-enemy, Sandy Saddler. Their last fight was a classic and which Pep himself described as: "The greatest fight of my life!"

This was the return match the boxing scribes had been clamouring for, it was also the fight the boxing fans eagerly wanted to watch. It was the third clash between the cultured flashy boxing professor, Willie Pep and the sepia slayer in boxing boots, Sandy Saddler. This confrontation needed no hype or build-up but it would receive massive newspaper coverage just the same. The demand for tickets was once again overwhelming. This was the reason the promoters had chosen a different and much bigger venue than Madison Square Garden. W.C. Heinz, writing in the Ring magazine in October, 1950 said: "If, on the night Willie won back his title on 11 February, 1949 they had made another return between the two for a New York ball park for the next summer they would have drawn $500,000 through the gates. These two are, as they say, merely featherweights, and they would have set a new record for men smaller than heavyweights, and they would have all gone home rich. But they didn't do it because Lou Viscusi wanted $100,000 guaranteed for Pep, and Charley Johnston wanted the same amount for Saddler and the same deal he gave Pep, which in their second fight was 30 per cent each. He finally agreed to 15 per cent, as against Pep's 45 per cent, just to prove how eager he was to get Saddler another crack at the champion. Johnston took less because he believed Pep was ready to be taken.

There was a complete blackout in force by the promoters. No radio or television. It was this which resulted in the massive turnout of fans. Once again the record gates and record receipts proved that the fans would still support boxing if they believed that a fight was worth it, and when they know that they can not watch the fight on television or get a blow by blow description on the radio.

There was a great deal of bad blood and unfriendly feeling between both camps. The feud was well and truly in evidence by now, due mainly to the financial aspects of the fight. The Saddler camp thought they were being treated like the poor relations again. What they seemed to fail to understand was the drawing capacity of the two fighters. Pep would bring thousands of supporters from Hartford, while Sandy would struggle to draw a few hundred from Harlem. The ring officials were referee, Ruby Goldstein, and the two judges were Frank Forbes and Arthur Susskind. These three were very experienced ring officials. And they would be needed if the pre-fight publicity was to be believed. Saddler said: "Pep has been deliberately avoiding facing me again. He has been fighting everybody and nobody. He wouldn't fight me because he knows that I'll hammer him and take my title back." Was it true? Well, a great deal of what was said was newspaper talk. One thing was crystal clear though, and that was Pep and

Saddler were now, not the best of friends.

The two gladiators had trained diligently for this eagerly awaited clash. Because of the difference in their purse money, there was certainly a great deal of needle and bad blood between the pair. It was quite evident for all to see during their training routines. After all the hype and the publicity had ceased it was down to these two superb craftsmen to do the business. By the time Pep and Saddler made their way into the ring in the Yankee Stadium, there were officially 38,781 paying spectators sitting down to watch this fight. This was incredible. $262,150 was taken in receipts at the box-office. If the champions of modern day boxing could draw gates like this, then boxing would be in a very healthy state indeed. And remember, these two were mere featherweights. Pep though, was the big drawing card, of that there was no doubt. He was highly popular throughout the States.

Once the contest got underway the fans were treated to superb boxing skills from the "Will-'o'-the-Wisp" he was up on his toes, dancing around the sullen faced challenger. Both exchanged jabs, but it was Pep's trusty left hand which was the faster. He was mixing his jabs with short, stinging right hands which were finding their target like radar on Saddler's chin. Willie was hitting the dark brooding challenger repeatedly. However, Sandy would not be denied. He was stalking forward throwing that power laden left uppercut through the middle of Pep's body. There was more action in these first two rounds than you would get from half a dozen heavyweight contests.

This was looking like a repeat of their last contest. Though Sandy was unable to inflict as much damage as he had done in their two previous battles, so certain were the betting boys that age and ring warfare had caught up with the Hartford warrior that they forecast doom for him. But after these opening two sessions they were beginning to change their minds! What the gamblers had failed to take into consideration was the cleverness and guile of Pep. He was also, at the age of 28 still very nimble on his feet and capable of making his opponent miss their target with such ease. Nat Fleischer, editor of the Ring magazine said: "Pep's movement stamps him as one of the truly greats of all time, only Sugar Ray Robinson compares with him in ring ability."

The large audience was enjoying the tension of the hostilities between these two bitter rivals. Pep had the old zip and sparkle and his brain was working like a machine, making no mistakes. He planned his battle and carried out his plans to perfect order. So perfect a fighting machine, he hardly gave Saddler a chance, except occasionally, as in the third and seventh rounds. The crowd could see clearly what Saddler's intentions were, it showed on his brooding face. He wanted to drill this dancing moth in front of him into the canvas. The night air was brisk and the swishing of Sandy's blows could be heard very clearly in the bleachers. Pep had his man dizzy at times by the use of his dazzling speed of hand and foot. This title fight was living up to all expectations in every way.

The third round was boxed again in a speedy manner with the champion boxing on the retreat, but using whipping counter punches at the oncoming fellow in front of him. This was beautiful stuff, none of the hustle and bustle which one expects from watching a heavyweight battle. This was vintage wine by comparison. Then, all in a brisk flash, Saddler threw a wicked curving long left hook. Bang! It connected on the champion's jaw, putting him down for a count of nine. The crowd were on their feet. Was this a repeat of their first encounter when the copper-haired Saddler flattened Pep? But after shaking the cobwebs from his brain, Pep got to his feet. He was more shocked than hurt. He then proceeded to show the fans why he was not only one of boxings finest champions, but also one of the bravest. After the knockdown, Pep gave as skilled performance as one would could ever hope to witness. The challenger's confidence soared after the knockdown. He cut loose more frequently and took more risks, trying to corner the champion at every opportunity. He ripped thunderous blows into the wiry champion's ribs and another devastating power-packed right hand followed through Pep's defence knocking his head back on his shoulders. But amazingly Willie fought back with a two-handed salvo of hard punches to both head and body, before skipping away again much to the astonishment of the Saddler fans.

Pep gave a masterful display of scientific boxing and hitting. In-fact, he duplicated the excellent performance of their second meeting in which he regained his title. The lanky challenger was losing control by searching for a knockout. There was cheering and shouting from all sides, but Pep was as cool as ice. Willie made his man miss often, so that Johnston was screaming at his fighter to slow down and pick his punches, but his advice was not heeded by Saddler. Had the champion been able to continue the pace which he had set from the start through to the sixth round, there would have been only one winner, that was clear enough for anybody to see. Pep was a master boxer, he was a few classes above the challenger. He was blessed with that something special which separates boxers like him from the rest, and all the indications were that he could continue. One incident in the fifth stood out in the spectators minds when Pep as he ducked a murderous left hook which fairly whistled past his chin, took two steps backwards, rested against the ropes, then grasped Saddler's left shoulder and sent him sprawling almost out of the ring. This angered Sandy. It was his inability to get Pep to stand still which bewildered him. He did not seem to be able to cope with Pep's brand of artistry.

Saddler was forever stalking his prey, ever willing to unload his punches. Strong and sturdy, he was more than willing to trade toe to toe with Pep. At times he was outdone in class and was made to look like a raw beginner. Though throwing bundles of blows he did not connect as often as he fired. He did, however, open a cut over the champion's left eye which brought blood flowing.

Saddler was also one of those special breed of fighters who happen to come along once in a fight fan's life. He was completely different to Pep in that whereas Willie traded on those smooth ring skills in which he excelled, Saddler dealt in violence and a style of fighting which was at times not pretty to watch, though nevertheless effective. It was said fighters such has Rocky Marciano were dirty and rough. It was a fact Rocky would do almost anything in order to win his fights. It's true Marciano would most certainly never have won any Sunday school prizes for his good behaviour between the ropes! But this fellow Saddler made Rocky look like a choir boy in comparison when it came to the rough stuff. He was the meanest of them all. He put the likes of Fullmer, Graziano, Basilio and the rest in the shade when it came down to ring manners.

In the fourth, fifth and sixth rounds, the defending champion surprised the crowd by his resilience and courage. He took these rounds clearly by peppering his opponent with the left jab, then hooking to the body besides landing effectively to the jaw. He did some spinning and twisting in those rounds which caused Saddler to retaliate when the opportunity presented itself. In these rounds this remarkable little champion was at his most effective. He outsmarted, outspeeded, outpointed and outclassed his foe. His blows were much more forceful, and he was hitting more solidly, jabbing straight and true, often sending five, six, or seven punches in rapid succession. Then calmly stepping back, while Saddler, the big puncher, was unable to land his wallops on Pep. At times the master boxer made a sucker out of his hard-hitting challenger, whose reputation as a one punch destroyer was second to none.

There was only one winner as the contest moved into the seventh round. And it wasn't Sandy Saddler, that's for sure. Pep started this session by using his immaculate left jab to the face and eyes of Saddler. But suddenly the ever dangerous ex-champion lashed out with a left hook which caught the champion in the solar-plexus. The punch thudded home. The crowd at ringside exhaled and let out a gasp! The venom of this blow almost doubled Pep in half. Three more punches landed in rapid succession. Pep was hurt, it was visible from his facial expression. Willie seemed to have weathered the storm as he had done previously. He went back to his fine boxing again, finding his target accurately. But just before the bell rang to end the seventh round, the whipcord punching of Saddler again found its mark. After 20 minutes of fighting with perhaps eight-hundred or more punches thrown by Pep, he threw another punch, a right cross but it missed. Before Willie could bring his hand back, the Halemite fired a terrific right hand shot under the Hartford warrior's kidney area. Again, this shot brought forth a gasp from the champion and he quickly fell into a clinch. He was now hurt more severely than in the previous attack. He hung on, grabbing Sandy's left arm in a vice like grip. This didn't stop Saddler, because with his free hand he was wailing away at Pep. His kidney took the full force of the blow, which transmitted the shock right through his body. It was as if his whole central nervous system shut down.

The ordinary man, even an ordinary fighter, might have lain there with neither breath nor shame. "When a fighter gets hit with a good body punch such as my guy took it does them more damage than a shot they take on the chin. A boxer cannot build muscle around his short rib, no one can," said Gore. As the bell sounded both fighters were grappling and twisting each other. Saddler had Pep's left arm pinned and bent at an awkward angle. He bent the champion's arm backwards before referee Ruby Goldstien could break them apart. Pep walked back to his corner, it was reported in several newspapers the following day, without any indication of pain or any kind of injury. He slumped down on his stool, placed his hand over his stomach. There were some frantic moments in Pep's corner, then suddenly came the news from Viscusi to Goldstein that: "The fight is over. My man has dislocated his shoulder," he said.

Pep was now shorn of his title when he failed to answer the bell for the commencement of round eight. Saddler was happy but annoyed at Pep's excuse for ending the action, stood up and shouted across the ring: "Dislocated shoulder?...Nuts. It was my kidney punches which made him quit." Charley Johnston, screamed out: "It was those solar plexus wallops which did the trick. I kept telling Sandy to keep digging those shots down below. I could see from Pep's discomfort that he didn't like taking these punches."

What Happened?

What really happened in this fight? Did Pep feign injury? Or had he just had enough for this particular night? The fight had taken an unexpected twist after the sixth round got underway. Pep was out in front and boxing majestically. Saddler's blows to Pep's kidney's changed events. There were plenty of accusations. It was said that because he had received his biggest ever purse of $93,000 and knowing there would indeed be a fourth meeting between him and the 24-year-old new champion, Pep had decided to take the easy option and quit on his stool. When the ending came, the champion was well ahead on points. Each of the three officials had him leading. Goldstein had it four to Pep, two for Saddler with one even. Forbes had the same tally as the referee, while Susskind scored it for Pep by five rounds to two. But remember, this was a 15 round contest, and Saddler had been connecting with those rib-bending body-shots and doing untold damage to the champion in the two rounds prior to the ending. The damage those kind of blows achieve is not visible to the human eye. However, the recipient of these punches certainly knows the amount of damage they are doing to his body because of the amount of excruciating pain he is left in.

The majority of boxing writers sat at ringside had Pep out in front by five rounds, with one round to Sandy and one even round. Because of his failure to fight to the finish, Pep was accused by the press and a great number of ringside fans of a lack of courage by quitting on his stool, claiming the shoulder dislocation. "Pep was winning the contest in everybody's tally prior to the abrupt interruption of the hostilities. Yet thousands of fans left the home of the New York Yankee's in doubt as to the real cause of Pep's actions by retiring in his corner," reported the Ring magazine.

Viscusi made the assertion that his fighter's injury had been caused by foul tactics employed by Saddler. Yet no official protest was filed by the Pep camp. Charges of roughness had been hurled by each boxer in all three of their fights. Was Willie really injured or, was he as Saddler claimed, frightened of taking more of those body shots which were causing him so much discomfort?

Saddler was scathing in his attack on Pep: "Pep stuck his finger in my left eye in the very first round. After that, I couldn't see properly for two rounds," he claimed.

Was there a contract for a fourth meeting between these two arch-rivals? Well the answer was yes! It was certainly true the contract called for a fourth bout in the event that their third contest was sensational, or, warranted another match. Harry Markson, managing director of the International Boxing Club, announced that it was already agreed the I.B.C. would stage the fourth encounter, but this time the fight would be staged at Madison Square Garden or the Polo Grounds in New York. The Yankee Stadium affair certainly warranted such a return engagement and one which it was believed would, if held in Madison Square Garden, set a new indoor record for a title match, judging by the keen rivalry and the interest shown by the fistically minded public in these two fighters.

Thousands of British boxing followers upon reading newspaper reports of the third battle between Pep and Saddler, and later watching the Pathe Newsreel film of the fight on cinema's throughout the country, were puzzled by the way the referee allowed the two fighters, especially Saddler, to use several kidney punches without issuing a warning to either boxer. The kidney punch was regarded as a foul blow under British rules and a boxer using this illegal blow could be warned by the referee, or, in most cases, instantly disqualified. Though it must be stressed in America this punch was not regarded as a foul blow! Meanwhile there was talk that Saddler might forfeit his newly won featherweight title and try to wrest the lightweight crown from the head of the champion, Ike Williams. If Sandy had fought Williams and beaten him, he would have be forced by the rules of the New York State Athletic Commission to relinquish his featherweight crown despite his return bout contract with Pep. And under the National Boxing Association rules he would have been stripped of his title the moment he signed for the lightweight championship bout.

World War Four

Three months after losing his championship to Saddler in their third epic battle, Viscusi and Gore set out to show the star of their stable, Willie Pep, how beating Sandy Saddler could be easily achieved...if he stayed strictly to their guidelines and did not let himself get involved in another roughhouse, trading blow-for-blow. It was common knowledge throughout boxing circles that, later in 1951, these two bitter rivals were going to cross gloves for a fourth and final confrontation, with Saddler's world featherweight crown up for grabs. But Pep's brain trust were already thinking and planning their strategy for that event. Lou Viscusi said: "Willie and Sandy, according to certain New York writers, hated the sight of each other. They weren't close buddies, but they were professionals. The reporters fuelled any kind of 'bad-blood' which existed between both camps. These guys were intent on making these two fighters detest each other. Myself and Bill Gore resented the implications which both Saddler and his manager, Johnston, had been spouting to the newspapers; saying Willie was scared and rather than go down fighting like a true champion in their last fight. He took the easy way out by quitting on his stool. This was absolute nonsense!"

On 6 December 1950, in Detroit, Sandy Saddler was matched with Pep's stablemate, the unbeaten St. Paul featherweight, Del Flanagan, who was of course managed by Viscusi and trained by Bill Gore. Flanagan was a slick boxer and good mover. He had helped Pep prepare for a great number of his fights over the past couple of years. Bill Gore, Pep's mentor and guru, was perplexed as to why Willie had made such hard work of his three fights against Saddler. "Willie has never had trouble with similar fighters like Saddler before. He has fought equally awkward guys with Saddler's style of fighting on many occasions in the past without much problem I think Sandy gets under his skin," he said. It was Gore's idea of having Flanagan box the world champion, Saddler. Sandy was unconcerned about the prospect of facing Pep's stablemate. As far as he was concerned, all opponents were the same. They were out to beat him, and he made it clear he had no intention whatsoever of letting them accomplish this. But he was in for a shock on the night he faced the 22-year-old Flanagan. He walked into a trap set by Pep's camp.

Del had been a very interested spectator at all three Pep-Saddler fights and had studied Saddler diligently. He strongly fancied his chances of beating the long-legged Harlemite. Flanagan was undefeated in 49 professional fights. When the Master of Ceremonies introduced the two fighters, Del was cheered loudly, while in contrast the champion was hissed and booed lustily. What followed was a mugging for Saddler. The rangy St. Paul boxer was moving in every direction, circling to his right, turning to his left, twisting, turning, and never standing still for a brief moment. The frustration was etched on Saddler's face. The champion was stalking forward with bad intentions, but he was jabbed silly. Ringsiders commented Flanagan was boxing like a carbon copy of his hero, Willie Pep. It has to be said had Flanagan been boxing any other fighter other than Saddler, and he had boxed in this manner "he" would have been loudly booed and jeered. But because of the physical advantages he held over other featherweights, and his no holds barred style of fighting, Sandy was perceived as a villain and a dirty fighter by the majority of fans.

Referee Clarence Rosen was kept very busy throughout the ten rounds. It was unfair the way Saddler was constantly booed by the fans throughout the fight. Several times tempers became frayed as Viscusi jumped on the ring apron protesting to the referee to take sterner action against Saddler for various infringements of the rules. Johnston, Sandy's manager, would jump up and down screaming at the official to take no notice of Viscusi. At the end of ten hard, brutal rounds, Flanagan was declared the winner. The

Pep camp were overjoyed. Flanagan had hardly deviated from the plan Gore had laid out for him. As a result of heeding his trainers preaching, the young man had earned himself the world champion's scalp and gained a momentous victory. Viscusi had taken a great deal of criticism for allowing his young prospect to face the rough-fighting Saddler. The usually wily manager would never normally sacrifice any youngster in his care, but it was muted that though Mr. Lou respected the champion, he did not think too highly of Saddler's all-round ability.

Speaking after the Saddler versus Flanagan contest, Viscusi said to the reporters: "If Willie had not veered away from our battle plan and used his own brand of boxing, he would have emerged victorious in each fight against Sandy. A boxer like Pep who uses his brains doesn't get beat by fighters like Saddler." Bill Gore was in full agreement. Turning toward Pep after Flanagan was declared the winner over Saddler, he said: "That's the way to beat this guy. Saddler doesn't like it when he can't find you. He loves guys who stand and slug it out with him. Keep him moving and guessing. You gotta confuse him. Hit and move all the time, he doesn't like movers, he can't handle that style. A fighter with your intelligence should never have problems with him."

Four months after the fiasco with Saddler, Pep was back in action. fighting in his home town of Hartford, he donated his entire purse to the Infantile Paralyis Fund. Fighting Tommy Baker of Chicago, the former champion needed medical attention himself after the contest ended in the 4th round.

Pep boxed briskly for the first two rounds but the third session brought a shock. In a collision with the Chicagoan, blood poured from a head wound, Bill Gore tried vainly to stop the bleeding between rounds but was unable to do so, however, Pep was permitted to answer the bell for the fourth, Pep went all out for a quick victory because it was obvious he would not be able to continue much longer. The fury of his attack drove Baker backwards, although badly outclassed, the Chicago fighter was never knocked off his feet, and when referee, Hugh Devlin, stopped the bout after one minute and twenty seconds of the round to save Baker from unnecessary punishment it caused some surprise. Baker protested loudly against the decision of the referee and pushed Devlin to the floor while spectators also showed their displeasure with loud booing.

It was reported that Pep needed 23 stitches in the cut. Yet amazingly, three weeks later, he flattened Billy Hogan in two one-sided rounds in Sarasota. Two weeks later, he was in New Orleans where he boxed briskly beating Carlos Chavez over the ten round distance. Twenty-one days after beating Chavez, he was fighting in Miami Beach in another lop-sided ten round points victory over Pat Iacobucci, who was a little human-dynamo. There was a brief halt to Pep's ring activity while he appeared in the Hillsborough County Court where his suit for divorce from Dorles Von Franckel was being heard. He arrived at the court with his young son, Billy, his friends, Sam Greenberg, Charley Green and Hartford boxers Al Magliera and Tommy Bazzano. The left arm he injured against Sandy Saddler a few months previous was injured again and in a sling. Willie sat and listened as witnesses for both sides gave evidence. Willie told the court his wife's behaviour stopped him from training because she stayed out late at night and sometimes for two or three days at a time, coming home under the influence of intoxicating liquors. Pep claimed she forced him to buy her a wedding ring for a thousand dollars and expensive fur coats which he could hardly afford but did so in order to keep the peace. He also said she would not let his five-year old son by a previous marriage live with them. He also accused her of "extreme cruelty" and declared she had greatly undermined his health and nervous system until he had become almost a nervous wreck.

She denied these charges and claimed he did not support her adequately and that he beat her up on several occasions. Because of his beatings, she said, she was not able to work and support herself. She related an incident in September 1950 when Pep hit her four times on the left ear and perforated an ear drum. Mrs. Pep also said her husband, after losing money gambling, would come home in a cranky mood and would slap her on the face and hit her. On one occasion, she continued, he hit her in the eye, broke her nose, picked her up and hit her head on the floor. She added he had an ungovernable temper. "He's worth between $100,000 and $150,000," she claimed, but forced her to seek charity of the world and her relatives and friends for support. It was a messy affair and the judge decided he would give his decision a couple of weeks later.

After the court case the Pep boxing road show moved on to St. Louis where he fought Baby Ortiz of Los Angeles. Willie was in sparkling form and displayed ferocious punching power bouncing Ortiz all over the ring, shaking the Californian up several times. Pep floored him for a count in the third round and continued his assault in the fourth, with Ortiz battered and soundly beaten by Pep's thundering fists, in the fifth session the referee stepped in and halted proceedings. The press reported that on this form Sandy Saddler would be hard pressed to hold on to his crown against waltzing Willie. Was Pep taking his anger and frustration out on these unfortunate opponents? Lou Viscusi gave the answer: "After the last Saddler fight ended so controversially, I decided Willie needed to get back into action as quickly as possible. He thrived on being active and fighting regularly kept him sharp and ready for his re-match against Saddler.

Had the adverse criticism effected him following his capitulation at the hands of Saddler? Well, the short but truthful answer was yes. It had hurt him deeply. After all he was a very proud man. He disliked the accusations which the critics were levelling against him that he quit rather than go down like a true champion. He loved being a world champion. He was pressing Viscusi to hurry up and seal a deal for a fourth confrontation with his bitter rival. There was a great deal of speculation and idle talk about where and when Pep and Saddler would fight again. There was a lot of money at stake and Viscusi would do his best to secure the best deal possible for his fighter. Charley Johnston, on the other hand, was claiming as champion, Sandy should now get the bigger purse. The arguments raged on. What was certain though, these two bitter rivals would duel a fourth time.

San Francisco was Willie's next port of call when giving another masterful scientific boxing display to outscore Eddie Chavez in ten rounds. This was vintage Pep, back to his breathtaking best. In the middle rounds of his fight against Chavez, he had the tough little slugger badly dazed and hurt. In fact, Chavez was on the verge of being knocked out. Pep appealed to the referee to rescue the stricken fighter, the referee insisted the bout continue and Willie took his foot off the pedal and allowed Chavez to last the distance. There were occasions in this contest when Pep looked sensational, using techniques other fighters only dream of being able to administer. Two more ten rounders were then put under his belt as he outpointed Jesus Compos in Baltimore before moving back to New Orleans where he boxed the ears of fiery Corky Gonzales. Corky a former National A.A.U. champion was regarded as a potential world champion. He himself predicted he would attain greatness from his ring exploits. But he never did become a world champion. Willie gave him a lesson he would never forget.

Just 22 days later he was at the Polo Grounds, in New York, facing the menacing, fearsome world champion Sandy Saddler. Pep had taken part in eight contests leading up to meeting the champion. He had won them all showing class and style, besides getting himself in terrific condition for Saddler. This schedule would be unthinkable in modern day boxing. The date set for the fourth and final showdown between these two worthy champions was 26 September, 1951. Sandy and Willie were classed as true super-champions, pure craftsmen of their trade of fist fighting, the like of which the boxing world would never have the privilege to witness again. These were the good old days of boxing.

As if things were not bad enough between Pep and Saddler themselves, and the feud between their respective managers, Viscusi and Johnston, the boxing scribes started their stirring again. By now, the "bad-blood" which the press claimed existed between the two camps really did exist. Yes, it was genuine now. The Saddler party kept harping on to the press that Pep was a quitter and he would do the same again. This upset Willie a great deal. "In our last fight Pep kept standing on my toe. It hurt like hell. In a clinch I yelled at him to stop doing that. What did he do? He kept on doing this all through the rest of the fight," said Saddler.

This was all good stuff for the newspaper reporters and made good copy, which in turn helped build up the gate. But Saddler failed to accept the slightest bit of blame for the rough stuff in their three fights so far. Everyone knew he was no angel. When one examined their respective styles, their fights should have been classic boxing matches instead of foul ridden excuses for boxing contests. Pep relied on consummate skill. He used the ring to the best of his capabilities by the use of his keen boxing brain. He was of slender build so did not make any sense to get involved in brawls with any opponents, and certainly not one as tough and as brutal as Saddler. It didn't make sense for Pep to fight Sandy's kind of fight, or try to enter into a contest of hard-hitting or any kind of rough stuff. It stands to reason he would have come off second best using these kind of tactics against the champion. There had never been any hint of any kind of rough house fighting from any of Pep's previous opponents. In-fact, many times Pep had received praise from his former victims and their managers for his sportsmanship. Saddler it would appear brought the worst side of him.

Bill Gore summed up his prize pupil when he said: "It is a fact of life, that in the main, Willie Pep was a clean and fair boxer. There was no evidence whatsoever to suggest he was a dirty fighter. He did not go in for rule flouting or anything else untoward Saddler brought the worst out of him. If Willie follows the same pattern Del Flanagan used on Saddler, then he will be champion again. In training, Willie has sparred hundreds of rounds with Del. We have gone over set moves and practised nullifying Sandy's awkwardness. I can tell you Willie was always in control of those sessions. We are pleased with his attitude."

In Sandy Saddler, Pep was facing a fighter who was not frightened by anybody. He was a dynamic puncher who also had the desire to stay a world champion. He was never reconciled to the fact Pep's reputation was bigger than his own at that time. After all, he had beaten this astonishing little boxing legend twice in three meetings. There were a number of doubts in Pep's mind concerning the next encounter with Sandy.

Usually for most fighters one bout against the likes of a Sandy Saddler was one fight too many. Yet here was this slightly built fighter having his fourth tussle with a fighter who he knew would fight every inch of the way. Pep also remembered the many cuts and bruises inflicted on him by the champion in their past fights.

Fighting really comes down to styles. A fellow like Pep could face every known type of fighter in the world. Nine times out of ten you could stake your last penny on the result. Pep would come out victorious. But that one exception would be a Sandy Saddler style of fighter. Saddler's particular brand of fighting would prove Pep's downfall, because he was a hard man to contain, he would not be denied. Sandy certainly had Pep's number. Saddler had the upmost confidence he could beat Willie Pep seven days a week. He was confident his style was the rock on which Pep would flounder time after time. He was also cunning enough to know his brand of aggressiveness was not to Willie's liking.

A Total Disgrace

By the time the fourth Saddler versus Pep battle was fought, New York boxing fans had become more than a little blase at the mere mention of world championship fights. The reason for this was because the Saddler-Pep affair would be the fourth world championship contest in five weeks to take place on Manhattan Island. Joey Maxim had set the ball rolling when he successfully defended his light-heavyweight crown against Irish Bob Murphy the San Diego sailor on 22 August at Madison Square Garden, a week later at the same venue, the Cuban Kid Gavilan was the centre of stormy scenes when a very disputed decision allowed him to retain his title against New York's stylish Billy Graham. A couple of weeks later, Britain's Randolph Turpin lost the world middleweight title he had fought so hard and majestically to win 60 days earlier against the flamboyant Sugar Ray Robinson with only eight seconds left of the tenth round the referee stopped the contest in the American's favour. When the end came, Robinson was suffering from an ugly gash over his eye and it looked extremely doubtful he would have been allowed to continue had the round ended. After so many world title fights it was little wonder that the fans were finding it hard to dig into their pockets and shell out more dollars for tickets for the Saddler-Pep contest.

The year 1951 will be remembered by Willie Pep for as long as he lives, and by the boxing historians for ever and a day. There were only 13,836 spectators in New York's Polo Grounds when the two men entered the ring for the fourth and final installment of boxing's bitter rivalry. The referee was former fighter Ray Miller, a tough and experienced official. The two judges were Arthur Aidala and Frank Forbes. Familiarity beeds contemp they say, and this ill-tempered contest between two world-class boxers might have been the reason for what followed in this bout, because any resemblance to a boxing contest was purely co-incidental in this foul infested excuse for a world championship contest. Quite honestly, it was a shambles and a total disgrace. The paying fans were cheated by the tactics of both fighters.

These two boxers who were classed as "great" were certainly far from that on this best forgotten night. Pep and Saddler should have been ashamed of themselves. They fooled nobody with claims that is was neither one of them who started the dirty fighting. Who did start it then? Because the nearly 14,000 paying spectators certainly wanted to know. They felt cheated and abused by both fighters. Saddler retained his title when Pep failed to answer the bell for the start of round ten of the scheduled 15 rounder. But what proceeded was a total disregard for the rules, ethics and regulations. It was a fight in which roughness and wild fighting were the standard and where ring discipline was absolutely non-existent. This bout surpassed anything seen in their previous battles. Those contests were quite tough in every respect, but this latest battle was disgraceful, with both pugilists guilty of rule flouting and scenes which did the image of boxing no service at all.

Even Marciano Blushed

"It was the roughest, dirtiest fight I have ever seen. It was more like a back alley brawl than a world championship contest. Both guys were guilty of breaking the rules," exclaimed Rocky Marciano. This sounded like the kettle calling the pot black, coming from Marciano who butted and elbowed many an opponent and who was no saint or shrinking violet during his ring warfare. But his remarks were accepted for what they were. Truthful! When a fighter such as Rocky cringes while watching supposedly two outstanding champions battle it out, it just shows how robust this war really was. Indeed, any resemblance to the accepted theory that boxing was a "fair-stand-up" exhibition of skill and sportsmanship between two well matched individuals was purely coincidental.

"No street fight was ever like this," said Rocky Graziano. "They wrestled, they tripped each other, they butted, they elbowed. And, if the referee had let them, they would've added their corner stools to their brawling tools."

There were heated arguments concerning the ending of the fight. One of Pep's cornermen was heard to protest, when Pep informed the referee, Ray Miller, he could not continue to fight because of the damage suffered to his right eye. Make no mistake, Pep was very badly bruised about the face. As he plopped onto his stool and stared into space through badly swollen and bruised eyes, there was blood dripping from a deep cut over his right eyebrow. Other red rivulets streamed from his nose and puffed lips.

He had also taken a very severe and sustained beating to his mid-section from the wiry champion's relentless body attack, when he decided enough was more than enough as he sat on his stool at the end of the ninth round, just as he had done in their previous meeting.

The State Athletic Commission Physician, Doctor, Vincent A. Nardiello, said: "When I inspected Pep in his corner, he told me: 'I am unable to continue'. His cornermen didn't say anything." Later, speaking to the press, Nardiello continued: "Pep said he could not see because of the blood which was going into his right eye. There was a bad cut which had been inflicted by Saddler in the second round. The blood was bothering him a great deal." Later the doctor said some disparaging things concerning Pep's retirement from this particular contest. "Even after the protest of one of his handlers, Pep decided to quit," added the doctor. Photographs of Pep's horrific facial injuries taken in his dressing room immediately after the brawl clearly reveal it was indeed impossible for him to continue. Pep was evidently convinced in this fourth installment of their ring serial, the distinction of being the first champion to regain the same crown was not to be his and that discretion was the better part of valour.

Who was the mystery cornerman who wanted Pep to continue the battle? There certainly was an unidentified voice heard to yell a commanding order to referee Miller, as the arbiter left Pep's corner after getting the former champion's official surrender. Miller took no notice whoever it was, and called for the ring announcer he then signalled an end to the contest. Miller summoned Doctor Nardiello to enter the ring and visit Pep's corner. The doctor examined the former champion who was found to be all right, but thoroughly indisposed and unable to leave the ring under his own power.

The confusion over the ending was nothing compared to the preceding events in the roped square. "For a world championship contest, this was a sorry spectacle indeed," said Nat Fleischer, in 'The Ring' magazine. Both fighters were equally as guilty of the many fouls which were committed throughout the time the fight lasted. It was a sorry day for sportsmanship said one disgruntled fan on his way out of the arena. They fought like two "ale-house" brawlers. By some small oversight they failed to bite each other or for that matter to start kicking the living daylights out of each other. If this so-called boxing contest had taken place anywhere outside the confines of a boxing ring, there is not the slightest doubt that both men would have been arrested and locked up.

At one stage, an embarrassed Ray Miller pushed Pep against the ropes and said: "if you do that again, I'll stop the fight. I have the power to disqualify you and deprive you of your purse." What promised to be a truly memorable championship contest disintegrated into a complete shambles. Both corners joined in and seemed to have gone stark raving mad. At one stage, Charley Johnston, during the minute rest period between rounds, suddenly stopped working with Saddler, rushed to where Dr. Nardiello, the was sitting alongside of of the judges, Arthur Aidala and screamed at him: "You are trying to dictate the judging of the rounds! You want Pep to win because he's Italian and my boy's a Negro!" At a later hearing, Johnston apologised for his behaviour to Nardiello and Aidala, but was banned for thirty-days and fined a hundred dollars.

The new chairman of the State Athletic Commission, Robert K.

Christenberry, had an unpalatable introduction to his new duties. Even referee Miller fell to the canvas in the seventh round while trying to separate the combatants from a death-like embrace, when it looked like they were trying to strangle each other. The crowd hated what they were witnessing and were not slow to voice their disapproval by long and loud hissing, jeering and booing. Saddler was twice wrestled to the floor at the end of the fifth and again in the eighth round. Then both fighters hit the deck from body holds in the sixth. They engaged in a mild exhibition of wrestling again in round eight. Only one warning was issued, and that was against Pep for unnecessary roughness.

The fight started with Saddler catching the Hartford fighter with a long, wide left hook to the jaw. This shocked Pep and he seemed to sense from that moment he was in for a very rough ride. The challenger fought back to win the round by the use of two-handed hitting and dancing away at breakneck speed. Saddler was cautioned by Miller for holding and hitting, both fighters were losing their tempers very early in the fight. What little boxing there was on view obviously came from the speedy former title holder. A whiplash left hook thrown by Saddler early in the second round cut Pep's right eye. When the two men were in a clinch in Saddler's corner, the champion connected with another left hook followed by a body punch. This was a dynamic shot flush on target, down went Pep for a count of eight. It was after this the rough-house fighting took over the contest and spoiled it as a worthy world championship match.

Banished For Life
On 6 October 1951, the New York State Athletic Commission held a meeting and all parties were called before the committee. Robert Christenberry had recently replaced Eddie Eagan as Boxing Commissioner, and he made his first official action a strong one. He suspended Saddler for 30 days for his part in the "dirty fight," and banned and fined his manager Charley Johnston. Then he slapped an "indeterminate" ban on Pep for "violating every rule in the book." An embittered Pep walked out of the meeting muttering: "I only did what he (Saddler) was doing. He made me fight rough." But those words were as empty as his future looked. Once a high-living, big-incomed fighter, Willie now had to go touring the sticks for his bread and butter.

Taking a closer look at the four fight series between Pep and Saddler, and taking account of Pep's views on the subject, the reader can draw their own conclusions about who was to blame in the most talked about feud in boxing's history. Talking to a journalist a few years after the last of their battles, Pep said: "Believe me, I wish I had never heard the name Sandy Saddler. He's caused me more trouble and misery than anyone else. I never boxed dirty in my life until I fought him. At the time of the first Saddler fight I'd had 136 professional fights. The only one I had lost was a non-title fight to Sammy Agnott. When I saw Saddler the first time, I thought he looked like Mahatma Gandhi. He was thin, with those spindly legs of his that reminded me of a marionette. I didn't figure to have trouble with him, although he had a good knockout record, 56 guys in 93 bouts."

The first fight at Madison Square Garden, saw the Hartford boxer much to confident and in the first round Saddler hit him on the chin with a terrific punch which took everything out of him. Willie knew where he was but he couldn't do anything. On top of that the challenger according to Willie was hitting him illegally, pushing him around, butting, thumbing and elbowing him. "He was dirty, that's the only way he can fight, or knows how to," said Pep. Sandy knocked the champion out with less than 30 seconds left in the fourth round. It was the first time in Pep's career that anyone had stopped him. He badgered Lou Viscusi to get him a return with Sandy as quickly as possible. Pep was ashamed of himself.

He had to wait until February 1949 for the return match. That turned out to be the greatest fight of Pep's life and possibly it was the greatest fight of Saddler's life too. Pep had four cuts over each eye which he claimed were caused by Sandy's head and his elbows. But Willie was always moving and he never got hit directly in the eye. "He butted me and thumbed me in the clinches, but he never hit me with a solid punch for six rounds," added Pep. In the sixth Saddler hurt the champion with a good punch on the chin, but he survived it. Pep was warmed up by now and Sandy didn't catch him cold like he had in their first fight, that's why Pep was able to stay on his feet. Meanwhile, it seemed Willie had found a way to get Saddler to break during a clinch. Every time he held, Pep would step on his toe. Sandy didn't like that. He had sensitive feet. The fight went the distance and at the end referee Eddie Joseph voted for Pep by ten rounds to five, and both judges gave Willie nine rounds. His face was a mess, but he was happy. It was the happiest he had been for a long time. As the new champion Willie fought 18 more times without ever coming close to losing, and then, in September, 1950 at Yankee Stadium, he had to defend the featherweight championship against Saddler again.

Pep had made up his mind that if Saddler fought dirty this time then he would too. The first three rounds went pretty well. Pep had an edge on points and he felt good. He was moving as well as he ever did, getting in quick one-two's, working the combinations, never letting Sandy touch him. Then in the fourth, referee Ruby Goldstein got in the middle of the two fighters in order to break a clinch and Saddler hit Pep. Willie never saw the punch coming and he went down. He was hurt, but managed to get up at eight.

He surprised Saddler by catching him with a solid punch under the left eye. It hurt him and got him angry. After that the two rivals got in all kinds of grips, but Pep was still ahead on points. By the end of the seventh it looked like it was Pep's fight. Then, near the end of the round, Sandy got his opponent in a grip against the ropes with his hand around Pep's shoulder, and he pushed Pep. "A terrific pain shot up my shoulder. Between rounds, Doc Nardiello grabbed my arm and tried to snap the shoulder back into place, but the pain was real bad. My manager wouldn't let me come out for the eighth," said Pep.

Their fourth fight was a disgrace. Everyone, including Willie Pep, has to agree with that assessment. After it was over the fans, officials and reporters said a lot of uncomplimentary things about Willie, how he fought dirty, how he quit to Saddler, how everything rotten about that fight was his fault. What really happened was that Pep was determined to win the title back and he was in the best shape of his life. In the first round Saddler grabbed him and hit him on the break, and Saddler drew the first warning. Willie remembers that clearly. All through the fight Sandy would hit Pep with one hand while holding with the other. "The referee, Ray Miller, wouldn't do a thing about it. In fact, Miller seemed to ignore Saddler's dirty fighting and concentrate on mine. At one point, after we had wrestled each other to the ground, Miller said to me: 'What do you want to do, start a race riot here.' Now what kind of a thing is that to say to me when I'm fighting like hell to win back my title?," said Pep.

By the second round Pep was already cut up quite seriously. By the eighth round his eye was bleeding profusely and he said Saddler was sticking his thumb in it. In the clinches Saddler gave Pep the business. He tried to get away and box but he couldn't keep it up. Every picture taken of that fight shows Sandy was the aggressor. At the end of the eighth, Pep said to Bill Gore: "Bill, I can't stand the pain." "You got the fight won," said Gore. "You're winning. You can't lose." "Then I went out for the ninth and Saddler kept sinking his big thumb in to my eye. I appealed to Ray Miller. I said: 'I can't continue' I wanted to add: 'if he keeps that up.' But Miller wouldn't let me finish. After I said: 'I can't continue.' Miller said okay and immediately raised Saddler's hand. I was jobbed out of the title. About the only good thing I can say about those four Saddler fights is that they were a big success financially. We drew a total of 86,399 people."

The End Of The Feud

That was the end of the most talked about series of fights in boxing's history. If you get the opportunity to watch the fights on video, judge for yourselves who was fouling and breaking the rules. But one thing is crystal clear in the last three battles, Pep boxed beautifully. Sadly, this would be the last world championship he would ever contest. What was also clear was that Willie Pep had a champion manager in Lou Viscusi. The negotiations for all four fights prove this point. Willie Pep received the largest share of the purse money for each of the four bouts. Did Pep sidetrack Saddler after winning his crown back in their second fight? Or, was it a case of Lou Viscusi simply looking after his boxers interest. And didn't other champions do exactly the very same thing as what Pep was being accused. There was no objection by any of the ruling bodies to any champion defending their titles against any opponent he chose, provided he took on the number one challenger every six months. Of course money ruled everything. Pep was accused of ducking Saddler before their third encounter, but one of the reasons, not the main one I hasten to add, was because Charley Johnston, Sandy's manager was a prime mover in the infamous managers guild, which at that time was in conflict with the International Boxing Club of New York over television fees and other matters.

Sandy Saddler boxed on until April 1956, before being forced to retire because of an eye injury suffered while travelling as a passenger in a taxi which crashed. Let there be no doubting this man's ability. He was a worthy world champion and his brilliant record testifies to that fact, he was undefeated world featherweight champion. His total record comprised 162 bouts of which he won 145 losing only 16, with two draws, but scoring an amazing 103 fights by clean knockout or stoppage. After his retirement, he became extremely bitter because of the treatment he received while attending various big fights in and around New York. He felt he wasn't being given credit as a great world champion, while Willie Pep was still introduced as an all-time "great." In later years Sandy mellowed and was delighted when he was elected into the "Hall of Fame" in the 1970s, an overdue honour. Sadly the passing years have not been too kind to this brilliant champion. After far too many hard, punishing battles in the ring, he suffered when some youths hit him over the head with a heavy weapon while stealing from him. Sandy now resides in a nursing home in New York, and can't remember much about what's going on in the world or of his past glory days.

Where does he go from here, the critics were all asking about the disposed and disgraced champion, Willie Pep. The newspapers and magazines were giving his banishment from New York plenty of coverage. Though bitterly upset at the treatment meted out to him by the New York Commission, he was never one to openly complain. Willie sat down and discussed future plans with Lou Viscusi. Both men knew things would be extremely difficult from now on. But Willie had no other job only boxing. Viscusi knew they could not base themselves in Hartford any longer. Boxing was going through a lull in the state, besides, Willie had fought in his home town only on certain occasions over the past few years and he would box in front of his home fans only twice more before his career would come to a full stop. Mr. Lou decided to move his base of operations to Tampa in Florida. He quickly organised his star boxer's comeback, and six months after his last battle against Sandy Saddler Willie commenced his campaign in Tampa. And what an occasion it turned out to be. Before the largest turnout to watch a boxing tournament for several years, Willie defeated a little Mexican tear-away named Santiago Gonzales in a ten round contest. He showed much of the old moxi which earned him on two occasions the world's 126-pound division crown. Gonzales was a spirited warrior and soon had the large crowd rooting for him. He was quite definitely not in the least overawed by Pep's reputation. One of Willie's greatest attributes as a boxer was his uncanny ability when under pressure and he displayed plenty of this during the ten hectic rounds. He also used a piston-like left jab to pile up points, and his Fred Astaire footwork, his hard and accurate punching was too much for Gonzales to cope with. But this Mexican was a proud fighter and though taking plenty of punishment he persisted in going forward throughout the entire contest.

Gonzales certainly endeared himself to the Florida fans who cheered and applauded him to the echo. In the eighth and ninth rounds Pep opened up with rapid-fire combinations and he almost scored a knockout, but Santiago ducked and weaved his way to safely as Barney Ross, the former lightweight and welterweight champion, who was refereeing the bout looked carefully for any signs of distress from the Mexican, but allowed the bout to continue. There was no dispute as to who won, Willie was a unanimous winner. The crowd booed lustily as Barney Ross raised Willie's hand in victory, they didn't like Pep's roughness against the Mexican. Bill Gore and Viscusi declared they were pleased with the little wizard's showing and believed Willie, after a few more fights under his belt would regain his sharpness and go on to meet Sandy Saddler again.

Return To The Big Apple

Teddy Brenner, the famous New York matchmaker, tells an amusing and interesting story about Willie Pep during his days after the last Saddler fight. Willie was on a visit to Jack LaMotta's nightclub which was situated in Miami Beach. After talking about their respective careers and having a few laughs, Willie told the former middleweight champion he was having an early night because the following day he was going to the track to watch the horse racing and have a bet. One of Jake's bar staff, a busty waitress, asked if she might go along with him. In-fact, she promised to use her car to transport the two ring greats. LaMotta said he would love to have joined his friend but could not make it. "Will you bet a double for me," he asked Pep. Jake selected the number one and five, and asked Willie to bet the numbers in a 50 dollar double. The following day the young lady turned up late saying her car would not start and she had to call a mechanic out to fix it.

Arriving late at the racetrack, Pep was too late to place LaMotta's bet, and sure enough the number one won the first race. Willie was fuming. What should he do now? He put the 50 dollars on number five in the following race and it won. The problem was that had he got to the track on time and placed the bet accordingly, Jake would have won $4,500. But Pep only got $350 for what he staked on the second race. Turning to the young woman he asked her to explain to LaMotta what had happened and give him his winnings. The woman immediately replied: "No, you know what's he's like, you had better come back with me." When they entered the club it was quite obvious LaMotta had forgotten about his 50 dollar bet, or infact, what numbers he had requested Pep to bet on for him. Willie explained about the waitress picking him up late, and he was unable to place the agreed bet so he put the 50 on the second race and he won the 350 dollars. "Forget it," replied LaMotta.

That, thought Pep was the end of that little episode. How wrong he was, for quite a while afterwards whenever Willie met old friends, boxing people and show business personalities they told him that Jake had told them he had been cheated out of his winning double. LaMotta even mentioned the story on a television show he was appearing on, and also while doing a radio programme. It was even in the papers about Willie cheating the Bronx Bull.

Frank Graham, a brilliant journalist wrote: "One day when going to the races in Miami, his pal Jake LaMotta gave him fifty dollars to bet on a daily double. But Willie, not sharing Jake's enthusiasm for this particular combination of horses, held the bet. When the double clicked at a staggering price, Willie took a plane to New Orleans and on his arrival, called Rocky Graziano in New York, asking him to pacify Jake who, he sensed, would strike him dead on sight. Rocky must have been very persuasive. Within a week, Willie was back in Miami making the rounds with Jake."

This had obviously gone much too far now. Pep phoned LaMotta and asked him to stop telling these stories, adding people were starting to really believe he had welshed. LaMotta, laughing told Willie not to take it so serious. "They love me telling the tale," he said. "And it's good publicity." "For whom?" asked an irate Pep. Later, the episode was finally put to rest once and for all and the two former champions are still friends.

New Yorkers were going to get their first glimpse of the former featherweight champion of the world since his banishment from their city almost two years before. He was topping the bill in the ten round feature contest at Madison Square Garden on the night of Friday, 5 June, 1953. This would be his first appearance in New York since his infamous, foul-infested war with Sandy Saddler which took place in September 1951, resulting in suspensions for both Pep and Saddler. Pep was facing a tough task for his return to the "Big Apple" being matched with young, highly-touted prospect Pat Marcune, an upcoming featherweight from Coney Island. Marcune was a hard-chinned, hard-punching scrapper. Pep, the former featherweight champion was 31, but was still one of the great names in the world of boxing, and was favoured to win at 12 to 5 to make his New York return a successful one. Since his last futile attempt to win back his featherweight title from Sandy Saddler in 1951, the Connecticut boxer had strung together a successful run of victories, losing only once in 18 contests, and that was to the heavy-punching Boston-Irishman Tommy Collins. In the bout before the Collins fiasco, Pep had beaten Claude Hammond in a tough ten rounder in Miami Beach, but had suffered a badly cut eye. Returning home to Connecticut, Pep entered the New Britain General Hospital and underwent surgery. The operation was to remove the scar tissue around his eyes and was performed by Dr. Bliss Clark.

I would like to digress slightly about Pep's defeat at the fists of the colourful, hard-punching Tommy Collins, the socking Irishman from Boston. To most Americans a Tom Collins is a long cool drink of gin with a cherry on top, but to Willie Pep a Tom Collins was a tall kid with plenty of power in both fists, and like the beverage too many would set you on your ear. Tommy Collins was one of the most popular fighters to ever come out of Boston. He was a contender for the world lightweight title and the best ticket-seller in the boxing business. Though a knockout puncher, he had only limited scientific boxing ability. When the Boston newspapers featured articles that the home town hero would be facing the "great" Willie Pep in the Boston Garden on 30 June, 1952, you could not get a ticket for love nor money. It was a complete sell-out the biggest ever attraction in the Boston Garden. And remember, the great Rocky Marciano came from this area as well.

When Pep was champion he used Collins as a sparring partner on several occasions. It was true to say Willie was in complete control during their many rounds of sparring. In fact on one occasion while wearing the heavy sparring gloves, Pep broke a couple of Tommy's ribs. Collins couldn't hit Willie with a bag full of confetti during their many rounds of sparring and the two fighters became firm friends. However, when they signed to fight each other, Pep thought it was a formality and merely went through the motions while training for the fight. "I knew I could handle him," said Pep. Bill Gore though, was worried by Willie's attitude and implored the former champion to train harder. Gore told Pep if he didn't put more effort into his gym sessions, then Collins would beat him. Still Willie took things lightly, he was far to confident and believed he had the beating of the Boston fighter seven-days a week.

On the night of the fight, the crowd of some 10,000 were yelling and cheering themselves hoarse. Willie boxed superbly for the first five rounds, he did everything but knock his opponent out. In the fifth, Pep had Collins against the ropes and was battering him unmercifully. The referee Joe Zapusta was looking carefully at Collins. Willie supremely confident, backed away to asses what damage to Tommy, he soon found out as Collins cracked home a terrific left hook which caught Pep flush on the side of the jaw and dropped him. The referee counted "seven" when the bell rang, and Willie had to be carried back to his corner where Bill Gore worked like a demon to bring him round. It was all to no avail because Willie had not recovered from taking that devastating left hook and the following round was met by a two-fisted barrage of punches to the head. That was the last Pep remembered until he woke up in the dressing room. He had been put down four times. That first wild left hook which connected flush on Willie's chin in round five had done the damage and he never recovered from this shot. It was one of the biggest upsets of the year and Willie's dream of winning the featherweight crown lay in ruins in the rasin dust on the ring floor.

Though this was only the fifth time he had lost as a professional, it was obvious Willie could no longer handle these young sluggers as easily as he had in the past. Pep demanded a return contest, but his request fell on deaf ears. In later years when discussing the Collins fight Pep said: "This was another fight which everyone thought was a 'bag-job' (fixed)."

In his 17 victories Pep had evidently lost little of his powers because he defeated Fabela Chavez, Armond Savoie the Canadian lightweight champion-and Jackie Blair. These were good class fighters who were among his victims. Pep was by now intent upon recouping further honours. He hoped to prove he was still a quality fighter and believed he could regain his old featherweight championship if given the opportunity. This was Willie's dearest wish and he knew he needed to convincingly beat Marcune and every other fighter who was blocking his path if he was to obtain another title contest. Training at Stillman's gym for the Marcune fight, Pep brought back nostalgic memories for many of the regulars. Noisy, colourful Stillman's took on a strange atmosphere whenever Pep went through his workouts while training there. Fighters and trainers would pause in their preparations and even the loud-mouthed hangers-on would stare in silence, as though a sacred rite was being performed. "No matter what they say about this guy, there's never been another boxer like him," said a big fellow with a twisted nose to his companion while pointing towards Pep rather sadly. The companion nodded slowly. "Yeah, it's too bad he didn't quit while he was ahead."

A wise observation, but not exactly a new one among ringsiders. They said the same thing about Joe Louis, Henry Armstrong and many others, fighters who dulled some of the glitter of their achievements and punished their ageing bodies by not hanging up their gloves soon enough. Pep was different, yes he perhaps should have retired while he was on top, and pleased the sentimentalist. But that is easier said than done. He was only 31, and when other fighters were trudging down the other side of the hill, here was Pep staging the battle of his life to regain some of the glory and the dollars he once had in his pocket. The battles were all uphill now, for some of the sparkle and talent had left him. Fame, a wise man once said, is the perfume of heroic deeds. It is also a fleeting thing.

"What most fans remembered about Pep was the fact that twice he sat on his stool and quit against Saddler. Once while he was winning, and again after he engineered one of the roughest and dirtiest fights which had ever disgraced the game," said a reporter in Stillmans. Pep's career might well have ended on that ugly blot, because he was banished from the ring in New York State for life. And, as every worthy fighter of note knew, there was no road back that detours New York. Pep didn't find many welcome mats dusted off for him. But he clung to one hope and kept fighting. For almost two years he had roamed the country, boxing in small arenas for even smaller purses. It was a heart breaking exile for this once-great champion.

A return from Exile

A few months before the Marcune fight, it was announced in the newspapers that New York Boxing Commissioner, Bob Christenberry, permitted Pep to return from exile, but no one gave it more than a sentimental nod in passing. Pep, they said, was a little old man now and almost broke. Christenberry's reprieve, perhaps, was just an expression of sympathy. For Willie, though, it was more than just a handout for coffee and cakes. It was the chance he hoped for so desperately, and he figured it had come just in time. Manager Viscusi got him booked into Madison Square Garden. Willie was overjoyed, after all, the Garden was the Mecca of boxing for Pep and every other American boxer.

On the day before the Marcune contest, there was a rivetting article in the "New York Times" by famed writer, Arthur Daley. The article was entitled: "A Pay Day For Willie." It was a brilliant piece of journalism by a first class writer. Daley was saying the wheel had spun full circle for Pep. "Once one of the most remarkable fighters of this generation, he's just a journeyman performer now, just another hungry boxer looking for a pay day," wrote Daley. The writer went on to say Pep's return to Madison Square Garden was purely for cash rather than glory. "He was virtually tarred, feathered and ridden out of town on a rail after his last appearance here. But, gosh, he was gifted. He was a wraith in the ring, swift of hand and swift of foot. As a boxer they just didn't come any better. But he is 31-years-old now and his future is completely behind him."

Daley was hard-hitting and got straight to the point in his article. Pep read Daley's article while resting on his bed in his hotel room. He smiled, then speaking to Gore and Viscusi who were sitting in his room, he said: "I wonder what Daley will write about me after I fight this kid Macune." Pep fully intended to perform to the lofty heights he was accustomed to. Gore, trying to cheer up his fighter, said: "Don't you worry too much about what you read in those newspapers." But Pep was not upset in the least by Daley's comments. He took these stories and reports in his stride, some were good, some were bad. But he reasoned: "They all have a job to do. Just like me."

On the night of the fight only 3,571 thought enough of his return from the "dead" to journey to watch him fight in the Garden for this main event, but millions were viewing the fight on television. The gate receipts came to $9,681. The sparse gathering were well rewarded, however. Pep did an "Old Master's" job on the 24 year-old Marcune, giving him a methodical two-handed shellacking. The fans saw a Pep in the image of the swift-handed kid who had come down from Hartford a dozen years before to win praise for his undoubted ability. In the same ring where he had alternately earned fame and disgrace, Pep staged an exhibition of boxing mastery which was a sight to behold. Feinting, slipping punches, firing away with both hands while he skipped about like an Arthur Murray disciple, he made onlookers forget many things and remember only the Willie Pep of yesterday. The former featherweight king brought matters to a dramatic climax by stopping Pat in 14 seconds into the tenth and last round. Marcune was not on the floor when the end came. The referee, Petey Scalzo, moved in to call a halt to the proceedings when it was obvious the gutsy Marcune was all through and with no chance of winning.

Although the newspapers called this contest a mis-match, because they stated Marcune's ring record suggested that he had no chance, he gave a very brave account of himself and was in with a chance right to the finish of the contest. In-fact, Marcune gave a wonderful display of courage as he absorbed the former world champion's best punches. One of those wallops caught Pat flush on the chin in the fifth round and put him on the canvas for a count of eight. There were several more quite hefty wallops thrown in a flurry which landed with Pep's full weight behind them in the ninth round, and these blows would have certainly dropped the courageous Marcune if the ropes had not held him up. Strangely it was in this ninth session that Pat made his best showing. Pep came out for the round with his left eye cut. Marcune made this cut his target and Pep was forced to hold on for dear life-things looked bad for the ex-champion. But within seconds Pep showed why he was one of boxing's biggest stars. Waiting for his chance, he suddenly let fly with a sizzling two-handed barrage of rapid quickfire punches.

This was a terrific onslaught of power packed punches to Marcune's face and jaw. Moments before the young prospect had hopes of winning because of the deep gash over Pep's left eye, but he was now rendered almost helpless by Pep's assault. When the round had ended, Marcune wobbled back to his corner very shakily. He had not recovered within the sixty-second break and was still unsteady on his feet when he came out for the tenth and fatal round. Marcune was still very shaken indeed as the graceful, stylish, "Will-'o'-the-Wisp," moved after his victim. After Pep's first exchange in this session, referee Scalzo stepped in and called a halt to the bout, because the plucky Marcune was in no position to defend himself. It went into the record books as a tenth round knockout to Willie Pep. Pep was obviously far more experienced and determined than the brave, younger fighter. But what a tremendous contest from the former champion. He really did give a splendid exhibition of boxing and ringcraft from the very first round, and he showed the younger rival tricks Pat could never figure out. Moving in and out and from side to side, Willie threw everything at Pat from the long range. When they came to close quarters, Pep tied his rival up very effectively. The former champion had a big advantage in the round scoring. The former champion weighed 127-three-quarters-pounds, while Marcune came in at 129-half-pounds. After his thrilling victory Willie was now persona grata in New York.

Back in his dressing room, Willie was sat on a bench, holding his head in his hands. His face was lumpy and scarred. The cut beside his eye was crescent-shaped and deep and seeping blood. He complained he had been butted. Commissioner, Bob Christenberry walked over to where Willie was sitting and smiling said: "Willie, you were the kind of fighter tonight I always heard about. That was a brilliant showing. I would like to offer my congratulations."

After thanking the Commissioner, Willie, looked in the mirror and said to nobody in particular. "What a way to make a living, but what else can I do? It's the only business I know." Lou Viscusi talking to reporters said: "Willie was on trial for his 'life' to night. Many people say he is well past his peak as a fighter, but he demonstrated boxing is his business and he could still fight with calculated fury that puts him above the run-of-the mill boxer. This was his 185th fight. This kid Marcune has a good record but was misguided in the notion that he could cope with Willie. You guys saw what happened. Willie is one of the classiest boxers the game as ever seen, and despite his years he still has not lost his touch."

There was a break of nearly five months before Willie boxed again. He needed the rest to allow the scars around his eyes to heal. Then it was back on his travels once again when he had four quick bouts all of which he won. He won three by tenth round decisions; the venues were in Charlotte, Palm Beach and Miami Beach. He also scored a second round count-out over Billy Lima in Houston, Texas. Pep kept hoping he would get another chance at the world featherweight crown. His record was far superior to most of the other contenders but the powers that be would not let him enter the world championship throneroom ever again.

Talking to Bill Lee, an old friend and a Hartford sports writer, Willie got discussing his punching power and his last big fight in Madison Square Garden. "I was never a one punch assassin, like those little Mexican guys, you know that Bill. But when I came down off my toes and set myself to use power, I could take a fellow out of the fight. My right uppercut came in handy against Marcune. Pat was a good boxer-puncher, but a better puncher than a boxer. I nailed him with an uppercut in the fifth, but he charged back and in the eighth he re-opened a cut over my left eye and the blood began to pour down my face. He must have thought he had me in the ninth because he came out like a wildman. Right away I began sizing him up for another uppercut. You've got to think ahead to land this punch. You've got to anticipate every move and then-at just the right second-wham! While Marcune was busy chasing me around the ring. I kept looking for that opening. Finally I found it, and fired the right. It was a beauty, Pat's eyes glazed and his legs went rubbery. As he reeled backward, I went after him, bombing him along the ropes. The bell saved him but the uppercuts had taken all the steam out of him and when he stumbled out in the tenth I swarmed all over him and finally the referee stopped it."

Very little was ever publicised about the voluntary work Willie Pep carried out. One of the things which received very little publicity was his eagerness to help any organisation which was doing work to help the young, old, infirm or mentally sick. A little example happened while Willie was in Tampa for his comeback fight with Santiago Gonzales, he heard about the the rise in juvenile crime and was concerned. The St. Petersburg Police Department were alarmed and in order to help curb juvenile delinquency they formed an amateur boxing club for the local youngsters to let of steam. Their imitative was to be commended. The police decided to stage an amateur boxing tournament and feature some of the reformed tear-aways on the show. Pep got to hear about their plan and immediately offered to help in any way he could. The kids and the officers were delighted at the former champions offer and he was invited to act as the guest referee, which he accepted and a wonderful night was had by all concerned. There were many occasions when he gave up his time freely to help the several charities and the Catholic organisation.

The Lulu Perez Fiasco and The Fix

After beating David Seabrooks on points over ten rounds in Jacksonville, Florida, Willie was sat in his dressing-room. It was January 1954. Then Lou Viscusi gave him the news he had been waiting and hoping to hear: "You might be topping the bill again at Madison Square Garden, in late February. I'm talking to the Garden officials in the morning. Negotiations are going well, I'll know pretty soon," his manager told him. Pep was thrilled. This was like music to his ears. He was overjoyed at this breakthrough. Because though he didn't mind boxing in the "sticks" as he called his travels to the likes of Jacksonville, Madison Square Garden was still the Mecca of boxing to him. It had a special ring to it. Since his fourth and final meeting with Sandy Saddler, he had only fought in the Garden once, when beating hot prospect, Pat Marcune, in the tenth and final round of an exciting fight in which he had performed with his old style of panache.

Though he had been boxing quite well since the last Saddler fight, it was a fact Pep's career had entered a long twilight period. Yes, he was still a big name attraction, still one of the greatest boxers ever seen in the ring, but he wasn't the best anymore, he wasn't the champion. Without the title, his fights were not as big, the purse money not as lucrative as previously, nor was the venues as crowded, the cheers were not as loud. But he knew nothing else but boxing, so he carried on fighting.

The 26 February 1954 must go down as the worst event in the long illustrious boxing career of this living legend. Willie was to be involved in one of the most controversial fights of his career and a contest which still causes controversy whenever it is discussed. As we shall see!

Willie was booked to oppose the 20 year-old Brooklyn prospect, the new knockout punching sensation, Lulu Perez, in a ten round contest. Pep was now 31 and in the twilight of his fantastic career. He was spurred on by the slim prospect of another shot at Sandy Saddler's world championship. A resounding victory over this young prospect would do his chances a power of good. Perez had one of the better professional records among the younger pretenders for the featherweight title, having won 34 from 36 bouts. Lulu boasted he intended flattening the former champion as quickly as possible. The fact was that Perez for all his punching-power, was no more than a tough, typical slugging brawler and very determined- but a fighter who was limited. He just walked forward, and in normal circumstances would have been tailor-made for a boxer of Pep's exceptional abilities. But, as many observers were quick to state, this was 1954, not 1944!

The New York newspapers were asking the question. "Can Pep Last The Distance?" Many writers openly stating that though he still possessed that asset of great speed which had in the past carried him to the heights, the Hartford athlete no longer seemed to have the stamina for a hard, gruelling distance fight. Pep was no more than even money with the betting fraternity a week before the proposed contest. Harry Markson stated: "Perez, was mainly a tearaway knockout walloper, who could bang with either fist. He could punch with the best of them. After all, most of his 34 wins had been via the quick route. In some quarters, Perez was a feared all-action man."

An Ugly Shadow

This fight was to cast an ugly shadow over the former world champion for many years to follow. It is still one of the most talked about fights when writers and fans discusses the "sleaziness" which exists within boxing circles. It resulted in Pep suing a magazine in the 1980s for millions of dollars, regarding an article which the publication printed suggesting he took a dive in the Perez fight.

During his comeback, Pep was still a bubbly little character. He would drop in at gyms anywhere he was booked to fight. Other boxers and trainers were delighted to have him use their workplace. He often trained in Stillman's Gym, New York. One of the many fighters who also trained there was Lulu Perez, these two sparred many rounds together. Talking about the Perez fiasco a few years later Pep said: "I worked a lot with Lulu Perez and I handled him like a baby. When they made the match with him I figured I wouldn't have any trouble. I said to my manager, Lou Viscusi. 'Don't worry Lou, I'll handle him easy. I didn't train too hard. I didn't think I had to. I figured I could put him away. I guess I was still reading the stories from the Marcune fight. I wanted to make an impression on the crowd by knocking him out."

Before the fight there was a great shift in the betting odds. At one time during the day of the fight there was a 7-5 swing in favour of Perez. But in Hartford, the home town of Pep, they had the former champion a 7-5 favourite. Reality prevailed over geography after both fighters weighed in at noon on the day of their bout. Pep was 127-one-half-pound, with the younger man coming in at 126-one-half-pound. The odds suddenly started to climb for the Brooklyn kid. By fight time, Perez was a firm favourite and this jump in the odds caused sinister talk among the steady fans. It was a black night all round for Pep. The lighting arrangements in Madison Square Garden were primitive, with most of the floor area cloaked in darkness which gave substance to the observations of some of those in attendance. Pep's fight plan it was said, was to try for an early knockout. Perez was prepared for the aging ex-champion to tire himself out. As it turned out, Pep tired very quickly indeed. True, Perez caught him with a cracking left hook in their first exchange. This punch hurt Willie badly. It shook him up, and he staggered back from the impact and the follow up left hook sent over by Lulu. Perez looked very menacing. Pep was backing up with Perez bearing down upon him looking to connect with another big punch. The swarthy Brooklyn fighter had his hands down on his chest, walking forward without a thought of what Pep might throw back at him. He had a compelling air of confidence about his fighting.

In the second round, Pep's fans cheered wildly when this once great champion sent a flurry of lightning fast left hooks into the teak tough advancing Perez. "Go for it Willie, you can knock this bum out," they shouted. Pep for a few fleeting seconds look liked the wonder boxer of a few years previously as he connected with his blows which brought spray from Perez's dark head. But it was all too brief, like a candle in the wind. Time was fast running out for this once greatest of boxers. His blows had not the slightest effect on his opponent. A rapid fire left-right which hit Pep on the head, dumped him on the floor. He got up after taking an eight count from referee, Al Berl. Perez was now tasting blood, Pep's. He was all over the Hartford boxer. A right-uppercut nearly took Willie's head off his shoulders, a follow up straight right cross hit Pep like a missile, direct on target the chin, putting him down once again. He was now in a sitting position shaking his head to clear the cobwebs but he was on his feet for nine. This kid Perez, knew one more knockdown would see the finish of this contest, and would bring him his biggest victory in his short career, the scalp of Willie Pep! Stalking the befuddled and dazed Pep, he forced the former champion to the ropes near Willie's own corner. With his hands down low, Pep was a sitting target. A piledriving right hand smashed against the Nutmegger's jaw. It came straight from Lulu's toes. Bang! A resounding noise could be heard like a gunshot all around the Garden. Down went Pep once more, pitching face forward onto the canvas, seemingly out to the world. Referee Al Berl didn't bother counting, he waved his arms as a signal the fight was over. It was a sorry sight to watch Pep's handlers administering attention to the stricken fighter who had graced this same canvas in glory many times in the past. Bill Gore was grim-faced, if he had any emotions he knew how to hide them on this occasion. There has to be a winner and there has to be a loser. But when it happens to a great and wonderful champion such has Pep, then it's doubly sad. In fact it's cruel. It was Willie's 190th professional contest, and only his sixth defeat.

"All I know is that I tried my best," said a very disconsolate Pep in his dressing-room after the fiasco. Then, a few years later in a magazine article he said: "Dr. Nardiello made a statement about how my reflexes were shot, which was a lot of baloney, and they banned me from fighting in New York ever again. Suddenly, I'm unavailable. What really happened was that the Wednesday before the Perez fight, I told Lou Viscusi. 'Lou, I don't feel too good.' You had better go and see Doc Nardiello, he told me. So I went right over to the Doc's office. 'What's wrong Willie,' he asked. I can't put my finger on it, Doc," I said. "I just feel listless, no energy, no life."

Doctor Nardiello explained that in his opinion Willie had been working too hard and told Pep. "I'll give you a needle." The doctor took out a needle and when Pep saw it he nearly fainted. He told the doctor he didn't want it. He would take a vitamin pill, but not a needle. People have talked about fight fixes and all that stuff. Pep said one day while he was training somebody came up and said: "Willie, would you throw the fight for 50 G's," Pep laughed at the person, thinking the fellow was kidding him. Maybe the man was feeling Willie out, Pep wasn't sure, but nobody ever got any satisfaction from him. He was never approached directly about fixing a fight. Then again, maybe the reputation came from the people he hung around with. Yes, he had met Frankie Carbo a few times, the so-called underground boss of boxing, and he was always nice and pleasant to Pep.

In the early days when nobody could touch him in the ring, Willie was a fighter, that was all. Then Pep got matched with Jimmy McAllister and that fight ended in a draw and all of a sudden there was talk of the fight being a fix. The fact is that all bets are off if the fight ends in a draw. So how could there have been a fix? Three months later, he met McAllister in a return. There were 13,914 fans waiting to see what would happen. All of a sudden the odds took a tumble and the word went out around Jacob's Beach and Stillman's that Pep was taking a dive. Well, there was no kind of dive. Willie pinned McAllister in his own corner in the second round, belted him with a left to the body and he went down. He never got up, but after that it seemed Pep's reputation as a shady character was made.

Then came those four fights with Sandy Saddler, and not only was he shady now, he was dirty too. There was idol gossip about a fix when Pep lost to Tommy Collins in 1952, but he was forgiven by the majority of the newspaper reporters even though Collins was never conceived as a legitimate world class fighter. But Collins was, after all, they reasoned, a fully-fledged lightweight who later would go on to fight James Carter for the lightweight championship of the world less than a year after demolishing Pep in 1953. But Perez was only a featherweight who would never even fight for the title. Was it because he was not good enough? Nevertheless, what ever the reason he was regarded as no more than a good all-action fighter who did not have that little something extra needed to become a champion. He was expected to be no more than awkward for the refined skills of the likes of Willie Pep, even in 1954.

After the Perez fight, Commissioner Bob Christenberry said: "Any evil talk is a slur on a once great fighter who took the beating of his life. The result speaks for itself. This is the end of an era. You can't hold back youth. Also he had had nearly 200 fights by then!" Some of the opinions expressed by the critics the next morning are worth recording. Jesse Abramson, perhaps the most perceptive and respected fight writer in New York, scoffed at the wild stories that Pep deliberately lost to Perez: "To me it was simply age catching up with Pep. His 31 years is comparable to age forty-five in a heavyweight. The tip off for me, even though I didn't see the fight, was when Tommy Collins, a nothing fighter, knocked Pep out. It's a long time since the Marcune bout and I've always been told that in older fighters it's a matter of how good they feel when they get up in the morning." Lester Bromberg, World Telegram and Sun: "Maybe Lulu Perez isn't that good. For sure, Willie Pep was bad. On the big time the show's all over for the once marvellously agile fighter who lost last night couldn't get out of the way of a kid's right hand. A sadsack in his second-round knockout at Madison Square Garden, Willie's dared mention a return but he's barred by the IBC."

Harry Markson, managing director, said: "There had been a nasty web of circumstantial evidence against the former champion in the betting which closed with the bookies refusing to take any action on Perez. A 13-10 price on Lulu had mushroomed to 4-1 and out in the late betting yesterday. Others wanted to know about Willie's failure to throw rights to the head, also his reasons for carrying his left guard so low that his youthful opponent spotted it quickly.

All three knockdowns were clean shots including the rights which sent Willie down into what some regarded as unnecessarily theatrical tumbles. And devil or not, giving him his due he took more punishment than he had to. It is possible that Lulu, only 20, has suddenly arrived at the state in which he can blitz name fighters. My personal view, and I confess a prejudice in Pep's favour is the little old man simply couldn't go. Please Willie, quit and a happy retirement."

Caswell Adams, of the Journal: "The odds went up and Willie Pep went down. Lulu Perez thus was credited by his curious coincidence last night by knocking out the former master of the world's featherweights in the second round. As a fight, last night's affair belongs in a bottle in a laboratory along with a three headed pig; it was that strange. He has the audacity to say he isn't through as a fighter. Once the queer quotations on the bookmakers have been noted, it must be noted also that Pep, through the short space of time when he was in the ring, never threw a right hand. And Wily Willie was always a good man with his right."

There is a little twist to the Lulu Perez story. Less than a year after flattening Pep, his handlers screamed blue murder that Sandy Saddler was afraid of their tiger and wouldn't fight him. Saddler duly fought him in Boston, and the champion utterly destroyed the aggressive little warrior in four brutal rounds, making a terrible mess of him into the process. This was a non-title affair and thirty-nine-days later Saddler defended his crown by beating Teddy "Red-Top" Davis in Madison Square Garden.

Was the Pep-Perez fixed as many people have claimed? Well I have my own feelings and observations. What I can say is this. I have watched the film of the fight hundreds of times, and I do mean hundreds of times. I have watched it from every possible angle, run it in slow motion and at fast speed. Putting aside my admiration for Pep, I can honestly say if he did not try in this bout, and, as it has been suggested he was not really hurt from Perez's punches, then he does indeed deserve the "Academy Award" for this pretence. But from my own observations of studying this particular contest, there is not the slightest doubt in my mind that Pep was badly hurt and stunned by the punches he took throughout the whole of the two rounds it lasted. He looked very shaky indeed. As a boxing coach myself, if I had been in his corner the night he fought Perez and seen the punches he took, I would have had no hesitation whatsoever of throwing in the towel or retiring him when he came back to the corner at the conclusion of that first round. The eyes tell the true story.

The fight film shows ever so clearly Pep was suffering from some form of concussion resulting from the accumulative punches which had landed like bullets on his head and face. Some reporters claimed Pep seemed reluctant to arise from the first two knockdowns. They also brought up certain other fights involving Pep which they cast doubts about. Everyone has their own opinions, they see it through their eyes and make their own judgements.

Years later Pep said: "The main thing to understand is this; a punch you get hit with when you are only 25 won't bother you. But when you get hit with the same punch when you're over 30, it will knock you down. And when you're 35 years old it will knock you out."

Where Does He Go From Here?
Where could Pep go from here was the question his braintrust were asking themselves. He had no other trade to fall back on. He had squandered most of his money on failed marriages and lousy business deals, gambling and loans to so-called friends. People had short memories. Pep knew deep down in his heart he was finished. But he could still fight in the "sticks" and trade in on his name. As long has his future fights were carefully selected he could still earn fair amounts of money. The true boxing fans would still pay to watch him perform. He had three more bouts in the five months following the Perez fiasco. He won three by 10 round decisions, over Mike Turcotte in Mobile, Til LeBlanc in Moncton and Mario Colon, in Daytona Beach. He knew these places were a long, long way from Madison Square Garden.

Sat at home many years after the Perez defeat, Pep was in a reflective mood: "The black marks are my three losses to Saddler and the knockout by Perez. Let me explain the Perez defeat. This is the fight that cost me more heartache and aggravation than any other fight throughout my career. Because of it I was banned from fighting in New York. It was Dr. Vincent Nardiello who listed me as "unavailable" after Perez knocked me out. Nardiello was the physician for the New York State Athletic Commission and he sat at ringside for most of the Madison Square Garden matches. He had a down on me because I lost that fight, that was the reason I couldn't get a fight in New York after the loss to Perez, even through the National Boxing Association allowed me to fight in the States under their jurisdiction and control. "If you want to know the truth, I had bet five-hundred dollars on myself in the Perez fight. Three times in my life I bet on myself; the Perez fight, another 500 dollars on the last Saddler fight and a small bet against Pat Marcune. I lost on Saddler and Perez, I won on Marcune, but I never had to bet. When I was winning all those fights, the first 63 in a row, then another 73 without defeat, I never bet a dime on myself. Who needed it?

The Fix!
"Did You Throw The Fight?" asked the gaunt-looking Mike Wallace, the aggressive and forthright host of America's top-rated chat show of the time "Nightbeat"... Willie Pep, straight faced, replied to this loaded question with an emphatic: "No"... I was never mixed up in anything like that. I had

an off night now and then, we all do. I always do the best I can. I wasn't in the best shape for the Perez fight because I drove all the way up from Florida. That took a lot out of me. But I don't want to take anything away from Perez, he caught me flush on the chin and knocked me out, fair and square."

The most publicised and talked about television show in the Eastern United States was "Nightbeat." Pep readily agreed to appear despite the fact many other celebrities refused to get involved in this telecast because of its probing and grilling type of questioning. "Pep, they say has more skeletons in his closet than Willie Sutton. Also, like Sutton, Willie the Wisp knows how to parry leading questions with the same grace he used to parry a left jab on the face," said the publicity handout for the show. The host of the show, Mike Wallace, was a nosy fellow to say the least. Wallace's strong point was pitching carefully prepared questions at his embarrassed guests and Nightbeat" strived to extract confidential information from those brave enough to venture onto its brassy spotlight. Pep provided Wallace's research staff with more juicy tit-bits than they had ever dreamed off. There were those "disgraceful" fights with Sandy Saddler; the "Dump" rumours of his fight with Lulu Perez; his banishment in New York State by Dr. Vincent Nardiello; and the accusations Pep himself had made in a magazine article.

When the battle scarred Pep sat down in front of the "Nightbeat" cameras, Mr. Wallace was ready and waiting. But after over fifteen minutes of trying to open Pep up, Wallace had to admit: "Willie, you know how to slip a question." Then Mr. Wallace fired this question directly at the former featherweight champion: "Willie, you are banned from boxing in the State of New York. Are you free to box in any other states?" Willie calmly replied: "Yes, New York is the only state where I can't box. They barred me there after my fight with (Lulu) Perez. That was a few years ago and I still can't understand why they did it." Pep went on to say one of the reasons why he was barred from boxing in New York was because it was claimed his reflexes were gone. "And that's just not true," he added. Mike Wallace shot back with a question: "Willie, speaking of that fight with Perez, I'm sure you are aware of all the talk about a fix connected with that fight." "Did you throw the fight?" Willie, looking right into Wallace's eyes replied: "No. I have answered this question before. No I didn't throw any fight."

In 1981 Pep sued Newsweek Inc. an Inside Sports magazine for $75 million in damages in a law suit he brought against them. Pep claimed their article libelled him. Newsweek published an article written by Paul Good, aptly called: "The Fix." It didn't mention Pep by name, instead he was simply referred to as "The Champ." The article told how Norman Brett, a compulsive gambler from Willimantic, befriended a professional fighter called "The Champ" in the 1940s and made some money when "The Champ" threw a fight for him. Pep was a champion in the 1940's and knew Brett, but he said Brett wasn't a "close friend" and he didn't throw a fight. Willie was 58. "It's not true," said Pep. "I'm known all over the world. It lets me down. I don't care how messy it gets, I didn't do it."

Norman Brett, a compulsive gambler, who was the source of the Inside Sports magazine story which accused Pep of throwing the fight, admitted in sworn testimony he was a "pathological liar" until 1977, when he joined "Gamblers Anonymous." Cross-examined by Pep's lawyer, John McKeon of Hartford, during a deposition at U.S District Court in Hartford, in supplying information for the article, Brett allegedly told Good Pep secretly revealed to him he would lose the prize fight when he was matched with Lulu Perez in 1954. Brett said he bet and won $9,000 when Perez won. Brett also told Good when he later joined Pep on a trip to Florida soon after the fight, he accidentally discovered $16,000 in cash in the glove compartment of Pep's car. "This money he implied, was to be used by 'The Champ' to pay off debts to unidentified gangland characters," said McKeon. McKeon asked Brett if he would agree with a woman who was ready to swear under oath that Brett is a pathological liar. "I would agree with her until 24 June, 1977," answered Brett, referring to the date he joined Gamblers Anonymous. "Then you do agree up until 1977 you could be fairly branded as a pathological liar? "Yes"

Attorney Stephen R. Froling of a New York law firm of Rogers and Wells represented Newsweek and Good at the deposition. Asked Froling: "Was your description to Paul Good truthful and accurate to the best of your knowledge about those events?" "Yes," replied Brett. "The statements in the article were accurate?" "Yes" The Inside Sports story indicated a man it identified as "Brownie" was in with Brett on early plans to bet against Perez because Pep had indicated to Brett he (Pep) would surely win. Brett said the plans were dashed when Pep on the eve of the fight told

Brett he'd lose because "my arm ain't a hundred percent." Brett claims he passed the information along to "Brownie" but, fearing a double-cross, "Brownie" refused to bet on Perez. During the deposition in federal court, McKeon produced "Brownie." Who identified himself as Edward Brown Sr. Brown had been characterised in "The Fix" as a "big betting oilman." Brown testified the account given to Good by Brett was untrue, adding he had never been contracted by Good or any other representative of Inside Sports to corroborate the story. Saying he had never bet on a fight, Brown scoffed at Brett's claim he was willing to plunk down a heavy wager. McKeon said he considered it shocking that a major national publication would rely entirely on the word of a convicted felon and an admitted liar. Brett was unable to produce a single living person to back up important details of the Inside Sports story.

It was claimed Brett's motive for giving the magazine the story was because he thought it would be made part of a book and that he had negotiated with actor Paul Newman to portray Brett on the screen in the event the book was made into a movie.

Pep's attorney, Norman Ebenstein, said there wasn't any doubt who was the subject of the article. "It's a vicious, defamatory article, and it is totally false," Ebenstein said at a press conference held in his Hartford office. Ebenstein said he believed the article was published to help promote the new magazine. "I suspect they (Inside Sports) felt the benefit to them in publicity would far exceed any cost to them of a judgement," he said, adding that it was totally "an effort to create sensationalism." Ebenstein said he hoped to prove that enough in the article is so false that the balance of the story is also false. "I hate to use the word, but I feel it's a piece of cake," he said. The suit filed in U.S. District Court, Southern District of New York, demanded $20 million in compensatory damages, $5 million in special damages and $50 million in punitive damages. It also sought a public written apology, a retraction and such other, further and different relief as the court may seem just and proper, to include costs and taxable disbursements.

It was a messy affair and something Willie could well have done without. It appears Mr. Good, when interviewing him, had said it was for material on a book he was writing on Brett, not for a piece on Pep. Good's story quoted the late Hartford Courant Sports Editor Bill Lee writing on the day of the fight: "The Broadway wise guys think (blank) will fade after five rounds and be beaten down by the pressure of the kid's youth and fast punches." Lee used Pep's name in the blank space, and "the kid" was Perez. Lee, who was one of Willie's closest friends as well as an astute boxing writer, filed the following news story moments after the fight. "New York-Lulu Perez knocked out the once fabulous Willie Pep in 1.53 of the second round tonight in a result which put gossip on the tongues of many who left the Madison Square Garden unconvinced the great former featherweight champion could have become as pitifully defenceless as he looked against his 20-year-old opponent. "Hoots of derision and angry boos came from those in the crowd who would not believe Pep had fallen so completely apart in the eight months since his spectacular knockout in the same ring over tough Pat Marcune. He was just a hopeless wreck of a once great fighter, and Perez in spots appeared almost overcome with surprise at the ease with which he won what he regarded as the most important fight of his career. The gossips murmured and muttered about the sudden rush of gambling money to Perez who became a 3-1 favourite an hour before the fight."

The following day Lee wrote a column in which he stated in part: "A vicious line of circumstantial evidence made it easy to charge Pep with throwing the fight, and the charges were hurled by more than the usual crumb bums who lost a sawbuck on the fight. The sun never sets on 'bag' talk in the ugly business of prize fighting. How can there be a betting coup when the 3 to 1 favourite wins? It would have to be the other way around for a killing. From where I sat, it was something more inexorable than larceny. It was the sad, sad finish of an old fighter who, like hundreds before him, stayed around one fight too many."

When the case got to court, Willie claimed he and thousands more reading the story knew straight away that the story in the magazine was about his contest in Madison Square Garden against Lulu Perez. Pep testified in a court of law. But Mr. Peter Fleming, the attorney for "Newsweek," told the jury that just as Pep did not stand up after his third knockdown in the second round, his story from the witness stand did not stand up. He called Pep: "A great fighter, who never threw a right hand punch in the Perez fight. The story that Pep had taken a dive in the Perez fight was part of boxing history," said Mr. Fleming. Sadly, Pep failed to prove that he was libelled by the article, and the Federal jury threw the case out on Monday, 28 February, 1984.

Set-Ups

Set-ups, fight fixing, gangsterism have always been part of the story of professional boxing which has always been tainted with corruption and been tarnished with malicious allegations from its very beginning. Yet it draws politicians, movie stars, rock singers, men of art and culture, wonderful writers like Bud Schulberg, George Plimpton, Norman Mailer, and Ernest Hemingway all have been touched by the boxing bug. These great writers and many more such as Gilbert Odd and Hugh McIlvaney have all written about the fight game in one way or another. Nat Fleischer was the founder and editor of the Ring magazine which became known throughout the boxing world as the "Bible" of boxing. The magazine was printed in New York. Fleischer was an authority on boxing and was acclaimed throughout the world. Several times throughout the years he wrote in his magazine a clean up of boxing was required, and the undesirable characters should be kicked out once and for all.

Two words which are most used in boxing for the big fights are upsets and set-ups. One has only to delve into Primo Carnera's career to find out there was corruption in abundance. In Willie Pep's case there were plenty of rumours flying about in the inner circles of the boxing world about a certain number of his fights. These were nasty and malicious remarks, scurrilous allegations without any substance. Were any of Pep's fights fixed? Certainly not. Why? Well there is no hard evidence, no facts to back up these allegations. Pep himself has appeared on radio and television, been interviewed by various magazine and newspaper writers all probing about fight fixes. He also went to a court of law and denied any kind of wrong doing during any of his 241 professional fights. It's a shame such evil talk should besmirch this great champion's integrity and reputation.

To write about the gangster element involved in boxing would take a book on this subject alone. But make no mistake, boxing in the 1940s was controlled by mobsters. To unravel this maze of intrigue I will briefly try and explain a few facts and leave the reader to make their own judgement. American boxing had been invested by corruption and the gangster element. Mobsters such as Al Capone, Owney Madden, Lucky Luciano, Frenchy Demange and Legs Diamond, were all involved in boxing in some capacity or other. The main reason these thugs were allowed into the sport was because there was no Federal control.

In the 1940s television sets became popular in America, boxing became one of television's most popular events. It also brought more money for promoters. For example, in 1952, boxing could be viewed almost nightly to more than five million homes who had a set, which was thirty-one percent of the market; within three years, the audience figures soared to 8.5 million. Even the popular "I Love Lucy" show failed to attract the figures which boxing generated. It was like a honey pot and it didn't take long to attract the undesirables who began buzzing around. Also about this time, Joe Louis was nearing the end of his astonishing ring career and he was advised to form the Joe Louis Enterprises Inc., Joe's friend, Truman K. Gibson, an associate and former prominent War Department aide, along with multi-millionaire James Norris and his partner Arthur Wirtz formed the International Boxing Club (IBC), which later would become known as "The Octopus." Shortly afterwards Louis left the group after receiving a hefty cash settlement.

Norris and his organisation then set about controlling all the major boxing venues such as Madison Square Garden, St. Nicholas Arena, Yankee Stadium and the Polo Grounds. Norris also owned the Chicago Stadium and other venues. The IBC soon gained control of the television fights and also control of the heavyweight, welterweight and middleweight divisions. It was of course a monopoly and was growing bigger and bigger and stronger and stronger. But they hadn't reckoned with the Boxing Managers Guild, a more villainous monopoly group than the IBC itself. This group was formed in 1944 chiefly as a protection union for managers and matchmakers and to keep the fighters in line.

The reader would be right in asking who was protecting the most important people in the sport-the boxers. Well sadly the simple answer was nobody. It was a fact that the fighters was there to be used, abused and to do what he was told. In 1949 there was a showdown between the Guild and the IBC. The outcome was that the IBC were forced to pay any boxer appearing on television a thousand dollars, in addition of course to his purse money. Later, the Guild caused more mayhem and the IBC were exasperated with the situation. Eventually Norris and Gibson paid the Guild $135,000 over the following three years. This was protection money to ensure there would be no more strikes.

Mr. Frankie. Carbo was once again back on the scene and his lady friend was put on the IBC payroll. Carbo had a police record which included among many other violations, grand larceny and murder. In 1939 along with "Bugsy" Siegal, Lepke Buchalter and other undesirables, he was involved in the infamous "Thanksgiving Day" murder of a member of Murder Inc. When the trial began, the chief prosecution witness mysteriously died when falling or by being pushed from his hotel window, while under the protection of police officers. The case of course collapsed. Carbo admitted he controlled Mike Jacobs during Mike's reign as the world's top promoter.

Carbo was also involved in one way or another with most of the big fights. It was reported that he began using his influence to arrange for Willie Pep, Carmen Basilio, Tony DeMarco and Jake LaMotta, four illustrious names to take part in IBC organised contests. It was Carbo along with "Honest" Bill Daly, who kept the Guild under control.

Ray Arcel and two associates started promoting independently of the IBC and the Guild. They ran weekly tournaments throughout America and were helped by television money. Arcel was a breath of fresh air to freelance and independent managers. He was giving them and their fighters a chance of getting fights without the necessity of being forced to "cut" in someone who was on the inside. The other two organisations were less than pleased and one Saturday afternoon in 1953, Arcel was stood outside the Manger Hotel in Boston, when in broad daylight he was struck from behind by thugs wielding a lead pipe concealed in a paper bag. Ray suffered a fractured skull among other injuries and was hospitalised for several months. This was a vicious cruel and unwarranted attack on Ray Arcel. There was certainly no case of mistaken identity. A reward of $7,000 was offered by the Boston newspapers to apprehend the scum responsible for this outrage. But those responsible for the flagrant attack against decent citizenship were not to be found around the New England States. They were based in and around New York City.

A few years later, Jackie Leonard a promoter on the West coast had run foul of Carbo and Blinky Palermo, he received a visit from Bill Daly. During their conversation in which Daly was very intimidating. He told Mr. Leonard that Carbo was extremely angry with him and he related what had happened to Ray Arcel. Explaining in graphic detail exactly what happens when a lead pipe is used.

In 1959 the F.B.I. arrested four well-known boxing figures and accused them of extortion. The government agencies were confident they had broken the link in the chain that had been tightly wound around American boxing by Carbo and his fellow mobsters. What surprised everybody was the arrest of Truman Gibson, president of National Boxing Enterprises' Inc. The four arrested were Frankie Carbo, Blinky Palermo, Joe Sica and Louis Tom Draga. In 1951 there had been a much bigger investigation and in 1955 the Guild was forced to end its manipulative reign. And shortly afterwards the IBC was ordered to disband. The clean-up campaign was underway and boxing would be the better for the cleansing. It has been said many times over the years that the reason organisations such as the Managers Guild and the International Boxing Club and other splintered groups were allowed to flourish in America was because there was no central controlling body.

The staff receive salaries and a pension. The licence holders do not know how much they are paid. because the BBBOFC will not disclose these facts. It would need a book on its own to unravel the running of this particular organisation.

Back to the story. Speaking in November 1956, Pep showed his anger about the fixed fight allegations or fights that were known as "bag" jobs with many sporting celebrities firmly pointing the finger at him Pep said: "The inevitable discussion began. 'You know how it is, how everybody says the greatest fighters of our age were Sugar Ray Robinson and Joe Louis. Sooner or later my name gets mentioned, but there is always a flaw. For instance, I was reading Jimmy Cannon, a well known New York columnist, and he quoted both Robinson and Louis, saying they never saw Pep make a wrong move in a fight when he was levelling. It always gets back to that when he was levelling. Well, I've got news for Sugar Ray Robinson and Joe Louis, there never was a fight in which I wasn't levelling. Now this may amuse a lot of people whose only memory of Willie Pep today is the seven times he lost, not the 200 plus fights he won. Willie had no good right to lose a fight, they say. Who says so? Am I a superman or something? An indestructable man? A robot that you can operate by machine and turn on and off at will? I'm made of flesh and blood just like everybody else. When I'm cut, I bleed good. "Women and money are my two biggest troubles. "I got arrested twice for shooting dice while I was the world champion. It was very humiliating and I've always felt bad about it. But getting back to my fights, I never threw any fight in my life, and that's the truth!"

Just over a year after the Lulu Perez affair. Willie was involved in another contest in which there was a great deal of controversy. After the Perez shock he had won five bouts when he accepted a contest with another young, up-and-coming fighter who was being groomed for stardom, Gil Cadilli. Cadilli was being built up as a contender and it would boost his prestige and drawing power if he could beat the former featherweight champion. The fight was staged at the Parks Airforce Base in California on 30 March, 1955. On the night of the fight, the Academy Award Dinner was being held in Hollywood. Even though Marlon Brando and Grace Kelly were awarded prizes for their outstanding performances of the year, there was no question they were being given preferential treatment, because the most logical candidates for the prizes must have been the two ringside judges of the Pep versus Cadilli contest.

A report in the Boxing and Wrestling magazine for July 1955 said: "It was the world's worst decision. Willie Pep was atrociously cheated out of a ten round decision over Gil Cadilli. Judges Eddie James and Tony Bosnich gave a ridiculous decision in awarding the palm to Cadilli after he was given a one sided pasting in nine out of ten rounds. The only round earned by Cadilli was the fourth in which he cut Pep's eye. In view of the exact scoring of the officials, it made it appear as if they were attending the Academy dinner because they certainly were not watching the Pep-Cadilli fight. Gil is only a youngster who seemed baffled and confused by Pep's mastery. There's no possible excuse for the verdict. Pep did everything but score a knockout and did it in convincing style. He won this fight, just as surely as Sid Flaherty controls boxing in Northern California."

The aftermath of this disgraceful miscarriage of justice toward Pep was that the California Commission removed Mr. James' name from the list of judges and also placed Mr. Bosnich on probation because of his inexperience. It was later revealed Bosnich was making his first appearance as a judge, and really should not have been selected to officiate in such an important contest. It was also revealed later Bosnich, a former fighter himself, used to be managed by Cadilli's manager, Sid Flaherty, who handled a stable of fighters which included Carl "Bobo" Olson, who was the world middleweight champion at this period.

The State Athletic Commissioner, Joe Phillips, said the outcome of the Pep-Cadilli fight warranted an investigation. The ringside judges score cards showed a great difference existed in the scoring. Who selected the the three officials? The nationally telecast bout was held at the Air Force base as part of the Air Force's recruiting programme. A spokesman for the Air Force base said the referee and two judges had been appointed by the State Athletic Commission as was customary, but Phillips said that was not the case. "The Air Base told us they would like to have Downey, Bosnich and James to handle the Pep-Cadilli fight and we had no objections," said Phillips. "But we had nothing to do with appointing them."

Thousands of television fans who had viewed the fight phoned the television station, wrote to the Commission and complained to the newspapers about the unjust decision rendered against Pep. In order to defuse the situation, Sid Flaherty said Pep should have been disqualified after the fourth round, because he claimed Pep's cornermen worked on repairing his eye injury for a full 37 seconds after the ten-second warning buzzer had sounded. "I had my stop watch and clocked them," said Flaherty. "Instead of clearing out of the ring in accordance with the state rule, they were nearly 30 seconds into the fifth round before the bell rang."

Pep, who rarely comments about his fights, said: "In all my years in the ring this was the worst job of officiating I ever saw. I'd love to fight this Cadilli guy again, but not in California." Less than two months later Willie fought Cadilli again, but this time in Detroit and Pep boxed the ears of the young prospect for a clear-cut points victory. A short time after the rematch against Cadilli, Willie was still trying to edge back into world contention. He was straining for new honours and the security and respectability he had been unable to find since the Perez scandal.

It was a brisk, sunny September afternoon in New York. Willie was passing the time of day in a lobby directly opposite Madison Square Garden.

With him was his 12 year old son Billy, Lou Viscusi, Bill Gore and Aldo Mente, a young lightweight who was being handled by Pep and Viscusi. The night before Pep had boxed in Holyoke, beating Pappy Gault for a ten round points decision. He was awaiting a plane connection to Miami, Florida, where he was due to fight another ten round contest. Viscusi was excited about Willie's performance the night before against Gault. The manager told friends Pep had boxed wonderfully well, and didn't get hit more than twice in the whole fight. "If only they'd give him another chance in New York," said Viscusi, who then outlined a plan he was hatching for Willie to fight Sandy Saddler for a fifth time in Miami. "If all goes well, it will be a big pay day for Willie and I'm sure Willie will beat

Saddler this time. If I didn't think so I wouldn't be trying to make the match," said Mr. Lou.

Pep listened to his manager, smiled and nodded his head. "Wouldn't that be some feat if I beat Saddler?" he said, clapping his hands together. "The champion of the world, banned in New York because his reflexes are shot."

He was of course referring to Dr. Nardiello's statement in 1954, that Pep's reflexes were no longer what they were. But there seemed to be a hollow ring in Willie's voice, like that of a man who wanted to believe it could happen, but deep down knew it was impossible. As Pep and his son walked out of the hotel. Viscusi followed them with his eyes and said to some friends: "Willie has been a target for the smear guys for a long time. It's about time they laid off him and picked on somebody else. People around New York would be amazed if they saw the way he paced himself last night. He set the clock back years and to be honest I was the most surprised guy in the place. He was just marvellous."

But time would reveal the whirling cycle of Willie Pep, all the way from a dirty narrow street in Hartford, through boxing's vicious back alleys, to the featherweight championship of the world, would never fight Saddler again, or fight for the title, (though he came close when he boxed Hogan (Kid) Bassey, but more about this in another chapter), nor would he make any more big money. Viscusi's dreams would be dashed away by the usual boxing politics. Instead it would be back on the fight circuit or as Pep himself called it, "playing the sticks," where his purses sometimes came to a thousand dollars, but more often the figure fluctuated to around the four-hundred dollar mark. And the result of his fight, would merit no more than a tiny agate line of type which would be lost among the half-dozen other out-of-town fight results. A few short years before a Willie Pep fight rated front page headlines, full page picture spreads in the centre fold and the centre sports page. It was a sad reflection of where he had come from to where he had been and now, at this moment in time where he was going.

The Best Sports Writer In America

Red Smith was a brilliant American sportswriter. He was virtually without peer in his profession. Winner of the prestigious "Pullitzer Prize" for distinguished commentary, in 1976 Smith became only the second sports columnist ever honoured with that award-Arthur Daley of the Times being the first in 1956. The "Pulitzer" committee cited Smith's work for being "unique in the erudition, the literary quality, the vitality and the freshness of viewpoint." He received innumerable awards and several honorary degrees. In the college textbook, "A Quarto of Modern Literature," between an essay by Winston Churchill and a short story by Dylan Thomas, there is an example of spot-news reporting by Red Smith. It is a column on a heavyweight fight between Joe Louis and Rocky Marciano, written on deadline. It is the only piece of journalism in the anthology, and the only sports story. He was pleased by the attention, but, not necessarily impressed.

Smith joined the New York Times, at the age of 66, which goes to show how highly this man was thought of in the newspaper trade. Mr. A.M. Rosenthal, who was the executive editor of the newspaper said: "We always felt bringing Red to our staff, even at an age when most men contemplate retirement, allowed us to fulfil a very special trust for sports. He was a wonderful writer and a wonderful man." Smith's three or four columns a week were syndicated by the New York Times News Service to 275 newspapers in the United States and 225 in about 30 foreign nations.

In 1956, when Red Smith and Frank Graham, another highly respected sports writer on the American beat, were covering baseball training camps in Florida they were in search of stories for their thousands of readers to drool over during breakfast. One afternoon while driving out of Tampa on the Tamiami Trail, heading back to Miami Beach, they were chatting away about what they were going to feature in their next day's column's. Over the car radio a sports report was being broadcast. It was announced Willie Pep would be fighting a tough Mexican fighter named Kid Campeche in Tampa that evening. So, without either of them saying anything, Red just turned the car around and headed back. Both had seen Pep in action from his early days as a fledgling young pro. Both admired his undoubted grace and ringcraft, along with his boundless enthusiasm for the boxing game. Smith in particular was charmed by Pep. Red loved Pep's approach to life and it's many pitfalls in the boxing business, his fighting zeal and zest for perfection. He had watched the valiant former champion's skill formulate. What Smith admired most about Pep though, was the way he got over the plane crash. Pep's brave attempt to revamp his career. "That took a lot of achievement. Willie was no quitter," said Red.

One day, while discussing his latter years in boxing, Pep told a young reporter: "It's funny how some things stick in your mind. Though thousands of stories have been written about my career, wonderful stories that still give me a warm feeling, I remember two above all the others. One was a column by Red Smith, commenting on my victory over Andy Arel in December 1955 in Miami Beach."

Pep had trounced his one-time sparring partner Arel on points going the ten round distance. Red Smith was sitting at ringside that night, and he wrote how beautifully Pep had boxed all through the ten rounds, and was moved to write the following: "Attending the very early Greek theatre must have been a great deal like watching Willie Pep fight. Those who claim to know say that in days before Aeschylus, the plot was always the same and audiences came only to see how well the players performed their roles." "Probably there are critics who would argue that theatre hasn't changed. At any rate, Willie hasn't. His drink is autumn wine now, but when you watch his televised shadow flitting across the screen you know time can not wither nor custom stale the little desperado's incomparable gifts.

"Cooped in an undersized ring in Miami Beach...Willie was Manolete and Michangelo in the handy pocket-sized package, with a dash of ponzi for seasoning...He is an endless delight and an unfailing surprise, and the longer he goes the more astonishing he becomes. Indeed, it was something of a surprise the camera was able to find him in Miami Beach. If Willie had chosen a life of crime he could have been the most accomplished pickpocket since the Artful Dodger. He may well be the only man that ever lived who could lift a sucker's poke while wearing eight-ounce gloves. In action he's a marvel, and in the record books he's a downright hoax. It is accepted as a fact of life in the ring that little fellows don't last long. Many of them start young and are burned out by the time they're 25. Willie had been fighting as amateur and professional, six years or more when he won the featherweight title from Chalky Wright, and that was way back in 1942. Sammy Agnott was the lightweight champion then, Red Cochrane had the welterweight title frozen, Tony Zale was succeeding to the spot left vacant by Billy Soose among the middleweights, Gus Lesnevich and Joe Louis bossed the big fellows. Where were they this year, 13 years later, when Willie was fighting once a month and winning 'em all." Red Smith wrote this article for the Chicago Sun Times.

So, for this man Smith to turn his car around and travel back to Tampa to watch Pep boxing in a nondescript boxing match that evening was a tribute to his own immorality. After watching Pep pitch a complete shutout against a very robust Kid Campeche on points after ten rounds. Smith smiled and shook his head. Willie had boxed in a manner forgotten, but brilliant to say the least. The old feints were still working, the dazzling footwork still immaculate and the all-round ringcraft impeccable as ever. In short, he had the Mexican baffled and bemused and totally outclassed with not a clue of how he could contain this little genius in front of him. After the fight ended, Red and his companion went into Campeche's dressing-room. As they knocked and walked in, they saw Campeche flat out on the rubbing table, he looked completely exhausted and downright dejected. His head was covered with a towel.

"Well, what was it like fighting Pep," said Smith. Throwing the towel to one side, the Kid replied: "What was it like? You really want to know. Well let me tell you, fighting Willie Pep is like trying to stamp out a grass fire." Campeche went on to explain how he was so confused he just lost all his rhythm and composure. "I would have hated to have fought him when he was younger," concluded the Kid.

Irregular Heartbeat

Smith would have found it more amazing had he known that just prior to the fight while training, Willie underwent a physical and the doctor, after examining Pep, told him his heart was not beating right. He was sent for more stringent tests to Miami University, where a prominent heart specialist examined him. After the examination was completed the specialist shook his head and said: "I have advised football players to retire because they had your condition." Pep was frightened, the medical expert added: "You have an irregular heartbeat." Pep excused himself, he wanted a second opinion. He rushed back to his hotel packed his case and took a plane to Massachusset where he spent four days in the general hospital. The hospital staff put him through four days of rigorous tests, really tough medical examinations. In the end apart from his heart being a little bit irregular he was told, "you can do anything you wish, you have a clean bill of health." His worries were over...apart from a hefty hospital bill.

Lou Viscusi, though, was getting concerned about Willie continuing boxing and after one fight he looked Willie in the eye and advised him to quit the ring. "What can I do," said Pep. "I can't hang around on street corners can I?"

"No" replied the manager. "Then let me be happy. I feel young, I'm sure I can get back to the top," concluded Pep. The year previously, after watching one of Pep's 13 contests of which he lost only one, a hotly disputed decision to Gil Cadilli, which he reversed a few weeks later, the prize winning writer kept a brief on all Pep's results, hoping the fighter would not end up getting badly hurt. He really did have a soft spot for the genius of Pep, as much as the former world champion admired and revered Red Smith's writing.

Pep's star had been on the wane since his last fight against arch-enemy, Sandy Saddler in 1951. He was still boxing all across the States, keeping his name alive. Giving fans a treat by watching a beautifully balanced boxing master. Willie was an ex-champion now and ex-champions have to fight in the sticks. He had to rough it, there were no more first-class hotels, nor eating in the best restaurants. Pep found himself eating in all kind of one-arm-dumps, and hanging around bus depots at night waiting for bus connections to all kinds of places. Even when an ex-world champion is making a comeback he has got to fight ordinary opponents and that means going to the small towns. Willie would have to arrive three or four days before the fight so the promoter could publicise it in the local press. Willie admitted life was very lonely being an ex-champion, but he was determined to keep fighting.

"I would have carried on fighting until I was 80 if I could have. I loved the involvement, I really did, of course I missed all the comforts and travelling by plane and eating the best food. But fighting was my whole life," he told friends. After beating Kid Campeche at the start of 1956 he won ten more fights over the next couple of years. He fought in places such as Beaumont, San Antonio, Lawton, Okla, Florence, South Carolina, El-Passo, Houston and Boston. Though he was outclassing his victims, he was nevertheless getting hit more often than he previously had, getting little cuts and nicks around his face. Nobody really cared whether he boxed or not, save for a few staunch boxing writers who had fond memories of Pep at his best. But he had to carry on as it was his living.

"There'll never be another champ like William Papaleo (alias Willie Pep)," that's what people were saying in Hartford in 1957. A glowing tribute indeed, but all this speaking in the past tense annoyed Willie. "Anyone would think I was dead by the way people are talking," he declared.

He had won his last 19 bouts. His old rival Sandy Saddler was by now retired due to eye trouble, and the new featherweight champion of the world was Hogan "Kid" Bassey. You could never take away a champion's ability. He would never forget his moves. But his legs and reflexes did not respond at the age of 34, which was Willie's age. He said his dream was a fight with Bassey for his old title. His recent record proved that the former champion was still too good for anyone but the real top-fighters. But Willie wasn't boxing rated fighters anymore.

In January 1958, he dropped a ten round decision to a good fighter, Tommy Tibbs, in Boston. This was only his sixth loss in some 200 professional bouts. He went on to win 11 more contests that year, beating the likes of Prince Johnson, Pat McCoy, who came from Galway in Ireland and two years previously had fought regularly in the British Isles, Bobby Bell, Louis Carmona, Jimmy Kelly and Bobby Singleton, among other lesser lights of the boxing world of that period. But then he was offered the chance to hit the big time again. He was booked to face the current featherweight champion of the world, Hogan "Kid" Bassey, in the Boston Garden in a ten round non-title fight. He was promised that should he be victorious, he would meet Bassey with the title at stake. He was delighted and trained harder than ever before. The Boston fans were buying tickets rapidly and it looked like being a sell-out.

A few weeks before fighting Bassey, Pep gave a radio interview outlining his plans and his desire to once again become the world featherweight champion. "I feel better today than I did five years ago," he told the listeners. Pep was looking in fine fettle and told the interviewer the most important thing about his boxing was keeping control. "The man who can make the other guy do what he wants him to do, will win every time. And he won't get hurt either. I admit that not getting hurt is the most important thing on my mind every time I climb through those ropes and into the ring, be it sparring or the actual fight, self preservation is the name of the game." Pep went on to explain how punches hurt just as much from fighters lower down the scale, as they did from those higher up the ladder.

Most of the fighters he was now fighting at this period were probably never heard of. In-fact Willie himself had never heard of some of them until the ring announcer shouted out their names during the introductions. Every once in a while though, he would run into a real hard-punching kid who had dynamite in his gloves. One particular night in South Carolina he was fighting a young aggressive fighter, and as the bell sounded for the first round the younger man tore out of his corner and belted Willie under the eye with a left hook. The former champion certainly felt that punch! He started to black out for an instant. Saddler never hit him any harder than that kid, but luckily the kid made the mistake Pep was hoping he would make. He started to throw wild looping rights at his chin. He could have thrown those kind of punches all day and all night without connecting once. Willie just let him swing and swing until he wore himself out, and all the time his head was clearing. Once Willie regained his composure, he pinned his opponent against the ropes and hit him at least 30 times to the body without reply. He never got hit again throughout the whole of the ten rounds. When he got back to the dressing room, Pep started to think what a fool he was, fighting for a couple of hundred dollars in a tank town and taking the same chances he would be taking if he was fighting a top fighter in New York where he would be getting a few thousand. It seemed stupid and wasteful.

Willie was asked his opinion on the current world featherweight champion, Hogan "Kid" Bassey: "This champion, Bassey, I think his name is, he is a good fighter, but nothing great. He's got a fast right hand and he moves good, but he's wide open all the time. Sure I know what you're thinking." "Pep must be nuts to even think about fighting him. How in hell can an old codger like him even think of fighting a real tough, strong youngster like Bassey? Well, don't kid yourself. I go ten rounds a couple of times a month, month in and month out, and I always feel like I can go five more rounds at full steam." Pep also said if he should ever be lucky enough to fight for his old featherweight title again he would train like never before.

It was unusual and very much out of character for Willie to criticise any fighter or his connections, but one day, egged on by a reporter, he said: "Well, suppose me and this clown Bassey was to fight for the title, I'd put in a solid month of toughening up in the woods some place. Roadwork every morning before dawn. In bed by eight every night. "Then I'd move into a nice out of the way training camp. Again daily roadwork and in bed early every night. At least six rounds of sparring every day with the best sparring partners I could get. I'd only employ guys who could really belt. I'd want them to press me every second I was in there. After a month in the woods, and another six weeks in camp, I figure I'd have an even chance against any featherweight in the world, Bassey, the champion, included." Again these comments were not like Willie Pep. He would never describe other fellow fighters as "clowns," especially a world champion. He had too much respect for anybody who put the gloves on and stepped into the ring. This outburst was obviously said for publicity reasons and nothing else. Willie had watched Bassey in action on television and said he wasn't impressed by what he saw. It was his opinion Bassey was always open to a counter punch and could be hit quite easily. The most important defect in Bassey's fighting style as far as Pep was concerned, was the champion had to set himself before he threw a punch. "I fought a lot of guys like Bassey in my time, said Pep. "Chalky Wright was one, Eddie Compo and Paddy DeMarco were two more. I loved fighting those kind of fighters because while they were setting themselves to punch, I would be banging them in the head and belly and moving out in the clear just when they are ready to tee off. That's exactly the way it would be against Bassey. I may be a little old, but I ain't sucker enough to stick around while some clown is setting himself to belt my brains out. I'd have quit a long time ago if that were the case."

Who Was Hogan "Kid" Bassey?

Who was Hogan (Kid) Bassey? Despite what Pep said about this world champion, Bassey could fight. Hogan was a sound boxer and more than average thumper, a worthy world champion who had won hard fights in America and the world title away from home. He also went on to destroy a dangerous Mexican challenger also in America in a title defence-no mean feat. British fight fans had accepted the squat, little Nigerian as one of their own, though at one time Bassey thought there was a "colour-bar" against him. This mode of thinking happened after Bassey had scored a terrific result in America. On his arrival back in London, he expected to be met by a full posse of reporters. Sadly, just one journalist was present. "Was it any wonder I thought there was some kind of colour-bar? Had it have been Dai Dower or Sammy McCarthy arriving back after such a prestigious victory in the States, I bet you would not have got on that air-strip for London pressmen," said a disconsolate Bassey.

By the time he reached his Liverpool home he was feeling much better. He received a civic reception at Liverpool Town Hall, where he was feted by a concourse of people with newspaper reporters and photographers in abundance. He was at this time married to a Merseyside lass, and had a young son, Hogan junior. Later, Bassey said: "It was very pleasing for me to know I had practically buried the racial prejudice which definitely existed in my early days in England." This little fighter Bassey was a national hero and the idol of the Nigerian youth.

Born in a small village called Ufok Ubet in Greek Town, Caabar, in Eastern Nigeria, Bassey started boxing amateur when he was 12. He was a member of the Paramount Boxing Club in Lagos, where well known fighters such as Ola Enoch, Sandy Manuel, Sammy Langford and Roy Jacobs, who all campaigned successfully in England during the 1950s, were among his team mates. Hogan won the Nigerian flyweight title in 1949 in his first professional fight while only 16 years-old.

In 1952 he set sail for England in an effort to advance his boxing career and a chance to meet better opponents. He was helped by Israel Boyle, an old Lagos fighter, who had already settled in Liverpool under the tutelage of Peter Banasko, a Liverpool boxing manager. His career in his new country got off to a good start when he forced Ray Hillyard to a fourth round retirement in a fight held in Liverpool Stadium. Bassey soon became a huge favourite all over Britain.

Bobby Boland, a tough Scottish fighter with a knockout record, was sensationally flattened in five thrilling rounds. There had been a great deal of friction between the two fighters which stemmed from Boland coming in over-weight and having to shed the excessive poundage. Annoyed, he made a scurrilous remark which incensed Bassey and a fight almost started there and then.

Bassey ran up 35 bouts in three-and-a-half-years, with many well known names on his record. Stan Skinskiss and Tommy Proffitt, two well respected fighters from the Manchester area; Tommy Higgins, Pierre Cossemyns, Louis Romero, two classy, tough Continentals; Denny Dawson, Johnny Butterworth, Percy Lewis, Joe Woussen, Enrico Macale, Harry Ramsden, Jackie Briers and Ken Lawrence. These were the days when there were regular tournaments in places such as West Hartlepool, Leeds, Blackpool, Manchester, Leicester, Newcastle, Liverpool, and of course, London. Great times, wonderful memories of a time when boxing was...just boxing!

His best victory though, was against "Smiling" Sammy McCarthy, the darling of the London promoters. Sammy had won all his 28 pro fights including a points win over the reigning British featherweight champion, Ronnie Clayton. McCarthy was among the smartest boxers in Europe at this time, great things were forecast for this 21-year-old. An added interest to the Bassey-McCarthy fight was both boxers putting up a £500 sidestake. Bassey clearly outpointed the London star.

Hogan was a little terrier of a fighter, always busy and punching from incredible angles, his best punch was the left hook, though his right also carried dynamite. He flattened Irish fighters, Joe Quinn and Billy "Spider" Kelly. He travelled to America and defeated Miguel Berrios on a 12 round points decision. This was a final eliminating match for the vacant world featherweight title.

"I would like to have fought Sandy Saddler for the title, but he did not seem in any hurry to defend his crown against me. I felt I could not afford to wait to long," said Bassey.

George Biddles had taken over as Bassey's manager after some difference of opinion between Hogan and Banasko. It was then on to Paris where he fought Cherif Hamia for the vacant world crown. Bassey was sensational, after being decked himself in the second round from a vicious right cross, he gathered his senses and knocked the Frenchman from pillar to post before stopping him in the tenth round and becoming the new featherweight champion of the world.

After a couple of non-title affairs, he was fighting in Los Angeles, defending his crown against a ferocious knockout brawler in Ricardo Moreno. After getting hit with a corking left hook on the bridge of his nose, he later described it as the hardest punch he had taken in all his 66 previous contests, Bassey went to work. It was a thrill-a-minute battle, just what the Los Angeles fight crowd love. He eventually knocked the Mexican born fighter spark-out with a left hook which smashed right through Moreno's guard with shattering effect, and sent him toppling down with never a chance of beating the count. The crowd were in hysterics, they had paid big money for the three rounds of non-stop action, but had enjoyed every second of those nine-minutes of fighting. "That is the way the Americans like their fighting. They have no time for ultra-scientific boxing, they want action and blood if they can get it!" said Bassey.

Shortly after this contest, Bassey was invited to Buckingham Palace to receive his M.B.E. (Member of the British Empire), a prestigious honour bestowed upon him by her majesty the Queen. Bassey was a very proud person indeed. "It was a momentous day, and something I look back upon with great pride."

The Impossible Dream

On 20 September, 1958, in the Boston Garden, Willie Pep tried to turn back the clock a dozen years, but found out this was an impossible dream. It was the present which counted when Willie, at 36, and with over 229 professional bouts in 19 years of busy campaigning, entered the ring. He received thunderous applause for this ten round non-title match.

Earlier in the day Bassey had been installed as an 8 to 5 betting favourite. He said: "I am certain Willie Pep's sole intention is to go the full distance, and get himself another crack at the title he once held with such distinction and honour. He was a unique boxer. I have the greatest of respect for him."

Waiting for the opening bell Pep was like a kettle steaming, waiting for the action to commence.

Sadly, his time had gone, and though he still showed flashes of his former brilliance against a much younger, tougher, harder-hitting, aggressive rival like the current world featherweight champion Hogan "Kid" Bassey, Willie no longer had the strength or endurance to box at top speed for long distance fights. But until he was battered into submission in 42 seconds of the ninth round the former ring master from Hartford gave a brilliant, never-to-be-forgotten display of boxing craftsmanship long since eclipsed from the fight game. He gave a remarkable account of himself.

From the outset, he began by boxing on the retreat, using nifty little feints, spinning his much stronger opponent and ducking and slipping dangerous punches. The crowd were in raptures for this was science, boxing science. The way Willie was making punches miss by moving his head a few inches either way was absorbing for the onlookers. Pep knew in his heart and soul this was definitely his last chance to enter the top flight of the featherweight class.

He was in tremendous physical condition. He had got himself ready for this bout with a series of 11 contests inside the previous eight months throughout New England. Yes it was true, most of those 11 victims were of the miscellaneous quality. But fights in the ring, even with inferior opposition, were far better than months of sparring in the gymnasium. He was ready for this battle with the British-based warrior, Bassey.

For the first five rounds, the former champion gave the 10,409 crowd, who paid $47,861 in gate receipts as there was no television showing of the fight, good reason to expect a miracle. They cheered his every move as he flitted in and out and even occasionally outflurried the determined champion. There was a 4,000 contingent of fans from Hartford who had made the journey in the hope of seeing their favourite pull it off and defeat the new featherweight king. Willie reached into his bag of tricks and embarrassed the champion on many occasions, jabbing and hooking and dancing around the ring as if on skates, but Bassey's body blows started to take their toll and slow Pep down. Pep was the crowd's sentimental favourite. Hogan had been coming forward throughout the bout digging hurtful punches to the Hartford boxer's solar-plexus. Willie's ancient and much-travelled legs grew weary upon taking these blows. It was an interesting and action-packed encounter. Pep used his caginess to befuddle the chunky, strong champion time after time. He had years of experience and knew every trick in the book and his ringcraft was magnificent. His technique was excellent and it took the African all his time to catch him with any solid blows, but Bassey was remorseless in his pursuit of victory. With only one round left, Pep was in front on two of the official score cards. Judge Savko had Pep leading by 79-77, while Judge Santore's card favoured the ex-champion by 77-75.

During the rest period between the eighth and ninth round, the crowd sensing Pep's stamina was on the wane shouted: "Come on Willie, you're nearly there, you can do it." But sadly the sands of time were running out for the Will-o'-the-Wisp. As the bell sounded to start round nine, both fighters came forward. They had barely reached the centre of the ring when Bassey tossed an overhand right which hit Willie flush on the chin.

This was a mighty powerful punch and Pep fell onto his back. His eyes were glazed and his legs were shaking and quivering from the impact. But he still had a fighting heart, and courageously got to his feet at the count of four, stumbled and reeled back towards the ropes. He was badly hurt and shaken up. The referee, Jimmy McCarron, restrained him until the count reached eight. Bassey was after him in a flash, using both fists he was winging away and threw another looping right which caught Pep again on the chin and settled the matter. He was across the lower strand, half in, half out of the ring. There was no chance that the brave former champion would beat the count but instinctively, Willie struggled to rise when the referee tolled ten. To many ringsiders it appeared McCarron had counted Pep out, but the referee insisted Willie had beaten the final decimal. Pep, however, was wobbling helplessly on rubbery legs and the referee called a halt there and then. The outcome appeared to prove once again that youth, strength and punching power could sometimes be too much for skill and experience alone.

Bassey became only the seventh fighter to defeat Pep during his long and colourful career. The Nigerian's victory crushed the Hartford maestro's hopes of ever getting another shot at his old title. No featherweight had ever won the championship three times. "I saw my opportunity and I seized it," commented Bassey. "I knew I had to do something drastic with only a couple of rounds left. However, I fought according to plan, especially going to the body to bring Pep's guard down."

Willie suffered cuts above the left eye and around the nose, and naturally was downhearted immediately after the defeat. But when asked if he planned to fight again, he quickly replied: "I don't see why not. This guy hits hard, and he hit me right. I made a mistake by pulling back instead of staying close, that was it. Bassey had been hitting me with good left hooks, but I wasn't tired and he wasn't hurting me. I noticed though, I wasn't getting out of his way fast enough." One reporter said later: "The little old champ made a chump of a young champ for the best part of eight rounds. Two more to go and he'd be home and a winner." But it wasn't to be!

Willies's Farewell To Boxing

"I have never lost two consecutive fights throughout my entire career. If that ever happens then I know it will be time for me to retire," said Willie Pep a few days after his defeat at the hands of Hogan "Kid" Bassey. He was not depressed about his loss to the current world featherweight champion, because for most of the contest he had boxed brilliantly until his stamina came to a sudden halt. And, as he pointed out: "I was in front on the judges scorecards. I felt good in the Bassey fight. Sure I'm 37 and it gets harder to get into top physical shape at this age. But I really did feel good in that fight. I was not feeling 37 during the bout I can assure you, 'I'm winning, I'm winning,' I kept telling myself, 'keep going and you're the winner,' I'm saying. But this kid Bassey has a tremendous one-punch knockout wallop," said Pep reflectively.

The former champion was offered a ten round contest in Caracas, Venezuela, against a local fighter named Victor "Sonny" Leon in January 1959. The purse was excellent so Willie willingly accepted the fight. Yes, he needed the money. In all his previous 200 or so contests, this was the first occasion he had fought outside America. He had of course crossed the border into Canada. "It's funny, but I never did do much travelling throughout my career. Boxing in the United States was much more active in my early days now, all the small clubs are dead thanks to television. All the action nowadays is in foreign countries," said Willie.

The people close to the former champion knew he was well and truly over the hill as far as world championships were concerned, or of him ever becoming a top ten contender again. But promoters refused to relinquish the picture of the skinny kid from Hartford who, a dozen years before, was able to move in and out, snapping jabs as he went, conserving his energy while controlling the fight. Years had passed since then and Pep was no longer the boxing genius he once was. Gone were the times when Lou Viscusi ran Pep with purpose and profit. Now Viscusi was ill. He could no longer look after Willie the way he once did.

Pep was now on his own. Life itself was his challenger. It had taken him up and down broad avenues where money rolled in and everything was bright. Now, time seemed to be running out on him just as the many thousands he had earned had gone down the drain. He could still box in breathtaking fashion for a few rounds, then he would become tired. Let's face it, he was performing wonders to keep boxing at this standard at his age, when the majority of lighter weight fighters are usually finished actively before reaching the age of 30. When he was a champion everybody was his friend, but now his money was gone and his fame was on the wane, so were most of his so-called friends except for Mike Tominiolo who knew Willie from the old days and stayed loyal during these hard times.

One of the reasons he kept fighting of course was he had by now been married and divorced a number of times, and each time he divorced he would settle outright by giving his ex-wives cash settlements, and that proved very costly indeed.

While training for his fight with Leon, Pep was doing a few days training at Stillman's Gym, in New York. One day after training, Willie was sitting on a chair on Eighth Avenue and he was having his shoes shined.

Two boxing officials walking up the Avenue toward Stillman's Gym, spotted Pep, one official turned to his companion and said: "I can't feel sorry for him. He had loads of money and let it slip through his fingers. If I feel sorry for anybody, it's the kids who have to fight their hearts out and never make any big money."

Though the big money had gone forever, Pep lived the same as always. While in New York, he stayed in a hotel on Eighth Avenue which had obviously seen better days. He drove a lavender Cadillac convertible up and down Broadway for everyone to see him. He always seemed to have a beautiful lady by his side. He was a restless spirit. "He can't sit still long enough in one place to do anything," said a friend who owned a bar on Broadway. Pep had an interest in a Manhattan saloon, but the saloon soon closed down. "All right, they say a famous fighter can open a saloon. Hell, this is a tough business. You have to work 14 or 15 hours a day or you ain't got a joint left. Willie couldn't stay in the joint for an hour a day. He's too nervous," concluded his friend. On his visit to the various race tracks Willie was well known to the jockeys. Con Errico, Joe Culmone and Tony DeSpirito, all famous jockeys, would give him tips on which horses to back. Willie maintained he lost over half-a-million dollars on horse racing, dice, bad investments and his ex-wives.

It was an eight hour flight to Caracas, plenty of time for Willie to do some hard thinking. A lot of the Willie Pep story was written on his face. The eyebrows were now thick with scar tissue and nicks and furrows marked his cheeks. "What the hell, I've had some great years in the ring," said Willie to a companion travelling with him to the fight in Caracas.

What can be said about his fight with Sonny Leon that has not already been said? Pep was adjudged to have lost a ten round points decision to the local star. This fighter Leon, was a fairly tough fellow but with limited ability, he wasn't a great fighter by any stretch of the imagination. In fact, for the first five or six rounds he had not landed a blow on Pep, not one single punch. "When I boxed Sonny Leon, the best I can say about him is that he's a fighter who can't fight. You know, for the past two or three years of my career, I had fought all over the States against ordinary guys. By that, I mean they weren't stiffs, but just ordinary. I mean I could always outwit an ordinary fighter. That's my style. I couldn't take a guy out with one shot, so I had to out-speed and out-think them," he said. Continuing Willie said: "Well I'm boxing this guy Leon and in the seventh round he hits me with a shot on the chin and down I go. I saw the punch coming but couldn't get out of the way. That's what its like when you're an old man of thirty-seven in this game. You just can't get out of your own way. As I say, this guy couldn't fight at all, but he knocked me down twice more and got the decision. I felt sure I'd licked him. Like I said, I saw the punches he knocked me down with coming, but I just couldn't get out of the way." "Hell, he was a tough kid, but I never used to have trouble with sluggers like that. One thing was clear, now I was on the same level with Leon and a lot of other fighters like him. I didn't want to be on that level." Pep said he wanted to have that little extra something that he had always had.

When he realised he no longer had it, he decided to quit. It had been a great life for him while it lasted. He recalled Bill Gore's words: "Willie, you get out of boxing what you put into it," that was sound advice for any youngsters who want to make it to the top of the boxing ladder. It was the first time in over 200 hundred fights he lost two fights consecutively. When he lost to Hogan "Kid" Bassey, at least he lost to a current world champion, and not a slugger like Sonny Leon.

On the long journey back to the States after the Leon fiasco, Pep decided enough was enough. He had stayed in the ring one fight too long. And he retired from the only occupation he had ever known and the only thing he was ever successful doing. He was hanging up his well worn gloves for good.

Sonny Leon never amounted to anything in the harsh world of boxing, despite his victory over one of the greatest exponent of it ever.

When he eventually got back to Hartford, Willie called into the office of Bill Lee, the sports editor of the Hartford Courant. Mr. Lee had followed Pep's career from the very beginning. "I did a great deal of thinking after the fight in Caracas and I decided it would be foolish to continue. Nobody made up my mind for me or influenced me in this decision. I made it myself. I would have liked to have ended my career a winner. Nobody likes to end up a loser, and I've lost my last two fights. So I thought it all out, and I'm through. There will be no comeback," Willie told Mr. Lee. "This time Willie Pep says he means it. After several 'Patti Farewells' to the prize-ring in the last few years, the one time Will-o'-the-Wisp insists his retirement now is final. He is definitely hanging up the competitive gloves. At 37, and after 229 professional battles spread across nearly two decades of industrious activity, Pep is convinced he's' had it.'

Two defeats in succession, for the first time in his long career, is the convincer for Willie," added Jersey Jones in a 1959 issue of the Ring magazine. "A guy could write a book on Gugliemo Papaleo, the son of a Sicilian immigrant. In-fact, to handle the job properly, one book would hardly suffice. To cover Pep's ubiquitous career, in and out of the ring, several volumes perhaps to fill an entire shelf library would be needed. The tragedy of it all is Pep, retiring from the ring, has little but memories to show for those 20 eventful years."

"No I'm not entirely broke," Pep remarked after reading the Jersey Jones article. "Maybe I'm short of cash, but I have a few assets left. I still have the house in Hartford that I bought for my parents. It cost me $18,000 then, but real estate values have been going up right along, and it probably is worth $25,000 to $30,000 now. Then I put some money away in a small annuity which will start paying off in a couple of years." "It won't be much, about 50 dollars a week, but it'll help," he concluded.

Let's hope he means it this time when he says he has retired, said Jersey Jones. There's nothing more pathetic in sports than a once great fighter refusing to quit and going on to be battered around by opponents who wouldn't have belonged in the same ring with him in his prime," finished Jersey Jones. How right he was. Boxing followers can never forget the sorrowful, pathetic sight of Joe Louis, Ezzard Charles, Ike Williams, Beau Jack, Sugar Ray Robinson plus many more wonderful champions and contenders who graced their lives, while we in England had only to look at Jackie Brown, Benny Lynch, Randy Turpin and many others who stayed around to long.

When Willie Pep retired it was as if a light had been switched off in millions of boxing fans hearts and minds. He stood for what the biggest majority wanted from their heroes...grace, skill, sportsmanship and the biggest of all...character.

Willie kept himself busy with guest refereeing engagements all over the world. He was the official in charge when Eder Joffre demolished Ireland's Johnny Caldwell in San Paulo, Brazil in January 1962. He would soon be flying to Manila to referee a Flash Elorde fight, he also had a bit part in the film: "Requiem For a Heavyweight." The money was not much but the former champion was enjoying travelling and meeting different people. He had not changed since his retirement from the ring. Always a fidgety fellow, laughing and joking and always with a gorgeous lady on his arm he was certainly not down and out as many of his old associates thought.

Election To Boxing's Hall Of Fame

In 1963, Pep was working as a sales representative for the Soundex Radio Electronics Company which was based in Brockton Massachusets, Rocky Marciano's home town. Willie's job was to travel and visit distributors. The idea being that the well-known celebrity would bring in more orders. The former undefeated heavyweight champion, Marciano was involved in this company in some capacity or other. In-fact, it was Rocky who got Pep this position. Marciano loved Willie Pep and treated him like an older brother. Rocky had great admiration for the flashy little exchampion who was still a snazzy dresser. Willie was only a year older than the Brockton man, but had been actively involved in boxing a great deal longer than his friend. Indeed, when Willie first won the featherweight title in 1942, Rocky was an obscure private in the Army. Marciano had often told friends how he envied the way Pep could box so elegantly, and that he had envied Willie's life style when he was the world champion and, he himself was just starting his climb up the boxing ladder. "Willie Pep, is a true and loyal friend, and he was a great, great champion," Marciano would tell people. Emphasising the word "great." Rocky loved Pep's witty sense of humour, his bubbling personality and the way the once great champion treated triumph and tragedy, everything about Pep fascinated Rocky. "Willie, has plenty of class, he possessed it both inside and outside the ring," continued the former heavyweight king, who was always dealing with some business tycoon or movie stars.

From 1956 onwards these two legends were often seen in each other's company. They travelled all over the states in search of action and excitement. But above all else...money, especially in Rocky's case. He was forever looking for sound business ventures.

Though working for Soudex, Willie was still involved with boxing. He was at this period acting as a manager himself, looking after a fighter named Paddy Reid, a fairly decent lightweight, who held the New England junior lightweight championship, and who had lost a very close points decision in New Bedford to Johnny Bizzaro, a very tough fighter and world class contender. He fought for the world lightweight title in 1963 but was stopped by the champion Carlos Ortiz.

Giving his views on his old pupils qualities as a manager, Bill Gore smiled, and said: "Willie is a great guy. But he was much too excitable to make a good manager or trainer. For a start he couldn't keep still or stay in the same place for more than was absolutely necessary. He did try his hand as a manager, but though there was no doubting when he himself was fighting, he was a pure genius, he found it difficult to understand other fighters could not do the things which came so naturally to him. He tried extremely hard to impart his vast knowledge to the kids he was looking after, but they did not have the nous to absorb what Willie was teaching them."

Around about this time there were rumours flying around that Pep was about to be elected into the boxing "Hall of Fame." Willie had heard the stories of course but refused to speculate on what might be. He tried his best not to get excited or show any kind of emotion, knowing from bitter experience how things had a nasty habit of rebounding back in his face. But deep down he was hoping against hope that the rumours were well founded, in fact he was overjoyed and absolutely thrilled that it might be true. When it was finally confirmed that he had in fact, received this prestigious honour, and he had been voted into the "Hall of Fame," he shed tears of joy. He was deeply touched and elated. Usually, this kind of honour is only bestowed on former champions or other boxing people long after they have retired. And in many cases, when the nominee has been deceased for a few years. When asked how it felt to be honoured and remembered by the boxing establishment Pep was very emotional, replied: "It's nice to know you're still remembered. This is a wonderful honour for me and I cherish this nomination. Yes, it's a big thing, real big, and I'm very flattered." Willie spoke the way he used to box-fast, excitable, with the use of his hands. The two-time former featherweight champion was gloriously elated at being the only modern-day boxer to be elected to the Hall of Fame in the 1963 balloting. A great award and it showed just how well perceived he was in boxing circles as a truly modern ring "great." Former boxing champions and old-time journalists were well-known for dismissing any fighter who did not box in their particular era. So for these people to cast their ballot for Pep's election was another example of what a sensational champion he had been. When asked by reporters how he felt about his election. Willie, with a huge grin on his face told them: "This is like winning the world title all over again." "Yes, I really do feel like a champion again. Everything except the money that comes with the winning of a world title. This is a big moment for me, a great honour. And you know something. This is something I can't lose. Nobody can come and take this away from me, ever."

Speaking in a restaurant with several journalists and friends, Pep started to reminisce about how he started out in this murky boxing business. He told them he made his Madison Square Garden debut on 12 December, 1941. "Lou Viscusi got me a four round bout against Ruby Garcia. I remember I really sparkled in that fight, I won clearly. I was only 19, and undefeated. The main event? Fritzie Zivic the former welterweight champion fought Young Kid McCoy, yeah, they boxed a draw," recalled Willie. What he failed to tell his captive audience was that after his Garden debut, it was he himself who the spectators were talking about as they were discussing the night's boxing in the bars and clubs or making their way home. The fans could not help but admire Pep's grace and style against Garcia. They tabbed him as one to watch for the future. Willie, warming to the conversation added: "Less than a year after making my first Garden appearance, I was appearing there again, against Chalky Wright for his featherweight title." The older people in the restaurant smiled as they remembered his fight with Wright which was an important first in boxing. It was the first fight in the long running television boxing programme, which was sponsored by the Gillette Safety Razor Company. It wasn't the first telecast. There had been other experiments. But it was the first in the series which became known as the "Fight of The Week." What they also remembered was the fact at the time, Pep was one of only 15 champions who were undefeated when winning their championships.

"Willie, I remember vividly your airplane crash," said an older sportswriter. "You were very fortunate not to have been killed." "I recall reading in the newspapers the medical staff at the hospital feared that you would never box again, but look how you surprised everybody. Mind you, I believe that along with many others, your injuries robbed you of much of your phenomenal speed. Though you were still a crafty, hardy fighter, I sincerely believe that you were never the same." "Jeez, Willie must have been really sensational before the crash," remarked a much younger scribe. "Because he was in a class of his own when I first recall watching him box, which was around 1949. And I can tell you I was impressed, very much so, spellbound in fact by his ringcraft and brilliance. So, he must have been absolutely exceptional earlier in his career.

Red Smith, who had been listening to the audience reminiscing about Pep's exploits turned to the former champion and said: "Willie, your return match against Sandy Saddler, when you won the title back in 1949, was, in my opinion the greatest piece of boxing I have ever seen. It was a masterful exhibition which I believe could not have been bettered."

Pep never attempted to win any heavier titles such as the lightweight. Willie Pep was a fascinating boxer, perhaps the greatest of his era. He lacked a big punch, but nothing else. On ring generalmanship he deserves a perfect score. He was a small guy. But he is up there with the best of them all," said Al Buck, in the Ring magazine. What a tribute these writers and friends paid Willie. He was very emotional upon leaving. They were absolutely correct of course in their assessment of his ability. This was a magnificent honour to bestow upon him. But he fully deserved it, because he really was something very special.

Save Your Dough
Rocky Marciano was one of the most popular and sought after sports personalities of the Fifties and Sixties. Everyone, it seemed, wanted to meet and talk to the former heavyweight king. Rocky had learned the hard way that a fighter needed to look after his hard-earned money. He knew from bitter experience that there was always somebody out there ready to relieve him of his rewards.

Just to digress for a moment, how ironic, that in June 1997, as this book was being completed, Mike Tyson the former world heavyweight champion who was preparing to fight Evander Hollyfield in the grudge match of the century in Las Vagas opened his heart in a remarkable interview in the Daily Mirror, in which he said he had no friends, and he had been dehumanised, humiliated, abused, betrayed and lost millions of dollars. "History proves that everyone in boxing probably makes out well except the fighter. He's the only one who basically suffers most, the only one on Skid Row most of the time," he stated. The Tyson story was so familiar in boxing. And over 40 years had passed since Marciano's last fight when he successfully defended his title with a ninth round knockout over Archie Moore.

Who then could blame Rocky for being careful with his money. He used to receive numerous invitations to attend functions, business dinners, sportsman evenings, charities, etc in towns and cities all across the states. He did of course charge a fee. There was a huge demand for his services.

To give the reader some idea of Rocky's popularity I digress again. I myself saw him in the 1960s when he came to Manchester with a fighter who was opposing Terry Downes at Belle Vue. After the fight I went to the Cromford Club, a well-respected and well-run establishment in the city centre. All the top stage, screen, and sporting stars frequented this club for a meal and a drink. When I arrived at the place it was past midnight and the place was heaving. I had never seen so many people in the club before. The reason for the huge gathering was because Marciano was there as a guest of the owner, Paddy McGrath, a former boxer from Collyhurst. Everybody wanted to shake Rocky's hand and get his autograph. He was asked to make a speech from the stage so big was the demand to see and hear him. Rocky looked a double for William Bendix an old-time film star.

"I can't sing, I'm no good at telling jokes, and I'm useless at giving speeches," said Rocky in his high-pitched New England accent. You could have heard a pin drop it was so quiet. "But just to be sociable I'll fight any man in the house." He brought the place down. The thunderous applause could not have been bettered at any of his championship fights.

Rocky was inundated with requests and often double booked for engagements. Rather than let people down, he would go to one event while he would ask Pep to attend another. Willie was brilliant at these functions and proved highly popular. He was witty, gracious and told fascinating funny stories about himself. He was always asked to return.

There is an amusing little story about these two scoundrels which took place in the early sixties when both Pep and Marciano were booked to appear at the grand opening of the Municipal Auditorium in Baltimore. Both champions were receiving a fee for their services. Rocky enjoyed it immensely when both himself and Willie were together on these appearances, he was basically rather shy and it meant he could leave the talking to Pep. When the official celebrations were over in Baltimore, both champions were invited to a luxurious, well-known night club as guests of a group of extremely wealthy businessmen. Pep was only too pleased to accept their invitation, and was delighted with his one-thousand dollar fee which he had received. He had no idea how much his friend Rocky received for his payment, and was not bothered in the slightest, being quite satisfied with his own payment and pleased Rocky was putting these personal appearances his way. Both men had been looked after splendidly. In the nightclub, which happened to be one of the most expensive in Baltimore, these rich businessmen were buying the drinks readily. Everyone was having a good time and in a happy, relaxed mood. These wealthy sports fans were thrilled to bits to be in the company of the two ring immortals. Both fighters could spin a good yarn and the company was swinging, the businessmen were fascinated listening to Rocky and Willie telling their stories about their careers. After several rounds of drinks and refreshments had been paid for by their hosts, Pep decided he must return their generosity. Reaching into his pocket he pulled out a wad of notes in order to pay the waiter. This was Pep's problem, and one of the reasons he ended up broke. Before he had chance to settle the bill, Willie felt a sharp kick on his shin, and he saw Marciano scowling and beckoning him to follow him outside. It is legendary the lengths Marciano would go in order not to spend his own money. Away from earshot, a red-faced Rocky was visibly shaking with rage, he gave his little pal a verbal dressing-down for having the audacity to spend any of his money. Realising he might have been a little harsh on his close buddy, he softened his voice and put his arm around Willie. "Willie, listen to me. I'm not going to spend a dime. And I don't want to see you spending any of your money either," he said. "Look, let these guy's spend their dough, put your money away and save it. These guys are loaded. They are quite happy to be sharing our company, and picking up the tab. So don't embarrass me," he concluded.

At first Willie was stunned by Marciano's anger, but later he admired the lengths to which his friend would go to avoid spending his own money. Pep himself had been foolish throughout his life where money matters were concerned. High living, and never worrying about where and how he spent his cash.

There were many occasions over the years when Marciano would introduce Pep to well-known politicians, movie stars, and several famous celebrities and show business stars such as Frank Sinatra, Al Martino, Bob Hope, Sammy Davies and Nat King Cole beside many others. During their trips around America together, the two former champions would travel by private aircraft, jets and limo's, they would stay in motels and fancy hotel suites. Staying a week here, two days there, then on to some other location where they get some "action," as Marciano liked to describe his lifestyle. These two were having a ball and thoroughly enjoying themselves. When they were alone, the thrifty Marciano realising Pep was broke and he would of course pay any accounts. To give an example of what a loyal friend Marciano was, during the late 1950s, Pep owned a little bar and grill on 57th Street, he named it "Willie Pep's Melody Lane." Every opportunity he got, Rocky would bring all his business associates and big shot celebrities into Pep's bar to eat and drink. Willie would willingly have fed Rocky and his company for nothing, but Marciano would not hear of it and always insisted his friends pay for everything.

Over the years, Rocky always tried to place Willie into some venture or other. One of Marciano's rich friends, an Italian-American businessman, gave Pep a job in his public relations business. The man did this only as a favour and to please the former heavyweight king. Willie acted as a sort of travelling companion, visiting different cities all over America. The fellow had his own private aircraft and pilot, a big limousine with a chauffeur.

Because he was close to Rocky, Pep could have anything he wanted from the man. The truth of the matter was, this fellow didn't need Willie under any circumstances. Friction soon developed between these two sons of Italian parents. This was inevitable. Pep was a proud man, and though he was grateful to his employer for giving him this position, he began to feel he was being used as some kind of stooge. After a few months, Willie flew back to Hartford. Around about this time, Pep's father was seriously ill and Willie wanted to be at home near the family. "I couldn't fathom this guy Pep, out," Marciano's business associate said. "He had no respect for money. I'll tell you one thing, Rocky Marciano would never end up like Willie Pep...broke."

Willie and Marciano still kept in touch, they continued their friendship up until Rocky's death in 1969. Rocky would tell everyone he met about how elated Willie was when he got elected into the "Hall of Fame." And how he himself felt so proud for his friend. Talking about Marciano as a fighter, Willie said: "Rocky started very late as a fighter. His problem was that there was nobody around for him to earn big money with once he became champion. He had fought all the top contenders and flattened them on his way up the ladder. He hammered everyone they put in front of him, beating the best of his period. His manager, Al Weill, was one shrewd guy. I have never seen any fighter before or since, train as hard as what Rocky did. He would lock himself away for three or four months preparing for a fight. That is true dedication. Rocky though, fought every fighter he faced. What I mean by that is simple, he would fight the good fighters in the same manner as he would fight the not so good fighters. He fought them all head on, no backward steps. He was offered vast sums of money to make a comeback but he had far to much pride in himself and would not be tempted. When a friend called me with the news that Rocky had been killed in a plane crash I cried for days. Beneath his tough exterior he had a gentleness about him which betrayed his ferocity and fierceness once he was inside the ring. I am proud we were close friends. "As I get older, I understand why Rocky was so hard with a buck. Though I couldn't be like that, it is just not in my nature. Money drained from me. I'll say this though, Rocky was a loyal and true friend, a beautiful human being," said Pep.

The Comeback

In December 1964, almost six years since retiring from boxing, Willie was on vacation in Florida. The truth was, he was bored with his life and the way it was progressing. Since his retirement he had been eating and drinking whatever he fancied and as a result, his weight had ballooned up to over 162 pounds and rising. It was all the rich Italian food. "Spaghetti and meatballs killed more Italians than all the wars put together," he said. He was always on the move, somewhere to visit, a few pals to meet, a racetrack to frequent and nightlife a plenty. He was a regular visitor to former middleweight champion Jake LaMotta's nightclub. And he was often seen in Rocky Marciano's company when the former heavyweight champion was in the state. Though busy and always on the go, Pep deep down knew he was lacking the discipline of his fighting days, the regimented early morning roadwork, going to the gym and watching his diet.
Artie Lupo, an acquaintance of Willie's who was also an ex-fighter, was also in Florida, training rigorously for a comeback in the ring. Lupo kept badgering the former champion to help train him for his forthcoming contest. "Why don't you help me prepare for this fight. Who better than you to get me ready?," he told Pep. Pep agreed to help his friend and he got up early every morning and did roadwork with Artie, he found he got back into a routine. Whenever Lupo ran, Pep ran. Artie worked out in the gym

and Willie watched him, then after a few days Willie worked out, too. He started to feel good. In the gym, Pep would put on his headguard and the big gloves, and spar a few rounds with Lupo. Truthfully, Willie, looked better than his friend. In-fact, it was Pep who was drawing the attention on the onlookers. That silky-smooth style was still there to be seen. His timing was a little rusty, but his defensive ability was untarnished as was his awareness of moves which was simply uncanny, even after being out of action for almost six years. His only problem, from what onlookers could ascertain, was his weight. He was having trouble shedding the pounds.

Lupo was booked for a six-round contest on 20 January, 1965 in Miami. Both Willie and his friend had trained all over the Christmas and New Year festivities. Lupo's manager, Mike Marino, was pleased at his fighter's progress under Pep's guidance. But it was to Pep's benefit also as he was enjoying the challenge of getting himself into some kind of condition again. Two weeks before Lupo was due to fight, he became ill. He could not go through with his proposed comeback, it was out of the question. Artie's knee's had swollen up like two balloons. Marino was now in a spot of bother with the promoter, who had done him a big favour in the first place, by booking Lupo. Desperate, Marino turned to Pep and begged him to help. "Willie, you take Artie's place on the bill. You have been looking great sparring with my guy. Please, I'm in a big fix."

After giving it some thought Pep agreed to box an exhibition bout. "I am not sharp, but you can tell the promoter I will box if he wants me," Willie told Marino. The manager could not wait to rush personally over to the promoters office and break the news. The promoter was delighted. He would now reap bigger rewards in ticket sales and publicity. "After all, it's not every day the punters can see a 'Hall of Famer' in action," he said. Pep made it clear he would only box on the specific understanding it was an exhibition. He still had his pride, and did not feel quite ready enough physically or mentally for a proper combative contest. After all it was six years since he retired from the ring.

The Little River Arena in North Miami was a small boxing club with a seating capacity of 630. Usually, minor talent play to tiny audiences, but on this very special night Little River went big time because Pep drew record crowds. He was in his forties, and weighing 142 pounds which made him nearly a welterweight. But there was still a magic attached to his name. More than 800 fans and celebrities squeezed their way into this tiny hall. Another 400 spectators had to be turned away. The police had to mount the entrances and stood by on patrol to help control the vast amount of traffic. The big boxing names around Miami turned out in full force to pay tribute to this immortal champion from their trade. Beau Jack was there, so was Ike Williams and Bobby Dykes. The Dundee brothers, Chris and Angelo, were also present. And so too was the current lightweight champion of the world, Carlos Ortiz. Pep looked as frisky as ever as he skipped down the aisle, swishing punches at the air and snorting through the nose which had been broken, reset and broken again more times than even Pep could remember.

Carrying his bucket and ready to tend his wounds was Charley Titone, a cracking fighter in his day and one who Pep had licked a decade earlier. The cheers were deafening, it was like a world title fight. A voice boomed out loud and clear: "Hey, Willie, watch out! That's Sandy Saddler in the other corner." This brought a mixture of laughs and booing and cheering. Pep grinned and slammed his big gloves together. Saddler wasn't in the opposite corner. Instead there was a spry local fighter named Jerry Powers, who was 26 and, for as long as he lives he will be able to boast: "I fought Willie Pep." Well, not exactly had he fought the living legend. Because this was billed as a four-round exhibition bout, with 14 ounce gloves, and both fighters wearing headguards. Powers was in that ring with a shell of a once great, great fighter. The illusion though was thrilling for everyone in attendance, until Pep shed his robe. Once he de-robed, stark reality snapped into sad focus. A roll of loose flesh hung around his midsection and when he moved it quivered like a bowl of jelly.

Pep showed flashes of sheer brilliance, and the fans stood cheering and applauding when he manoeuvred Powers off balance with a feint, or spun him into the ropes with a tap of the elbow. "I have never run into that one before," remarked Powers. But the moments were far too few and Pep was the happiest fellow in the hall when the final bell sounded. Back in his dressing room, he said: "I'm glad we wore those heavy gloves. This kid hit me with a couple of good shots on the head, but did you notice that he never hit me any-place else?" The promoter was overjoyed at the box-office takings from the big turn-out generated through the turnstiles by having the former champion on the bill.

The promoters offered Willie more exhibition matches, plus an official eight-round contest against a young up and comer named Hal McKeever in the same arena. Pep readily agreed to this comeback bout. He had the taste and the smell for active fighting again. His purse for fighting McKeever was to be $1,500. Though McKeever was described as a good prospect by some newspapers, the fact was he had fought only 18 times in six years and had lost three of his last four contests. While training to meet McKeever, Pep was sparring with a husky young welterweight in a Miami gym. It was a demanding session and Willie was feeling shattered. After the workout he was lay on the dressing room table. "How far is Key West from Miami," he asked an old-time fighter who was fixing someone's headguard. Key West was where the promoters had him already booked for another fight. The old fellow replied: "Willie, that ain't so far." Then looking rather ruefully, Pep said: "Tell me how far is it from Miami to Madison Square Garden?" The old-timer shook his head a couple of times and said: "Too far, Willie. Much too far for you."

For his official comeback fight, there was another sell-out crowd. Again Pep displayed several flashes of former brilliance during the bout. He won, and won clearly. But at a cost. His face was cut and bruised with a deep gash above his right eye and a nasty cut below his left. It was his 221st victory from 232 bouts in his distinguished career. He had drawn a capacity crowd, which was the way it used to be 15 years previous when he was topping the bill at Madison Sqaure Garden. But this was several light years away from the Garden. This was an old Masonic temple known as the Miami Grotto, which became the Little River arena or auditorium on fight nights.

The winner sat slumped in a chair in the corner of his dressing room. Asked afterwards how he felt, Willie replied: "I feel very good." He certainly didn't look it as the sweat dripped from his forehead, a purple welt under his right eye and a jagged gash over his right eye and a nasty looking half moon cut under his left eye. He looked like a 42 year old man trying to recapture a forgotten and glorious past. When reporters asked McKeever his opinion about Pep's performance he shook his head and said: "My name should never have been in Willie Pep's record. There are guy's out there who are a lot more rougher, tougher and hit harder than me and they will hurt him. He should quit right now."

Gone was manager Lou Viscusi and trainer Bill Gore. They were now looking after other top fighters, among them was the top welterweight contender, Manny Gonzales, who had just defeated the brilliant world welterweight champion, Emile Griffith in a shock upset. "Manny has a great deal of Pep's savvy and ability," said Gore. Instead of his tried and trusted mentors, Gore and Viscusi, Pep now had Mike Marino working his corner and George Sheppard, as his booking agent. George was a matchmaker in Hartford when Willie was just staring out in professional boxing. It wasn't like the old times of course, but it wasn't too bad. Sheppard didn't book Pep against any really top-class fighters. And he certainly tried his best to look after the former champion. "Look," said Sheppard. "Willie's not going to get hurt while I'm looking after him. I take care of all my fighters. If he goes into any fight I book for him and gets hurt or looks bad, I'll advise him to quit straight away. I've got 25 years experience in this game, I know what I'm doing."

After beating McKeever, Willie had a further eight bouts that year which he won. He would out-fumble the older boxers and out-smart the younger fighters. He was making a few dollars and claimed he wasn't getting hurt. This of course wasn't strictly true. Though he was winning, he was getting plenty of little nicks and bruises around his face and eyes. While in Philadelphia for one of his comeback bouts against a local taxi driver, Jackie Lennon, Willie was in the city's Svlania Hotel, reliving, deja vu but not quite, the rituals of his twenties. "But I want no tears," he said while talking in the hotel lobby. "I'm not destitute. I can can get a job any time I want. It's just that this is what I know best." He was wearing a grey hat with a black band and a red feather and its movements announced the small man's emotions. When he sat down in the lounge with an old Navy friend from South Philadelphia, named Chris and writer Steve Gelman, Pep laughed about his life, but each laugh seemed to arouse a private corresponding sorrow. He kept his company entertained for a couple of hours with stories about happenings throughout his life. Willie was a brilliant speaker and very excitable while talking, he could hold his company almost captivated and spellbound with his stories, he was that fascinating. Finally, Willie stood up and excused himself while he retired to his room. "My future?" he said, "Leave it blank."

When Pep retired in 1959, he ranked with Joe Louis and Sugar Ray Robinson as one of the three top fighters of his time. "Trained in no profession except boxing, Pep worked as a night club manager, a brewery customer relations man, a boxing referee, a restaurant greeter. With very little of the one million dollars he had earned left, he drifted-Hartford, Miami,

New York, Las Vagas and California," Gelman said. "Some fighters," Pep told him. "Can adjust when they're through. I've had trouble adjusting." It was 10-30 the next morning, and Willie was sitting on a couch reading the Philadelphia Daily News. He read the racing form and a moving boxing story by Jack McKinney, who wrote no one was really happy about Pep's comeback with the logical exception of his opponent, Jackie Lennon. Willie's brown eyes searched the ceiling. He tugged his hat forward, then stared at the paper. "People don't understand that I'll Know", he said. "I'll know when I've had it. Archie Moore fought until he was 50. Jersey Joe Walcott was older than me. Sugar Ray Robinson is older than me right now. We're not catchers. We can last. You can always fight with your face. I don't fight that way. My thinking is alright. Believe me. I'll know. A few weeks ago I fought Hal McKeever, I didn't get hit in eight rounds but after coming out of a clinch, he butted me. I got cut from a butt, but blood was streaming down my face and I looked all battered up and the writers wrote about poor Willie Pep got beaten up. They wrote after that fight and quoted me as saying: 'Tonight I got cut for $500. The last time I got cut it was for $90,000.' They wrote on the usual theme, that once it had been Joe Louis and then Sugar Ray Robinson and now it was Willie Pep refusing to acknowledge that for athletes, unlike other men, the sundown inevitably comes early."

During his retirement Pep often said: "If I only had back the money which is owed me, I'd have nothing in the world to worry about." Yet, when he got his purse money in Miami, Willie began giving away several dollars. Psychologists say handouts help a man feel important. Fighters simply say handouts are part of the business. "I understand an awful lot about this business," Pep said. "I'm not deluding myself. I'm not thinking of winning any championships. But I can still demonstrate the art of self-defence. I'm just an ordinary guy trying to make a few dollars and fight. There are some ordinary kids around and I think I can beat 'em," added Pep.

George Sheppard, Pep's manager walked into the hotel. Sheppard was bald, full of face and jowl. He wore a black suit and black overcoat and he drew circles in the air with an eternal cigar. He seemed to launch his voice, deep and raspy, from his bowels. "Did you read that McKinney? Sheppard asked Willie. "You'll make him eat crow." Minutes later, after stepping out into the fog and rain before going into the hall for the weigh-in. Pep grabbed Sheppard's arm. "George," he said. "George, I got nine-thousand headaches. My dad's got scirosis of the liver. Who knows what'll happen to him? I got kids, I hardly see them. Yes, I got headaches. Oh, what the hell, George? Forget it." Charley Goldman, who was 67, all five-foot of him, bald, wearing glasses walked into the dressing room. Charley, was of course the famous trainer of Rocky Marciano and other champions. He was going to work the corner for Pep's fight. "How you feeling, Willie," said Goldman. "You got to do things slowly you know. No sense in rushing things at your age. You pick up sprains and little nicks around the eyes." Pep, started joking with the gnome-like trainer. It helped take his mind of the upcoming fight. Just then, Joey Giardello, the world middleweight champion walked into the changing room and went over to where Pep was getting his hands taped. "Gee, you're looking good, champ. Looking good." Willie smiled at the newer champion. "Hey, I used to listen to this guy's fights when they were broadcast on the radio when I was only eight years old," Giardello shouted to everybody in the room. "How's it going old man?" "What do you mean old man," responded Pep, laughing. "Look at this licence. See, I was born 1925, I'm only 39. I could prove it, but the courthouse in the town I was born burned down." As Pep walked into the doctor's room, Giardello said: "I never usually go to fights. I'm here because of Willie. What a guy. What a boxer."

That night Pep gave the tough Jackie Lennon a boxing lesson and beat him clearly to take the six round points decision at the Philadelphia arena. As the crowd of over 2,168 walked from the arena there were comments such as: "What a great fighter he must have been in his prime," an older fan eager to tell the younger spectators remarked: "He was a marvel. Take it from me. The guy was a marvel." Between boxing some fairly untalented if tough opponents in legitimate matches, interspersed with a few exhibitions here and there. Willie was earning some much needed cash. To make extra money, he was still guesting as a referee on occasions. While attending the Liston-Ali second fight in Lewiston, several well-known figures and older reporters were expressing concern to Pep about his welfare should he continue to keep boxing at his age. Willie replied: "Please, don't worry about me. I can take care of myself real good." He was obviously embarrassed by their concern and sorrow for his decline. It really was a tough time for him because to keep fighting he risked injury and his reputation as the "greatest" featherweight ever!

It Nearly Stopped In Providence

His comeback campaign nearly came to a sudden stop in Providence. He nearly came unstuck. He spluttered and stuttered when he faced Tommy Haden. It is true to say that Haden would not have got within touching distance of the maestro in his prime. But he wasn't in his prime, this was 1966, and boxing against this young New England junior lightweight champion Pep had to delve deep into the memory bank just to survive. Rocky Graziano, the one-time dead-end kid, former middleweight champion of the world and a friend of Willie's was brought in by the promoters to act as guest referee and, of course, help swell the gate. After two strength sapping and robust rounds Haden was trying to make himself a reputation by flattening Pep, it looked like Willie might need his friend, Graziano, to help him beat this kid. In the third round a slice of luck came Pep's way. The local boy received a very nasty-looking cut around the right eye and the blood was cascading down Haden's face. Willie threw punch after punch at the injury, slicing the wound open further. Shortly after, the bout had to be stopped in Pep's favour. The old champion breathed a sign of relief. It was getting harder and harder every time he fought. The ring was no place for a 40-year-old trying to earn a living. It was pathetic watching Willie trying to regain his youth. "When you're young you fight and in spots, you try to remember to pace yourself. When you're old you pace yourself and, in spots, you try to remember to fight," said Pep.

Talking later to some friends, Willie remarked: "I didn't box champions or near-champions, I just boxed ordinary kids and I found out it's just as hard to fight ordinary fellows as it is fighting against good fighters because they're all trying to beat the hell out of you." A reporter visited Willie at his home in Hartford to find out just why he was hanging around in the fight business and to try and get a new slant on something about the former champion. But Willie told the reporter he was now a bug on physical fitness. "When some people reach 40, they lay down and play dead. I'm not playing dead. I'm keeping in shape. But the main thing why I'm continuing fighting, is that I want to show people the real art of self-defence. Too many fighters today, they go into the ring with the sole intention of trying to knock each other's brains out. They don't know how to move in and set a guy up by using a left jab, they don't know how to slip, duck, feint, all that jazz. Me, I'm not a strong guy, so I have to use my wits."

About this time The Ring magazine published a no-holds barred article about Pep and Sugar Ray Robinson. These two former ring greats had recently fought on the same bill at the Cambria War Memorial Arena in Johnstown, Pennsylvania. The promoter, Don Elbaum, said it had been his lifelong dream to feature the two greatest fighters of all time on one of his promotions. He had hundreds of posters printed and hung all over Johnstown advertising the appearance of Sugar Ray and Will-'o'-the-Wisp. The modern arena had a capacity to seat 5,000 people. But by the time the two former champions skipped down the aisle into the ring for their contests, there was less than a thousand fans spread throughout the empty arena. Fifteen years before, this arena would not have been big enough to hold the crowds that would have turned out in their droves to watch these two greats in action. Pep scored a three-round ko over Willie Little, while Sugar Ray beat a fellow named Peter Schmidt on points over ten rounds. Afterwards Pep and Robinson had a few laughs in their hotel and talked about the old days.

George Girsh, the writer of the Ring magazine, article, urged these two former ring "Greats" to quit active boxing while the quitting was good. "These two former greats are active far longer than they should be. There's no doubt about the reason why Pep is back fighting after nearly six years. It's for dough," said Girsh. "Never again should Pep obscure the memory of the game little scrapper who scored triumphs over many worthy champions and contenders, such as Joey Archibald, Chalky Wright, Allie Stolz," "Sal Bartolo, Jackie Wilson, Willie Joyce, Manuel Ortiz, Lulu Constantino, Phil Terranova, Paddy DeMarco, Eddie Compo, Ray Famechon and Sandy Saddler. In other words, fellas, quit while you are lucky enough to be in one piece. Go home before you get 'hoited.'"

Other boxing and sports publications, joined in the crusade to get Willie to hang up his gloves for good. Sandy Saddler, who was still a fitness fanatic and weighing only a few pounds above his best fighting weight, shook his head sadly after watching his former arch-enemy struggling in one of his comeback fights which was screened on television. Rocky Marciano, though not directly telling Pep to retire, kept putting jobs Willie's way. But as always Willie did his own thing. "Don't feel sorry for me. Don't send me no flowers," he said.

The Final Showdown

If Willie Pep would have earned 25,000,000 dollars, he would have found a way to get rid of it. In March, 1966, he was asked to go down to

Richmond in Virginia to box a four-round exhibition match with a local boy called Calvin Woodland, a lightweight who was quite a decent fighter and a lad who the local promoters were building up for bigger things. The promoters, a fellow Pep called "Sam the Mumbler" and his partner named "Snake-Eyes," requested the ex-champion to arrive a week or so in advance of their tournament in order for Pep to drum up ticket sales and as Willie was a "Hall of Fame" living legend, who the local reporters and radio and television stations would be delighted to have on their programmes or in their newspapers. To all intents Willie had accepted in his own mind that after knocking out Ray Coleman in five rounds in October 1965 in Tucson, Arizona that was it. A final wind down of his career, with a victory. He had won his 11 fights since embarking on his comeback, and he felt it was the right thing to do, by going out with a victory. He was happy to oblige the promotion by travelling down early and doing the public relations work on behalf of the show. He was booked into a decent hotel and enjoyed himself reliving past memories. He was a reporter's dream. Witty, with a good sense of humour, brilliant at giving exact times and places of his past fights, always quotable and very, very interesting.

In places such as Richmond, which was a sort of backwoods type of place where the locals had hardly ever seen a live championship match, it was a marvellous occasion for them to have one of the greatest ever boxing celebrities in their city. But his visit to Richmond would end in sadness for the former champion. On the day of the tournament Willie was asked to attend the weigh-in. Bill Brennan the commissioner, told Pep to get changed and hop on the scale. Pep willingly obliged and he was 135 pounds. Brennan, according to Pep quietly whispered to him as he was putting his clothes back on. "Willie, you're fighting a proper fight tonight." Pep looked puzzled and explained to the commissioner as far as he was concerned he was promised a thousand dollars plus expenses and it was a four-round exhibition. Brennan looking very officious said: "Willie, this is going to be a genuine fight and not an exhibition." Pep protested, and told Brennan what he had agreed with the promoters. "If you don't agree to fight, you will not receive a cent, and I'll make certain that the World Boxing Association blackballs you in future." At this time Willie was doing refereeing jobs in different parts of the world for the WBA and he respected them and wanted the refereeing engagements, he also needed the thousand dollars. "So I had to go through with a fight which I wasn't prepared for. Calvin Woodland, was a darn good lightweight, I was 45 and out of shape. He beat me by decision over six rounds. That, I decided, was my last fight. And so the boxing part of Pep's life was now finished for good.

There would be no more comebacks, he was finished with active fighting for ever. He did box in benefit exhibitions for the Cerebral Palsy, the Heart Disease, Polio and Leukemia and other such charitable agencies which was organised by former fighter Chico Vejar, and other well-known fighters. These exhibitions were not serious, more like a comedy sketch with the celebrities wearing pillows (sixteen-ounce sparring gloves) the crowd loved it and the money went to help people less fortunate to have a bit of pleasure and happiness especially at Christmas time.

"How would you like to be remembered Willie?" a sportswriter asked the former champion in 1970. Pep looking back in time, fell silent while contemplating the question. "My last remaining ambition in life is to redeem my name. I think I'm on the right track now, but I feel people want to remember me as Willie Pep the fighter, the guy who won all those fights and was once rated as the greatest fighter of his age. They should forget about the Willie Pep who lost 11 fights, the guy who got decked those few times by guys who never should have touched him. It's like what John Lardner wrote about me once a couple of years ago. 'Your correspondent will remember little Papaleo, Willie Pep, longer and better than the others, because he had the nonchalance and the blinding speed to move within a half-inch of danger and stay there all night. I hope history will end up by giving him everything he wants.' That was very nice. But what I want the most is for it to be like that day when I was in the Army as an Military Policeman. They used to send me down to pick up the drunks. One night I had to go into town to bring in this guy whose hand had been shot off in the war. He was mean. I guess he was just looking for somebody to take it out on. I tried to talk to him quietly. "I didn't want any trouble with him, but he said to me: 'I'm not going.' I didn't want to fight with the guy, so I talked to him some more, but all he said was. 'You trying to make me go, I'm not going.' Then some guy in the crowd mentioned I was Willie Pep, and the soldier turned to me and said: 'Willie Pep? You've been my idol ever since you came up through the rankings.' And he gave me his arm and walked as meek as a lamb to the car. As soon as they found out I was Willie Pep, they all liked me, I want it to be that way again.

Willie Pep Irked, Irritated, Insulted By British Board

This was the headlines in The Hartford Courant on Monday, 12 February, 1967. Willie was in London as a guest of the Anglo-American Sporting Club. The club were hoping to feature the great boxer in an exhibition with the British and European featherweight champion, Howard Winstone. Winstone had been compared with Pep has boxer who relied on his brains rather than brawn. Mickey Duff the matchmaker said: "We applied to the British Boxing Board of Control for a licence to put on the exhibition. We received a letter from the B.B.B OF C. saying our application could not be granted. No reason was given." It was said privately an official of the board regarded the idea as gimmicky and in bad taste. He did not say why they thought that. Pep who was now 46, was fuming. "I've boxed exhibitions all over the world and only a month ago I boxed an exhibition against former champion, Sandy Saddler. I don't understand the Board's attitude. At least I think they should have seen me before turning down the exhibition. It's an insult. In any case we were going to use headguards and just fool about a bit. Howard was delighted at the idea. Nobody was going to get hurt." Willie was honoured by the club and presented with a silver salver inscribed "To Willie Pep, former world's champion, a champion of Champions, from the Anglo-American Sporting Club, 27 February, 1967." The audience rose to their feet and gave him a standing ovation. Among the many guests and well-known celebrities in the audience was Sammy McCarthy and Joe Lucy, two former British champions. Mark Rowe the new "Golden Boy" of the late 1960s was also present. Later, Willie told Len and Dennie Mancini, who had looked after him during his stay in England that he was deeply touched by the reception accorded him by the members.

A couple of years later Pep's magic monicker was destined for the marquees. He was to be the subject of a motion picture to be produced by Falcon International Pictures, Incorporated, a new company, based in Los Angeles. Willie had of course appeared in bit parts in a few New York films. His wife, Geraldine was expecting their baby, Willie's third child, the others being from his other marriages. Geraldine was from a basketball family. Her father, Nat Volpe, a former Manhattan College star, was the coach at Scranton University in Pennsylvania. A meeting was held at the Hartford Hilton and it was disclosed Frank Martin, president of Falcon, would be the producer, with Falcon vice president Martha Dykstra. The script writer who was also going to do the research of Pep's life was Frank James. Vito Motola had the film's music rights. Willie's role would be limited to technical advisor. Casting would have to await the completion of the vital ingredient-the script. The film was to place the emphasis on Pep's character, rather than a newsreel of his pugilistic prowess. It would take time to finalise, time to develop the story, time to cast the roles, time to shoot the scenes and time to edit and cut footage to satisfy everyone involved in the film's ultimate fate.

It was an unusual press party with nobody taking charge and delivering the information required. Sad to say, the project seemed to fade into oblivion.

Another project which Willie tried, but which did not bring the rewards it deserved was the book "Friday's Heroes." It was like a trip down memory lane as Willie reminisced about the Friday Night Fights from Madison Square Garden; hence the title of Pep's book. It was full of wonderful memories for fight fans who remember those days and it featured Joey Giardello, Chico Vejar, Chuck Davey, Kid Gavilan, Tiger Jones, Ralph Dupas, Kenny Lane, Vince Martinez and many more. "The book didn't sell too good," Pep said a few years later. "I don't know what was wrong, whether it wasn't marketed properly or what. What I do know was that I ended up with a garage full of books. Ah well, that's the way it goes in this business."

Actually, this book is now a collectors item. It took a friend of mine, Richard Jones, years to obtain a copy!

The Passing Of a Great, Great Trainer

In November 1975, Willie was sat at home in Hartford, when the phone rang. The voice on the other end of the line gave the former champion some dreadful news. Bill Gore had passed away in a hospital in Tampa, Florida. Willie's 83-year-old former mentor had been ill for quite some time. Willie thanked the caller and placed the phone down, tears streamed down his cheeks as he remembered the brilliant man who groomed him to stardom. Gore, a native of Providence, was already a trainer of repute when he accepted the job of tutoring the young 17-year-old Pep. Bill had helped train three world champions at light-heavyweight in Mike McTigue, Melio Bettina and the great Bob Foster. He also trained Joe "Old-Bones" Brown, the lightweight king. Altogether the tall, white-haired trainer worked in 29 corners in which his boxer was boxing for a world title. He took fighters to every corner of America and made several trips to Europe.

Many years after Willie Pep's retirement from active fighting, a journalist asked Lou Viscusi what was the secret of Pep's phenomenal success. Without stopping to gather his thoughts, Mr. Lou replied...Bill Gore!

Willie, over the years was always gushing in his praise for his old trainer and teacher. He recalled Bill Gore's methods of training were designed to not only get him in the finest physical condition possible, but also taught him how to avoid getting hurt. He preached that it was far better to hit your opponent and not let him hit you. Bill Gore devised manoeuvres for Willie to practice whereas he could avoid taking full-blooded punches by a simple movement of his head or feet. Unfortunately, it is virtually impossible for any boxer not to get punched while taking part in a boxing contest. Willie wanted to dissect the style of boxing he learned from the maestro, Bill Gore. He would have liked the teachings of Gore documented for posterity. Many years later, Johnny Famechon the nephew of Pep's old challenger Ray, became world featherweight champion, he also had a great teacher in Ambrose Palmer, who was similar to Bill Gore.

Robinson Couldn't Tie Willie Pep's Laces

In September 1981, Willie Pep, the old champion, stood on the fringes of the crowd in the State Senate Chambers quietly watching as the new champion was being hailed. Marlon Starling was being honoured this day for his courageous knockout victory over Olympic super-star, Mark Breland in August, which earned him the World Boxing Association welterweight crown. Forty-five years before Pep himself had stood where Starling did now. Willie then blinked a scar-etched eye and it was all over. He thought about that as he watched; the fleeting fame, the fortune won and lost, the glory which was his youth flashing through his mind in random vignettes. They introduced him, finally, and he gave one of those boxers waves. It was a short ovation, nice, but a formality. Still, his eyes glistened when the applause subsided and it was all over.

Now a senior citizen, he keeps active by doing after dinner speeches and travelling where ever he is requested. At these functions he is very witty and easy-going with a pocketful of one-liners: "Lay down," he'll say to another boxer, "so I can recognise you." Or, "You're the guy with all the broken hands. The referee kept stepping on you." And then his standard: "When I told the doctor I was marrying a 33-year-old woman he said I could be taking a chance. I told him hey, if she dies, she dies." He always got a good laugh even from those who have heard it all before. It's all about the delivery, and Willie Pep is a natural.

"A prophet is not without honour, save in his own country," someone once said about Willie Pep. "Hey, I had my day," he said. "I had my time, my kick. Now I fight the same fight everybody else does. I ain't complaining. The young people today, they don't even know who I was." Perhaps it is about time they did know who Willie Pep was. To conclude this account of the life and times of boxing's history maker I include a few words from Paul Pender which was published in Peter Heller's brilliant book. "In This Corner."

Robinson Couldn't Tie Willie Pep's Laces

Former world middleweight champion, Paul Pender, caused uproar in boxing circles when he said in an interview for the book: "Sugar Ray Robinson couldn't tie Willie Pep's boxing boot laces when it came down to boxing ability."

What a statement from this champion from the 1960s period! What qualified Pender to make such a dramatic and controversial declaration?... Well for starters he had two victories over the fighter voted the greatest pound-for-pound fighter in the world...Sugar Ray Robinson. Is Pender right in his assessment? After all boxing is about opinions. To try to attempt to rate the all-time greats of boxing is to try and achieve the impossible. I must confess that watching the 1995 version of 40odd-world-champions in the various splintered organisations, I pine for the likes of Pep and Robinson and yes, even, Pender and fighters from the 1940's and 1950's to be active today and sort out the mess which boxing finds itself sullied with. Yes, there are certain fighters who would have achieved greatness in any era. Robinson and Pep were but two of these "special" champions. Sugar Ray Robinson and Willie Pep started their pro careers about the same time, in 1940 both were exciting, breathtaking champions in their own right. Both possessed exceptional grace, speed and boxing ability, though Robinson had the equaliser for any occasion...a knockout blow in either fist. Both these fighters had iron chins and their courage was never in doubt. Robinson also had another advantage given to him by mother nature...height. He stood nearly six-feet which for a welter or middleweight was a huge advantage. Robinson threw bunches of punches at his opponents, three, four, five left hooks in a split second. Then in a blinding flash, he would throw four or five right hands, switching them to uppercuts or whatever method he chose. There is no dispute Sugar Ray threw better combination punches than any other fighter in the history of boxing, apart, perhaps, from the other Sugar Ray Leonard. Ray Robinson was majestic, when he opened up on his victims he was awesome, a class-apart. Robinson scored thrilling, spectacular count-outs over the likes of Rocky Graziano, Carl "Bobo" Olson and many others. Who could ever forget his one-punch knockout over the teak-tough, Gene Fullmer, who he dropped like a log with his pulverising left-hook? But because of his sensational blast-outs, fans were apt to gloss over his boxing ability when assessing him as an all-round ring general. While I marvel at Sugar's fantastic punching power, I also vividly recall his fights against Carmen Basilio, Fullmer, Pender and fighters of this ilk where Ray for me at least, spent far too much time propped against the ropes taking punishment. This of course was late in his career when he was way past his best. Like Muhammad Ali later, Sugar Ray paid a very heavy price for hanging around the ring for longer than was good for him. It was a sad decline for a super champion. Boxing can be cruel to its own. It has little mercy for fighters who carry on trying to beat "Father-Time," Joe Louis, Henry Armstrong, Sugar Ray, and poor old Sandy Saddler and Ali, all paid, or are paying dearly for their involvement in this brutal, tough business.

When I met Pep at his home in 1994, he was quite candid about his longevity in the toughest sport in the world. "As a kid, my idol was Tony Canzoneri," said Willie. "Like myself Tony was from Italian stock. Also like me, he worked as a shoeshine boy to earn money for his family. Canzoneri was one of the most exciting fighters of the 1930's." "He fought for four world championships and won three. He was the only fighter in history to win the world lightweight championship twice." Tony Canzoneri was held up as an example for Pep to follow when Willie was a youngster. The fight crowds loved Tony's aggressive brand of all-out fighting. But though Willie was full of admiration for Canzoneri's achievements, there was no way he was going to try and emulate Canzoneri's fighting style. Tony took far too much punishment for Pep's liking. It seemed to him the best way to endure the rigors of the ring was to avoid getting hurt, or take the minimum of punishment while doing what was necessary to win each contest. Henry Armstrong was another exciting fighter of that period, but he took fearful punishment in return. Pep said kids used to copy Armstrong's style of fighting in the gym, but this kind of fighting was certainly not for him. "Sugar Ray Robinson, he was fabulous," Pep told me. "But he had no defence, especially later in his career. His defence was his offense, if you understand what I'm saying. While he was attacking his opponent, then they couldn't hit him back. Ray also had a hard, stunning, accurate jab.

They said I couldn't punch, yet, I stopped 65 opponents in my career. I lasted so long because I had a saying: 'He who fights and runs away, can fight till he's forty.' Even in training I never used to take punishment. Oh, when I was a kid starting out, I would have wars with certain guys in the gym. But an old fighter wised me up and gave me sound advice which I adhered to strictly throughout the remainder of my fighting career. 'Box, use your brain. Out-think these guys,' this old guy told me. And that's the same advice I would hand to any youngster taking up boxing today." Talking about a fighter of more recent times, Willie thought Sugar Ray Leonard was a really good boxer. He considered Leonard the best of the 1980s. He said he himself was always in shape because if he wasn't then Lou Viscusi wouldn't let him fight. He said that this was what he couldn't understand, that modern day fighters, especially heavyweights, seemed almost exhausted after six rounds. Willie added: "That's why Muhammed Ali beat so many of his opponents. Because he could fight for 15 rounds."

In my humble opinion, Willie Pep was the greatest wizard the boxing ring has ever seen. The facts are in the record books. The fighters who I have mentioned were also great. But punchers are punchers and boxers are boxers. I happen to believe a brilliant defensive boxer such as Pep is what boxing should be about.

He lasted so long in the meanest, toughest, hardest sport in the world, because he put his faith in skill. Brain over brawn. He was a magician between those ropes. He was like an optical illusion to his 241 opponents. First they saw him. Then they didn't, it was if he had vanished into thin air. He possessed boxing "nous" by the bagful, and he used it to his full advantage. The boxing world will never witness his like ever again. He should be treasured for what he brought to the noble art of self defence. Tommy Bazzano, an ex-fighter from New York stated: "The difference between success and failure in boxing is the fighter has to have the 'killer instinct.' There are very few exceptions, Willie Pep was one of them because he was a genius."

Years after Pep had retired, Lou Viscusi, who managed him for over 20 years, told a gathering of boxing celebrities: "When you manage a guy for as long as I managed Pep, through the good and the bad, the fat and the lean, you don't have to think up trick phrases to describe him, and you don't have to impress the writers. After 20 years with a guy, you can afford to tell the truth. Shaking his head and smiling, Mr. Lou continued: "Willie was the greatest," he said fondly, shaking his head a little. "He's the greatest, Believe me, he was a once-in-a-lifetime kind of boxer." The celebrities made a comparison between Pep and Ezzard Charles, the former heavyweight champion. "It isn't hard to understand Willie," said Viscusi as if talking about a favourite son whose wild ways he couldn't quite understand. "The secret is his charm; he's basically 'simple' in the good sense of the word. That, in a nutshell, was the secret of why he had so much success and the secret of his genius."

The Greatest Winning Boxer Ever!
Pep is the greatest winning boxer who ever lived. Boxing records are written in something less that indelible ink. Sometimes they seem to change like sand with the tide, giving rise to wonder as to the arithmetic of boxers and the memory of their managers. "I had the good fortune of winning 230 professional fights while losing only 11," said Pep. Nobody before ever won more fights, and his record is safe for all time. It will never be broken. John L. Sullivan won a paltry 38 bouts, Rocky Marciano 49, Muhammed Ali 56, Joe Louis 62 and Jack Dempsey 61. Great champions all, but not even close to Pep's 230. Benny Leonard won 89 fights with 115 no decisions.Then we start getting warm with Sandy Saddler's 144, Sugar Ray Robinson's 174, Henry Armstrong's 195 and finally Archie Moore with 199 professional victories. "That's it, that's the record," said Willie. "I won more fights than any other fighter who ever lived. What else can I tell you?" Pep's amazing record will probably never be equalled, boxing historians and record compilers agree. "With the money modern fighters receive today, guys don't need to fight much," Pep said. "There are good fighters around today, but we had a lot more back when I was boxing. Now you can pick out the good ones."

In my travels around the boxing circuit throughout the British Isles and in America, I have met and conversed with many boxing people, boxers, officials and ordinary fans. When the conversation got around to who was the best boxer ever, almost everyone replied...Willie Pep. Teddy Brenner, is a well respected boxing figure on the American boxing scene and was a famous matchmaker at the St, Nicholas Arena, and later Madison Square Garden, in New York. I met Teddy in December 1992 and he told me: "Unfortunately I was never involved with any of Willie Pep's fights. Though I was very friendly with his manager Lou Viscusi. I vividly remember though being at ringside for his second fight against Sandy Saddler. It was the best featherweight bout I ever saw. Sandy was at his peak then, but Pep beat him, he was masterful." Teddy then told me about how many fighters expressed the opinion Pep was in a class by himself when it came to pure boxing skill. He also told me Sugar Ray Robinson was one of his own favourite fighters. "I was very friendly with Sugar Ray Robinson. One day as we sat having a meal in a restaurant on Broadway. I asked Ray who he thought was the best boxer he had ever seen. He didn't hesitate for a minute...Willie Pep, he replied. 'He was the best I ever sáw.'" Sugar Ray then told Teddy about their bootleg amateur bout many years previously, and smiling told his friend: "Do you know something Teddy, though I got the decision over him in our fight, I outweighed him considerably, but he gave me hell. I saw a great many of his fights throughout his career, and I always learned something from watching him. If anyone has any lingering doubts about how great Willie Pep was, let me reassure them that he was a pure genius!"

While in Hartford I was in a cafe with a friend, Tom Jones, not the singer but a lawyer. Tom had accompanied me to Willie Pep's home. Later, while having a cup of tea in the cafe we were marvelling at how well the old champion looked when a stout, senior citizen on the next table turned to us and said: "I take it by the sound of your accents you guys are English?" When we replied yes, and explained our visit to Hartford was to meet and speak to Willie Pep, the man smiled, introduced himself as Thomas Donza, and told us he was a neighbour of the former world champions when both were kids. "I remember my old man taking me to watch Willie fight Sugar Ray Robinson at Capitol Park. What a thrilling encounter that was," he told us. Mr. Donza, then recalled events and happenings from that period. "I listened to his fight with Chalky Wright the radio while stood on Columbus Boulevard, everyone was cheering wildly. Time seemed to stand still. When he came home the city gave him a civic reception but the Italian section in Hartford, also gave him a huge reception." He told us that in his opinion Pep was the finest boxer, not fighter, he said with emphasis on boxer, he had ever watched. "I saw most of the fights Willie had right here in Hartford. There was the Hartford Auditorium which was once an old trolly car depot, Willie boxed there a lot." "He was a wonderful boxer, he hovered across the ring, he could do everything. I often close my eyes and see his image flitting on the screen when he beat Sanddy Saddler and won by the title. Lord above, that was some fight. Willie was splendid that night. Though in my opinion I don't think he was ever the same again after that battle. He seemed to lose that extra zip which he was famous for. I hope you guys tell it the way it was," he told us emphasising again that Pep was the greatest boxer of his generation.

Joseph W. Duffy, from Wethersfield, Connecticut, is a writer and historian and an avid boxing fan. He recalled how as a kid he grew up watching "The Greatest Fights of the Century" and the "Friday Night Fights" which were a regular weekly feature on television. His father was also a staunch fan and enjoyed the blow-by-blow description given by Jimmy Powers on their old black-and-white set. Madison Square Garden and Saint Nicholas Arena in New York never felt far away. Ruby Goldstein, the referee and ring announcer Johnnie Addie were familiar names to him. Mr. Duffy inherited an intoxicating, indelible impression of Willie Pep from his father. "Pound for Pound, Pep was the greatest boxer who ever lived," Mr. Duffy Snr told his son. The historian recalled first seeing Willie Pep. A large car passed near his home one day and a neighbour remarked: "There goes Willie Pep!" A few years later, Mr. Duffy was near the front of a long line of people outside the Hartford Civic Centre, waiting to enter for a Frank Sinatra concert. He was excited at the prospect of seeing and listening to Sinatra, but got a bigger thrill, when a tuxedoed Pep passed him on his way into the Centre. Willie thanked Mr. Duffy for stepping aside. The writer mentioned Eddie Dillon, an old-time fighter and a friend of his father's. "He was a good guy, old Dillon," Pep said. Mr. Duffy recalled being in Goodwin Park one afternoon, as Pep, who was in his late sixties jogged past him wearing Bermuda shorts pulled over thermal bottoms. No fancy designer tracksuits for the former champion. Mr. Duffy shouted: "hey, Willie! You're still the champ!" Willie smiled and quipped; "I'm getting old." The historian was delighted and watched his former idol jog further along, stopping to throw punches while halting periodically to touch his toes and do some excersises. "He was the greatest," he said. "Pound for Pound, one of the greatest boxers who ever lived."

Bill Corcoran from Manchester, New England, was a former boxer and an eyewitness at several of Willie Pep's fights, especially the first 10 years. He waxed lyrical about the former champion. "Pep was a tough fighter with the energy of a uranium atom," he said. "He had the grace of a ballet dancer. He boxed his way into the record books by using a brilliant left jab." Mr. Corcoran claimed that Pep could jab at a ratio of eight to every opponent's one. "Every cell in Pep's hand was made for the furious jab," added the former boxer. He said Rocky Marciano could throw heavier punches, but emphasised the fact Pep delivered faster punches. "Willie made the decade of the 1940s memorable for sports firsts that stand unsurpassed into the present. He endured 29 years as a professional boxer. Conventional wisdom said that little fighters weren't supposed to last, but he was a hit-and-run artist. He made his opponents miss a great deal. He had ring vigour."

Billy Kearns, who was a former welterweight and acted as Pep's sparring partner was another who was full of praise for Willie Pep's boxing ability. Kearns recalls boxing Pep in his Hartford gym early in his career. "He had magical feet," said Kearns. "He could spin you and be behind you in a flash. He was already a legend in 1948 when he faced Sandy Saddler. He had a winning streak of 73 straight victories on the eve of his first title defence against Saddler. And remember, among the fighters he'd faced, five had beaten Saddler. He got knocked out, but he was geared up for the big rematch and the world saw how great Willie really was. In 1947 he was involved in a plane crash. He could have played on his injuries and held out for a big insurance payout, but Willie loved boxing and honoured it." Hartford-born Jim Murray, a Pulitzer prize winning sportswriter for the Los Angeles Times, ranked Willie Pep among the three greatest fighters of all time. Few in Hartford would disagree with this assessment.

Hugh Devlin was bantamweight champion of Massachussetts many years ago, he was also a director for the Connecticut Boxing Commission. Devlin said Pep's greatest fight was the second Sandy Saddler affair. "Willie was great," he said.

Gilbert Odd a boxing historian and one of the best ever boxing writers said of Willie Pep: "Wives and dice were the ruin of Willie Pep." Gilbert then went on to explain that in his opinion Willie Pep was a throw back to the times when world champions were truly craftsmen of the squared ring. His admiration of Pep's boxing skills was plain to see.

Don Dunphy, was described as the best ever blow-by-blow boxing commentater of his generation. In a television studio for a programme "The Way It Was" Dunphy was a guest of the host Kurt Gaudy. The song "Happy Days Are Here Again" echoed around the studio and Willie Pep and Sandy Saddler were both sat in easy chairs. "These two were the greatest featherweights ever," said Mr. Dunphy.

Bert Randolph Sugar, a one time editor and publisher of The Ring and an established author said that watching Willie Pep box was like watching a tap dancer with gloves on. "Pep was boxing's artful dodger, said Mr. Sugar. "He was not a lethal puncher. Most of his victories, came not from single devastating blows, but from his opponents falling to the canvas in utter exhaustion. He stayed at the top of his craft by being shifty, cunning, and quick. He never did develop an appetite for getting hit."

Tom Edrington a sports writer for the Tribune newspaper in Florida was another who waxed lyrical at the mere mention of Willie Pep's name. "There never was and there will never be another boxer as perfect as Willie Pep," he said. Adding, "Tell me a modern day fighter who could survive 241 professional fights. Let me see him winning 229 of them. Could a modern day pugilist fight twice a week, four times a month. Let them try surviving three years wartime service and surviving a plane crash that breaks your back. Willie Pep, the 'Will O' the Wisp' did those things and more." Mr. Edrington went on to explain how a few years ago, he was seated next to Pep at a banquet at the Showboat Dinner Theatre in Florida, the talk obviously got round to Pep's career in the ring. Tom was telling Willie how much he admired his defensive tactics, Pep listened intently and said to him: "You know something Tom, I was a very religious guy when I was fighting. I always felt strongly that it was better to give than to receive. Especially in the ring."

Jack Bates, the Manchester trainer of Jackie Brown world flyweight champion, Johnny King, British Bantamweight champion, Jock McAvoy the hardest-punching middleweight ever produced in the British Isles and Johnny "Nipper" Cusick, British featherweight champion, always regarded Willie Pep among his ten all-time greatest fighters who ever lived. That was some compliment coming from Bates who was not known for praising "modern" champions. "When you watch Pep boxing, you can almost see his brain thinking out his next move," Jack use to say. "He was so superior to everyone else in the forties," he added.

Jack Cuddy was the United Press International boxing editor for 32 years and co-author of Jack Dempsey's book "Championship Boxing," who in 1965 retired after fifty years in boxing. Cuddy talking about Willie Pep said: "The fastest fighter I ever saw has to be Willie Pep. Willie's quickness and skill were phenomenal until January 1947 when he was injured in an airplane crash. It should be remembered that Willie's four historic rough-and-tumble fights with Sandy Saddler occurred after those plane injuries to Pep's spine and legs. In his prime he was breathtaking."

Frank Johnson was twice British lightweight champion during the 1950s. One of his close friends and Frank's regular sparring partner was Syd Smith from Rowtenstal in Lancashire. Frank Johnson often told Mr. Smith how much he admired Pep's brand of boxing. "Frank was one of the most skillful boxers one could ever wish to see. I must have sparred hundreds of rounds with him and he would always end by talking about Willie Pep. I think Frank based his style of boxing on the American," said Syd.

In October 1996 Angelo Dundee came to Manchester to visit a friend, Duggie Flood. Mr. Flood also happened to be a friend of mine and he brought Angelo to our gym. I was preparing Robbie Reid for his WBC world super- middleweight challenge against Italian Vincente Nardiello, which Robbie won by a seventh round knockout. Angelo was his usual bubbling self and was helpful with suggestions for the forthcoming contest. Later when the training session was finished and we got talking about Angelo's former pupils such as Willie Patrano, Jose Napoles, Muhammed Ali and Sugar Ray leonard to name but a few, I asked Angelo for his opinion on Willie Pep. At the mere mention of Pep's name, Angelo's eyes lit up as if I had switched on the lights and he became so enthusiastic while talking about Pep that everyone in the gym stood riveted and listened attentively as Angelo recounted how Willie Pep was the finest boxer he had ever seen in action. "Ali and all the other fighters you mention were great, and I do mean great," said Mr. Dundee. "But for pure boxing skill, trickery, footwork, determination and courage, Willie Pep was the greatest I ever saw. His second fight with Saddler was the most perfect exhibition in the history of the ring" Later, Angelo told me that Willie had a wonderful straight left jab and explained that Pep worked diligently in the gym to cultivate this punch. "Willie relied on fistic science backed by strength and intelligence," concluded Angelo.

Hogan Kid Bassey, who defeated Pep in 1959, had nothing but praise for the former champion, he told me: "When I was starting my climb of the boxing ladder, I was a great admirer of Willie Pep and Sandy Saddler. When I fought Pep he was obviously past his peak but he was a very swift mover and extremely hard to hit. The boxing officials wanted him to win, because they could promote a re-match for my title. But what man proposes God disposes and I knocked him out. I was told at the end of round eight the judges had me behind on points and I could only win by a knockout. He was indeed a truly great fighter. He would stand in the ring and as I fired my punches at him, he would pull away from them and avoid them like no other boxer I ever fought. But this move proved his downfall. However I must say that Willie Pep's contribution was the complete display of boxing artistry as one could imagine."

Stephen B. Acunto, a former boxer who was trained by Charley Goldman, Rocky Marciano's trainer is the founder of the American Association for the Improvement of Boxing Inc. In the early 1990s Steve was putting a video cassette together in order to help young boxers. "The purpose of making the film was to engender in young boxers the idea of reducing to an absolute minimum the amount of blows they assimilate in a career, by learning to box scientifically and treat the sport as an art." said Steve. "And who better to use as an example but Willie Pep. Willie was very helpful and extremely co-operative while we were putting together the video. Willie Pep was one of the greatest boxers who ever laced on the gloves. His boxing displays were works of art. I shall treasure the many memories of his contests, he put brain before brawn and made boxing look easy, which it's certainly not. Boxing could do with a Willie Pep performing today. He would be a sensation."

Bill Heinz, a well-respected journalist in America recalled an incident which took place a few years after Willie Pep had retired from active fighting. Heinz wanted to speak to the former champion and phoned him one evening. Pep was surprised at receiving the call. "How did you find my number?," he asked Mr. Heinz. When the journalist explained he was still a famous name so it wasn't hard to obtain his number Willie replied: "I'm a has-been, nobody remembers me." Mr. Heinz said he remembers Willie Pep as the greatest creative artist he had ever seen in the ring. "When I watched him box, it used to occur to me that, if I could just listen carefully enough, I would hear the music. He turned boxing contests into ballets."

Oscar De La Hoya was the 1992 Olympic gold medal winner. He has won four world championships in different weight divisions. Oscar is another great admirer of the Willie Pep brand of boxing. While training for his fight with Mexican legend, Julio Chavez, Oscar's trainer showed him a tape of some of Pep's contests. De La Hoya who had only read about Willie Pep's ring achievements but had never seen any film footage of the former featherweight champion was instantly captivated as he watched Pep in action and confessed his admiration.

Johnny Butterworth was a top-class professional fighter in the Fifties, who was known as the "Rochdale Thunderbolt" because of hie terrier like style of fighting and who took part in over 80 professional contests while campaigning in British rings and also in America and Australia. Johnny trained with Willie Pep during his stay in the states, he could hardly contain his admiration for the former featherweight champion when I spoke to him. "Willie Pep was great," Johnny told me in his heavy Lancashire accent. "He was the best boxer I ever saw," he added. He then told me how he watched in complete admiration as Pep would go through his workout in a New York gym. Apparently nobody bothered training when Willie trained, because they wanted to watch the master at work. "English fighters would tear into the punch bag," said Johnny. "But Willie made the bag do all the work. He would move round it lightly digging a few punches whenever he chose to deliver them. He was a captivating boxer. I wish I could have been blessed with just a slice of his ability. A truly great, great boxer."

The last word on Willie Pep falls to well-known International Boxing Manager and Agent, Dennie Mancini. "I have represented Willie Pep in Great Britain for over 30 years, and I keep in constant touch with him. Everything about Willie Pep is full of kindness to other people. I remember when I was a little boy and being bombed out three times, I wrote to the then great featherweight champion of the world in America, requesting a signed photograph. I sent the letter more in hope and never thinking for one second that I would receive a reply, but a reply I certainly received and with it was the autographed photo. I have treasured this all through my life. Later in life I met Willie when he came to England and obviously we spoke a great deal about boxing and his remarkable career. One day he turned to me and said: 'Dennie, you know I was extremely lucky, because

I had a great trainer in Bill Gore and a great manager in Lou Viscusi. I was a dam good runner so between the three of us we got some good results.' Willie was always a very modest man. I asked him why, after surviving that terrible plane crash where he broke most of his body, and he amazingly fought again about eight months later. His reply will always remain with me. 'Dennie, if I had been a plumber I would have had to go back out to work because I needed to make a living. I was a fighter, so I went back to fighting.' He fought and beat Jock Leslie, a very good box-fighter in one of his early comeback fights. They don't come any better than Willie Pep as a fighter and a man."

Pep would undoubtedly have been knighted had he have been born in England because he was a "Peerless Jim Driscoll, Walter McGowan, Howard Winstone, Ken Buchanan and Maurice Cullen and Prince Naseem Hamed all rolled into one. That's how good little Willie Pep was!

Willie Pep's Boxing Record

1940
July 3	James McGovern. ven	Won Pts 4. Hartford.
July 25	Joey Macus.	Won Pts 4. Hartford.
Aug 8	Joey Wasnick.	Won KO 3. New Haven.
Aug 29	Tommy Burns	Won KO 1. Hartford.
Sept 5.	Joey Macus.	Won Pts 6. New Britain.
Sept 18.	Jack Moore.	Won Pts 6. Hartford.
Oct 3.	Jimmy Riche.	Won KO 3. Waterbury.
Nov 22.	Carlo Duponde.	Won KO 6. New Britain.
Nov 29.	Frank Topazip.	Won KO 5. New Britain.
Dec 6.	Jim Mutane.	Won KO 2. New Britain.

1941
Jan 28.	Augie Almeda.	Won KO 6. New Haven.
Feb 3.	Joe Echevarria.	Won Pts 6. Holyoke.
Feb 10.	Don Lyons.	Won KO 2. Holyoke.
Feb 17.	Ruby Garcia.	Won Pts 6. Holyoke.
Mar 3.	Ruby Garcia.	Won Pts 6. Holyoke.
Mar 25.	Marty Shapiro.	WonPts 6. Hartford.
Mar 31.	Joey Gatto.	Won KO 2. Holyoke.

Willie Pep's Boxing Record

Apr 14.   Henry Vasquez.   Won Pts 6. Holyoke.
Apr 22.   Mexican Joey Silva.   Won Pts 6. Hartford.
May 6.   Lou Puglose.   Won KO 2. Hartford.
May 12.   Johnny Cockfield.   Won Pts 6. Holyoke.
June 24.   Eddie De Angelis.   Won KO 3. Hartford.
July 16.   Jimmy Gilligan.   Won Pts 8. Hartford.
Aug 1.   Harry hitlian.   Won Pts 6. Manchester.
Aug 5.   Paul Frechette.   Won KO 3. Hartford.
Aug 12.   Eddie Flores.   Won KO 1. Thompsonville.
Sept 26.   Jackie Harris.   Won KO 1. New Haven.
Oct 10.   Carlos Manzana.   Won Pts 8. New Haven.
Oct 22.   Connie savoie.   Won Ko 2. Hartford.
Nov 7.   Billie Spencer.   Won Pts 4. Los Angeles.
Nov 24.   Dave Crawford.   Won Pts 8. Holyoke.
Dec 12.   Ruby Garcia.   Won Pts 4. New York.

1942

Jan 8.   Joey Rivers.   Won KO 4. Fall River.
Jan 16.   Sammy Parrota.   Won Pts 4. New York.
Jan 27.   Abie Kaugman.   Won Pts 8. Hartford.
Feb 10.   Angelo Callura.   Won Pts 8. Hartford.
Feb 24.   Willie Roach.   Won Pts 8. Hartford.
Mar 18.   Johnny Compo.   Won Pts 8. New Haven.
Apr 14.   Spider Armstrong.   Won KO 4. Hartford.
May 4.   Curley Nichols.   Won Pts 8. New Haven.
May 12.   Aaron Seltzer.   Won Pts 8. Hartford.
May 26.   Joey Iannotti.   Won Pts 8. Hartford.
June 23.   Joey Archibald.   Won Pts 8. Hartford.
July 21.   Abe Denner.   Won Pts 12. Hartford.
Aug 1.   Joey Silva.   Won Ko 7. Waterbury.
Aug 10.   Pedro Hernandez.   Won Pts 10. Hartford.
Aug 20.   Nat Litfin.   Won Pts 10. West Haven.
Sept 1.   Bobby Ivy.   Won KO 9. Hartford.
Sept 10.   Frank Franconeri.   Won KO 1. New York.
Sept 22.   Vince Dell'Orto.   Won Pts 10. Hartford.
Oct 16.   Joey Archibald.   Won Pts 10. Providence.
Oct   Bobby McIntire.   Won Pts 10. Holyoke.

Oct 27.	George Zengaras.	Won Pts 10. Hartford.
Nov 20.	Chalky Wright.	Won Pts 15. New York.
	(Won world featherweight championship)	
Dec 14.	Joe Aponte Torres.	Won KO 7. Washington.
Dec 21.	Joey Silva.	Won KO 9. Jacksonville.

1943

Jan 4.	Vince Dell'Orto.	Won Pts 10. New Orleans.
Jan 19.	Bill Speary.	Won Pts 10. Hartford.
Jan 29.	Allie Stoltz.	Won Pts 10. New York.
Feb 11.	Davey Crawford.	Won Pts 10. Boston.
Feb 15.	Bill Speary.	Won Pts 10. Baltimore.
Mar 2.	Lou Transparenti.	Won KO 6. Hartford.
Mar 19.	Sammy Angott.	Lost 10. New York.
Mar 29.	Bobby McIntire.	Won Pts 10. Detroit.
Apr 9.	Sal Bartolo.	Won Pts 10. Boston.
Apr 19.	Angel Aviles.	Won Pts 10. Tampa.
Apr 26.	Jackie Wilson.	Won Pts 12. Pittssburgh.
June 8.	Sal Bartolo.	Won Pts 15. Boston.
	(Word championship contest)	

1944

Apr 4.	Leo Francis.	Won Pts 10. Hartford.
Apr 20.	Harold Snooks Lacey.	Won Pts 10. New Haven.
May 1.	Jackie Leamus.	Won Pts 10. Philadelphia.
May 19.	Frankie Rubino.	Won Pts 10. Chicago.
May 23.	Joey Bagnato.	Won KO 2. Buffalo.
June 6.	Julie Kogon.	Won Pts 10. Hartford.
July 7.	Willie Joyce.	Won Pts 10. Chicago.
July 17.	Manuel Ortiz.	Won Pts 10. Boston.
Aug 4.	Lulu Constantino.	Won Pts 10. Waterbury.
Aug 29.	Joey Peralta.	Won Pts 10. Springfield.
Sept 19.	Charley Cabey Lewis.	Won KO 8. Hartford.
Sept 29.	Chalky Wright.	Won Pts 15. New York.
	(World championship contest)	
Oct 25.	Jackie Leamus.	Won Pts 10. Montreal.
Nov 14.	Charley Cabey Lewis.	Won Pts 10. Hartford.

Willie Pep's Boxing Record   349

Nov 27.	Pedro Hernandez	Won Pts 10. Washington.
Dec 5.	Chalky Wright	Won Pts 10. Cleveland.

1945

Jan 23.	Ralph Walton.	Won Pts 10. Hartford.
Feb 5.	Willie Roache.	Won Pts 10. New Haven.
Feb 19.	Phil Terranova.	Won Pts 15. New York.

(World championship contest)

Oct 30.	Paulie Jackson.	Won Pts 8. Hartford.
Nov 5.	Mike Martyk.	Won KO 5. Buffalo.
Nov 26.	Eddie Giosa.	Won Pts 10. Boston.
Dec 5.	Harold Gibson.	Won Pts 10. Lewiston.
Dec 13.	Jimmy McAllister.	Draw 12. Baltimore.

(This was the only draw on Pep's record)

1946

Jan 15.	Johnny Virgo.	Won Ko 2. Buffalo.
Feb 13.	Jimmy Joyce	Won Pts 10. Buffalo.
Mar 1.	Jimmy McAllister	Won KO 2. New York.
Mar 26.	Jackie Wilson	Won Pts 10. Kansas.
April 8.	Georgie Knox.	Won Ko 3. Providence.
May 6.	Ernie Petrone	Won Pts 10. New Haven.
May 13.	Joey Angelo	Won Pts 10. Providence.
May 22.	Joe Aponte Torres.	Won Pts 10. St. Louis.
May 27.	Jimmy Joyce	Won Pts 8. Minneapolis.
June 7.	Sal Bartolo	Won KO 12. New York.

(World championship contest)

July 10.	Harold Gibson.	Won KO 7. Buffalo.
July 25.	Jackie Graves.	Won KO 8. Minneapolis.
Aug 26.	Doll Rafferty.	Won KO 6. Milwaukee.
Sept 4.	Walter Kolby.	Won KO 5. Buffalo.
Sept 17.	Lefty LaChance.	Won KO 3. Hartford.
Nov 1.	Paulie Jackson.	Won Pts 10. Minneapolis.
Nov 15.	Thomas Beato	Won Ko 2. Waterbury.
Nov 27.	Chalky Wright.	Won KO 3. Milwaukee.

1947

June 17.	Victor Flores.	Won Pts 10. Hartford.

(Pep's first fight since he was injured in areoplane crash)

July 1.	Joey Fortuna.	Won KO 5. Albany.
July 8.	Leo LeBrun.	Won Pts 8. Norwalk.
July 11.	Jean Barriere.	Won KO 4. North Adams.
July 15.	Paulie Jackson.	Won Pts 10. New Bedford.
July 23.	Humberto Sierra.	Won Pts 10. Hartford.
Aug 22.	Jock Leslie.	Won KO 12. Flint.

(World championship contest)

Oct 21.	Jean Barriere.	Won Ko 1. Portland.
Oct 27.	Archie Wilmer.	Won Pts 10. Philadelphia.
Dec 22.	Alvara Estrada.	Won Pts 10. Lewiston.
Dec 30.	Lefty LaChance.	Won KO 8. Manchester.

1948

Jan 6.	Pedro Biesca.	Won Pts 10. Hartford.
Jan 12.	Jimmy McAllister.	Won Pts 10. St. Louis.
Jan 19.	Joey Angelo.	Won Pts 10. Boston.
Feb 24.	Humberto Sierra.	Won KO 10. Miami.

(World championship contest)

May 7.	Leroy Willis.	Won Pts 10. Detroit.
May 19.	Charley Cabey Lewis.	Won Pts 10. Milwaukee.
June 17.	Miquel Acevedo.	Won Pts 10. Minneapolis.
June 25.	Luther Burgess.	Won Pts 10. Flint.
July 28.	Young Junior.	Won KO 1. Utica.
July 25.	Teddy "Red-Top" Davis.	Won Pts 10. Hartford.
Aug 17.	Teddy "Red-Top" Davis.	Won Pts 10. Hartford.
Sept 2.	Johnny Dell.	Won KO8. Waterbury.
Sept 10.	Paddy DeMarco.	Won Pts 10. New York.
Oct 12.	Chuck Burton.	Won Pts 8. New Jersey.
Oct 19.	John LaRusso.	Won Pts 10. Hartford.
Oct 29.	Sandy Saddler.	Lost KO 4. New York.

(Lost world featherweight title)

Dec 20.	Hermie Freeman.	Won Pts 10. Boston.

1949

Jan 17.	Teddy "Red-Top" Davis	Won Pts 10. St. Louis.
Feb 11.	Sandy Saddler.	Won Pts 15. New York.

(Re-won world featherweight championship)

June 6.	Louis Ramos.	Won Pts 10. New Haven.
June 14.	Al Pennino.	Won Pts 10. Pittsfield.
June 20.	John LaRusso.	Won Pts 10. Springfield.
July 12.	Jean Mougin.	Won Pts 10. Syracuse.
Sept 20.	Eddie Compo	Won KO 7. Waterbury.

(World championship contest)

Dec 12.	Harold Dade.	Won Pts 10. St. Louis.

1950

Jan 16.	Charley Riley.	Won KO 5. St. Louis.

(World championship contest)

Feb 6.	Roy Andrews	Won Pts 10. Boston.
Feb 22.	Jimmy Warren	Won Pts 10. Miami.
Mar 17.	Ray Famechon.	Won Pts 15. New York.

(World championship contest)

May 15.	Art Llanos	Won Ko 2. Hartford.
June 1.	Terry Young.	Won Pts 10. Milwaukee.
June 26.	Bobby Timpson.	Won Pts 10. Hartford.
July 25.	Bobby Bell.	Won Pts 10. Washington.
Aug 2.	Proctor Heinold.	Won Pts 10. Scranton.
Sept 8.	Sandy Saddler	Lost KO 8. New York.

(Lost world featherweight championship)

1951

Jan 30.	Tommy Baker.	Won KO 4. Hartford.
Feb 26.	Billy Hogan.	Won KO 2. Sarasota.
Mar 5.	Carlos Chavez.	Won Pts 10. New Orleans.
Mar 26.	Pat Iacobucci.	Won Pts 10. Miami.
Apr 17.	Baby Ortiz.	Won KO 5. St.Louis.
Apr 27.	Eddie Chavez.	Won Pts 10. San Francisco.
June 4.	Jesus Compos.	Won Pts 10. Baltimore.
Sept 4.	Corky Gonzales.	Won Pts 10. New Orleans.
Sept 26.	Sandy Saddler.	Lost KO 9. New York.

(World championship contest)

1952
Apr 29.	Santiago Gonzales	Won Pts 10. Tampa.
May 5.	Kenny Leach.	Won Pts 10. Columbus.
May 10.	Buddy Baggett.	Won KO 5. South Carolina.
May 21.	Claude Hammond	Won Pts 10. Miami.
June 30.	Tommy Collins.	Lost KO 6. Boston.
Sept 3.	Billy Lima.	Won Pts 10. Pensacola.
Sept 11.	Bobby Woods.	Won Pts 10. Vancouver.
Oct 1.	Armand Savoie.	Won Pts 10. Chicago.
Oct 20.	Billy Lima.	Won Pts 10. Jacksonville.
Nov 5.	Manny Castro.	Won KO 5. Miami.
Nov 19.	Fabala Chavez.	Won Pts 10. St.Louis.
Dec 5.	Jorge Sanchez.	Won Pts 10. Palm Beach.

1953
Jan 19.	Billy Lauderdale.	Won Pts 10. Nassau.
Jan 27.	Davey Mitchell.	Won Pts 10. Miami.
Feb 10.	Jose Alvarez.	Won Pts 10. San Antonio.
Mar 31.	Joey Gambino.	Won Pts 10. Tampa.
Apr 7.	Noel Paquette.	Won Pts 10. Miami.
May 13.	Jackie Blair.	Won Pts 10. Dallas.
June 5.	Pat Marcune.	Won KO 10. New York.
Nov 21.	Sonny Luciano.	Won Pts 10. Charlotte.
Dec 4.	Davey Allen.	Won Pts 10. Palm Beach.
Dec 8.	Billy Lima.	Won KO 2. Houston.
Dec 15.	Tony Longo.	Won Pts 10. Miami.

1954
Jan 19.	David Seabrooke.	Won Pts 10. Jacksonville.
Feb 26.	Lulu Perez.	Lost KO 2. New York.
July 24.	Mike Turcotte.	Won Pts 10. Mobile.
Aug 18.	Til LeBlanc.	Won Pts 10. Moncton.
Nov 1.	Mario Colon.	Won Pts 10. Daytona Beach.

1955
Mar 11.	Myrel Olmstead.	Won Pts 10. Bennington.
Mar 22.	Charley Titone.	Won Pts 10. Holyoke.

Willie Pep's Boxing Record

Mar 30.	Gil Cadilli.	Lost Pts 10. California.
May 18.	Gil Cadilli.	Won Pts 10. Detroit.
June 1.	Joey Cam.	Won KO 4. Boston.
June 14.	Mickey Mars.	Won KO 7. Miami.
July 12.	Hector Rodriquez.	Won Pts 10. Bridgeport.
Sept 13.	Jimmy Ithia.	Won KO 6. Hartford.
Sept 27.	Henry "Pappy" Gault.	Won Pts 10. Holyoke.
Oct 10.	Charley Titone.	Won Pts 10. Brockton.
Nov 29.	Henry "Pappy" Gault	Won Pts 10. Tampa.
Dec 12.	Leo Carter.	Won Ko 4. Houston.
Dec 28.	Andy Arel.	Won Pts 10. Miami. 1956.
Mar 13.	Kid Campeche.	Won Pts 10. Tampa.
Mar 27.	Buddy Baggett	Won Pts 10. Beaumont.
Apr 17.	Jackie Blair.	Won Pts 10. Hartford.
May 22.	Manuel Armenteros	Won KO 7. San Antonio.
June 19.	Russ Taque.	Won Pts 10. Miami.
July 4.	Hector Bacquettes.	Won KO 4. Oklahoma.

1957

Apr 23.	Cesar Morales.	Won Pts 10. Fort Lauderdale.
May 10.	Many Castro.	Won Pts 10. South Carolina.
July 16.	Many Castro.	Won Pts 10. El Passo.
July 23.	Russ Taque.	Won Pts 10. Houston.
Dec 17.	Jimmy Connors.	Won Pts 10. Boston.

1958

Jan 14.	Jimmy Tibbs.	Lost Pts 10. Boston.
Mar 31.	Prince Johnson.	Won Pts 10. Holyoke.
Apr 8.	George Stephany.	Won Pts 10. Bristol.
Apr 14.	Cleo Ortiz.	Won Pts 10. Providence.
Apr 29.	Jimmy Kelly.	Won Pts 10. Boston.
May 20.	Bobby Singleton.	Won Pts 10. Boston.
June 23.	Pat McCoy.	Won Pts 10. New Bedford.
July 1.	Bobby Soares.	Won Pts 10. Athol.
July 17.	Bobby Bell.	Won Pts 10. Norwood.
Aug 4.	Luis Carmona.	Won Pts 10. Presque Isle.
Aug 9.	Jesse Rodriques.	Won Pts 10. Painsville.

Aug 26.	Al Duarte.	Won Pts 10. North Adams.
Sept 20.	Hogan "Kid" Bassey.	Lost KO 9. Boston.

1959

Jan 26.	Sonny Leon.	Lost Pts 10. Caracas. Ven.

(Announced retirement, 27 January, 1959)

1965

(After Six years retirement Willie Pep made a comeback)

Mar 12.	Hal McKeever.	Won Pts 8. Miami.
Apr 26.	Jackie Lennon.	Won Pts 6. Philadelphia.
May 21.	Johnny Gilmore.	Won Pts 6. Norwalk.
July 26.	Benny Randell.	Won Pts 10. Quebec.
Sept 28.	Johnny Gilmore.	Won Pts 6. Philadelphia.
Oct 1.	Willie Little.	Won KO 3. Johnston.
Oct 4.	Tommy Haden	Won KO 3. Providence.
Oct 14.	Sergio Musquiz.	Won KO 5. Phoenix.
Oct 25.	Ray Coleman.	Won KO 5. Tucson.

1966

Mar 16.	Calvin Woodland	Lost Pts 6. Virginia.

(After this contest, Willie Pep announced his retirement from boxing. He was forty-five-years-old)